Tom Medwell

ANDREW MUELLER was born in Wagga Wagga, Australia, and lives in London, England. He writes about various things for various titles, including *The Financial Times*, *Monocle*, *The Guardian*, *The Times*, *Esquire*, *Uncut*, *Australian Gourmet Traveller*, *New Humanist* and, frankly, anyone else who'll have him. Another book of his, *I Wouldn't Start From Here: The 21st Century and Where It All Went Wrong*, was lauded as "not bad for a guy from Wagga Wagga," by *The Wagga Wagga Advertiser*.

Andrew Mueller is also the singer, songwriter and rhythm guitarist with The Blazing Zoos, an incipient alt-country phenomenon who released their debut album, *I'll Leave Quietly*, in 2010. Mueller plans to spend the royalties generated by its success on an immense and triumphantly gauche Nashville mansion with rhinestone-studded gates and a guitar-shaped swimming pool. Or, a sandwich.

His hobbies include swearing at televised sporting fixtures, sighing at newspapers and the maintenance of a minutely annotated list of people who'll be sorry when he's famous. Form an orderly queue, ladies.

ROCK
AND HARD PLACES

★ ★ ★ TRAVELS TO ★ ★ ★
BACKSTAGES
FRONTLINES
AND ASSORTED SIDESHOWS

ANDREW MUELLER

SOFT SKULL PRESS

An earlier version of this book was published in 1999 in Great Britain by Virgin Books.

Library of Congress Cataloging-in-Publication Data

Mueller, Andrew.
  Rock and hard places : travels to backstages, frontlines and assorted sideshows / Andrew Mueller.
    p. cm.
Includes bibliographical references and index.
ISBN 978-1-59376-268-1 (alk. paper)
1. Mueller, Andrew—Travel. 2. Music journalists—Travel. I. Title.

ML423.M84A5 2010
781.66092—dc22

                                                2009052518

Cover design by Goodloe Byron
Interior design by Neuwirth and Associates, Inc

Printed in the United States of America

Soft Skull Press
An Imprint of Counterpoint LLC
2117 Fourth Street
Suite D
Berkeley, CA 94710

www.softskull.com
www.counterpointpress.com

Distributed by Publishers Group West

10 9 8 7 6 5 4 3 2 1

For Mum and Dad

★

"Many shall run to and fro, and knowledge shall be increased."
—DANIEL 12:4

★

"Road (n): A strip of land along which one may pass from where it is too tiresome to be to where it is futile to go."
—AMBROSE BIERCE, *The Devil's Dictionary*

CONTENTS

THE GREAT LEAP FOREWORD

Introduction

IT IS A fitting happenstance of deadline that I'm writing this here and now—in Zagreb, Croatia, in between U2's two shows at Maksimir Stadium. As the thrillingly witty pun that serves as this book's title suggests, the reportage gathered in this volume straddles, with varying degrees of chafing, the realms of rock'n'roll and conflict, and it's a version of that same ungainly feat that U2 are attempting here. The two nights U2 are playing in Zagreb are their first shows ever in Croatia, and their first anywhere in the former Yugoslavia since they took their gaudy, glitzy *PopMart* circus to the shattered Bosnian capital of Sarajevo in 1997.

That these shows are essentially a long-delayed sequel to the Bosnian outing was acknowledged last night in Bono's introduction to "One," U2's supremely versatile lament for the loss of love, faith or whatever you're (not) having yourself. "The next song," he'd said, "means a lot of different things to a lot of different people. Tonight, we want to play it for everyone in this region who has had their warm hearts broken by cold ideas." As the crowd recognised it, there was a palpable shift in the atmosphere: a warm summer night suddenly felt a few degrees chillier. I've heard this song played dozens of times in dozens of cities, Sarajevo in 1997 among them, but it has never sounded better than it did last night, which is to say it has never sounded more wounded and reproachful, Edge's scuffed-up guitar itching like an unresolved tension. U2 faded "One" into an excerpt from The Righteous Brothers' "Unchained Melody"; in the Balkans of all places, the phrase "time can do so much" hit a note somewhere between a threat and a promise.

If this book is about any one thing—which, just so we're clear on this, it very definitely isn't—it's about moments like that, when music steps beyond its boundaries of verse and chorus and becomes a soundtrack or accompaniment to something somewhat larger than itself.

THIS IS THE second introduction I've written for this book. I wrote the first a little over a decade ago, when a slightly different version of *Rock and Hard Places* was published in the United Kingdom to widespread indifference (it was, however, a minor if weirdly enduring cult hit in Eastern Europe and the Balkans, from where I still receive emails about it with baffling regularity; I can only conclude that the entire print run was mistakenly loaded onto a barge bound down the Danube, where it ran aground and was subsequently looted by delirious locals in some sort of *Whiskey Galore* scenario). Having just re-read said introduction for the first time in nearly that long, I've decided to lose almost all of it except the headline.

It's not that I believe the original introduction is bad, exactly. Indeed, for something composed in a hungover fog in a hotel room in Boston—where I was, at the time, on tour with The Cardigans—it's reasonably coherent, and contains what I still think is quite a good joke about orangutans. It's just that ten years is a long time, in which much has happened, both to the world in general and to the journalist meandering about in it. The difference between the world this book was first published in, and the world this book is being re-published in, is neatly illustrated by the blurb which appeared on the cover of the first edition—and which, for reasons which will become clear presently, does not appear on the cover of this one. It was contributed by the very great P.J. O'Rourke, who very kindly appended his name to an observation that the writing about rock music and various screwed-up locations contained herein was "as spectacular as a Taliban attack on Lollapalooza—which come to think of it, isn't a bad idea." Which is to say that, back in 1999, the idea of a gaggle of religious cranks based in Afghanistan threatening the destruction of an American institution seemed so preposterous as to be the stuff of throwaway whimsy.

All the pieces in this book were first commissioned as journalism by various publications (except the last one—incredibly, nobody wanted to spend money on an account of taking a country band on tour in Albania. And they wonder why nobody's buying newspapers anymore). The versions of them collected herein are, however, longer than those which were originally printed, which is to say I've put back in all the jokes, digressions, tangents and a crashingly self-indulgent flourishes which are invariably—and usually quite rightly—the first things to perish when an editor swishes his machete at one's copy. As will be noted by the dozens of owners of the initial pressing of *Rock and Hard Places*, as they while away long winter evenings by comparing that with this, some old stories have been jettisoned in favour of some newer ones. The older ones appear, despite the occasionally retrospectively horrified urges of the author, unaltered from last time out—except for a few excisions of trivial and now irrelevant references to contemporary phenomena, which really didn't merit the explanatory footnotes that leaving them in would have necessitated. The new ones don't have quite so many trivial and irrelevant references to contemporary phenomena: let it not be said that I've learnt nothing these last ten years. And all the stories have introductions composed especially for this volume, seeking to place them in their proper context, wrap up what happened next, and/or basically explain to the reader what the heck the author thought he was doing at the time.

Rock and Hard Places is not intended to be a serious, or even a frivolous, portrait of our times (my other book, *I Wouldn't Start From Here* is, however, and remains freely available) or of anything else. The stories gathered here have nothing much to do with each other except that I wrote them, so taken as a whole, this tome doesn't really demonstrate much besides the sorts of things that can happen when someone decides to be a rock journalist, and then a travel writer, and then a foreign correspondent and, finally, a country singer. I have gleaned some insights along the way, however. Young men carry electric guitars and rifles with the same insouciant swagger, both implements prized as they are by vindictive and resentful males for the instant, if often ill-deserved, gravitas they confer. In countries at war, the food is invariably worse than in countries at peace, but the coffee is always better. The more alcohol a people drink, the worse they look, except in Iceland. The major difference between America and the rest of the world is that America is unconcerned about becoming Americanised. Finally and most importantly, travelling yields no answers, but it does, if you keep your eyes and ears open, occasionally give you ideas for better questions.

IN A BLUE YORKE STATE OF MIND

Radiohead in America
OCTOBER 1995

ALMOST ALL TOUR features in all almost all music journals are frauds perpetrated against the reader. The wretched reality masked by the "On the road with . . ." headline is almost invariably as follows. The journalist is flown somewhere at the grudging expense of the band's record company. Arrangements are made for said hack to attend two—perhaps, if they're incredibly lucky, three—consecutive shows of the tour in question, ideally in towns not too inconveniently and expensively far apart. A formal interview will be scheduled in a dead hour one afternoon along the way, after lunch and before soundcheck, so that sufficient quotes to fill the writer's word count may be prised from the half-asleep singer. An invitation may also be extended to one or more after-show parties. In the event that the band actually deign to turn up at one of these wing-dings, the ranking of the journalist in their order of priorities may be precisely calculated by counting how many famous people, influential music industry panjandrums, and attractive young women are also in the room (one swiftly learns to avoid the rookie error of pitching for the gigs in big, glamorous cities: the solidarity fostered by adverse circumstances, and the absence of anything else to do, ensures that you'll generally get far more out of any given band when they're marooned in some misbegotten midwestern swamp than you will when they're larging it in Los Angeles or New York). After all of which the journalist will transcribe his tape, decipher whatever notes he might have scrawled, meditate briefly upon the relative nature of truth, and compose a few thousand words subtly conveying the impression that he had bonded with the group in question to the extent that they had all but asked him to join.

The story that follows, originally written as a cover feature for Melody Maker, was an exception to the above rules—as are, in general, all the tour stories gathered in this book (the ones about underwhelming encounters with Belgian art rock ensembles, and waiting three days in Seattle's Four Seasons hotel for a fifteen-minute interview with a band whose management were suffering terrifying delusions of majesty, are being saved for a subsequent, woefully inferior and utterly shameless cash-in volume). It isn't a definitive portrait of the subjects. Indeed, it would be ridiculous to have entertained any pretensions of that sort—how firm a grip on the essence of your being would someone have who'd just hung around and watched you at work for a few days? It is, however, a reasonable summation of what sticks in the memory after a few days on tour: the fleeting impressions, of unfamiliar places and people, smudged at the edges by drink, jetlag and exhaustion, haphazardly focused by the oncoming deadline.

★ ★ ★

"IT'S A VERY good idea," nods Thom Yorke. "It's not the idea I'm arguing with. The idea, in itself, is fine."

Thom, sunglassed and shrouded in an enormous fake black fur coat, is sitting on a luggage trolley in the lobby of the Sheraton Hotel in Hartford, Connecticut. He has just stumbled off the tour bus after a long drive from Philadelphia. Behind him, a bow-tied porter hovers vaguely, as if unsure whether to heave this bedraggled apparition into the street, or ask him which room he'd liked to be wheeled to. Crouched on the floor in front of Thom, Radiohead's bassplayer, Colin Greenwood, is earnestly outlining his plans.

"My question," continues Thom, at pains to sound reasonable, "is where the fucking hell we're going to find five hundred fucking ping-pong balls at short notice in this fucking place on a Sunday afternoon."

A pensive silence ensues. Thom has a fair point. I'd hardly been able to find a cold beer in Hartford at eleven o'clock last night.

"We'll just have to think of something else," says Thom, and chews on a thumbnail.

AN HOUR LATER, with everyone washed, changed and infused with caffeine, we pile into a minibus to the venue, and Colin explains a few things. Tonight, Radiohead will play the last of their shows as the support act on R.E.M.'s "Monster" tour. They have been warned to expect some sort of practical joke by way of farewell. Clearly believing that revenge is a dish best served pre-cooked, Radiohead (Thom, Colin, drummer Phil Selway, guitarists Ed O'Brien and Jonny Greenwood—from whom, presumably, Thom stole the "h") have been plotting their retribution in advance.

"Mike Mills," says Colin, "told us not to wear anything we want to wear again."

"Paint," speculates Thom, gloomily. "It'll be paint. Or custard pies. Oh, God."

"So the idea with the ping-pong balls," continues Colin, "was that we'd get the roadies up in the lighting gantries above the stage to drop them on R.E.M. during the last song."

A contemplative hush settles as we drive through Hartford. If you've never driven through Hartford, the effect can be recreated in the comfort and safety of your own home by going to sleep. I flew in from London last night with Melody Maker photographer Pat Pope and Radiohead's press officer, Caffy St Luce. Our efforts to hit Hartford and paint the town red had come to nought; we couldn't even claim to have painted the town beige. The first place we tried was a sports bar, decorated with fading hockey pennants and populated by four lone, middle-aged men staring morosely into their drinks. We asked the barman what people in Hartford did for fun. "They come here, sir," he replied. We finished up in a deserted cocktail bar where the star turn was a drink called a Zombie. "Limit two per customer," said the menu. I asked a waitress what happens if you drink three. "You can't walk," she replied.

"I wonder why people build cities in these places," says Thom, balefully surveying the fist-chewingly unremarkable scenery. It's a real graveyard with streetlights, this place, the kind of town where you could fire a Gatling gun down the main road without hitting anybody—and if you did, you'd be doing them a favour.

The venue for tonight's show is the Meadows Music Theatre, a giant half-indoor, half-outdoor affair, something like Wembley Arena with a back yard. It's early afternoon, hours before showtime, but we've arrived early so Radiohead can soundcheck and do some of the aimless milling about that constitutes the major part of any rock'n'roll tour. In Radiohead's commodious dressing room, Thom draws a smiling face and the words "Thanks for having us, you've been brilliant, love Radiohead" on a scrap of paper and gives it to a roadie who will secrete it amid the sheets on Michael Stipe's lyric stand. This gesture is at odds with the received wisdom on Thom Yorke, which is that he's slightly less amenable than a cornered mongoose.

"Yeah, well," he shrugs. "They've really been brilliant to us. We're getting a whole hour to soundcheck every night, and you know how often that happens to support bands in real life."

Gratitude notwithstanding, the other members of Radiohead have been talking, and a Plan B prank has been hatched. R.E.M.'s stage set is an extravagant homage to Alexander Calder that includes a backdrop of enormous red lampshades, swinging from the stage roof. The idea now is that as R.E.M. close their show with "It's The End Of The World As We Know It (And I Feel Fine)" the lampshades will be joined in flight by all five members of Radiohead, suspended from harnesses. Colin, Jonny, Phil and Ed look well pleased with this scheme. Thom looks rather less so.

"It'll never work," he says.

Radiohead go off to do their soundcheck, which I watch from the hill at the back of the empty arena. Between songs, Ed plays snatches of "Radio Free Europe," R.E.M.'s first single. I've often thought that it'd be a great gag for a support act to close their set by playing the headliner's biggest hit, but I suspect Radiohead want to be invited back one day.

Back in the dressing room, Radiohead are informed that the harness jape is off—R.E.M.'s tour manager isn't having it. Someone else says, probably quite rightly, that Radiohead's insurers would pop a rivet if one of their clients got injured in a mid-air collision with a giant item of lounge furniture.

Phil brings one of the big red props into the dressing room for further discussion.

"We could," he offers, "just put them on our heads and run around the stage."

He tries it on. He looks silly beyond description.

"I can't see," he announces, muffled.

"Typical," snorts Thom, momentarily recalling, as he sometimes does, the deadpan snarl of John Lydon. "Very bloody Keith Moon, aren't we? Other bands seem to be able to misbehave without looking like utter wankers. I wonder what our problem is."

He clomps off to wait in silence for showtime, fidgeting with some artwork he's got stored in his Macintosh laptop. Jonny, meanwhile, is trying to evade a phone interview with some local radio station. He asks if I fancy doing it. "They'll never know," he says. He explains that several Japanese and Taiwanese magazines currently trailing exclusive interviews with Radiohead's right-angle-cheekboned guitar hero are, in fact, running with the thoughts of his mates, cousins or anyone else who was sitting around his house in Oxford when the phone rang.

"Go on," he goads. "It's easy. How are you finding touring with R.E.M.? Do you feel under pressure to follow the success of 'Creep'?"

It's a tempting offer, and the trust Jonny is offering at such early acquaintance is touching—after all, there's nothing to stop me saying, "We're only supporting R.E.M. for the money, all of which we plan to invest in companies which test cosmetics on baby seals and pay Malaysian children three cents an hour to drill those pointless little holes in the ends of toothbrushes and I am sleeping with your sister." However, I've done more than a few phone interviews myself, I know how prone they are to literal and metaphorical crossed wires even when you're talking to who you think you are and I don't want to wind up a fellow hack unnecessarily. There is some honour among scoundrels.

"Suit yourself," he says. "I'll ask one of the crew."

Jonny tells me that his driving ambition is to leave America having said "Wanker" and "Bollocks" on every radio station in the country.

GIVEN THAT HARTFORD is what it is—the kind of place where they'll have to close the zoo if the chicken dies—it's not surprising that the venue looks full to its 30,000 capacity an hour before Radiohead are due on.

To get to the arena from backstage, I have to run an ideological gauntlet of stalls operated by the organisations R.E.M. have invited on tour with them: Greenpeace, Rock the Vote, the National Coalition to Abolish the Death Penalty, and some people who'd like it to be more difficult for other people to buy handguns. There's a couple of groups with more nebulous names, like People for the American Way and Common Cause, which sound excitingly like rogue shotgun-wielding militias of squirrel-eating far-right rednecks that have snuck under R.E.M.'s wire, but these also turn out to be cheerful liberals encouraging others to be cheerfully liberal. I talk to a few of them. I probably even agree with most of them. I've just never grown out of that shockingly juvenile reflex of rebelling against any opinion that is being thrust at me in tones of righteous certainty, even if it's my own. By the time I get to my spot on Radiohead's mixing desk, I'm almost goose-stepping.

Radiohead are brilliant tonight, but as they rarely display any aptitude for being anything else, it's not surprising. As for R.E.M.'s threat of practical jokes, this pretty much turns out to have been the practical joke itself. Ed is briefly tormented by a radio-controlled car operated from the wings by Mike Mills, but no custard pies or paint bombs are deployed. Nevertheless, Radiohead have convinced themselves of the worst: as soon as the last note of their last song (a rousing version of "Nobody Does It Better," dedicated to R.E.M.) fades, they down tools and leg it as fast as they decently can. As Radiohead complete their flight, R.E.M. wander on stage bearing a tray of champagne glasses, seeking to toast their support act, and find nothing but 30,000 people laughing. After a couple of agonising minutes, Thom, Ed, Jonny, Colin and Phil are retrieved, and the R.E.M./Radiohead mutual admiration society drinks its health to sustained applause.

Backstage at the end of the night, every friend or relative of every member of R.E.M. and Radiohead makes both bands stand together for souvenir last-night pictures. Peter Buck gently taunts Radiohead for their eventual, agonised decision not to storm the stage during the encore. Colin brings me a beer.

So, Colin. Do you feel under pressure to follow the success of "Creep"? How are you finding touring with R.E.M.?

"I can remember listening to R.E.M.'s first couple of albums on my

Walkman on the way to school," he says. "They're one of the reasons I wanted to be in a band. This is still really strange."

During R.E.M.'s set, Colin had shepherded me out onto the stage, to a position just behind Peter Buck's amplifiers, where we spent the set giggling like two starstruck teenagers who'd snuck into someone's soundcheck.

"They've been so good to us, and it's been really good for us, especially Thom. This seems to have been his year for meeting his heroes. Elvis Costello introduced himself at this thing we did in Italy. I think that kind of thing has helped Thom a lot."

Bill Berry, R.E.M.'s drummer, comes over to say goodbye. He's wearing a purple Radiohead t-shirt.

THE FOLLOWING NIGHT, in a New York City feeling the first chills of winter, Radiohead are due to play a secret show at the Mercury Lounge, a tiny venue on East Houston. The band leave Hartford by minibus while Pat, Caffy and I get on a train, which breaks down, then a bus, which gets a flat, and then another bus, whose unspeakably sadistic driver hits upon *Planes, Trains & Automobiles* as just the video everyone is going to want to see by this stage.

When we get to the Mercury, almost hysterical with irritation, Radiohead are mid-soundcheck. I stand up the back and try to be inconspicuous, which isn't easy in a brightly-lit venue almost too small to change your mind in.

"There you are," grins Thom from the stage. "Any requests?"

Someone's in a good mood, at least. I suggest "Sulk," a deliciously bitter tune that sounds roughly the way you feel when trapped in an interminable bus journey while being subjected to a film which could have been based on your misery, except that you know Steve Martin is going to get home eventually.

"We were going to do it anyway," says Thom, with a smirk. They play it, and things suddenly seem like they could be worse: my favourite band of the moment play a four-minute concert for an audience consisting of me and the bloke on the mixing desk.

Thom and I head for a coffee in a place up the street. The waitress is wearing a Sleeper t-shirt—evidently one of New York's sub-species of ardent Anglophile indie-rock fans. She double-takes at Thom, but obviously can't quite place him. She carries on double-taking while we talk.

"The thing that's really freaked me out about doing a tour with a band as big as R.E.M.," begins Thom, "is seeing how being so famous can change the way everybody, and I mean absolutely everybody, behaves towards you."

Someone once wrote that the curse of being Marlon Brando, I think it was, was that you'd never see people being themselves.

"Absolutely. And it is really hard to do, to be yourself in front of somebody famous."

The waitress is beyond double-taking and is now staring. She's worked it out.

"I find it . . . fuck, you know, I don't want it to happen. But that's presuming we're even going to make another record that people like."

Colin was saying last night that you'd found meeting a few people in your position helpful. What happens? Do you have those magnificent, unfathomable conversations that artists always want everyone else to believe that artists have, or do you just stand around gawping like a fan?

"No . . . it's more . . . you're there, and there's millions of things you can ask, but just the fact that you've met them becomes enough. I mean, even someone like Elvis Costello you can still judge on first impressions to some degree, and he was really nice, really trying to be nice. He can obviously be extremely sour, just like I can be, just like a lot of people under pressure can be, but he was really nice."

I think the reputation he's got—rather like the reputation you've got—is more than anything to do with an inability to suffer fools gladly, or even at all. If you can't cope with imbeciles, and you work in the music business, you're going to upset people.

"You're right, and the music business is quite bitchy and competitive, but after all that, you meet people you really admire, and suddenly that whole competitive thing is just not important. I found that helpful. Just being able to say I've met him. That's enough."

So you just talked shop, like everyone else.

"I bloody hope not. Although, to some degree, you do find yourself in the same boat, having gone through the same experiences, and they're quite a limited set of experiences, and they can turn you into quite a limited personality. So, I think, it's a shock when you discover that there other people who have gone through that, who are a few years ahead of you in the time machine, and have come back and said it's okay, you know, they're still alive."

Since Radiohead's debut single, "Creep," went supernova in the States in 1994, the band as a whole, and Thom and particular, have reacted to the fame thrust upon them with the bewilderment and disgust of a Methodist who inherits a brothel. The common take on "The Bends," the title track of the album Radiohead made against the backdrop of that success, was that it was a vicious, splenetic rail against the fact that stardom is not the liberating force that people imagine. It's actually incredibly limiting, and ultimately, unless you can ignore it, rise above it or find a way to have fun with it, utterly cretinising. "The Bends," like The Byrds' "So You Want Be A Rock'n'Roll Star," Costello's "Hand In Hand" and "Pump It Up," or Nirvana's "Serve The Servants" and "Pennyroyal Tea," sounded like one of those records often made by newly successful bands—they've got what they always wanted, and discovered that they don't want it.

"Well, no. . . ," says Thom, sounding almost apologetic for tearing down this hastily-constructed theory. "That song was really just a collection of phrases going round in my head one day. The crazy thing about that song is that there was no calculation or thought involved—it was just whatever sounded good after the previous line. It was written way before we'd ever been to America, even, but yeah, it's always interpreted as this strong reaction against the place and everything that went with it for us."

Understandable, though. The lyric is loaded with sleepy-eyed views from aeroplane windows, an alcohol drip-feed, the fear that the surface everyone sees is all you've got left.

"Oh, absolutely, but that hadn't started at all. I wrote it before we recorded the first album. We hadn't been anywhere. Is that the time?"

I imagine so.

"Shit, we're on in half an hour."

I pay for the coffees while Thom waits outside, polishing his sunglasses on the hem of his baggy jumper.

"Is that the guy who sang 'Creep'?" asks the waitress.

STREWN AROUND THE Mercury after another typically incendiary show are record company flyers plugging *The Bends*. These trumpet excerpts of the blanket critical praise *The Bends* has attracted. Radiohead have predictable difficulty taking any of it seriously.

"Radiohead toss and turn like the best Pearl Jam and U2 anthems," recites Jonny, from one leaflet.

"With the emphasis on toss, presumably," adds Ed.

"Thom Yorke's voice," reads Thom Yorke's voice, "is as enigmatic as Billy Corgan's."

Thom blinks a few times.

"Thanks a fucking bunch," he splutters, less than enigmatically.

Colin, meanwhile, is perturbed by the critical line taken by *Rolling Stone*. "It's four stars in quotation marks," he grins. "Does that mean they just swore at it?"

Outside on the pavement, a few dozen people have waited for Radiohead to emerge so they can tell them that they're, like, rilly rilly awesome. One woman apologises to Thom for her boyfriend, who'd been making a nuisance of himself down the front during the gig, and had come very close, at one point, to having Thom's guitar shoved down his throat. Sideways on, to judge by Thom's expression.

There's a record company meet-and-greet bunfight we're supposed to be at, though nobody is keen on the idea. Thom and I get in the last of the fleet of taxis that Caffy has flagged down.

"Right," he says. "Here's the plan. We hit the room, we charge around it as fast as possible, we shake hands with and smile at as many people as we can, whether we know them or not, and then we get out and go back to the hotel. I hate these things."

Right.

"If it doesn't kill us," says Thom, "it makes us stronger."

It turns out to be fairly low-key and relaxed, and everyone eventually stays for more than a few drinks. Even Thom could be mistaken for a man who's not having all that terrible a time. When we get back to our lodgings at the Paramount Hotel near Times Square, it's long past midnight, so we stage a chaotic photo shoot in Pat's tiny room—to allow all of Radiohead to get in front of the camera, I have to sit in the bath. Pat's efforts to encourage Radiohead to look like stern, seen-it-all road warriors are not aided by Jonny who, as Pat loads new film, reads choice titles from the catalogue of the hotel's in-house video library. "I will give anyone in this room five dollars in cash," he announces, "if they will ring reception and ask for *Honey, I Blew Everybody.*"

When Pat finally despairs of getting any sense out of them, Thom and I head downstairs to a table overlooking the lobby. The Philip Starck-designed Paramount is a triumph of style over substance. Everything in the hotel has been built or chosen to look good, regardless of whether it's any use—this creed applies equally to the furniture, the staff and most of the guests. If everything written about Thom Yorke was true, there's no way he'd come in here except with a beltful of grenades and a flamethrower, but he seems to find the place amusing. We order a tableful of beers, though we're both well on our way already. Thom peers over the glass balcony at a tottering catwalk mannequin loitering in the lobby below, bulging out of a dress that could scarcely be less comfortable if it was made of barbed wire and nettles.

"Fashion victim," says Thom, pointing unabashedly. "Dear oh dear. Though what I really like is those Versace jeans that cost £300 and still look like jeans."

I've never seen the point of spending that much money on something you're only going to spill coffee on.

"Makes you feel good."

This from a man who is still wearing a fake fur coat that looks like it was assembled from the pelts of a dozen bathmats.

"Colin spent £900 on a suit, but he only wears it now and again. Doesn't want to get it dirty. I did have a lovely pair of £100 sunglasses, but they got nicked."

My point exactly. So. Have you made a load of money, then?

"Ed's the person to ask, because I find it all ultra-confusing. One minute we'll have half a million in the bank, the next minute we'll have nothing. Ed keeps saying 'It's okay, it's all about cash flow, it'll all come through in the next six months.'"

You might want to keep an eye on him. It won't seem so funny when you're back busking outside Oxford station and Ed is sipping julep on the verandah of a plantation homestead with commanding views of Lake Tanganyika.

"Yeah . . . bloody hell."

Thom's squinting over the balcony again, this time at one of the under-dressed, alabaster-skinned goddesses that the Paramount seems to pay to saunter languidly about the building. We play a short game of she's-looking-at-me-no-she's-looking-at-me-no-she's-looking-me-yeah-right-I'm-the-pop-star-and-she's-looking-at-you-fat-chance.

"It's when they start coming up to you and saying hello that you get completely freaked out."

Happen often?

"No. I mean, yes, Andrew, it happens all the fucking time. I mean, no. The crew cop off a lot more than we do."

Always the way. Though that can be kind of funny. Other people's sex lives usually are.

"That borderline," says Thom, "is interesting, that duplicity between extremely cheap and extremely beautiful. But someone coming up to you after a show and invading your body space ridiculously, or . . . or being in a lift! I was in the lift earlier on, with my fur coat on, and this woman—she's obviously into teddy bears or something—got in the lift, and she was, like stroking me, and her opening line was 'Hey, we're in the green lift.'"

Classy.

"Mmm. Maybe I should wear it more often."

Thom smiles, which he does more than he's given credit for. If he's relaxed into his role over the last year, he still seems unduly spooked by the way other people react to his work. He has bridled at several interviewers who've accused him of relentless miserabilism, of preaching to a constituency of adolescent misanthropes who regard his lyrics less as songs and more as pre-packaged suicide notes.

"There's a few key words that keep coming up . . . I mean, you're asking for my hard disk, and it's really only the RAM working at the moment. Um, what people actually usually say is that the songs are beautiful, and they say nice stuff about the way I sing and the atmospheres and things, and the lyrics. Which I find quite weird. I was trying to get away from that on *The Bends* by printing them on the sleeve. I was trying to burst the bubble, saying they're just words, it's . . ."

They're important, though. You wouldn't bother writing them otherwise.

"The problem is having to deliver that sense of importance all the time. That's where the problem lies, because then you get into that

Morrissey territory of contriving situations simply to perpetuate the way that you think people think you are."

How do you rate yourself as a lyricist?

"Inconsistent. Definitely inconsistent."

What's the best one you've written?

"Um . . ."

There's a very, very long pause. It's hard to say whether Thom is indecisive or embarassed.

"Suck your teenage thumb," he decides. "Toilet trained and dumb. When the power runs out, we'll just hum. This is our new song. Just like the last one. Total waste of time. My iron lung."

He rattles it out in an everyday, conversational tone.

"Some woman gave me Dylan's *Highway 61 Revisited* the other day," he continues. "She said, 'Thom, you're a poet, listen to this,' so I listened to it, and then I read the sleeve notes and just burst out laughing. I mean, hang on a fucking minute . . ."

That was Dylan's act, though. Impenetrable, spurious nonsense that, for some reason, sounds like it explains everything. Michael Stipe does a fair bit of it as well.

"Well, I'm coming to the conclusion that your brain functions more honestly in spurious crap like that than it does in . . . things like 'My Iron Lung' happen every Saturday, say. The rest of the week it's just that spurious crap. When I was much younger, I did this four-track demo, and this girl, a really close friend of mine, listened to it and said, 'Your lyrics are crap, they're too honest, too direct and too personal, and there's nothing left to the listener's imagination,' and I've had that somewhere in the back of my head ever since. So now I want to write that spurious stuff that's coming straight out of my head. There's a song on *Blood & Chocolate* by Elvis Costello, the one that goes on and on for yonks . . ."

"Tokyo Storm Warning."

"Yeah. Gibberish! Complete fucking gibberish! And it's just wondrous. Because you open yourself up to that, because that's the way human brains think. I just think Radiohead are in a really dangerous position at the moment, where we could end up supplying that pathos and angst all the fucking time, and I think there's a bit more to it than that."

A closing line, if ever I've heard one.

"Mmm. I'm dying for a piss, as well."

THE INTERIOR OF the urinal in the Paramount's lobby is covered—ceilings, walls and floors—in gleaming, mercilessly reflective, polished steel. There is nowhere you can look without seeing everything else that's going on while you're in there, and from an alarming variety of angles. Thom and I pause, aghast, just inside the door.

"You go first," says Thom. "I'll wait outside. I'm still too British for this."

I'M THE TURBAN SPACEMAN, BABY

Afghanistan under the Taliban

MAY 1998

WHAT FOLLOWS STANDS as an example of the sort of thing that used to happen back when the absence of email made it necessary for editors and writers to interact in person. I was having lunch with Craig McLean, then features editor of *The Face*, the venerable British monthly style and culture periodical. Britain was, at the time, still invigorated by the removal, the previous year, of a decrepit, incompetent Conservative administration which had often seemed at least as bored and annoyed with Britain's people as Britain's people were with it, and by the election of the Labour government of Tony Blair, who had ostentatiously embraced pretty much everything that *The Face* had spent years promoting as an edgy counter-culture. The appalling phrase "Cool Britannia" was being routinely deployed to suggest the accession of a gilded new generation.

Which was balls, obviously—Britain's new prime minister was, after all, a mid-forty-something lawyer. Craig thought it might be fun, therefore, to write a story about a place where the people of our generation really were in charge, and suggested Afghanistan, then under the control of a disproportionately youth-run Islamist cult trading as the Taliban. In many crucial respects, Craig noted, the Taliban were typical *Face* readers: crazy students who sold drugs and had firm opinions about facial hair. He suggested I go and meet them.

I still feel a bit weird about the piece that resulted. I was, I think, seduced by how easy it was—both journalistically and morally—to regard the Taliban's lunacy as amusing rather than malevolent (that said, I think America and the West could have lurched yards ahead, these last few years, by depicting Osama bin Laden and his fellow travellers as dimwitted, ranting wingnuts rather than omnipotent evil geniuses). I was possibly a few years' more hard travelling from shedding my final vestiges of idiot relativism (although my brief experience of the world as the Taliban would prefer it has been useful, subsequently, as ammunition in disputes with idiot relativists). And it didn't occur to me, even for a second, that these people could ever pose any threat to anybody other than those sufficiently unfortunate to live in their dingbat fiefdom. (It's not much consolation that entire western intelligence services made approximately the same assessment.)

So, I wish I hadn't written this story. I wish—for all the difference it would have made—I'd come home and written an impassioned jeremiad demanding a massive international intervention in Afghanistan. I wish I'd demanded that the civilised world send bombers, troops and aid on the grounds of elementary human compassion. I wish I'd suggested that we harry the Taliban up hill, down dale and out of business. I wish I'd urged that surely, whatever else we may respectfully disagree about, some ideas are such obvious transgressions against sense and decency that we can occasionally get together as a planet and solemnly, forecfully declare: this is bullshit. We said it, or words to that effect, about South Africa when it treated black people like barnyard animals; I fail to understand why so many other countries continue to get a free pass to do the same to women.

As I write, of course, a massive international intervention in Afghanistan has been under way for some time, and I am yet to read a report describing the place as the Vermont of central Asia. I nevertheless believe the ongoing war there to be an effort worth making. Aside from considerations pertaining to self-interest—allowing Afghanistan to fester as a failed state worked out pretty badly for the rest of the world—it strikes me as a supremely elegant match of supply and demand. On one side, fervid holy warriors who declare that their dearest wish is a martyr's deathfighting the infidel. On the other, the awesome military forces of NATO and its allies. An offensive named "Operation Form An Orderly Queue, Weirdbeards" is surely overdue.

Finally, I apologise to American readers for the cricketing references in the opening paragraph, but that's what you get for disdaining this supremely noble sport in favour of the boorish playground pastime of baseball, and as further punishment you may strap yourselves in for the following. A few months after the reported conversation took place, the player at the centre of it stepped into cricketing legend just over the other side of the Khyber Pass. In October 2008, while captaining Australia in a Test match against Pakistan at Peshawar's Arbab Niaz Stadium, Mark Taylor piled up a colossal innings of 334 not out, equalling what was then the Australian record for runs scored by an individual batsman in a Test match, set sixty-eight years earlier by Sir Donald Bradman. I remember reading of Taylor's triple century at the time, and hoping that the officer who'd been so excited to meet someone who shared Taylor's birthplace had been able to get leave to see at least some of Taylor's epic knock. Even if Mark Taylor was—it turned out, upon further investigation—actually born in Leeton, a bit to the northwest of Wagga Wagga, just past Narrandera.

★ ★ ★

"MARK TAYLOR," SAYS the young Wing Commander of the Pakistan Army's Khyber Rifles, "is a very good batsman."

We're outside in the stifling heat, incessant noise and choking dust of the border crossing at Torkham. He's examining my passport, making sure my visa entitles me to come back into Pakistan at some stage. I'm kind of concerned on this point myself.

"You were born in Wagga Wagga," he continues. "Like Mark Taylor. Very, very good batsman."

Behind me are the CARE Afghanistan truck and driver that have borne me along the vertiginous Khyber Pass road from Peshawar, along with the armed military guard that any foreigners silly enough to travel the intermittently bandit-prone route must be accompanied by.

"Very good batsman."

Well, I don't know, I tell him. Without wishing to cast aspersions at Australia's redoubtable captain, or his efficiency as an opener, I've always found him a bit prosaic, as a spectacle. Certainly no Dean Jones.

"No. Very good batsman." He emphasises the "Very" with a fervour that suggests further disagreement would be foolish.

The border crossing point is an open gate between two white

turrets that would be more appropriate to a mediaeval theme park. Between them, unchecked traffic teems in both directions: battered cars and gaudily decorated trucks; camels and mules; people toting sacks, suitcases and wheelbarrows; lone, swaggering turbaned Afghans slinging rifles; shoals of Pakistani traders in various shades of pyjama suit; women blundering about under veils, trying uselessly to control squawking flocks of children, chasing and scrapping in the dirt. On the fence next to the gate, six Japanese tourists perch and chatter like mutant galahs, and fire their cameras into Afghanistan.

"But," the Wing Commander concedes, "he has been having a bad patch lately. Please enjoy Afghanistan."

This conversation is the least peculiar thing that will happen to me for a week.

ACROSS THE BORDER, I change some US dollars for Afghanis, the local currency. The Afghani is not one of the greats—children in low-slung hessian tents by the roadside sell it pretty much by weight, exchanging an inch-thick wad of purple 5000-Afghani notes for every 20-dollar bill. One kid holds my American money up to the sun and scrutinises it with an impatient eye, which is a bit rich considering that if I walk 50 metres back in the direction I've come, the notes he's giving me will only be useful as novelty bookmarks.

The Afghan customs officer is friendlier than his appearance, which isn't difficult, and asks about the purpose of my visit. I mumble some obsequious platitudes about coming to learn the truth about his beautiful, historic country and its sensitive, cultured, deeply misunderstood people. This is all true as far as it goes, though it's interesting to reflect that a dangerous-looking chap with a gun and an attractive woman will, if for entirely different reasons, reduce the average bloke to spouting exactly the same sort of fawning drivel.

For my purposes, anyway, it serves better than "Well, think about it: you've got a country with no rule of law, other than that dictated by the whim of a bunch of crazy students, and not only that, but crazy students who control the world's richest natural resources of recreational drugs—on paper, this place should be one gigantic Glastonbury. But, if we believe what we read, it's a total no-fun zone populated by ill-educated peasants living in perpetual fear of bearded wackos with rocket-launchers who think they're working for God. What's all that about?"

The customs officer stamps my passport, and walks me out to the bus station: a muddy lot behind the money-changing tents, full of merchants trying to sell each other shoes, bread and watches. He helps me buy two seats—one for me, one for my pack—on a crowded minibus headed for Jalalabad, shakes my hand, and waves me off.

THE REASON FOR my visit to Afghanistan is the reason that's motivated every hack who's come here since 1994. The Taliban, Afghanistan's rulers, are the journalistic equivalent of an open goal with a keeper lying injured somewhere near the halfway line. You can't miss. The Taliban are extremists so extreme they can't be bothered pretending they're not, and oppressors so oppressive they excite the liberal outrage of Iran. As if that wasn't enough, they have an undeniable comedy value—the global guffaws that greeted the Taliban's edict on facial hair were probably audible from deep space—and are also a convenient cipher for the image of Islam that so much of the western media, either through mendacity or ignorance, is keen to project. The Taliban, and their creed of the Koran and the Kalashnikov, are bloody good value, as long as you don't have to live in Afghanistan.

Under the Taliban's uncompromising reading of Islamic sharia law, Afghanistan is the most repressive society on earth, a place where everything is illegal, except beards and praying, which are compulsory. If you're trying to have fun in Afghanistan, you can forget the following: cinema (closed), drink (punishable by flogging), dancing (illegal), or being outside for any reason at all after 9:00 PM (curfew, about which the Taliban aren't kidding—a few days before I got into Afghanistan, two foreign aid workers, lost on their way home in Kabul at 9:15 PM, flagged down a Taliban patrol vehicle, apologised, and asked for a lift, whereupon they were arrested, locked up for four days and threatened with a public beating, before the poor sods' employers interceded and the Taliban settled for driving them to the border and throwing them out of the country). If you're male, you can go out for a meal, but you can't take your girlfriend, because eating would necessitate her removing the mesh face-mask from her all-over veil—the burqa—and women may not show any part of themselves in public, on pain of a sound thrashing.

And if you decide, all things considered, to stay in and watch telly, you're in for a slow night—there isn't any. The only broadcaster permitted in Afghanistan is Radio Shariat, which offers a schedule consisting of religious programmes and heavily censored news bulletins, and is light on chuckles.

The sole legal amusement I detect in a week in Afghanistan is pestering foreigners. Everywhere I walk, I get followed by droves of people, children and adults alike, a few begging, most just curious. One afternoon in Kabul, while I'm standing outside a mosque watching punters arrive for prayers, a kindly shopkeeper scuttles up with a chair. When I sit down, I am surrounded by dozens of people, staring and gawping. They eventually crowd so close that the first few rows land in my lap. I have a sudden insight into how deeply tiresome it must be to be famous.

THE SPINGHAR HOTEL in Jalalabad is situated at the end of a gravel drive amid pretty and well-kept gardens. By the front door is a sign bearing a picture of a Kalashnikov assault rifle with a red cross painted over it. Classy place, obviously.

Jalalabad, capital of the province of Nangarhar, is a grim footnote in British imperial history. It was here, in January 1842, that an early attempt at bringing this wilful country to heel came to an end, when a Dr. Brydon, the only surviving member of a 17,000-strong British army that had marched to Kabul three years previously, rode into the city on a lame horse.

There's not much of anything in Jalalabad today, except dust. The streets are paved with it, the people covered in it, the buildings apparently built from it, and the chicken I'm served at the Spinghar tastes of it. Jalalabad does have a bazaar, and though it's a common fantasy among middle-class western dilettantes that markets in remote third world towns are full of picturesque natives selling each other exquisite hand-crafted jewellery and organic hair conditioner, there's nothing for sale in Jalalabad except whatever crap fell off the back of the last truck that came through: plastic crockery from Uzbekistan, Azerbaijani chocolate and a startling amount of Pepsi Cola, stacked everywhere in blue crates.

In the centre of Jalalabad, there's a traffic roundabout, around which a large crowd is gathered. I gather with it for a bit to see what they're waiting for. After an hour, I decide that maybe 300-a-side staring-silently-into-the-middle-distance has been decreed a right-on Islamic sport, or something, and leave them to it. That evening, when I go to meet someone in the UN compound, I'm told that the mob had been gathering to watch local Talibs administer a kicking to one of their own— for "dishonesty," apparently. At the hotel at dusk, a few local women are sitting gossiping beneath a tree. When they see me approaching, they pull their masks back down over their faces, and fall silent.

I leave Jalalabad for Kabul the following morning with Noel Spencer, a genial Northern Irishman who, after years defusing things for the British Army in Northern Ireland and the Kuwaiti Royal Family in Kuwait, now does the same for the UN's mine clearance operation in Afghanistan. His experienced driver and his new 4WD pick-up take nine hours to negotiate the 200 or so kilometres between the two cities. At best, the road, devastated by decades of neglect, tanks and mortars, is appalling. At worst, it just isn't there, degenerating into interminable sequences of ridges and cracks that engender the strange feeling of being seasick on dry land. More than once, the horizon disappears behind the lip of potholes big enough to fit the entire truck in.

Which, given Afghanistan's horizons, is an accomplishment. If the people of Afghanistan take the Almighty a little more seriously than most, they could rightly argue that this is where He's done some of his best work. Snow-white and basalt-black mountain ranges as jagged as an Albanian bank's profit-and-loss charts cradle the sort of sweeping green plains that make me wish that I had a troop of cavalry I could charge across them. Next to the road, the mighty Kabul River flows green, then grey, then silver, before disappearing as the road heads up to the plateau on which Kabul sits, and winds through immense gorges which look awesomely forbidding and final, like exits from the entire universe.

Villages, made entirely from mud, hunch along the roadside. In one, too small to merit a name, we stop for lunch in a mud room where the floor is also the table, and the only way to pick the difference between the flies and the sultanas in the stew is that the sultanas are marginally less animated. In another town, Sarobi, there is a shop, operating out of a converted shipping container, offering for sale an impressive range of used assault rifles, mortars, grenade-launchers and anti-tank weapons. The shipping container next door is piled high with more crates of Pepsi.

WEDNESDAY MORNING, THE first thing I do is the first thing all visiting media in Kabul have to do: check in with the Ministry of Foreign Affairs. The press office is run by a cheery old buzzard called Dr. Aminzai, a career civil servant who had a reputation, during previous regimes, as an impeccably groomed, Armani-clad dandy trailing clouds of imported aftershave. He wanted to keep his job, and so now wears a traditional robe and turban, and a beard you could hide crates of bootlegged Pepsi in. He makes me fill in some forms, gives me a Taliban press card, and reads me the riot act.

"You must stay," he says, "at the Intercontinental Hotel."

I checked in last night. It's up on a hill commanding glorious views of Kabul, though the swimming pool and the cocktail bar haven't seen use in some time. It has 150 staff and 200 rooms, but only two are currently occupied—mine, and one up the hall by a hotel employee who opens his door and booms, "Hello, Mr. Andrew!" every time I walk in or out (as the week wears on, I will try to catch him by leaving again straight after arriving, or creeping out at four in the morning to run up and down the deserted upstairs corridors, but he doesn't miss a trick).

"You must not take pictures of people," continues Dr. Aminzai.

I wasn't going to try. Several photographers have been attacked by the Taliban for committing photography, though it isn't illegal, as such—I later get a smudged black-and-white portrait of myself taken by a bloke on a street corner with an ancient box camera.

"And," he says, "you will not be able to talk to women."

That's okay, I tell him. It's like that at home.

"It will mean trouble for you," he says, ignoring my feeble, if heartfelt, attempt at levity, "and more trouble for them."

With that, Dr. Aminzai introduces my Taliban-appointed translator/minder, whom I'll call Akbar. Akbar is a twenty-one-year-old student at Kabul University. He's not Taliban himself, but is happy to make a few dollars conducting journalists around town for them. Akbar speaks excellent English, and we get on surprisingly well, given that we both, I think, feel like we're trying to explain earth to a martian.

"You are not married?" enquires Akbar over lunch one day.

No.

"But you are twenty-nine."

Correct.

"How is this?"

Oh, I don't know. Stuff.

"But you have had girlfriends?"

Mmm.

"And you have. . . lain with them?"

In general, yes.

"What becomes of them, when you have finished with them?"

They struggle on.

"But what other man will want them?"

It's a topic we return to frequently, especially when Akbar—a devout Muslim, and engaged to be married—introduces me to other people. The first thing he explains to them is my unattached status, which he seems to find more extraordinary the more he thinks about it—the people he tells couldn't seem more surprised if he told them that I had a tail. I begin to wish that I'd said to Akbar from the off what I'd been saying to the equally curious merchants in the bazaar back in Peshawar ("Yes, her name's Winona, she's an actress. Yes, three sons, Jehosophat, Ezekiel and Susan—we're a bit worried about Susan").

In the Herat, one of Kabul's few tolerable restaurants, we meet Kalahan, a twenty-four-year-old student (married, four children). He asks me earnestly about "prostitution houses."

Brothels, I correct him.

"Please—what is that word?"

He writes it down as I spell it out.

"Please—are they legal where you live?"

I've no idea. Sort of, I think.

"But please," he asks, "if everyone is allowed to sleep with each other anyway, what is the point of them?"

I try asking Kalahan about the civil war that ravaged Kabul and killed thousands of its citizens in the early 90s. There's enough of Kabul still standing up to give me the idea that it must have been quite an attractive city, once. It was also rather fun, according to long-serving expats I meet in the UN Club, now Kabul's only licensed premises

("In 1992," recalls one Belgian doctor, "you could stay out all night, and it was only about as far off the pace as Budapest, or somewhere like that"). Today, several suburbs of Kabul are uninhabitable ruins, though people still inhabit them. Even the less damaged areas look like English football fans have been staying in them ("And culturally," the same doctor tells me, "this place has gone from 1976 to 1376").

Kalahan and others his age don't really want to talk about the war, or the Soviet invasion that preceded it, or the Taliban takeover that followed it. This is understandable—it's all they've ever known. UNICEF estimates that 70 percent of Kabul's children lost a family member between 1992 and 1996. It's like trying to get Mauritanians excited about discussing drought.

"The Taliban," explains Kalahan, resignedly, "stopped the war."

But aren't you frightened of them?

"Of course. But they won't last. Nobody does."

Nobody, least of all the Afghans themselves, has ever succeeded in governing Afghanistan's volatile mix of tribes (half Pakhtun, with the balance made up by Tajiks, Turkomans, Uzbeks and Hazaras). Many have tried: the Sikh and Persian empires, Tsarist Russia and Victorian Britain. In 1979, the USSR decided it was the nation for the job and, just as America had done in Vietnam, found its immense, sophisticated army locked in unwinnable combat with motivated guerillas—performing the military equivalent of trying to swat wasps with a steamroller.

When Mikhail Gorbachev admitted the jig was up in 1988, Red Army casualties stood at 50,000. The road between Kabul and the Pakistani border is still littered with rusting remains of dead Soviet tanks. The tribesmen of Afghanistan, the dashing horse-mounted mujahedin who had opposed the initial Soviet invasion with rusty cutlasses and flintlock rifles, were by this stage bringing down MIG fighter planes with Stinger surface-to-air missiles. They hadn't found these lying around—America, reasoning that the enemy of its enemy was its friend, spent $3 billion equipping and training the mujahedin. In creating this army of Islamic holy warriors to fight the godless communists, decadent Christian America forged the heavily armed and anarchic environment in which the Taliban would flourish. Funny old world.

The common enemy defeated, the mujahedin took their shiny new American weapons, and their captured old Russian ones, and fought amongst themselves. Throughout the early 90s, former mujahedin chiefs and sundry warlords—notably Ahmed Shah Massoud, Gulbuddin Hekmatyar and Rashid Dostum—fell in and out with each other at such a rate that the favoured black humour fashion item among foreign aid workers at the time bore the legend "My party raided Kabul and all I got was this lousy t-shirt."

Enter, in late 1994, the Taliban. The Taliban—the term is a plural of Talib, or religious student—formed in the madrasas (Islamic schools) of the southern city of Kandahar. They had Allah on their side like everyone else, only more so. They had weapons supplied by local merchants tired of the beatings, robberies and rapes perpetrated by the bandits who preyed on the roads around Kandahar (Noel Spencer had told me that, pre-Taliban, he'd been hijacked several times along the Kabul-Jalalabad road). The Taliban were tough on crime, and tough on the causes of crime. They rounded up 50 local highwaymen and hung them off the barrels of tanks.

To a population as harassed as it was uneducated (53 percent of Afghan men and 85 percent of women are illiterate), this robust approach to enforcing civic order had a definite appeal. Over the next two years, the Taliban annexed swathes of Afghanistan, recruiting as they went from Afghanistan's uncountable gangs of freelance brigands, who knew a winning side when they saw one. In September 1996, the Taliban hoisted their flag over Kabul, a city which the mostly southern, rural talibs had always regarded with the same pious repugnance that Utah Mormons harbour for Las Vegas. The Taliban's all-white—or rather, given Afghanistan's chronic filth, all-grey—banner was alleged to be a symbol of peace. The Taliban removed Soviet-era President Muhammad Najibullah and his brother from their sanctuary in Kabul's UN compound, and hung them off a traffic observation kiosk.

Casual brutality and an enthusiasm for Islam were hardly innovations in Afghan politics, but the Taliban really weren't messing about. They introduced a blizzard of laws. Some were biblically severe (public amputation of hands for theft, public execution for murder, often by relatives of the victim). Some were faintly hilarious (the criminalisation of kite-flying, the compulsory flowing beards for males). Except that

even these really weren't funny. According to a report in Peshawar's
Frontier Post, 500 Kabuli men were lashed the week before I arrived for
having trimmed their beards. Akbar solemnly tells me that he has been
warned about his fringe.

One afternoon, when Akbar is taking me shopping for a rug on
Chicken Street, a young, correctly hirsute Afghan approaches me and
asks if he can practice his English. Over tea in a nearby cafe, he and
Akbar ask me about Australia. I tell them about the Sydney Gay Mardi
Gras, which I'd been to a few months previously. Their minds boggle
almost audibly.

"What were the police doing while this was going on?" demands
Akbar.

They marched in the parade.

"You have sodomites in your police?"

Akbar clearly thinks I'm winding him up.

"I was in Herat in March," says our new friend, blandly. "The
Taliban caught two sodomites there. They pushed a wall over on them
with a tank."

The department that enforces these laws is the Ministry for the
Propagation of Virtue and Prevention of Vice. The name, like many
aspects of Taliban rule, manages to evoke both George Orwell's satire
and Monty Python's comedy (the Spanish Inquisition sketch comes to
mind more than once, especially one morning at the Intercontinental
when eight turbaned Talibs appear behind the waiter to hear me order
breakfast—Rice Krispies, I decide, to general muttered approval).
This Ministry's operatives are the public presence of Taliban justice,
scowling beneath black turbans and behind blacker Ray-Bans as they
sip Pepsi and patrol Kabul in Toyota pick-ups with tinted windows.

Akbar and I go to the offices of Vice & Virtue, which are situated
just opposite the roundabout where Najibullah and his brother were
killed. I ask to see Alhaj Mawlawi Qalamuddin, the Deputy Minister.
I am treated with customary Islamic courtesy, provided with tea and
biscuits and kept waiting for ages before being told that Qalamuddin is
away at the front line (fighting continues 20 kilometres north of Kabul,
against forces loyal to Massoud). This happens every morning for a
week, which suggests that one reason nobody can figure the Taliban
out is that the Taliban themselves aren't too clear on what they're

doing. The chap who runs the shop, a one-eyed thirty-something called Mullah Mohammad Omar, stays down in Kandahar and doesn't do much press. There are, in theory, Ministers, but none of the ministries I visit know where the bloke in charge is—"Away at the front line" is, I suspect, a convenient shorthand for "Shagged if I know, and what's it to you, anyway?"

"There's no power structure, no accountability," one aid worker tells me, back at the UN club. "They're just young guys with guns who think they know everything."

ON SATURDAY MORNING, outside the offices of the Taliban's intelligence service, the Estekhbarat, I wait to see some young guys with guns who think they know everything. While Akbar is inside making representations on my behalf, I sit at the gate with the guard. Like a depressing proportion of young Afghans, he has the soaring cheekbones and blazing eyes of a 50s matinee idol—if the women are as pretty as the men are handsome, the burqa is as great an affront to aesthetics as it is to human rights. The guard is keen to test an English vocabulary apparently acquired from satellite transmissions of *Play School*.

"My nose," he says, pointing at his mountainous Afghan beak.

"My eyes," he continues, gesturing at two iridescent irises of a limpid aquamarine that suggests someone in his gene pool didn't object too strongly to either the British or the Russians.

"My ears," he announces, resting his rifle on his lap so he can hold them out for emphasis.

"And," he says, "my . . . bread?"

He has his fingers in the thatch trailing off his chin.

It's your beard, mate. Beard.

"Beard," he confirms. "Very good. Thank you."

Inside the Estekhbarat building, I am ushered into an office that smells of feet and resembles a student bedsit, except that the groovy oriental rugs on the walls were made locally. Inside, cross-legged on two camp beds, are two terse young Talibs in white robes and white turbans. One gives his name as Abdul Haque Waseeque, and claims to be Acting Director of Intelligence. The other declines to give a name or a title, but mentions that he's just been away at the front. Ah, so it does exist.

As the inevitable tea and biscuits arrive, I start with the easy stuff. Like most Talibs, they're of Pakhtun descent, and from outside Kabul—they both grew up in Ghazni, to the south, and were raised to regard Kabul as a sink of depravity. They're in their mid-twenties, and won't go into detail about their work, but say they're the Afghan version of the CIA.

"Laws made by humans have flaws," begins Abdul. "The rule of Allah has none."

The tone is set for the next couple of hours: God said it, they believe it, and that settles it. But why does divine rule have to be this . . . miserable?

"For the time being," says Abdul, "it is delicate. How can cinema be right in war conditions? The Taliban pledged Islamic law and peace, and we have created that."

Granted, Kabul is no longer at war, though the airport was rocketed by Massoud just before I arrived (I'd originally hoped to fly to Kabul on the the Red Cross shuttle from Peshawar, but flights were suspended when Massoud started acting the goat). There are fewer guns visible in Kabul than on the streets of Belfast or Beirut. Crime, which was rampant, is now so rare that for the last few weeks there haven't been any amputations or executions before the Friday football match at Kabul Stadium. Akbar and I had gone to the game the day before, a dismal 0-0 draw between two teams wearing shorts like you've only seen in footage of 1920s Cup Finals (the Taliban decided that football was un-Islamic for a while, but changed their minds). A few thousand people turned up, and mostly talked amongst themselves, though the wild, two-footed tackles that punctuated the match were greeted with appreciative laughter. Akbar, who I increasingly suspect of being a closet liberal, glumly admitted that on afternoons when someone's due to get something lopped off, the place fills to its 30,000 capacity.

But I still don't understand how security is abetted by forcing women to drift silently about looking like pantomime ghosts.

"The burqa is the rule of Islam," says Abdul. "The rule of Mohammad, Jesus and all the messengers is that women should be covered."

I take the sort of deep breath you take before arguing with armed fanatics on their own terms. According to my Penguin translation, the Koran says that "the wives of true believers should draw their veils close round them." It doesn't say that they have to cover themselves totally. It certainly doesn't rule them out of work, education and life the way the Taliban have.

"The burqa is the rule of Islam," repeats Abdul, though the news that I've read the Koran cheers him up a bit. "I must ask if you are concerned about the years you have wasted in preparing for the next world."

I change the subject. When the Taliban took power, they made extravagant fulminations against the drug trade: evil, corrupting, the ruination of us all, etcetera and amen. In 1997, according to the UN Drug Control Programme, 200,000 Afghan farmers grew 58,000 tonnes of opium, mostly on Taliban-controlled land. The British government estimates that 95% of the heroin in Britain is grown in Afghanistan's poppy fields. Afghanistan is also the world's biggest exporter of hashish— those who consider their narcotic recreation a victimless crime may care to contemplate whose wages they're paying.

Now, the Koran doesn't explicitly forbid making a fortune shipping smack to the infidel, but . . .

"The purpose of Islamic law," intones Abdul's friend, "is to protect life, property, religion and the brain. Heroin is forbidden."

So why not forbid it?

"We cannot stop the poppy from growing."

Yes, you can. Get some flamethrowers in amongst all those poppy fields I saw alongside the Jalalabad-Kabul road. It'd be a start.

"It is not our people who consume it. It is yours. In the West, society is riven by drugs and prostitution. In the Islamic environment, young people have more love for Islam."

It's odd, then, that they find it necessary to beat people for failing to attend prayers.

"If a person does everything in accordance with Allah, then everything will be good. If not, we must implement the will of Allah by any means."

Eyes beginning to glaze, desperate to hear an answer that doesn't invoke Allah, Mohammed or the Koran, I ask Akbar to ask them who they fancy for the World Cup.

Abdul doesn't blink.

"In accordance with the teachings of the Holy Koran, no human being knows the future, only Allah almighty."

Oh, come on. Brazil? France? Argentina?

"Only Allah . . ."

Okay, okay. What do you do for fun?

"To relax, we recite from the Koran."

The depressing thing is that I believe him. If I thought there was the slightest chance that, as soon as I'd gone, Abdul was going to turn to his mate and go, "There's another dopey gringo sold on the gimlet-eyed holy warrior tip, you go and round up some birds and I'll get some cans in for the match," I'd be a lot less worried about Abdul and his mate and the country they're running.

When I get up to leave, two strange things happen. The first is that Abdul stands as well, clasps my hands in his and asks Akbar to ask me to stay in Afghanistan, become their brother and join their jihad. The second is that while I'm trying to think of a polite way to decline this kind offer, the room starts shaking. At first, I think it's just me—nobody else notices, or if they do, they don't care. After a few seconds, with the shaking growing more violent, and things starting to come off shelves, I ask Akbar what's happening.

"Abdul wants you to join the Taliban," he says, wobbling.

This isn't what I'm worried about; I'm thinking that maybe Massoud's rocket batteries have lost interest in the airport and are trying out a new target. Or that Abdul really does have friends in high places.

"Oh," says Akbar. "I think it's an earthquake."

I will later learn that a few hundred kilometres north, 5000 people have just been buried alive. Funny, in a country so forsaken by God—scenery aside—that people should be so keen on Him.

WONDERING IF AN older head might prove more reasonable, I drop in on the mayor. Mullah Abdul Majid, even by Afghan standards, is an imposing figure. He has one severely mangled hand and one missing leg, legacies of his time as a Mujahedin commander—a common CV among senior Taliban figures. He begins by welcoming me to his city "in the name of Allah, the compassionate and merciful," and pours me the first decent coffee I've had in two weeks. An elderly secretary beside him writes down every detail of our conversation, so that it may be broadcast to an enthralled nation on Radio Shariat (I listen to the daily English-language bulletin that night, hoping to hear that "His Excellency the Mayor today briefly tolerated some scruffy hack from *The Face*," but I can't make out a word through the static).

"It is our religious duty to implement the basics of Islam," he explains. "No other country has shed so much blood. We must ensure that we have a result for the price people paid."

He deflects questions about women ("The burqa is not new to Afghanistan, just to the outside world") and drugs (shrugs). He only gets excited when I raise foreign reaction to the Taliban—nobody but Pakistan, Saudi Arabia and the United Arab Emirates has recognised the Taliban as a legitimate government.

"Five years ago," he glowers, "the world was wondering how to bring peace to Afghanistan. The Taliban did, and world still recognises robbers like Massoud."

Laughing Boy at Estekhbarat had said the same, and it's a hard point to argue with. It's not like the world doesn't do business with human rights black holes like China, Israel, Saudi Arabia and Turkey. Maybe the Taliban are suffering for being too honest or too artless or too thick to dress up their regime as anything other than mediaeval barbarism. But maybe if they moderated their approach, the embassies might start reopening.

"You cannot," says Majid, "moderate the will of God."

THE ONLY MODERATING influences on the Taliban are Kabul's aid agencies, or non-governmental organisations (NGOs). They are doing what they can to drag this hopelessly poor nation into the current century. Afghanistan's poverty is best illustrated not by per capita wages as percentages of gross domestic product, or anything like that, but by a uniformed policeman who accosts me one afternoon in Kabul's market.

"You are very rich," says the cop. "I am very poor. Give me some money, please, so I may spend it."

You're supposed to arrest me first, I tell him.

This destitution exists despite Afghanistan's situation astride one of the most lucrative trade routes on earth—unfortunately, the kind of merchants who'll shift crates of Pepsi across places this politically unpredictable and riddled with landmines are not the kind who pay import duties. It also seems incompatible with Afghanistan's glorious natural beauty, which, given a few years of peace, tourists would happily pay enormous sums to see. The only ones I meet are a pair of dour French passport stamp-collectors, in Afghanistan only because it's the fifth-last country they haven't been to. They ask me if I know anything about getting visas for North Korea, and if the Taliban will hassle them much.

The few hundred other foreigners in Kabul all do far more useful things than checking off place names in their atlases, or asking nonplussed secret policemen who's going to win the World Cup, and the Taliban hassle them a lot. The NGOs do the things governments are supposed to do—pave roads, build bridges, heal the sick, educate the young—while the Taliban pursue such crucial concerns as caning taxi drivers for carrying women unaccompanied by male relatives (this happened to ten cabbies the week I was there), or drafting ludicrous visa regulations (having spent a week in Peshawar getting a visa to get into Afghanistan, I have to spend a day in Kabul getting another one to get out—the Talib who signs off on my exit visa lectures me about irregular verbs and asks me to make sure that I tell my readers how nice the weather in Kabul is compared to Peshawar). The Taliban are at pains to tell me how grateful they are for the work the NGOs do. NGO workers say they're sure the Taliban would run them out of town if they thought they could afford to, and make me promise not to mention them or their organisation.

To justify their paranoia, one NGO worker shows me a memo, dated May 24, 1998, from my perpetually absent friend Qalamuddin at Vice & Virtue. It refers to a much-gnawed bone of contention—employment for women. The Taliban are not keen on the idea, though they're less keen on healthcare for women being provided by men. So, compromises allowing local women to work in this area have been made, and broken, and made, and . . .

"Inspectors have been ordered to identify and arrest such people. Offenders will be treated in accordance with Sharia law. You will have to bear any further responsibilities in this regard."

"This," I am told, "is what we're up against, every day, about every damn thing."

The same NGO worker tells me about a local woman, formerly employed by their NGO, who'd come in one day tearful because she was an hour late. The reason was that her twelve-year-old son had refused to come with her. Women who leave home unaccompanied by a male relative do so at their own very real risk.

"Can you imagine a twelve-year-old boy having that kind of power? That's what worries me, that people are already accepting this as normal."

Wandering around Kabul the last few days, though, I've been wondering if the women of Afghanistan are beaten yet. Oppressed people, consciously or not, will reach for whatever means of rebellion are available, however trivial, and beneath many of Kabul's shambling burqas are expensive-looking, open-topped leather shoes with high heels. Given Kabul's chronically potholed streets, shrapnel-ravaged footpaths and open sewers, that's as fine a definition of heroism as you could want.

I HAVE TO leave Afghanistan by road, as well. I hadn't been able to get in on the Red Cross shuttle flight between Peshawar and Kabul because of Massoud's rockets, and I can't fly out because the airport is closed by rain (there's no radar, no air traffic control, and an awful lot of mountains—if pilots can't see, they can't land). I find a lift back to Peshawar with a truck-load of European doctors, all trying to connect with planes and choppers heading up to the earthquake zone. It takes us just short of two days, via Jalalabad—the roads are not improved by rain.

It's only after we've crossed the border, collected our armed guard for the Khyber drive, that I can identify the single strangest thing about the Taliban's Afghanistan. It's something that wasn't there, rather than something that was, and I encounter it blaring from a tinny speaker outside a roadside tea shop. It's one of those regrettable hybrids of Asian folk and European pop, it's got a beat that sounds like a washing machine with an unbalanced load, an arrangement that suggests the contents of a tool kit being emptied down a lift shaft and a vocal apparently recorded by a cockatoo with one wing in a wringer but it's. . . music.

3

BALKAN AFTER MIDNIGHT

Sarajevo's rock'n'roll scene

March 1996

THIS TRIP WAS a penance, of sorts. I have few meaningful regrets, but among them is a failure to make more of an effort to write more about the war that beset Bosnia-Herzegovina in the 1990s (that regret is, of course, tempered significantly by the knowledge that Bosnia-Herzegovina was, at that time, the kind of place in which a young and clueless interloper could very easily have ended up dead—and that, of course, is at least part of the reason why I didn't make more of an effort). The failure of the civilised world to act decisively to halt a genocide in the heart of Europe struck me as an atrocious and inexcusable dereliction then, and seems even more so in retrospect. The spectacle of Muslims being slaughtered with impunity, for year after unnecessary and avoidable year, was a viciously radicalising catalyst for more than a few angry, vindictive and malevolent souls: the route to 9/11 leads through Sarajevo and Srebrenica.

I did end up making one visit to Bosnia's war, almost by accident, which is described elsewhere in this book, but I didn't get to Sarajevo until after the war had (more or less) ended, and I still feel pretty bad about that. Not that I imagine my presence would have made any difference to anything, but it's a stand I would like to feel I'd taken when it counted: on the side of a city with a tradition of amiable plurality, against the forces of bigotry and backwardness seeking to destroy it—and, not insignificantly, against the agents of ignorance and indifference, possessed though they were of air forces big enough to put a stop to the nonsense in an afternoon, who watched Sarajevo burn for a little over four years.

What follows is what I felt I could do—which, at the time, was write about rock music, quite a lot of which, I'd heard, had been made during the siege. I secured a tentative commission from a now-extinct magazine called *Blah Blah Blah*. I rustled up some phone numbers from some friends at an aid organisation called The Serious Road Trip, whom I'd got to know in London. I flew, via Frankfurt and Zagreb, to the Croatian port of Split, where I cadged a lift with a French NGO as far as Mostar, who handed me over to another NGO who took me to Zenica, from where the Road Trip drove me to Sarajevo in a hot pink Land Rover with flames painted down the side.

As it turned out, showing up in a war zone and writing about rock'n'roll was easier and more rewarding than I'd anticipated. Sarajevans were, not unreasonably, bored sideways with war as a topic of conversation, and once word of what I was doing spread among local musicians, my days and nights filled up profitably and agreeably. I was assisted above and beyond the call by Jim Marshall, a splendidly laconic Scot who had suffered none of my qualms and spent most of the siege in Sarajevo as an aid worker. He's still there today, and provides the following updates of the characters you're about to meet. Enis from C.I.A. became a DJ, spent some time in Berlin, but is now back in Sarajevo. The members of Z.O.C.H. have been spotted, it seems, "hill-walking and pushing baby strollers." Pedrag "Paja" Pasic still runs his football school. Zelimir Altarac-Cicak is a radio personality, and has a Sarajevo music website every bit as excellent as his haircut at www.cicak.ba. And Sikter are still going, as well—www.sikter.com.

The image, or idea, that has stuck with me hardest from this trip was that of the kids gathered in the club called Obala, urging the DJ to turn it up so loud that they couldn't hear the explosions of the shells landing outside. I've often wondered since if that isn't the reason that human beings have always made and listened to music: to obliterate reality, and to replace it with something beautiful, or at least with something that makes some sense to us at those moments when little else does.

★ ★ ★

ALONG THIS STRETCH of the south bank of the Miljacka River, the front lines were so close that, with a following wind, it would have been almost possible for the Bosnians defending their city to spit on the Serbs besieging it. Near the bitterly contested Jewish cemetery, the barricades are still in place, separated by a no man's land which is the width of an inner-city street, because the no man's land is an inner-city street. A few blocks farther along the river today, history is being made. Grbavica, the last of Sarajevo's suburbs still held by Bosnian Serb forces, is being handed back to the government of Bosnia and Herzegovina under the terms of the four-month-old Dayton Peace Agreement.

Myself, a veteran Scottish photographer and aid worker called Martin Kennedy and a young rock'n'roll band called C.I.A. are picking our way through what were, less than six months ago, Bosnian army positions. We're looking for suitably dramatic backdrops for photographs for our story about Sarajevo musicians, and we're spoilt for choice. Film studios spend millions to create this kind of picturesque destruction.

On an inside wall of one half-destroyed house that had functioned as a Bosnian army sniper post, there's a lurid, hand-painted cartoon portrait of Dr. Radovan Karadzic. Karadzic is the retired psychiatrist, useless poet, convicted fraudster and nationalist maniac who, as leader of something amusingly called the Serbian Democratic Party (SDS), presided over the attempted murder of Sarajevo. The anonymous artist has perfectly captured Karadzic's hooded, punch-drunk eyes, mean, lopsided mouth and extravagant, blow-dried bouffant, and made his opinion still clearer by ramming a sickle through the good doctor's ears, jamming a hammer, handle-first, into the top of Karadzic's fussily-coiffed head and dubbing the picture with the caption "CCCP Koza." CCCP was what the Soviet Union used to call the Soviet Union. "Koza" is Bosnian for goat.

Outside, a section of the street has been dug up and turned into a trench. It is still littered with banal testaments to the urban nature of Sarajevo's war: crushed soft drink cans and soggy pizza cartons. I wonder if the soldiers picked up their take-outs on their way to battle, or if they radioed their orders in from here, and if so, how much extra it costs to get a deep pan with added anchovy delivered to an active front line.

Martin thinks he's found his spot, and starts organising C.I.A. into something that looks like a photograph. He's just about to raise his camera when Enis, the ponytailed one of C.I.A.'s two vocalists, waves to stop him.

"Excuse me," says Enis.

Martin sighs the sigh universally deployed by photographers whose subjects have started having ideas of their own.

"I was wondering," continues Enis, "if we could do the pictures in that trench over there."

"I suppose so," shrugs Martin. "Any particular reason?"

"Well," says Enis, apologetically, gesturing at his bandmates, "that's where we met."

ESCAPE HAS ALWAYS been the most precious of rock'n'roll's renegade imperatives. As soon as the first guitar was electrified, it was identified as an ideal weapon with which to vent dissatisfaction with the world, as noisy as a gun, nearly as dangerous and almost as likely to get you arrested. Young people ever since have been forming rock'n'roll bands to escape homes, hometowns, families, expectations, tedium, frustration, poverty, the prospect of having to work for a living, or even just a vague, incoherent ennui which they have a hard time explaining, man.

In Sarajevo, they formed rock'n'roll bands to escape the literally inescapable: the three-and-a-half-year siege of the city by the motley assortment of drunks, hillbillies and thugs trading as the Bosnian Serb Army. The siege of Sarajevo—a city surrounded by steep, ridged hills that might have been designed as cover from which cowards could wage war against civilians—began in April 1992. In late 1994, a new independent radio station called Radio Zid broadcast a request for demo tapes from local bands. They received submissions from twenty-five groups they'd never heard of. Something was clearly afoot.

Something still is. I've come to Sarajevo at the behest of my friends at The Serious Road Trip, unarguably the world's most rock'n'roll non-governmental organisation. They'd been telling me for months that there was much here to interest an itinerant rock journalist, and they weren't kidding. Every Sarajevan still the silly side of thirty seems to be in a band, or to have several dozen very good friends who are in bands. Or to have been in a band once. Or to be thinking about starting one. Or to be very keen for me to come and spend a few hours being deafened by enthusiastic renditions of their material in some tiny, sandbagged rehearsal space in some disused basement of some shrapnel-shattered building.

It would be enormously gratifying to be able to report that the quality is as startling as the quantity, and that as soon as the smoke lifts, Sarajevo will be hosting an A&R gold rush to rival the boom years of Seattle or Manchester. It would please me no end to be able to write that Sarajevo is an El Dorado of rock'n'roll genius, mostly because the musicians in Sarajevo's bands are, by and large, decent people who've put up with more than enough, but at least partly because most of the musicians in Sarajevo's bands boast military service histories that would make the Dirty Dozen look a bunch of simpering lightweights.

The truth is that Sarajevo's is a fairly typical European rock'n'roll culture, comparable with those of Berlin, or Stockholm, or Tel Aviv, where genuine brilliance only fitfully upstages big fish/little puddle mediocrity, and where earnestness is having a real field day at the expense of wit. In fairness, nobody pretends otherwise. Everyone agrees that Sarajevo's favourite song of Sarajevo's war was written by Americans (Rage Against The Machine's "Killing In The Name," which, as one local musician puts it, "was the 'Blowing In The Wind' of this war"). Everyone also points out that the difficulties of procuring guitar strings and plectrums in a city where you couldn't take food and water for granted would have hobbled The Beatles at their most fecund.

Sarajevo's rock scene today revolves around three venues. Trust, across the street from Veliki Park on Sarajevo's main road, Marsala Tita, opened in late 1995, and is now a popular meeting place with fine coffee, a tiny balcony on which bands play twice a week, and a pool table. Trust's patrons have a tendency to hastily invent something called "Bosnian rules" on the rare occasions that I look like I'm going to win, insisting that the black has to go in off one cushion, or into the same pocket as my last coloured ball, or be potted left handed or, in one desperately fought frame, all three.

Kuk—the Bosnian word for "hip"—is a short walk away up Kralja Tomislava. Kuk is a low-slung, circular room that was originally built as a morgue attached to the nearby university, but was turned into a nightclub during the 1950s. Kuk was commandeered by the

Bosnian army shortly after the siege began, and handed back, minus all equipment and fittings, in 1995. Since then, under the supervision of The Serious Road Trip, Kuk has been refurbished as an exhibition hall, music therapy centre and rock venue, the intermittent availability of PA sytems permitting.

The best-loved of the three clubs is Obala, which opened in 1993 in what had been an academics' cafe by the river, not far from Sarajevo's shattered library. There are two ways into Obala. One is to walk along the footpath and go in through the front door. Until recently, this was an option only for the foolhardy or the very, very fast. The more trodden route starts a few blocks back on Vase Miskina—the pedestrian arcade that winds through the old city's market district, Bascarsija—then winds up alleys, down side streets, through a derelict building, across a playground and enters Obala through an emergency exit. Such circuitous detours are now second nature to every Sarajevan. Ida, the unfeasibly attractive translator I've borrowed from The Serious Road Trip, explains that the route we've just taken would not have been observable from the hills, and would therefore have been safe from snipers.

And mortars?

"Well," she says, "those can get you anywhere."

The people who run Obala are justly proud of the fact that they closed only five times during the entire siege, and that the place was nearly always full, even when the chronic shortages of pretty much everything and attendant inflation pushed the price of a beer up to fifteen deutschmarks (£5.50, or thereabouts) and a shot of whiskey to eight, making Obala nearly as expensive a night out as any bar in Copenhagen. When the shelling was especially bad, the Obala DJs would crank the music up so loud nobody could tell how close the explosions were. Every band in Sarajevo cut their teeth as a live act in here. On the nights that Obala staged concerts, they tell me, the place was so full that people stood out in the halls.

I'm shown round Obala by Adis, one of the club's founders. He also plays drums in a band called Z.O.C.H., which, I am gleefully informed, is an acronym standing for Zlatom Optocene Cune. Zlatom Optocene Cune, I am even more gleefully informed, is Bosnian for "Gold-Covered Dicks." I file this phrase alongside the only other Bosnian I have managed to retain—the vivid admonishment "Popi govno," which means "Drink shit." As luck would have it, I have interrupted Adis in the middle of a Z.O.C.H. rehearsal in one of Obala's back rooms, and he invites me to sit in on the rest of it. He dusts off a sandbag for me, tells me to make myself comfortable and apologises in advance for the volume.

"If it's any help," he grins, tapping at his snare, "we did this to Bono when he came here in January."

While I wonder how loud sound has to be before the human eardrum implodes, Z.O.C.H. crash and clatter their way through half a dozen songs of proficient enough grunge ordinaire, before we return to the club to talk. The members of Z.O.C.H. are all in their late twenties and early thirties, older than other Sarajevo musicians, and perhaps more realistic than most about their situation.

"Everything here stopped in 1992," explains Soba, the guitarist, who says he was an officer serving in a Special Forces unit until his demobilisation last December. "It's impossible to do any proper recording. There are hardly any facilities, and what producers there are have never heard of Steve Albini, for example. We can't talk to them, never mind work with them."

At present, the only outlet for Bosnian rock'n'roll is Radio Zid, who released, in early 1995, the only available recording of Sarajevo bands—a roughly-recorded live CD called *Rock the Under Siege*, which featured such local luminaries as Sikter, Protest, Gnu, Bedbug and the rather gloriously named Hindustan Motors, among others. Z.O.C.H. were not featured on *Rock the Under Siege* for the same reason they're not featured on Radio Zid: they've been banned by the station. This is ostensibly due to the graphically sexual nature of some of Z.O.C.H.'s lyrics, but I get the impression that the real reasons might be more personal—Sarajevo's rock scene is as hopelessly riddled with petty jealousies and rivalries as anywhere else's.

"It's hard," shrugs Soba, "but we do what we can. We've been somebody here, you know, and it doesn't mean a lot. We want to go and play in other places now. Anywhere. Except Serbia, obviously."

Whatever merits Sarajevo's rock groups possess, variety is not one of them. They are exclusively male, and almost as exclusively keen on riff-heavy guitar rock, heavily in hock to Green River, Pearl Jam,

Soundgarden, Mudhoney and the Seattle grunge lineage in general, though Nirvana's stock in Sarajevo has fallen rapidly since Kurt Cobain's suicide, which elicited some sorrow, but little sympathy ("When I heard about Kurt," one drinker at Trust tells me, "I had just finished a shift at the hospital, and run home through the shelling, and . . . well, for fuck's sake, you know?" There is no mistaking the disgust in his voice).

I unearth only one band who don't look and sound like they should be haunting the coffee shops of Seattle in silly beards and plaid shirts: Beat House Project, an unabashed techno act from the name down. Sarajevo's dance scene appears pretty well dormant—the first rave in the city was staged by Radio Zid the week before I arrived—although the bleak, otherwordly, electronic atmospherics of Massive Attack and Portishead have touched many a nerve. Most ascribe this torpor to the fact that, in Sarajevo, ecstasy is as rare as non-smokers—and even if you can find a tablet going spare, you won't get much change from 200 Deutschmarks. Beat House Project have a litany of funny stories to tell about the peculiar difficulties of making music like theirs in a city where, for long periods, there wasn't any electricity. They have some less amusing anecdotes concerning the five wounds that the trio collected between them during the war.

Sarajevo's conversion to loud guitars and inchoate screaming about alienation is a relatively recent development. Zelimir Altarac-Cicak, the veteran Bosnian journalist, DJ and promoter, explains that tastes started shifting dramatically with the beginning of the siege.

"Before the war," he says, "only pop music."

The sort of anodyne europop he's talking about was generally sung in Bosnian—or, as the language was known before the war, Serbo-Croatian—and is best exemplified now by the work of a singer-songwriter called Muha, a shy and painstakingly polite man in a beret and an overcoat, who looks and sounds completely unlike someone who wrote his last album in hospital, recovering from wounds sustained in the defence of his city while fighting with a Special Forces unit.

"But now," confirms Zelimir, "everything is rock'n'roll, everything is noise."

Aida Kalendar, one of Radio Zid's indefatigable volunteers, puts it another way.

"You do not," she says, "spend the whole day being sniped at and shelled and then go home and listen to Blur."

The Moron Brothers are another typical Sarajevo rock group. In fact, The Moron Brothers are just typical Sarajevan youth, or even just typical youth. They're friendly, funny, like a drink and are gratifyingly excited about being interviewed by someone who has met Eddie Vedder twice. And then . . .

"I met Doma, the bassplayer, in the army," says Tela, the Moron Brothers' guitarist. "I'd rather not say which unit, because, well, you know, we don't know what's going to happen next."

The Moron Brothers formed in 1993, and have averaged one gig a month since.

"We already owned most of our equipment," continues Tela. "We got strings and things like that from friends outside. It was just good to have something to do. Musicians were lucky that way. It helped to be able to get together and sing about . . . well, everything we didn't have during the war. In fact, about everything, and anything, except the war. We'd had enough of that."

ON THAT COUNT, The Moron Brothers are speaking for an entire city.

Six months since NATO's criminally overdue airstrikes ended the siege, Sarajevo is still palpably exhausted by its long ordeal. Nobody has yet bothered to take down the hand-painted "Pazi—Snajper" ("Danger—Sniper") signs that hang at the city's exposed intersections. Many of the metal barricades and tattered blankets that were erected and hung to deter and distract the killers in the hills are still in place. I've also noticed that quite a few people tie their shoes strangely, threading the lace straight down one side and straight back up the other, without crossing them over. I initially assume that this is some obscure craze, like the wallet-chains or baby pacifiers that occasionally become regrettably popular with the kids back home, but when I mention it to someone, they say no, people used to do that so it would be easier to get their shoes and trousers off if they were hit. More than once, I'm nearly run over by cars coasting silently downhill, according to frugal wartime habit, with their engines switched off.

My other narrow failure to become the single most pathetic casualty of the Bosnian conflict occurs in the monumental ruins of the library. The library, or what's left of it, totters near the spot where, on June 28, 1914, a young Bosnian Serb nationalist called Gavrilo Princip shot Archduke Franz Ferdinand of Austria. This assassination preceded a train of events—world war, lopsided peace, world war, cold war, collapse of communism, rise of nationalism—that may well have happened anyway, but the symmetry is eerie. It's as if the echo of Princip's pistol, gathering momentum down the decades, somehow rebounded on its point of origin, magnified a millionfold. Along this street, the 20th century began and ended.

The library is—or was—a magnificent Austro-Hungarian building, a repository of thousands of priceless documents, books and treasures. It was destroyed in August 1992 by Bosnian Serb Army incendiary shells—a deliberate act of vandalism, a cultural genocide to serve notice of the attempted human one to follow. As I walk out onto the remains of the first floor balcony above the entrance, I hear an enormous crash immediately behind me. When the dust settles, I see a lump of exquisitely carved ceiling masonry lying on the floor. It has missed me by about three feet.

There are almost certainly other near misses—Grbavica on the day of its handover finally seems like too interesting a thing to pass up, and we figure if we stick to the footpaths and don't go barging into closed flats and opening cupboard doors, we should be fairly safe from mines and booby traps. Photographer Kennedy and I go to visit the ravaged suburb with Chris Watt of The Serious Road Trip, also visiting Sarajevo for the first time, and Jim Marshall, a Scot who spent most of the siege in Sarajevo with the Road Trip and now works for the Office of the High Representative (OHR). Jim offers to take us to see Grbavica because "I want to see where those fuckers were shooting at me from" (they hit him once, wounding him in one leg).

Grbavica is unbelievably creepy. There isn't an undamaged building in the suburb, and few blocks lack the scars of fires, some of which have been deliberately lit over the last few weeks by Serbs determined that the Grbavica that they hand back to Bosnia should be of as little value as possible.

These sorts of scenes were supposed to have faded from history along with 1945-vintage newsreel footage of liberated Europe. The buildings all look like they're waiting for demolition teams to come back from lunch and finish the job. Trenches fortified with rusty hulks of wrecked cars connect the high-rise ruins. A steady drizzle of clothes, books, furniture and other household flotsam flutters from balconies and windows: the possessions that the departing Serb population didn't want to carry. Some of this stuff is being flung overboard by people who were evicted from these apartments before the war and are now returning, some of it by opportunists hoping that perhaps the original owners are dead, or refugees, or emigrants, yet more of it by looters. From below, it's as if the wrecked buildings are vomiting their diseased, hungover innards into the streets.

These blocks of flats were notorious throughout the siege as high-rise Bosnian Serb Army positions—not for nothing did the expanse of trunk road that runs past Grbavica on the other side of the river become internationally infamous as Sniper Alley. As recently as two months ago—which is to say two months after the signing of the Dayton Accords—a rocket-propelled grenade launched from one of these buildings hit a crowded tram, killing one person and wounding several others. We climb up the dark, damp staircases to the top of one of them for a sniper's-eye view of Sarajevo. Even without a telescopic sight, it's sickeningly easy to imagine how simple a job it must have been for whoever sat up here with his rifle. I look out over the city, and the people walking around it, through the windows and the holes in the walls that he fired from, and I wonder what he's doing now.

Grbavica's principal landmark—there's about enough of it still standing upright to qualify as such—is its football stadium. Before the war, it was the home ground of Zeljeznicar FC, one of two teams from Sarajevo that used to compete in the Yugoslavian League. This afternoon, it looks like it's just hosted an especially exuberant Old Firm derby, right down the splintered Celtic FC mirror in what used to be the bar. Scraps of shrapnel litter the terraces and the stands are spotted with bulletholes. On on the concourse behind the burnt-out snack bar, Martin finds a spent Bosnian Serb Army mortar casing.

The pitch is on fire. Half of it, anyway. The blaze has been started by troops from the NATO-led United Nations Implementation Force (IFOR) patrolling Bosnia's peace. It's a reasonably risk-free way of clearing any mines that might have been laid in it by thoughtful Serbs as they departed.

"How big a bang will they make if one goes off?" asks Chris, worriedly.

"Not that big," says Jim. "We're okay."

Martin has noticed something infinitely more distressing. At the end of the pitch that isn't ablaze, the goalposts are still standing, and around those goalposts, some kids are playing football. Martin sprints off towards them, waving his arms and bellowing frantic warnings in strangled, Scots-accented Bosnian. They ignore him.

"That's the most frightening thing about this city," says Jim. "It's full of people who just aren't scared of anything anymore."

Outside the stadium, there are more children clowning around in the rubble. These children are, as children will, playing at soldiers, which in these wretched surroundings is both saddening and kind of funny. One of them has found himself an even more impressive souvenir than Martin's mortar round. This kid is maybe eight or nine years old, and he's equipped with all the usual kids-playing-war stuff—a yellow toy pistol tucked into his tracksuit bottoms, a black toy rifle in his right hand—but it's what he's got slung round his neck that has attracted my attention: a khaki, and very real, rocket-propelled grenade launcher. As any primary-school-age boy would, he looks utterly delighted with it.

My reasons for calling Martin over are not, initially, entirely journalistic: while there's a hell of a picture waiting to be taken here, Martin also knows more about this kind of hardware than I do, and I'd be happier about life in general if I knew the thing wasn't loaded.

"No," says Martin. "We'd have noticed by now. There'd be one less building around here, for a start."

Martin crouches in front of the kid, whose smile by now is almost wider than his face, prepares to shoot, and lowers his camera.

"Bollocks," he says, laughing.

Problem?

"It's too good," he says. "Do you really think anybody, anywhere, is going to believe I didn't set this up? I'll take it, okay, but you have to buy it."

THE VISIT TO Grbavica Stadium reaps an unexpected bonus: back in Trust, I mention it to someone, who mentions it to someone who

knows something about football coaching classes that were run for
Sarajevo's kids throughout the siege, and a few days later I find myself
sitting down to lunch with someone who played in a World Cup. Cool.
Pedrag Pasic, known as "Paja," represented Yugoslavia in the 1982
World Cup Finals in Spain. He first made his name as a striker with
his hometown club, FK Sarajevo. Later, he moved on to FC Stuttgart,
where his partner up front had been Jürgen Klinsmann. He returned
to Sarajevo after injury ended his playing career in 1988.

Paja could probably have got out of Sarajevo. He obviously had
connections in Germany and, it seems to safe to assume, more money
than most. And though these things matter less to most Sarajevans
than the outside world has come to believe, Paja is neither ethnically
Bosnian nor Muslim, hailing—like Radovan Karadzic—from the
nominally Orthodox Christian Yugoslav republic of Montenegro.

"Sarajevo," Paja shrugs, "is my home."

Paja's weekly coaching classes ran under cover in Skenderija
Stadium, one of the arenas built for the1984 Winter Olympics—the
upper rows of seats have been sandbagged and fortified, and were used
during the siege as Bosnian army sniper posts. There's about a hundred
yards of open ground between the entrance to the stadium and the
nearest buildings. I ask how on earth the kids had crossed it to get to
football practice every week.

"Quickly," says Paja, and smiles.

Back at Obala, I meet again with C.I.A. Enis does most of the
talking, running through what is becoming a familiar list of influences,
reasons and ambitions. They liked The Beastie Boys, Rage Against the
Machine and Biohazard. They formed a band because it was a welcome
distraction, even if they had to rehearse with acoustic instruments
and then wait for a gig at a venue with a generator to see if any of
what they'd come up with worked for real. They'd like to go and play
outside Bosnia, and see if people will think they're interesting for any
reason other than where they come from. Lazily, I'm beginning to tick
the answers off in my head in advance, when Erol, the other vocalist,
says something horribly accurate.

"It's important that people understand what happened here," he
says, quietly. "I don't think enough people do. But what we want to
do is present ourselves to the world and show that we are normal, or

as normal as we can be. I know what people think. People think we're savages."

He's right, of course. The western governments who fiddled while Sarajevo burnt sought to justify their indolence by suggesting that internecine violence was the natural state of the Balkan peoples, as if the war in Bosnia and Herzegovina had started of its own accord, as if the overweening ambitions of one murderous barbarian in Belgrade and another bellicose mountebank in Zagreb had nothing to do with it.

Wars are not natural disasters. Nor are they spontaneous occurrences. An operation as vast as the attempted genocide of the people of Bosnia and Herzegovina requires planning—planning which could, and should, have been aborted by depositing a cruise missile through the letterbox chez Milosevic. It's instructive to compare Yugoslavia to another European country which is a federation of linguistically similar but culturally different peoples with centuries of hostile history behind them, and to wonder what the world would think if the government in Westminster armed the English-born population of Wales and sent them on a rampage through the valleys, dealing murder and rape for the crime of being Welsh, and laid siege to Cardiff.

I wonder whether this would look like "the inevitable result of age-old ethnic tensions"—to paraphrase the conventional wisdom on Bosnia—or like there was a dangerous fruitcake in residence in Downing Street. The Irish writer and commentator Conor Cruise O'Brien, who should certainly know better, articulated the prevalent attitude when he wrote in 1992 that "There are places where a lot of men prefer war, and the looting and raping and domineering that go with it, to any sort of peacetime occupation. One such place is Afghanistan. Another is Yugoslavia, after the collapse of the centralising communist regime." It'd be interesting to learn how he'd feel about that last sentence if the words "Yugoslavia" and "communist" were removed and replaced with "Ireland" and "British."

The language used to describe the Bosnian war was riddled with perjoratives: the three sides were invariably divided, by media and diplomats alike, into "Serbs," "Croats" and "Muslims." It would have been just as accurate, and just as silly, to talk about a conflict between Bosnians, Croats and Christians, or between Serbs, Bosnians and Catholics. It's hardly surprising that Sarajevans are given to wondering, bitterly, how long the siege would have been allowed to continue, had it been a nominally Muslim army in the hills blazing away at the citizens of an ostensibly Christian European city.

"Have you heard about our new Bosnian anthem?" someone asks me one night in Obala. "It's called 'Too Many Muslims, Not Enough Oil.'"

FRIDAY AFTERNOON, I'M walking along Marsala Tita with Faris Arapovic, with whom I'd got talking and drinking the night before at Kuk. Faris, it turned out, is the drummer in one of Sarajevo's better bands, Sikter. Today, I've been round at his family's flat, where he's shown me a video of Sikter playing in front of 100,000 people at Milan's San Siro stadium the previous July. Several Bosnian bands had been invited to appear at the concert, headlined by Italian megastar Vasco Rossi, but only Sikter had been able to make it, as they'd been in Amsterdam at the time, while the other groups were marooned in besieged Sarajevo.

As we walk, I notice a vast column of smoke winding up into the cloudy sky from a couple of miles away in Grbavica, where I'd been the day before. I wonder if there's some kind of trouble.

"Don't know," says Faris.

If there is, Faris has probably seen worse—his family's flat overlooks the spot where, in August 1992, sixteen people were blown to pieces when two Serb mortars hit a bread queue. If Faris had got up that morning when he'd been supposed to, he'd explained earlier, he'd have been queueing up with them.

"They must be burning rubbish," he says, squinting towards Grbavica.

Possibly. They were going to have to do something with all that junk that had been tossed out of the windows. But that's a lot of smoke for a bonfire. We bump into Jim, whose office is across the road.

"Bit of Barney Rubble in Grbavica this afternoon," he says.

It seems that an attachment of Bosnian Serb Army troops from Vraca, the suburb up the hill from Grbavica, had decided they weren't going to take the Dayton Agreement lying down. They'd taken a slap at the Bosnian police who were moving into the area, and the Bosnian police had fired back. IFOR, evidently intent on showing both parties who was in charge, had despatched Apache helicopters, which had clobbered the building occupied by the marauding Serbs. Hence the smoke.

"Well, there you are," says Faris, triumphantly. "I told you they were burning rubbish."

4

YASSER, I CAN BOOGIE

The Prodigy in Beirut
MAY 1998

A STORY STRAIGHT OUT of the "What could possibly go wrong?" file, and indeed everything pretty much did, except that it all sort of worked out eventually. And so it should have: it was a good thing that The Prodigy decided to do this. For all that the rock'n'roll tour is mythologised as a devil-may-care bacchanal, it is, in the main, a tediously hidebound ritual, in which, year in and year out, the same bands play the same venues, in the same cities, to the same crowds, get reviewed in the same publications, are asked the same questions on the same radio stations, and wake in the same hotels before being herded aboard the same bus to do it all again at the next stop down the track. This routine, like all routines, is a function of laziness—the reality is that once any band reaches a certain stature, they can play more or less anywhere they like, so long as they're occasionally willing to take a slightly relaxed attitude to getting insured and/or paid. They also find, when they do make the effort to steer their caravan off the beaten track, that the audiences tend to be much more excited (you don't even have to go to a picturesquely screwed-up recent war zone to prove this—I grew up in Sydney, and well recall the disproportionate adulation showered upon anybody who deigned to come all that way to play at us). It's a valuable and important cross-pollination: the band are exposed to new influences, new ways of understanding their own work, and those who come to see them get to feel like that they are citizens of the pop culture universe, rather than observers squinting through telescopes.

For me, this turned out to be the first of several trips to Beirut, which is now immovably lodged very near the top of my list of favourite places to visit. There is no wearier cliché in the travel writer's lexicon than "land of contrasts," but Beirut is exactly that, to degrees both tragic and hilarious, a city of materialist decadence and observant abstemiousness, of cheerful hedonism and holy fury, of affable, pluralist civilisation and vicious, sectarian barbarism: an accurate municipal coat of arms would feature the cocktail and the Kalashnikov.

★ ★ ★

YOU WOULD IMAGINE that anybody who has served in Lebanon's armed forces for as long as the sentry in the airport baggage hall clearly has would have seen just about everything, but right now he couldn't look more amazed if his rifle turned into a snake that spoke Gaelic. He stares at Keith Flint, and at Keith Flint's twin-blade mohawk haircut and earrings and nose-ring and tongue-stud and tattoos, stares unabashed and unblinking for minutes on end, as Keith talks to a film crew from Reuters and tries to ignore him.

"I don't really know anything about Beirut," Keith is telling the reporter. "It's somewhere to play, isn't it?"

Keith shrugs, finally, and turns to the gawping soldier with a slight, pained grimace. "Alright?" he asks. The sentry walks away, shaking his head.

TURNING UP IN this part of the world in funny outfits and confusing the natives is a British tradition dating back to Richard the Lionheart, but an interesting perspective on The Prodigy's visit to Lebanon is provided by a local fan quoted on the front page of the following morning's *Beirut Daily Star*: "This is the greatest thing ever to happen in the Middle East." The report does not say whether or not twenty-year-old Rania Attieh was subsequently incinerated by a lightning strike.

Beirut, on first acquaintance, is at once as dismal as a ruin and as optimistic as a building site, which is because just about all of Beirut is either a ruin or a building site. Beirut, all the storybooks say, was a beautiful town. Few of the houses, churches and mosques that earned it this reputation survive. Those that do are scarred with shrapnel pocks and bulletholes as tragic and pathetic as acne on a handsome face.

Beirut has been the definitive and archetypal victim of the sort of war that has become bafflingly fashionable in the latter half of this century: the sort of war where one bunch of a country's inhabitants decide they don't like one or more other bunches of the same country's inhabitants. Everyone then spends years demolishing everything that might have made the place worth fighting over in the first place. Then, when there's hardly anything left standing up, the squabbling parties realise that not only have the neighbours they didn't like not gone anywhere, nobody's got a roof or running water either, and the country is now run by people who didn't even live here when it all started (in Lebanon's case, Syria and Israel).

My parents' and grandparents' generations were wrong about a lot of things, but they had this one pretty much sorted out: if you're going to have a war, have it somewhere else. If you lose, at least you've still got what you started with. What every one of Beirut's barely countable squabbling factions did, in effect, was held a gun to their own temples, announced "Everyone do as I say, or this guy gets it," and pulled the trigger.

"So . . . what went on here, exactly?"

We spend the day before the gig wandering Beirut's noisy, dusty, crowded streets with those of the touring party who can be bothered. These include the invited press contingent, which is myself, and Mat Smith and Steve Gullick from the New Musical Express. Last time we'd all been away together, it had been to Sarajevo to see U2. Next year, we hope to go to Mogadishu with The Spice Girls. We are accompanied this warm afternoon by blue-haired and somewhat unfortunately named Prodigy guitarist Giz Butt. Giz wants to know why, according to the morning's paper, there was a gunfight a few blocks from our hotel last night. We all slept through it. Four men were wounded.

"Hezbollah and Amal," explains someone from the gig promoter's office. "They fight like this all the time. Who knows why?"

Giz and a couple of other members of the band have brought

portable tape recorders with them, on which to collect the sounds of Beirut. We can look forward, therefore, to the next Prodigy album making extensive use of samples of car horns and people yelling about their carpets.

THE PRODIGY ARE not the first western pop act to visit Beirut since Lebanon's seventeen-year civil war ground more or less to a halt in 1992, but they are, by some distance, the most interesting and most contemporary. The people of Beirut, as if they hadn't suffered enough, have spent the years since independence enduring such meagre musical pickings as epically tedious German heavy metal time-wasters Scorpions and pensionable crooner Paul Anka. Later this year, they can look forward to performances by Julio Iglesias and Joe Cocker, unless they reach the not unreasonable conclusion that a return to internecine slaughter might be preferable.

It would be an exaggeration to suggest that The Prodigy's visit to Lebanon has been motivated by any deep-seated sense of history or empathy with the suffering. The Prodigy have come here for the same reasons they've previously gone to Poland, Macedonia, Russia, Iceland, Hong Kong and other places off the path usually beaten by touring bands.

"It keeps it fresh," says Liam Howlett, The Prodigy's songwriter and keyboardist. "You don't hear of many mad gigs anymore. You hear about Oasis going to America, you know, and that's boring. I know U2 do their share, but nobody else does."

A few hours before showtime, Liam and Keith are lounging about, picking at a small room-service banquet in Liam's suite at the Lancaster Hotel. The Lancaster, a new building a short walk from the seafront, is a good sign: you don't build a hotel like this if you think there's a meaningful chance someone's going to knock it over again. The Lancaster gleams and sparkles and has obviously been constructed in anticipation of a return of the glory days; my suite downstairs is bigger than my flat back in London.

Liam and Keith didn't go out today. Despite Liam's professed hunger for new frontiers, they seem completely indifferent to their surroundings.

"We get involved this much," says Liam. "Do we want to go there? Yes. Is it safe? Yes. Right then, let's do it."

It's nine months since I went to U2's concert in Sarajevo. They'd gone to Bosnia on a self-appointed mission of solidarity with the people of a city that had been walled off from western pop culture for three and a half years. They'd slashed ticket prices, talked up the healing properties of rock'n'roll, displayed a commanding knowledge and understanding of local politics and history, and gone round for tea with the president. The Prodigy aren't even holding a press conference.

"I find it very hard to understand politics," admits Keith. "I like to go to places and just take them in at a surface level."

Last night, I'd been telling Keith about U2's Sarajevo show, and trying to get him interested in the idea of taking The Prodigy to Bosnia and Herzegovina, where they are massively popular. "We've been," Keith said. No, I said, they hadn't. Otherwise I wouldn't have had so many Sarajevan friends bending my ear about whether The Prodigy would ever go and play there. "I'm sure we have," Keith had insisted, distractedly. Eventually, I'd suggested that maybe it had been Zagreb or Llubljana. Easy enough mistake to make if you spend your life on tour, I guess, though it would be a bad idea to make it while actually in any of those cities. "That's it," Keith had said. "The one starting with L." Someone else later explained that The Prodigy's Balkan show had been in neither Croatia nor Slovenia, but in the Macedonian capital of Skopje.

"It's funny being here, though," muses Keith, looking out the window. "Because it's like a joke, this place, isn't it? If you go on holiday and stay somewhere shitty, you come back and say it was like Beirut, don't you?"

I'm sure Brian Keenan did.

"Who?"

Hostage. Him and John McCarthy. You know.

"Fucking hell. Was that here?"

The really frightening thing is that I know that Mat from the *NME* has had exactly this same conversation with Keith already today. Despite Keith's fearsome appearance, there's something of the mildly batty but loveable maiden aunt about him.

"Hey!" he announces, gesturing at the television. "That's, um . . . whatsit Square, we played there!"

It's a story from Moscow. Boris Yeltsin's fallen over again, or something.

"Red Square," says Liam.

"That's what I mean," says Keith. "I mean, you spend your life while you're growing up watching these geezers with fur hats marching up and down it with guns and bombs, and then one day you find yourself playing in it, and it doesn't really register at the time, but three months later, like . . . well, like this, you'll see it on telly and think fuck me, did I really do that?"

"We don't get involved with the politics," says Liam, "and we don't get involved in the set-up of the gig, although I know this one has been a nightmare, and still is."

He isn't joking. As he speaks, we don't know if the show is going ahead. It had been called off for the first time three days before, after an argument about the suitability of the venue. Other arrangements had been swiftly made, and it was all on again. This morning, The Prodigy have seen these other arrangements for the first time, and are less than impressed. An open-air stage has been erected in a car park near the Green Line that divided Christian East Beirut from Muslim West Beirut during the war.

"The power," explains an incredulous Keith, "comes from the mains lead, which has been dug out of the ground, sawn through, and the bare wires from that are taped to the gear, no insulation whatsoever—I tell you, it's fucking lethal."

The weather isn't helping. We've heard reports that the fierce wind, which is currently turning Beirut's formidable reserves of dust into a million tiny tornadoes of corrosive, eye-stinging grit, has also taken the canopy off the stage, exposing the dubious electrics to the rain which looks sure to follow.

"I'd be betting against it, at this point," admits Liam, glumly.

AT ABOUT SIX o'clock, four hours before The Prodigy are due on stage, we get word that all systems are go. Paul Fairs, The Prodigy's tour manager, explains that there has been a fair bit of telephone traffic this afternoon between The Prodigy's lawyers, the promoter's lawyers and the Lebanese Ministry of the Interior, and there is a general feeling that "if we don't do this show, we may have trouble getting home."

Down at the venue, as the first punters begin to arrive, I speak to Philip Kfoury, the worried-looking twenty-three-year-old whose company, Power Productions, has brought The Prodigy to this unlikely destination. He reckons to have sunk US $250,000 in putting tonight on, and reckons he'll lose most of it, though he's hoping the kudos he accrues for getting The Prodigy this far will pay back his losses with interest in the future.

His difficulties, he explains, have been manifold. Not the least has been trying to get publicity for the gig without bringing The Prodigy's often contentious subject matter to the attention of the Lebanese authorities, who are not a rocking bunch. They have previously deep-sixed proposed Beirut concerts by Pink Floyd and Aerosmith, and once turned Iron Maiden away at the airport. It is sadly unlikely that any of these have been purely aesthetic judgments.

The Floyd, the Smith and the Maiden are three bands who, in their own countries, are rightly regarded by all bar the most demented wowsers as about as grave a threat to public morality as a seaside pantomime. The Prodigy, however, are nowhere near their artistic sell-by date, and are still capable of inciting genuine controversy. They quoted Josef Goebbels, albeit ironically, on the sleeve of their *The Fat Of The Land* album—though this may have been a ruse to distract attention from an even less forgivable inscription elsewhere on the same cover ("Guest vocals, Crispian Mills"). They recently had a hit with a single called "Smack My Bitch Up" (and, I thought, handled the subsequent controversy about misogyny and violence badly; Liam Howlett, instead of defending his view of women to every scandalised hack in pursuit of an easy why-oh-why story, should have issued a statement saying it was about feeding heroin to his dog).

The really important thing about "Smack My Bitch Up" is that it's a great way to start a rock concert. The Prodigy appear on time on their jerry-rigged carpark stage. Keith and The Prodigy's other two rapper/dancers—the unfeasibly tall Leeroy Thornhill and the kilt-clad Maxim Reality—make up in presence and activity what the set lacks in The Prodigy's usual volume, and the overwhelmingly teenage crowd, mostly children of Beirut's wealthy, make up in decibels what they lack in numbers (the tickets were a distinctly uncharitable US $30 a go, which is why only 5,000 of 6,500 have been sold; also, about another 5,000 people have spotted that an excellent, and free, view of the show is afforded from a nearby highway flyover).

The security presence is considerable. Groups of camouflaged soldiers huddle at both sides of the stage, bearing the baleful expressions of people who feel that their current assignment is beneath them. A few songs in, they get bored enough to pounce on one of The Prodigy's lawyers, who they have spotted taking pictures with his instamatic. He is hustled off to their makeshift command post, where they attempt to confiscate the camera. I push through the crowd after him, and try something that occasionally works in situations where people are basically confused and nobody speaks any English, which is waving my press card and barking drivel in a crisp, authoritative manner. I find Bob Dylan lyrics helpful: "Maggie comes fleet foot! Face full of black soot!" They give him back his camera and let him go with a warning.

The Prodigy leave the stage suddenly after about forty minutes, and the mob applaud politely and start filing out. I haven't seen The Prodigy for years myself, but something doesn't seem quite right. It seems a short set to play, having come all this way, and they haven't done "Firestarter," either. Ten minutes later, they return, play another half dozen songs, and leave again.

At the hotel afterwards, Liam explains that this gap was due to a light sprinkling of rain that was threatening to turn the stage into something that might have given new meaning to the phrase "live circuit." They'd come back on when the cloud had passed.

In the Lancaster's bar, Liam decides that we should all go out and have ourselves a night on the town, or at least on the parts of it that aren't being torn down or rebuilt. This notion is scotched by the hotel's security staff, who seem concerned that we may end up staying in Beirut rather longer than we'd planned. "Not safe," they say, making that Mediterranean finger-waving gesture beloved of Italian footballers disputing offside calls. By way of compromise, Giz is dispatched to reconnoitre a nightclub around the corner. "Not good," he says, on returning. "Old blokes in suits with really young women, and everyone wearing lots and lots of gold."

Liam gets the drinks in. Keith goes to bed.

BY BREAKFAST TIME on Sunday, The Prodigy have left the building, departing Beirut on the early flight. Mat from the *NME*, the lawyer type whose camera caused all the trouble at the gig and I have stayed, determined to do some sightseeing. This is less easy than it sounds. It could be said that Beirut has not yet come to terms with the idea of tourists wandering around it for its own sake, especially if you were trying to win some kind of award for understatement.

We explain to a driver from the hotel that we'd like to see Beirut's peace monument. He doesn't appear to have heard of it, which is a surprise, as we'd have thought that a seven-storey high sculpture made of tanks and concrete would be a hard thing to miss. One of us has a picture of it in a guidebook, which we show him. He charges off into Beirut's genially chaotic traffic.

The peace monument, the work of a French artist called Armand Fernandez, was unveiled in 1996 outside the Lebanese Ministry of Defence complex on the outskirts of Beirut. It consists, as we'd explained to our driver, of a couple of dozen tanks, armoured vehicles and artillery pieces stacked on top of each other and held into place by a tower of concrete. It is every bit as bewildering, ugly and ludicrous as the civil war it commemorates.

Naturally, we wish to photograph this monstrosity. Our driver asks some soldiers standing nearby if this is permissible. Armies are supposed to operate according to a chain of command; the Lebanese military has a chain of indecision. The soldiers don't know, or don't want to decide, so they go and get their senior officer. He, in turn, goes and asks a completely different bunch of soldiers, who go and get their senior officer, who asks the first soldiers the driver had spoken to.

After a lengthy discussion, a verdict is reached. We may take photographs of the monument, but only from one of three preordained angles, lest we accidentally get any of the MoD buildings themselves into our pictures. This is only reasonable, given the undoubted havoc my family and friends could wreak with underexposed, badly framed long-distance shots of a nondescript office block.

On the way back to the hotel, we pass the racetrack, where a meeting is in progress. We decide this looks like fun, and ask the driver to come back in a couple of hours. We stand amid the entirely male crowd in the crumbling grandstand and watch the horses go round the red dirt track a few times, admire the picturesque backdrop of shattered buildings for a bit, completely fail to decipher the betting system, get bored, and resolve to leave.

"No," says the guard at the gate.

What?

"No," he repeats, indicating that we may not leave the course until after the day's racing is complete. There are still four races to go. We're bored now. We make to push past him.

"No," he says, again.

"Don't be silly," says Mat, and tries to prise his hand from the gate.

"No," he says, again.

We do a bit of standing around looking impatient, folding and unfolding our arms and stomping our feet. After a few minutes of this, the guard relents and asks us to follow him. He leads us back inside the course to the on-site police station. A policeman fills out a few forms and leads us to a sweaty man in an office, who directs us to another office with three other men in it. I wonder if this is what happened to Terry Waite. The three other men all sign one of the forms filled out by the policeman, and send us back to the last office, where the sweaty man stamps it and gives it back to the policeman, who then writes something in Arabic on a piece of paper and gives it to Mat. The process takes nearly twenty minutes.

The piece of paper gets us through the gate where we'd been stopped the first time, but we get pulled up again on the other side of the course at the main entrance. Mat flourishes the paper with a triumphant cackle, but there's a problem—the note gives permission for three people to leave the track early, and there are now four of us. An expatriate American, who has seen us going, is trying to sneak out on our ticket of leave. He apologises, sheepishly, and is led back to the stand while we're waved out of the gate.

"We'll light a candle for you," Mat calls after him.

We spend the afternoon tooling about on the Corniche, the wide pedestrian promenade that winds along Beirut's waterfront, and fills up every weekend with perambulating families, preening adolescents and kamikaze rollerbladers. Despite the fact that all present should have grown out of such things, we visit Luna Park, a rusty, melancholy little funfair. Mat and I take a couple of turns on the dodgems, though having now spent a couple of days running for cover from Beirut's traffic, we suspect that preteen Lebanese regard these less as a sideshow ride, and more like the beginnings of driver education.

Luna Park also boasts the world's most pissweak ghost train, which could certainly be livened up with some local colour—they could replace the decrepit plastic skeletons and flaking rubber ghouls with animatronic keffiyeh-clad fanatics which throw blankets over the passengers, stick guns in their ears, handcuff them to a radiator and yell at them about Israel. Thrillseeking tourists would be round the block. As things are, the ghost train is a good deal less daunting a prospect than the ferris wheel, which looks to be on the verge of slipping its moorings and rolling out into the sea. Out the front of Luna Park, a street trader is doing a roaring trade in toy rifles.

WE HAVE A night free. We have directions, thoughtfully provided by some journalists from Beirut's English-language paper, *The Lebanon Daily Star*. We are going out. We flag a taxi. This is a mistake.

"We want to go here," says Mat, slowly and patiently, pointing at our hand-drawn map. "It's a club called Zinc. Do you know it?"

"Very good hotel," confirms the driver. "I know very good hotel for you."

We have high hopes for Zinc. We have been told that it's where all Beirut's cool and happening people go. We have been assured that it is even more convivial than Che's, the place we'd visited two nights previously, where the walls were covered in portraits of Senor Guevara, and people we didn't know kept buying us drinks.

"Very good hotel," says the driver again.

He plants his accelerator foot, and we head off in a cacophonous symphony of squealing tyres and honking horn. I suddenly realise what it is John Coltrane's records have reminded me of all these years.

"Very good hotel," says the driver again, and again every five minutes after that. We ignore him until we begin to get the sinking feeling that he knows Beirut as well as we do. I am sure, for example, that we have been past this tank before.

"Have you," asks Mat, evenly, as we pass another checkpoint for the third time, "got any idea where you're going? I mean, any idea at all?"

"I know very good hotel for you."

Oh, God. Do you speak any other English at all?

"Very good hotel."

There's not much we can do but sit tight, see where we end up, and try not to dwell on what became of a few other visitors to Beirut who sat tight in the backs of Mercedes-Benzes, waiting to see where they'd end up, and trying not to dwell on what became of other visitors to Beirut who sat tight in the backs of Mercedes-Benzes, etcetera.

"Very good hotel for you."

After blundering through another dozen dark, demolished blocks, apparently at random, we pull up in front of what does, we would normally be happy to agree, look like a very good hotel.

"Very good hotel," grins the driver, triumphantly. "Very good hotel for you."

Presumably he picks up tourists all the time who are wandering around Beirut of an evening with no baggage and no idea where they're staying that night.

"We don't want a fucking hotel," explains Mat, barely audible over the sound of his teeth gritting. "We're quite happy with the one we've got. We want to go HERE," he says, pointing forlornly at the map.

"Very good hotel."

We pay him and head off on foot. We ask directions from the soldier at the checkpoint we've been driving past, from a variety of angles, for the last hour. He's got no idea, and the streets around here look depressingly unpopulated. On a unanimous show of hands, we admit defeat. We stop another cab.

"Do you," we ask, broken men each, "know the way to the Hard Rock Café?"

5

EVERY WHICH WAY BUT MOOSE

Green Day in Canada
OCTOBER 1995

THE PREMISE FOR this trip, originally undertaken as a cover story for *Melody Maker*, was that it was pretty weird that Green Day, of all people, were quite possibly the biggest band in the world at the time. The idea that Green Day might still have a plausible claim on that title fourteen years later would, at the time, have struck all parties concerned—including, doubtless, Green Day themselves—as entrancingly preposterous. While I don't much care for Green Day's recent umpty-platinum punk rock operas *American Idiot* and *21st Century Breakdown*, I don't begrudge Green Day their success: I'm always able to recall meeting three people whose hearts, it seemed to me, were lodged in the right place with unusual unbudgeability.

I'd like to conclude this introduction with an unreserved apology to the people of Fredericton, New Brunswick, for the fusillade of cheap shots taken at their town throughout this piece. They reflect far more poorly on the hapless assassin than his intended target, and while I did consider consigning them to oblivion with repeated, rueful tappings upon the "delete" key, I decided to leave the passages in question, not only in the interests of maintaining the integrity of the original piece, but also by way of visiting richly merited self-inflicted punishment upon the author for having flaunted his twenty-six-year-old smart-arsery quite so egregiously.

★ ★ ★

FREDERICTON IS THE capital city of the Canadian province of New Brunswick. When any place touts as its principal claim to fame the fact that it is the capital city of the Canadian province of New Brunswick, you'd guess that it's not got much going for it, and in Fredericton's case you'd be right. Fredericton consists mostly of the kind of wooden houses that have flagpoles in their front yards, and is populated largely by the kind of people who'd fly flags on those poles. The standard joke to make about a town like this is to suggest that it's the kind of place where folks still point at aeroplanes, but there's something stilted and slow-motion about the way people here talk and walk and think that makes me reckon they'd be more likely to fling themselves to the ground in supplication to whichever strange god has filled their skies with giant metal eagles. Older residents can probably still remember a time when local people ate hay and worshipped the sun.

Other than its status as the administrative hotbed of New Brunswick, Fredericton also boasts a university: the imaginatively named University of New Brunswick. Inside the campus is the Aitken Centre, an ice hockey arena that serves as home ground for the Fredericton Canadiens, a nursery side for their infinitely more illustrious Montreal namesakes. This makes the Fredericton Canadiens roughly the hockey equivalent of Tottenham Hotspur reserves. Nonetheless, perhaps due to the—entirely plausible—possibility that there's not a lot else happening around here on the long winter nights, at least not since witch-burning was outlawed, the rink provides seating for up to 8,000 of Fredericton's population of 60,000.

Four surnames between the lot of them, doubtless, but they bought tickets for tonight's Green Day show fast enough to sell the Aitken Centre out three weeks in advance. Even up this dismal side-road from nowhere, the devotion commanded by Green Day, this apparently unprepossessing trio, is impressive, bordering on the phenomenal.

Or even the ludicrous.

PHOTOGRAPHER STEPHEN SWEET and I had not arrived in Canada in the most optimistic frame of mind. We had been told two weeks previously where and when our photo session and interview would happen, and how long they would last. We had been told we couldn't travel with the band, or spend any informal time with them at all.

We were told that Green Day had a low opinion of press, and didn't want to endure any more of us than they really had to. We had been led, basically, to expect all the pettiness and egotism that tend to run rampant in the entourages of big American bands.

Sweet and I had braced ourselves accordingly. We both knew well, by now, the truth of Charlie Watts' oft-quoted adage that his twenty-five years in The Rolling Stones had been "Five years playing, twenty years hanging around," and its little-recognised corollary that rock journalism is the same, but without the five years' playing. We spend the flight to Toronto, and the connecting flight to Halifax, and most of the Green Day gig we see in Halifax, and the flight to Fredericton, and the time we spend trying to stay warm by walking laps of what passes for Fredericton's main street, telling each other that this assignment is going to chomp out loud, that we'll be doing well to go home with a picture of the drummer raising a finger through the back window of the bus, and a quote of two words from the singer, one of which will be "Get," and that if we'd both paid more attention in school, we could have got real jobs.

Our contact in Green Day's crew is the tour manager, who rejoices in the name Randy Steffes. Sweet and I have become gloomily obsessed with this unlikely monicker. "Randy Steffes," one of us will murmur, apropos of nothing, to break the frequent despondent silences. "Christ on a bike," the other will respond. We have developed a mental image that we feel fits: a large, middle-aged man with a receding hairline, an over-compensating ponytail, a tour jacket embroidered with the dates from a mid-80s James Taylor tour, a small constellation of unnecessary laminates giving his neck a permanent crick and a half-hundredweight of equally pointless keys hanging from his straining belt. He will hate us. We will hate him. He will make Sweet take pictures of the gig from the back of the hall. He'll make me sit through the entire soundcheck before giving me five minutes with the band.

"Randy Steffes," sighs Sweet.

Christ on a bike, I reply.

WE GET TO the venue, persuade the student security of the truth of our story that we've come all the way from England—they don't appear to have heard of it—and announce ourselves at Green Day's production office. On the door hangs a sheet of photocopied paper, headlined "The Daily Whiner," which lists the day's travel arrangements (Green Day are heading out of Fredericton straight after the show—perhaps they've been here before), crew schedules, press commitments and a couple of in-jokes. *Melody Maker* is mentioned in this dispatch, and they've not been unduly rude about us, and as this is more than *Melody Maker* can say it's been about Green Day, we're inclined to be pleasantly surprised.

We're looking for Randy Steffes, I tell somebody, being careful to neither mispronounce nor giggle.

"I'll call him," somebody says.

The next thing we hear is a lawnmower-like buzz from around the corner behind us, followed by a loud shriek of "Fuuuccckkkkloook-oooouuuttt." Sweet and I take cover as a blond apparition riding what appears to be a motorised skateboard with handlebars screeches to a skidding halt in front of us.

"Sorry," says this creature, from somewhere beneath a dishmop of blonde dreadlocks.

"Randy Steffes," the thing on the scooter explains.

Is . . . ?

"Me," it says. "I still forget how quick these things seem when you drive 'em inside."

Ah.

"Anyway," he continues, still getting his breath back. "The band are here. That's the good news. But they've just seen the review you guys ran of the album, so they're likely to be a bit hostile."

Tremendous.

"Put these on and wait here," he says, handing over two VIP laminates, each bearing a cartoon picture of an unshaven drunk pissing on a visibly distressed daffodil. "I'll go and get 'em." He zooms off down the hall, bellowing "Coooommmminggggthroooo."

He returns, on foot, with an obviously recently woken young pop group. "Green Day," he announces. "Da-naaa."

The introductions are awkward. To Green Day, I am an agent of a paper which has just reviewed their new album, *Insomniac*, in much the same way that Air Marshal Harris could have been said to have "reviewed" Dresden. My esteemed colleague Neil Kulkarni has dismissed *Insomniac* as the work of "quacks and mountebanks peddling placebo enervation which is in fact tranquiliser to kids stupid enough to know what they want and how to get it," before informing the sections of our readership that mightn't have followed that argument that "Green Day suck for real."

To me, Green Day are three people who have no real reason not to make my life difficult—sell ten million copies of one album and one *Melody Maker* cover more or less doesn't make much difference. The photographs seem a good place to start, so Sweet suggests some seats down by the football field outside the venue. This elicits a massed negative response.

Aha! Spoilt whingeing brats who can't cope with the idea of getting their fingers cold for ten minutes?

"Um," says Billie Joe Armstrong, Green Day's singer and guitarist, "the trouble is that there'll be people out there who'll be waiting to see the show."

Yes! Stuck-up nouveau megarich who reckon they're now too good for the people who made them what they are!

"And, well," he shrugs, looking monumentally embarrassed, "we do get hassled. I mean, really. Especially in small towns."

There's a bit of self-conscious giggling as the absurdity of the situation comes into focus. Green Day's current status is the stuff of the most piquant silliness. I keep thinking, and I suspect they do too, that they're just a spirited, if straitlaced, power-pop outfit, a standard-issue one-two-three-four ramalamalama three-chord garage band with better than average tunes. But Green Day are, unarguably, much more. That number again: ten million.

It occurs to me that I wouldn't have thought of suggesting to Robert Smith, or Bono, or Michael Stipe, or Eddie Vedder, that they run the gauntlet of the kind of people who might have travelled across a state to watch them play. Green Day's last album, *Dookie*, sold more than any of the following: The Cure's *Wish*, U2's *Zooropa*, REM's *Monster*, Pearl Jam's *Vitalogy* or, come to that, Nirvana's *Nevermind*. It is possible that the three dopey, dishevelled wretches before me are the component parts of the biggest band in the world right now.

"Look," says Billie Joe, who seems to find the situation as baffling as we do, "you think about it, and we'll see you after the soundcheck."

Green Day wander off, leaving Sweet and me feeling like we've fallen through the looking glass.

GREEN DAY FORMED longer ago than most people give them credit for in Rodeo, the unfashionable end of the fashionable Californian town of Berkely. Billie Joe and Mike Dirnt, Green Day's bassplayer, assembled their first band when both were aged eleven. Sweet Children, as they were known, failed to make a significant impact outside their own bedrooms, and the project was abandoned in favour of a succession of punk covers acts. Under a variety of long-forgotten names, Billie Joe and Mike took skiploads of speed and played around the Bay Area of San Francisco during the boom years of the peculiarly ascetic version of punk spawned by such grimly conscientious acts as Dead Kennedys and True Sounds of Liberty, and developed by the likes of Operation Ivy and Neurosis. At one of the all-ages concerts that characterised the hey!-if-the-kids-are-united ethos of the genre, Billie Joe and Mike met Tre Cool, a drummer. There is a possibility that Tre's name is some sort of cunning fraud.

The three became Green Day, an invigorating fusion of the hardcore they'd grown up on and the pop sensibilities of their transatlantic infatuations: The Who, The Clash, The Buzzcocks and The Kinks. They took more skipfuls of speed, played more gigs, and released two albums, *39/Smooth* and *Kerplunk* on an excitingly obscure local label. These sold about 30,000 copies each and got ecstatic, semi-literate reviews in fanzines with names like *Pocketful Of Vomit* and *The Urine Sample*.

In 1993, some bright spark in an A&R department in a thumping great American record company noticed that every other thumping great American record company was signing punk-influenced guitar groups and making shedfuls of money: at the height of the Nirvana-inspired grunge goldrush, it seemed that a major deal and major success were there for the taking for anybody who could operate a guitar without hurting themselves, whinge convincingly about nothing in particular and cope with a few fashionable indignities being wrought with their hair. Green Day, present and correct on all three counts, were offered a deal. Hoping that here lay a way to make a living from their music, they signed it. Green Day were pleased with *Dookie*, their major label debut. It seemed to them a solid and likeable piece of work, well recorded but not oppressively polished. Who knew, with a bit of luck, it might sell 100,000 copies.

It did. Then it sold another 9,900,000, and counting—a turn of events that has confused nobody more than Green Day. When they talk about their good fortune now, they do so with the perplexed air of people who've been knocked down in the street by a runaway dustcart full of cash. They're defensive, almost paranoid. They almost sound like they feel guilty.

In Britain, the conventional critical wisdom on Green Day, for what little it's worth, is that they're smart, cynical charlatans, living high on some spurious notion of adolescent alienation, and milking the affections of their deluded fans for every last cent. This case collapses within seconds of arriving in their dressing room.

Bands of Green Day's status generally ensure that they're well looked after backstage. There will be ample food of the junk and fresh varieties, a selection of drinks alcoholic and non, magazines, a couple of contractual eccentricities like fresh socks or bowls of M&Ms with the red ones carefully separated—even televisions, stereos and video games are not unusual. Green Day's backstage rider consists of one espresso machine, and whatever eye-reddening herb the room is reeking of, and they bought all that with them. This self-imposed austerity is all in the name of keeping overheads, and therefore ticket prices, as low as possible. For similar reasons, Green Day travel with minimal crew— Randy doubles as a soundman—and subject themselves to a punishing tour schedule that often sees them playing stretches of fifteen gigs in as many nights, travelling between them overnight on the tour bus, thereby obviating the expense of hotels.

"It is now two weeks since I had a shower," grins Tre, welcoming us in. Tre, from the vertiginous blond bouffant, to the immovable deranged grin, to the continuous high-pitched giggle, is going to walk one of the parts if anyone ever casts a stage production of *Beavis and Butt-head*. When I tell him this, he replies, without missing a beat, "Huh-huh. You said 'parts.' Huh-huh." The ice is breaking, slowly but surely. "Do you want an espresso? We don't have anything else."

Billie Joe and Mike are sitting on benches, and seem warily amicable. Their determination to keep their shows as accessible as possible for their growing legion of fans is laudable, but Green Day are hampered by their tendency to protest rather too much. The first minutes of conversation sound like a rehearsal for Monty Python's "Four Yorkshiremen" sketch.

"I guess," begins Billie Joe, "that the biggest misconception about Green Day, at least as far a Britain is concerned, is that we all come from rich backgrounds, which is bullshit. Rodeo, which is where we come from, doesn't have a low, low class, but it doesn't have a really high, high class. It has no class. It's a refinery town, a smudge on the map of California."

"My mom was living in a trailer last year," adds Mike. "And she's a Native American."

Tre is engaged in single combat with the espresso machine, preventing him from regaling us with tales of a childhood spent in a shoebox in t'middle of t'road, or something very like it.

"I was the youngest of six kids raised by a single parent," continues Billie Joe. "She had a waitressing job. She is still a waitress. But if people read a few things from various British publications . . ."

We both know who he's talking about.

". . . they'd just think we brought together by some record company or something."

Would that matter?

"Well, yeah . . . I don't want people to think we were this thing that was put together."

The American strain of punk is plagued by the same craving for "authenticity" as every other form of American music. American musicians talk about being "real" and "meaning it" with genuine fervour, believing that the central virtues of rock'n'roll are sincerity and credibility. To the British pop consumer, such considerations as background, motivation and underlying morals appear rather quaint. Whether Green Day were raised in paper bags in septic tanks or are all architecture graduates whooping it up on trust funds is a matter of supreme irrelevance, surely. They've made at least three belting pop singles ("Basket Case," "Longview," "Stuck With Me") and those are all the credentials they'd need, you'd think.

"I know what you're saying," nods Mike. "When I was growing up, I didn't really think bands had backgrounds. They weren't real. But we have ideals that we carry with us, and they matter. I'm a momma's boy, totally, and that instilled good morals in me, I think. I'm not saying our backgrounds were completely fucked, but they weren't great. We've been through as much shit as anyone, but we keep reading that we're rich college kids."

Let's drop the college thing. That leaves "rich"—and you must have made a few bob by now—and "kids." Your average age is around twenty-three. So "rich kids" is hard one to refute, surely.

"I bought my mom a house, yeah," says Mike. Mike stares at his shoes. He seems a bit frail, and will later tell me that he suffers from a heart condition that gets exacerbated by stress. "But we don't have high standards of living. People think that once you gain money you suddenly have no feelings and no problems. We all have a life to live, and monetary stability brings another list of problems that comes with it. I can't expect people to understand or relate to that—they'll just say 'You're a rich rock star, what are you bitching about?' Well, I'm bitching because I've been gone from my fiancee for a year and a half. That still hurts."

Go and see her, then. That's the whole point of being rich. You don't have to do this (Green Day all have other concerns—Billie Joe is married with a young son, Joey).

"When we stop having fun, we will stop," says Billie. "I'm still having a total ball playing gigs. I don't know if you noticed the other night in Halifax, but I was having fun."

People don't usually come on naked for the encore when they're feeling a bit downbeat, no.

"If people pay to see us play—and we are entertainers—we have to put out as much as we possibly can. We can't go, 'Duh, I'm a rock star, this sucks, the people who are paying to see me now are the kind who used to beat me up in high school, I want my mummy.'"

Billie Joe is starting to lighten up a bit.

"I don't want to sit here and complain about being a rock star. I don't want to be whining and moaning. Fuck that, you know. I'm not gonna take for granted the fact that I have the ability to play music for the rest of my life if I want to. That's all I've ever wanted. For one or two or a few people to understand what the hell I'm talking about in my songs, that's more than I've ever asked for, for people to fuckin' get it."

WHICH BEGS THE question of what people are getting when they get Green Day. You don't shift ten million records without hitting a fairly significant seam in the cultural firmament. Nirvana's astonishing, and astonishingly sudden, success demonstrated that America was crying out for a punk-influenced rock trio articulating a large and hitherto unrecognised undertow of alienation, but it all got a bit messy and ugly for comfortable consumption when Kurt Cobain reacted to the fame, acclaim and wealth visited upon him by shooting himself.

Enter Green Day with their cute, catchy songs about television and school and masturbation, their pop-eyed cartoon of a singer, their funny videos, their implicit assurance that it's all just a lark, The Ramones all over again, and here's your licence to print money.

"Mmm," nods Billie. "That's the bleakest analysis I can come up with. It's what kids are talking about in their high schools, or their grammar schools, for that matter. I don't like to belittle people, though, because they happen to be liking my music at the same time. There again, kids are some of the most brutally honest critics there are."

If I could just play devil's advocate for a second, do you ever wonder—as a parent, even—what effect your relentlessly bleak lyrical view has on the kids buying your records?

"Maybe people take it the wrong way," says Billie. "I don't think I complain that much. A lot of our songs, I guess, are kind of about other people that whine. 'Brat' is about waiting for your parents to die so you can get your inheritance. That's where everyone starts saying, 'Oh, you're rich kids.' But that song's not about me, it's about fucking college kids. I mean, I don't know if you're a college kid . . ."

No, I'm not. Or at least wasn't. Or at least not for long enough to deserve the name. But we've done this bit.

"Well, we're not coming out with some tits-and-ass beerfest. We say obnoxious things and stuff, but I'd rather have my kid go to see Offspring than Poison, because at least I'd know there was some kind of sensibility associated with the band. Because . . ."

Billie Joe takes a deep breath and goes into rant mode.

"In America in the early part of the 90s, mainstream music was starting to get more interesting, Nirvana breaking big, Pearl Jam—who I don't like that much, but they're still more interesting than Bon Jovi—taking off and punk rock starting to get everywhere. Lots of cool stuff. Then, suddenly, in 1995, you get a bunch of fucking golf-playing fraternity boys putting out music. I mean, have you heard Hootie & The Blowfish?"

I have. While having no objection in principle to golf-playing fraternity boys releasing records, the appeal of Hootie & The Blowfish eludes me. In a sane world, they would play to modest audiences whose average age and IQ coincided somewhere in the high forties. In reality, there's hardly a venue in America they can't fill.

"Regular guy rock. Jesus. And Jay Leno is beating out David Letterman for ratings. Can you believe that? Things really are going backwards."

Green Day, presumably, see themselves on the side of the angels.

"There's more to us than people think," says Mike. "We do more than whine. There are a lot of subjects on the new record if people want to decipher them. 'Westbound Sign' is about the time Billie's wife moved out. 'Tightwad Hill' is about where we come from. 'No Pride' is like the anti-anthem, it's an anti-nationalism kind of song."

Ah, Green Day whining about nationalism.

Billie Joe gives me the look this last remark deserves, but decides to let it go.

"Listen," he says. "We've got to go and play, but come and have a beer afterwards, huh?"

This seems a reasonable offer.

WE STAY UP pretty late afterwards, while Green Day's crew pack crates, roll cables and give the buses the sort of meticulous clean you give buses when you're about to drive them across the border into America and you don't fancy becoming an extra in some lonely customs post's remake of *Midnight Express*. Tre helps the process along by smoking what remains of Green Day's stash, and entertains himself by smashing empty beer bottles against the dressing room wall. Mike shuffles quietly about, chatting to passing crew, and Billie Joe and I get into a frankly embarrassingly detailed argument about whether or not *All Shook Down* is a better Replacements album than *Let It Be*.

The Replacements were one of those bands whose commercial success was directly inversely proportional to their musical merit, which is to say they had almost none of the former and a lavish wealth of the latter. Bands like this have a way of turning their fans into crusaders, passionate bores who will seize at the slightest opportunity to make a convert. Woe betide the stranger in the seat next to me who makes a passing reference to The Go-Betweens or The Fatima Mansions at the beginning of a Heathrow–Los Angeles flight. Where The Replacements are concerned, Billie Joe and I have met our matches in each other. A glazed look begins to descend on everyone else in the room (Tre had one already, but for different reasons).

While I'm just delighted to have met someone else who can quote the line "Anywhere you hang yourself is home" from "Someone Take The Wheel" (The Replacements' peerless lament of the touring life), Billie Joe is trying to make a point. Green Day are in this for the long haul, he says. Earlier, he'd drawn a comparison with The Beastie Boys, who started out with multi-platinum success as a puerile novelty act, and went on to achieve genuine respect and the cult-level fame that Billie says he'd be more comfortable with. A shame that The Beastie Boys accomplished this transition by ceasing to make such splendidly cretinous records as "(You Gotta) Fight For Your Right (To Party)" and "No Sleep Till Brooklyn" and turning into a bunch of smug, self-righteous hippies in silly jumpsuits, but that's not relevant to Billie's argument.

The Replacements, Billie Joe reminds me, filled their first couple of albums with songs called "Gary's Got A Boner," "Dope Smokin' Moron" and "Fuck School." They made Green Day sound like Soren Kierkegaard. They went on to make some of the most haunted and glorious music in the rock'n'roll canon.

"That," says this determined, and brighter than expected, young man, "is what we're here for."

6

FRIDAY I'M IN CHICAGO

The Cure in America and Canada
JUNE 1992

ONE OF THE joys of travelling as a reporter is the opportunity to work with great photographers, and I've been unusually blessed in that respect—as I was on this trip, travelling with *Melody Maker*'s Stephen Sweet. And one of the frustrations of working as a writer is realising how little impact thousands of your words might have in comparison to a single frame snapped by a great photographer, which was what happened when this story originally ran. I'd mumbled something to Sweet about maybe focusing on the odd relationship between The Cure's Robert Smith and his mascara-smeared legions of look-alike fans, and Sweet nailed it the first night, outside the band's hotel in Chicago.The scene is described, and done insufficient justice, below Sweet's shot of Smith's encounter with an especially ardent adherent from behind the singer's shoulder, deftly capturing the worshipper's supplicant gawp and Smith's wincing, forehead-rubbing awkwardness. I still think it's one of the best illustrations of the dysfunctional relationship between celebrity and celebrator I've ever seen, and its potence is diluted not even slightly by the knowledge that the anguish discernible in Smith's expression was due principally to the fact that he was just plain sloshed. The camera, in those pre-Photoshop times, may not have lied, but it didn't always declare the whole truth.

What is lacking in the story that follows is much in the way of any meaningful attempt to understand the cult of Robert Smith from the perspective of its adherents. This was partially due to constraints of time, but mostly down to your correspondent's pathological aversion to boring nutters. I could understand being a fan of The Cure, because I was—and am—one: indeed, a little over two years before I did this trip, I was living, back in Sydney, in a room dominated by the black-and-white *Boys Don't Cry* poster, and I would still doubt the sanity of anyone prepared to argue that *The Head On The Door* wasn't one of the dozen best albums of the 1980s. I just don't understand the urge to appropriate your favourite singer's haircut and taste in misshapen jumpers, and regard his every pronouncement as freighted with Delphic sagacity. Which is to say that I don't understand uncritical reverence for anything, which is, I suppose, to say that I don't understand quite a lot of the rest of my species terribly well. However, I believe that the analysis of his own flock that Smith delivers later in this piece is both astute and compassionate, or at least blessed with more of both those qualities than anything I might have come up with on my own.

Fame is a phenomenon that generally conspires to make both the admired and the admirer look ridiculous: I suspect that this is what I was trying to demonstrate with the random observations of The Cure's celebrity inserted throughout the narrative. The best that all concerned can do with any variety of notoriety is refuse to take it seriously, and I've rarely since seen anyone cleave to that attitude quite so splendidly as The Cure.

★ ★ ★

"HERE, LOOK. NO, over here. See, I've invented this game for you. And I'd like you to play it."

The face—that great grinning shambles of lipstick, pancake and hair gel that I've only previously seen on magazine covers, television screens and, I'll admit, the walls of the bedrooms I occupied during my teens—is inches from mine. We're in a dressing room backstage at The World, a modestly-named arena an hour and a half's drive from Chicago, where The Cure have just played a superb show in front of 15,000 people. I'm sandwiched between Robert Smith and long-serving Cure bass player Simon Gallup on a black leather couch that might conceivably seat one in any kind of comfort.

"Look. On the table."

While Gallup has been asking me about a couple of friends of his back at the *Melody Maker* office, Smith has been arranging the contents of a bowl of M&Ms on the polished black table in front of us. From where I'm sitting, there doesn't seem to be much rhyme or reason to what Smith's doing, but as we've only just met and I've got to get a cover story out of this, I figure it's as well to humour him. I nod, and smile, and wish I wasn't quite so sober.

"Right," Smith continues. "Now what you have to do—and pay careful attention to this, right—is move that red one there at the bottom up to the top without," he pauses for effect, "touching any of the others."

Ah. Smith, it must be said, is drunk. Heroically so, in fact, and operating according to the deranged and indecipherable logic the state engenders, which is to say that while I'm sure this is all making cast-iron sense to him, I haven't a clue what he's talking about. I turn to Gallup in some faint hope of support, but he's got his head in his hands, is muttering intently to himself and clearly has no wish to be disturbed. I'm on my own.

"Come on," says Smith. "I'm waiting."

I'm thinking that somewhere, in some little-regarded footnote in a dusty thesaurus stashed in a dank corner of a cobwebbed attic owned by some mad, bearded, elderly professor, there's a cracking French or Latin phrase for "the fear of making an irredeemable plum duff of oneself in front of one's adolescenthood heroes within five minutes of meeting same for reasons you can neither control nor comprehend." Still, I steel myself, extend a trembling digit to the small red sweet, push it around the others to the spot Smith had designated at the top of the table, and sit back, trying to look nonchalantly triumphant. There follow some seconds of confused silence, broken only by Gallup's mumbling.

"Right," says Smith, eventually, and buries his fingers deep in his hopelessly congealed thatch. "Ah . . . okay. I can see I'm going to have to make this more difficult."

I'M STAYING IN the Claridge Hotel in Chicago, a renovated terrace house in which the halls are lined with glass cabinets full of antique toys. Amusingly, the hotel also has a complimentary stretch limousine service, and a driver with enough of a sense of humour to cope with directions like, "Oh, I don't know, just drive around for a bit and let me wave at people." When I come back and turn on the television, there's one of those uncountable, indistinguishable sub-*90210* teen angst soap operas on. This particular episode revolves around an outwardly normal, obviously beautiful, and tiresomely overachieving young woman who takes a stack of pills in an effort to kill herself. On her bedroom wall, looming above her as she belts back the downers, is what the show's producers doubtless imagined was a definitive signifier of tormented youth: a poster of The Cure.

IT IS DECIDED, after a couple more hours of drinking and slurring by all present, that The Cure will give me and photographer Stephen Sweet a lift back to Chicago on their tour bus. While we huddle on a couple of couches, The Cure's crew move into fluent action, packing up and rolling out everything non-human in black flight cases. Someone takes off the Sensational Alex Harvey Band CD that has been playing at excruciating volume since I arrived. "I was enjoying that . . . ," protests Smith, half-heartedly. "Someone threw it on stage tonight . . ." He stops, looks slowly around the room, then embarks on an animated ramble about how Alex Harvey reminds him of his wife, Mary, and about something that once happened with his brother and some French women, which I can't follow at all.

Gallup, meanwhile, is flinging surplus crisps, unwanted carrot sticks, empty cups and Robert's M&Ms at the nearest available target, which turns out to be The Cure's record company boss, Chris Parry of Fiction. One of The Cure's minders makes him stop. Smith, by now, is wrestling on the floor with another of the band's minders. It's hard to say how serious it is. Given that Smith has the upper hand, it's probably fair to surmise that he's trying harder than the minder (I mean, Smith is a big bloke, and probably more than capable of looking after himself, but the chap he's locked in combat with has arms thicker than my entire body and looks like he could kick-start a 747). A couple of crew prise the two apart and organise everyone onto the bus. As we pull out of the venue, the few dozen cars that have been parked, waiting, in the darkness alongside the road, start their engines and follow us.

The bus is as well-appointed as you'd expect, given that it's carting about a bunch of thirty-something millionaires whose singer is pathologically terrified of aeroplanes (The Cure crossed the Atlantic on the QEII). There are lounges fore and aft, a small kitchenette, a toilet, at least two televisions, a VCR and, inevitably, a stereo capable of broadcasting to all points within six zip codes in any direction. The Cure's on-board listening this evening rather belies their reputation as arch miserabilists: T-Rex's "Hot Love," Gary Glitter's "Didn't Know I Loved You Till I Saw You Rock'N'Roll" and, perhaps surprisingly given the bickering over stolen basslines traded by the two groups down the years, New Order's "State Of The Nation." It's while Smith is on all fours in the bus corridor, cradling a beer in the crook of his elbow, bellowing along to Middle of the Road's "Chirpy Chirpy Cheep Cheep" in a hearty roar quite removed from his patent wracked whine, and trying, for reasons known only to himself, to tie my shoelaces together, that Gallup, entirely unprovoked, makes an announcement.

"I can cook, me," he informs the bus at large. This is greeted with total indifference.

"I said," Gallup says, focusing this time on Sweet, "I can cook. I can."

"I, uh, don't doubt it," replies Sweet, polishing his lenses with a view to recording the carnage unfolding around us.

"I'm one of the greats," continues Gallup, swaying back and forth for reasons not entirely to do with the movement of the bus. "And I'm going to prove it. To you all. To you, my people, to whom I am a river."

Gallup approaches the stove and begins waving ingredients around. The dusting of herbs and generous squirt of Worcestershire sauce that congregate on one shoulder of my jacket suggest that the tottering gourmet is working on Welsh rarebit. Smith, meanwhile, has hauled himself upright via my left knee, a table and a handful of my hair, and has descended again on his long-suffering minder, whose job description appears to encompass punchbag as much as protector.

Gallup's culinary tour-de-force stumbles to a finish. He arranges it on a paper plate, and with a slurred "Ta-daaa," taps Smith on the shoulder and presents it to him, having evidently forgotten who he set out to impress in the first place. Smith disentangles himself from a headlock, takes the plate from Gallup, looks at it briefly, emits a maniacal cackle, and flings it across the bus, where it bounces off the wall just above where guitarist Porl Thompson is sitting, quietly reading.

"Piss off," he murmurs, without looking up, and turns the page.

WISH, **THE ALBUM** The Cure are in America touring with, went straight into the American Billboard Chart at Number Two. It was kept off the top spot by Def Leppard. Robert Smith claims that this doesn't bother him. I can't believe he means that.

AT THE CURE'S hotel on the bank of Lake Michigan, there's a bigger crowd waiting for us than most bands ever get coming to see them play. This happens everywhere The Cure go, but the Chicago crowd are going to be luckier than most—depending on how sociable the band are or aren't feeling after a show, the tour bus is often sent off empty, while Smith and company are spirited away in anonymous, windowless minibuses.

An obviously time-served plan is immediately in effect: two minders get off the bus, explain that the band will be coming out shortly, and will sign things and chat for a bit, but they're all very tired, need to get up early and so forth (Gallup and Smith, at this point, are waltzing, cheek-to-cheek, unsteadily up and down the bus, each humming a different tune). The minders arrange the mob in an orderly queue between the bus and the hotel door. Porl Thompson, drummer Boris Williams and guitarist/keyboardist Perry Bamonte make their way briskly along it, signing t-shirts, shaking hands, exchanging brief pleasantries. The queue is then re-straightened, and Simon and Robert appear, holding hands and smiling shyly, like children being presented to friends of their parents.

It takes Smith half an hour to get inside. Most of the fans are just enthusiastic and excited, though there's a few who give every appearance of being unhealthily obsessed. At least three are in floods of tears and hyperventilating, and there's one that Smith just can't seem to get past—the kid is a lot shorter and slighter than Smith, but in every other respect looks exactly like him, from his oversize white sneakers to his baggy black shirt to his powder-pale face to his artlessly smudged lipstick to his uproariously tangled black hair. The scary bit is that the kid doesn't say anything, just gazes up at Robert with a daft, adoring smile. "Look . . . ," Robert starts saying, then rubs his eyes. "I mean . . ." One of The Cure's minders notices what's up, and hustles Robert past him.

Another earnest mascaraed waif, who's seen me get off the bus just before Robert, comes up to me with her *Wish* tour poster and a marker pen.

Uh, I'm not in the band.

"Yeah, but you know them."

Well, I only met them a couple of hours ago, and I meaningfully doubt that they're going to remember it in the morning. I don't know if that counts.

"Oh, please. Would you?"

I take her pen. With love from Andrew. *Melody Maker*, every Wednesday. Still only 65p.

ON THE PLANE to Toronto, I'm reading the entertainment liftout of *The Toronto Daily Star*, which has Robert Smith on the cover, his face bathed in a green ink that makes him look like a QEII passenger who's wishing he'd flown after all. Inside, the *Star*'s resident rock'n'roll hack has bashed out one page of cribbed Cure history and a couple more pages of the usual lazy rubbish about doom, gloom, misery and despair, all rounded off with a few of the standard jokes about Edward Scissorhands and how, gosh, Robert Smith looks a bit like him. Also included for the edification of the readership are "Ten Frightening Facts about Robert Smith." Among these lurk the revelations that "His mummy knitted him ten pairs of socks to take on the current tour" and "He has a habit of sticking his fingers in his mouth when he talks, which makes him look silly."

IN TORONTO, THE Cure are playing the Skydome. The Skydome is a vast concrete barn that can be configured to hold 80,000 fans for a Blue Jays home game, or 25,000 for a Cure gig. When weather permits, Skydome's roof can be opened to the heavens. The fact that the heavens above this gaping slit are dominated by the endlessly upright form of the CN Tower must make Toronto something of a must for holidaying Freudians.

Backstage tonight, after a performance that was perhaps more competent but rarely as passionate as the one in Chicago, the mood, appropriately, is more subdued and, not to put too fine a point on it, sober. Members of The Cure and the support band, Cranes, sit quietly waiting for the tour buses, lost in Skydome's labrynthine tunnels, to find them. Assorted press, record company types and examples of that breed who always end up backstage without anyone knowing quite how, or why, or who they are, mill aimlessly about. Thanks to the increasing road fever being experienced by The Cure's tour manager, the backstage passes these people have affixed to their jackets don't read "Guest" or "VIP" but "Freeloader," "Blagger" and "No Idea." Mine says "Poser." Porl and Simon are playing with Porl's new toy, a sort of cross between a Polaroid camera and a fax machine that instantly prints out blurred, grainy, black and white images of whatever has just been photographed.

"See?" says Porl, pointing at a hopelessly blotched and smudged sheet of thermal paper. "It's you and Gallup."

After being hit by a tank, possibly. What's it for?

"For?" asks Porl. "Well, it's for . . . for rich idiots with more money than sense."

He goes off in search of a more appreciative subject. Smith appears with two handfuls of beer bottles and apologises, definitely more out of politeness than remorse, for the carryings-on in Chicago. "It was just a good show," he says, "and everyone was just in a good mood, and that can tend to get out of hand."

Smith suggests that we should go and sit somewhere quiet and talk about stuff before the buses find us. At no point does he put his fingers in his mouth. I forget to ask about the socks.

"It's a funny tour, this," he begins. "Everyone's been in such a good mood the whole time. Staggering! There's only been one violent row in twelve weeks, and that was really early on, when we were all still settling in."

As I saw in Chicago, The Cure kidding around and unwinding backstage could be mistaken for a Wild West all-in. An actual violent row must be something to see.

"Yeah . . . the arguments, when they happen, do get pretty intense. I mean, one-on-one, we've had few set-tos, but there's only been one big group row, which was very easily sorted out. I think it just comes from a constant reappraisal of what we're doing. The first couple of weeks were quite intense. We had a lot of MTV and record company bollocks which we went along with, which was a bit dumb of us, really. We used our days off very badly. Since then, we've used them wisely."

What do you do?

"Do? We don't do anything."

Smith, as he points out himself, is more constrained than most people in his position in terms of going outside for a bit of a walk, or trying to see the sights. He . . . there's no other way to put it. He really does look like Robert Smith. This isn't as fatuous a statement as it sounds: a lot of famous people, in the cold light of reality, look nothing like they do on television, or at least can get away with not looking quite like they do in magazines. The hair alone ensures that Robert Smith is unmistakeable. Robert Smith, possibly uniquely, has a famous shadow.

"Last time we were here," he says, "we were also playing stadiums, but somehow people still didn't know who the fuck we were. People in, like, Reno didn't know who The Cure were, but this time they do, and it's quite strange confronting that."

It has its points. Having previously fronted American customs to tell them that I'd come to interview bands called Violent Femmes or Hole, it was nice to be able to say something that impressed them.

"Exactly. And it's the first time that's happened. And because of that, it's still quite funny. Like, playing the Rose Bowl still just feels like . . . like a mistake, like it shouldn't be us playing there."

THAT AFTERNOON, ON CNN's *Entertainment News*, a reporter at the Chicago show accosted one of the legions of Smith lookalikes on hand and attempted to gain some sort of insight into The Cure's success. "They're great," replied the Smithette. "Really alternative."

"THE FANS . . . I dunno. Things started bothering me on the last American tour. We'd reached a certain level, and people knew where we were staying, and they'd check into the same hotels, so I'd have people camping in the hall outside my room, not just one or two but lots, sitting in the corridor and listening through the door, and it made me very . . . uncomfortable."

Smith sounds almost as if he thinks he's being unreasonable.

"But at the same time, I couldn't really go out and tell them to fuck off, because really I should be pleased. But I wasn't. So I'd just lie there and agonise over it, and it was driving me mad. So this time we're all checked in under ridiculous assumed names, our hotels aren't listed in the itinerary, so only we know where we're staying, stuff like that."

It still must be bloody strange looking out at an arena full of people all trying their damnedest to look like you. A bit *Life Of Brian*, I'd have thought. You know: "Yes! We're all individuals!"

"Well, we went to this funny little diner a couple of weeks ago, somewhere between Denver and St Louis, or wherever. Anyway, horrible little town, full of people who aren't particularly friendly to people who look like us. Anyway, we went in, and what must have been the only two Cure fans for miles around arrived just as we were finishing our meal—someone must have phoned them and tipped them off. And they were all dressed up, and made up, and wearing black, you know.

"I mean, I don't know why they did it, but at the same time . . . when they walked in, everybody in the place went, 'Oooh,' like they were obviously the local weirdos. But when those people put two and two together, they had a kind of newfound respect, like, 'Oh, we know this band, and these people are fans of this band.' So I think people do it for that reason, to step outside the norm. And in some of the places we're going, that must take a lot of courage. I think, really, it's just like warpaint, or tribal feathers or a . . . I dunno, a kilt, or something."

On *Wish*, there's a song called "End," which contains the repeated line "Please stop loving me / I am none of these things," which . . .

"Yeah, in part. But it's mainly directed at me. The bit about 'All the things you say / And all the things you write' is me talking to myself. There's an irony there when I'm up on stage doing it, but I realised that there would be. I do feel quite self-conscious that people are taking it as if it's directed at them, though."

People come over roughly every five seconds to tell Robert that the bus is on its way, or about to arrive, or here now, but he doesn't seem in any hurry—it's not like they're going to go anywhere without him. He carries on talking about the tour, musing on the irony that when The Cure came out to America a few years ago to tour the epic doom-fest

Disintegration, crowds threw flowers and teddy bears onto the stage, "Whereas this time, when we've come out with a much more upbeat record, you know, 'Friday I'm In Love' and all that, we've been getting a lot of phials of people's blood and Baudelaire books." He bites quickly when I try to bracket The Cure alongside Simple Minds and U2 in a peer group of post-punk bands that have gone megaplatinum—Smith dismisses both, with a theatrical snort, as "Competitors for the title of most foolish-looking-into-the-middle-distance band in the world."

He's also entertainingly indiscreet about his former bandmate and pending legal adversary Lol Tolhurst, gleefully reciting choice excerpts from the universally appalling reviews garnered by Tolhurst's post-Cure band, Presence ("I can't fucking wait for the court case"). In the piles of stuff being stacked onto the bus is a gift that has given to Robert by an associate of the band: a Lol Tolhurst dartboard.

"The thing to keep remembering," says Smith, finally, "is that we're a very foolish band. And we always have been."

AS SWEET MADE his way into the photo pit in Chicago, he was approached by a couple of local kids, who wanted to know if he'd be meeting the band. When Sweet said yeah, they gave him a passport-sized photograph and asked if Sweet could get Robert to sign it. It was, they explained, a picture of a friend of theirs, a huge Cure fan. She'd been killed six months ago in a car-surfing mishap. Sweet took the photo, and the kids' addresses.

In Toronto, when Sweet gives Smith the photo and explains the story, Robert looks utterly at a loss. After staring at it, shaking his head silently for a few seconds, he borrows a pen from someone.

"What," he scrawls across the top of it, "can I possibly write?"

And he signs his name to the bottom.

7

APATHY IN THE UK

On book tour in Britain
AUGUST 2008

THERE IS NO aspect of the rock'n'roll life more mythologised than touring, and I should know. Having given rock'n'roll the proverbial best years of my life, writing about music for *Melody Maker*, then assorted others, I did my little bit towards furthering the idea of touring as a splendid and enviable mobile Saturnalia. Which is to say that I lied. Not lied as in related palpable untruths, but lied in failing to pass onto readers the whole truth, which is this: tours are only fun when they're someone else's tour, in which case they're about the most fun you can have. When they're your own tour—as most people who undertake such things will confide, after a few drinks—they're an excruciating, dignity-destroying process which will steadily cause you to loathe, in this order, your most recent work, your audience, yourself, everyone, everything. I once interviewed Harry Shearer, now best known as the voice of much of *The Simpsons*, but a genuine rock'n'roll immortal due to his portrayal of bass player Derek Smalls in *This Is Spinal Tap*, the purest essence of the touring experience ever distilled. While wrangling my tape recorder, I remarked that I'd first seen the film as a teenager, and thought it amusing satire.

"Well, thanks," said Shearer.

And then, I continued, I became a rock journalist.

"And now," grinned Shearer, "you know better, right?"

I embarked on my own tour, therefore, with some trepidation. In order to interest the British reading public in the UK edition of my book, *I Wouldn't Start From Here*–an account of one peripatetic hack's bewildered stumbling around the political, philosophical and actual front lines of the 21st century– my British publisher, Portobello, arranged for me a series of manifestations in bookshops and associated establishments. Naturally, I became gripped with visions of Artie Fufkin, the hapless press officer from Polymer records, penitently inviting Spinal Tap to "kick this ass for a man" after organising an in-store appearance at which even the two men and a dog of fable have failed to show.

Nevertheless, I agreed, largely out of curiosity–always the best and the worst reason to agree to anything.

★　★　★

IN FAIRNESS TO all concerned, it starts well. At London's Frontline club—a haven for foreign correspondents, and similar—I do an onstage interview with my good friend James Brabazon, a reading and a Q&A session. A decent crowd show up, some of whom I don't know. James is a kind and thoughtful interrogator, despite the patent truth that he's survived any number of adventures much more interesting and alarming than anything I'd even attempt. During the readings, one about Gaza and one about Albania, people laugh when I hope they will, the questions from the floor are smart and pointed, and we sell all the books we brought along, and there's no point in even trying to be smart or glib or self-deprecating about the feeling of people asking you to sign a book you wrote: it's just brilliant. The following night, I appear at the Corner Club in Oxford, and contrary to all expectation— this is, after all, a university town in August—a reasonable gathering awaits, which is to say less than twenty, but more than a dozen, which is enough that reading aloud and fielding questions doesn't just seem weird for everybody.

Nevertheless, I reflect, on the way back to London, the economics of it are insane. If I sold half a dozen books tonight—the most optimistic of estimates—that's a gross return of about fifty quid, of which about a fiver goes towards defraying my advance (although the Corner Club did throw in dinner, which was very good). The outlay to accomplish same was £19 in rail fares, and about that again on magzines and newspapers to read on the train, and coffee. I understand that it's about generating word of mouth, building an audience, and all that, and I don't mind doing it—again, it's fantastic that people turn up, and listen, and ask questions, and stick around for a drink afterwards. But a jolt of perspective is provided within forty-eight hours, with the broadcast of the episode of BBC Radio 4's *Excess Baggage* in which I'm interviewed about the book (again, vexingly, by someone who'd regard the hair-raisingest moments in it as a rest cure—in this case, the explorer Benedict Allen): within minutes of the programme airing, *I Wouldn't Start From Here* is tenth on amazon.co.uk's travel chart.

It doesn't last. By day's end, not that I'm checking every hour or anything, *I Wouldn't Start From Here* is clinging grimly to the Top 100 travel books, digging in its nails while Charley Boorman's *Race To Dakar* stamps on its fingers, and so the road beckons. After we'd recorded *Excess Baggage*, Benedict Allen remarked that he'd just done a reading in Bristol, in the same shop I'm due at. I asked what sort of crowed he'd pulled. "Eight," he'd beamed. I can't wait.

SINCE *I WOULDN'T Start From Here* was published in my Antipodean homeland in 2007, I've received a flattering, if bemusing, number of emails from folk younger than myself soliciting advice. I have been unsure what to offer by way of reply, as the only utterly infallible contribution I've ever felt I can confidently make to the sum of human wisdom is this: if you go home with a woman for the first time, and discover, in your exploratory survey of her CD shelves, that she possesses more than one album by Joni Mitchell, climb out of a bathroom window at the earliest opportunity, and run like the fucking wind.

To that pearl, I can now add this: don't invite your friends to your book signings. This because that when you do invite your friends to your book signing, and no other bugger shows up, you forfeit the consolation of subsequently lying to said friends that the event was a riotous outpouring of adulation next to which Barack Obama's Berlin speech looked like Gary Glitter's homecoming parade.

Which is to say that the spectre of Artie Fufkin looms forbiddingly at Borders on London's Charing Cross Road, and he's about the only one who does. I'm parked by the till, next to a cardboard marquee bearing my name and the book's cover, and a stack of volumes awaiting purchase and signature. It's a set-up that might well work were I a much-garlanded literary titan, or a gormless, ghostwritten halfwit who plays football, or is otherwise on television occasionally. But I am none of these things. I am a semi-retired rock journalist who has written a strange book about screwed-up places, and I have neither admirers nor fans, just an agent and a bunch of mates making helpful morale-boosting comments, like for example "Do you want a hand brushing off the cobwebs?" and "How much longer before you pack it in, Mueller? We're getting thirsty." Eventually, though, three honest-to-goodness members of the book-buying public appear. In the circumstances, attempting any sort of reading would just seem odd, so we have a chat, instead. They seem nice, and afterwards I stomp into Soho with my friends, attempting to make my improvised soliloquy about the advantages of quality over quantity audible over their sniggering.

The Brighton leg of the tour was supposed to be the basis for a proper old-school, wacky *Summer Holiday*-variety travelogue. My publicist at Portobello, Hannah Marshall, owns a bright orange Zastava 750— a more or less automotive relic of Yugoslav communism. We had intended to drive to Brighton and back in it. However, it is raining on the day we are due to head to the seaside, and because the car is—as I understand it—constructed largely from papier-mâché, straw and turnip peel, she doesn't fancy our chances. We take the train. I spend the trip half-heartedly inventing prima donna rider demands—bowls of blue M&Ms backstage, a polar bear cub to stroke during the reading and so forth. Hannah spends the trip ignoring me.

After the Charing Cross experience, I pitch up at Brighton's Borders store willing to regard anything north of total humiliation as a result. A pleasant surprise awaits. The manager, Neil, a grinning, shaggy-haired sort in a Nirvana t-shirt, gives every impression of being someone motivated to work in bookselling by a fizzing zest for books, and he's made an effort. There are signs, posters and displays touting my tome and my appearance, and though the dozen or so people who fill the seats seem a meagre return for Neil's heroic labours, it's a dozen or so more than I was expecting. I give a short talk explaining myself and the book, and read from the chapters about Albania and

Gaza. The latter—in which I do, I fear, imply that the state of Israel is in some respects imperfect and fallible—provokes a brief irruption of controversy. "Nazi!" snorts one punter—the one who seems to be storing a considerable percentage of his worldly chattels in the plastic carrier bags he is clutching to his chest—and shambles off; another satisfied customer.

But there are good questions from the floor afterwards, and some books are sold, and I head for Bristol two nights later suffused with an optimism which, it proves, is as hilariously misplaced as an air horn at a chess tournament. Despite the lengthy interview I'd done with the local BBC radio station, my audience at the Borders branch on Bristol's handsome Clifton Promenade consists, in its entirety, of the parents of an ex-girlfriend. I add the entire populations of Somerset and Gloucestershire to the burgeoning list of people who'll be sorry when I'm famous, sign all the copies of the book the store has in stock so they can't send them back, and at least get taken out to dinner, and to meet my ex's parents' new dog, so it's not a complete write-off.

THE FOLLOWING WEEK, I head north, in neither hope nor expectation. An Australian, such as myself, who seeks triumph in Leeds, labours in a dauntingly long shadow. In July 1930, on his first tour of England, a 21-year-old batsman from Bowral, New South Wales, called Donald Bradman, piled up 334 runs at Headingley. "As to its extraordinary merit," declared the venerable cricket annual *Wisden* of this titanic innings, "there could be no two opinions." It is humbling indeed, then, to arrive for my reading at the Borders outlet on the shopping street of Briggate and discover that I have, in a very real sense, equalled Bradman's accomplishment, at least if one values each attendee at a book reading as worth 55.66 runs, and doesn't make any deductions for the fact that one is a member of staff, and another is a palpably insane transient seeking shelter from the astonishing rain, and who spends most of the time muttering into a mobile phone—a call which, I cannot help but suspect, has been going on for some while, possibly some years, and does not involve anyone else.

Nevertheless, that leaves four honest-to-goodness members of the reading public whose presence has not been compelled by professional obligation or voices in their head, and I am genuinely pleased to see them (I am, following last week's debacle in Bristol, genuinely pleased to see anybody). I give my explanation of myself, and my book. *I Wouldn't Start From Here* is, I tell them, the first history of the 21st century: a publishing landmark. Given the tumultuous rain, the meagre attendance, and the ever-present, over-arching knowledge that I'm never going to sell a thousandth as much as Bill fucking Bryson, this feels pleasingly preposterous. I do a couple of brief readings: one I haven't done before, about traipsing around some of the less glamorous reaches of Kosovo with soldiers serving with KFOR, then the reliable crowd pleaser recalling my first meeting with Edi Rama, the extraordinary mayor of Tirana, Albania. Afterwards, a pleasant young chap called Sean wants to argue about politics for a bit. As I have nothing better to do but ink my signature into the forlorn pile of books stacked on the table, in the hope that an "autographed copy" sticker will persuade someone to part with £8.99, I'm happy to argue back. Sean takes his leave, and my scrawling is interrupted by a tall, twitching, bearded apparition in a mouldy greatcoat and deerstalker hat.

"Have I missed something?" he asks.

Not really, I tell him.

"Did you write this?" he continues, lifting one of the volumes.

I did, I confirm.

He—I swear I'm not making this up—whips a magnifying glass from a pocket, and regards the cover intently.

"I've never heard of you," he concludes.

Him and everybody else in explored space, I reflect, as I plod out into the rain, back down a near ankle-deep Briggate, to tonight's lodgings at the Malmaison hotel. I order room service, and watch a DVD of a recent Australian Rules football fixture which my folks have sent me. The forces of all that is good and righteous (Geelong) vanquish the evil empire (Hawthorn). I reassure myself that this is all going to be worth it eventually.

"Eventually," happily, turns out to mean "almost exactly twenty-four hours." York is brilliant. Not just the event, but York itself. Beautiful, walkable, riddled with fantastic antique bookstores. I find a 1923 edition of Hilaire Belloc's history of Napoleon's retreat from Moscow. I decide that £30 asking price is worth it, on the grounds that it serves as both a heartening totem (it is, after all, a book about conflict by someone who liked to think himself funny) and a useful dose of perspective (in that it reminds that some journeys are a rather greater struggle than the one I am presently undertaking).

When I report to York's Borders store, things look unpromising, which is to say about like I expected them to look. Just two of the seats arranged in front of the table heaped with books are occupied. The staff tell me not to worry—they've been giving this plenty, printing their own posters, building displays, mentioning it to customers, and they're quietly confident. They're also absolutely right. By 6:30, all twenty-odd chairs are filled. I read the section about meeting Tirana's mayor again, and a bit about talking to American soldiers in Baghdad just after they'd taken the city. When I solicit questions, there's an intriguing contribution from an officer's mess-sounding sort who explains that his interest was piqued because he'd also worked in the Middle East. I ask in what capacity. "I'd rather not say," he beams (later, after everyone else leaves, he explains himself further, leaving me in no doubt that he's genuine—however, were I to pass on what he relates, I'd be in the invidious and inconvenient position of having to kill all of you). Others want to know how I'd characterise my politics ("Increasingly bewildered," I answer) and there's a good discussion about the intersection of tragedy and comedy. Best of all, at least from the perspective of the author whose ego has, of late, endured a bit of a kicking, there's an actual queue for signed copies.

Nevertheless, as I contemplate the looming conquest of Scotland, I feel like I'd rather be me than Napoleon. Which is unusual.

BY THE TIME my train from York pulls into Edinburgh's Waverley station, I am ensconced in a not unpleasant fug of cheerful resignation. I'm already prepared for Scotland to go badly. A scheduled appearance at a Borders store in Glasgow has been cancelled. According to the email from the store's management, this was for reasons beyond anyone's control, but I was pretty sure I'd detected, between the lines, sentiments to the effect of "Who the fuck is he? He couldn't pull a crowd if he was paying people fifty quid a time to take his book away. Why do you keep sending us these losers? Can't you get us Paul Theroux, or Charley Boorman, or at least somebody we've ever heard of?"

As for Edinburgh, I know I haven't a hope. I've arrived in the middle of the city's annual festival, without even any official attachment to the literary component of the event—and even for big names with bottomless resources, attracting attention in Edinburgh during the festival is difficult, for the fairly fundamental reason that in Edinburgh during the festival it often feels like there are more performers than there are punters. For the duration of the festival, the normally famously staid city goes, in the most genial and least pejorative sense of the word, crazy. By which I mean that if, after the previous Edinburgh Festival I'd attended, in 2006, I'd entered some hypothetical contest to find the most bizarre one-line reminiscence of the event, my own submission ("I hosted a three-night stand at the Underbelly by England's greatest living songwriter, shook hands with Sean Connery, accidentally kidnapped a waitress and compared favourite *Onion* stories with a former Vice-President of the United States"), though no word of a lie, would have struggled to crack the top ten thousand.

What minimal delusions of grandeur I may still be harbouring are vanquished by the experience of apprising myself of my accommodations. The only parts of the bedsheets through which it would be difficult to read a newspaper are the stains which are holding them together, the ventilator shaft outside the only window offers an intriguing suggestion of what life might be like inside a 747 engine, and the plumbing is obsolete and diabolical even by British standards. However, the festival is on, which means that they are charging my publisher for the night what they would probably, at any other time of year, be grateful to get away with charging for the freehold of the entire hotel, and its indolent, surly staff.

Still, I reflect, I shouldn't complain. I should struggle, at moments such as these, to spare a thought for the millions for whom a published book, and a subsequent publicity tour, however ill-attended, are wildest dreams plus tax. I tell myself that, in some sense, I'm doing this not for myself, but for all those thwarted authors with yellowing manuscripts in the bottoms of their wardrobes, sheaves of rejection slips in a desk drawer—and probably, I reflect further, as I grimly roll up a newspaper in preparation for single combat with the moose-sized cockroach who presides over the bathroom, some semblance of a settled, functional, adult life.

My only engagement in Edinburgh is at Word Power, an independent bookshop on West Nicolson Street. It is, of course, hopelessly cliched to become sentimental about independent bookshops, menaced as they are by the internet and by the chain stores I've spent the last couple of weeks visiting. It is also absolutely right and proper to become sentimental about independent bookshops, especially ones like Word Power, which compensate for their relative lack of shelf space by their surfeit of enthusiasm and knowledge. The rampant nature of their optimism is attested by the twenty-odd seats they've arranged in front of the lectern.

Failing to pull double figures in Edinburgh at the height of the festival on a sunny Friday afternoon prompts, I'm pleased to discover, significantly less in the way of existential despair than tanking just as badly in Leeds on a rainy Tuesday night. After all, I can reassure myself, it's Edinburgh during festival. If I didn't have to be here, I wouldn't be here either.

8

NO SLEEP TILL TRAVNIK

China Drum in Bosnia

JULY 1996

MORE THAN ANY other piece in the book, this account of a little-known punk group's attempt to be the first British rock band to play in post-war Bosnia requires a glossary. Not only does it contain cultural references which are specific to the English, it contains cultural references which are specific to the sub-group of the English who hail from the city of Newcastle-upon-Tyne, in northeast England—or, as these folks are known, by themselves and by others, Geordies. The stereotypical Geordie is cheerful, funny, insatiably—if not occasionally wearisomely—sociable, utterly likeable, fond of a drink and distinguished by a rich accent and picturesque dialect all but completely baffling to outsiders (indeed, many of the words attributed to the band in what follows are not so much quotations as translations). It is intended only as the highest of compliments to the stout fellows of China Drum to observe that I remember them all, in every sense that matters, as hilariously stereotypical Geordies.

So, some explanations are in order—many of which may make more sense after reading the piece, but anyway. Being Geordies, China Drum are all ardent supporters of Newcastle United Football Club, whose fans are known, en masse, as the Toon Army (Newcastle, unusually for an English conurbation of its size, is a one-club city, so Newcastle United are held to be representing "the town"—or, when rendered into Geordie, "the toon").

And, being from Newcastle or thereabouts, China Drum affect to dislike nobody in the world more than the people of Sunderland, just thirteen miles down the road—hence the gloating singalongs about Sunderland's football team, who had, the previous season, come off the worse in the both of the Newcastle vs. Sunderland derby matches (Freud's famous "narcissism of minor differences"—the syndrome which dictates that people tend to hate most intensely those most similar to themselves—will find a means of expression everywhere, and the recent history of the destination of China Drum's journey demonstrates that there are far more destructive vents for it than football rivalries).

Frequent reference is made, below, to attempts to recreate, in assorted carparks and forecourts along the way, key moments from something called Euro '96. This was that summer's European Football Championships, which had been held in England, and in which England's team had acquitted themselves in the manner for which they have become justly famous, i.e., fumbling, fluking and flattering to deceive through the group stages before being knocked out in the semi-finals in a penalty shoot-out against Germany. The players referred to en route all took part in the tournament: England and Geordie icon Alan Shearer; England's Paul Gascoigne, a player who might have joined the pantheon of all-time greats had his surging genius on the field been allied with the smallest soupçon of common sense off it; Gary McAllister and Colin Hendry, who had been members of Scotland's characteristically hapless squad.

England's infuriating exit from Euro '96 may have contributed to the anti-Hunnish sentiments which were expressed during the pertinent portion of our drive, but as the English rarely require much in the way of prompting to loudly remind Fritz who won the bloody war anyway, probably not (the admonishment not to mention the war, obviously delivered ironically, is a quote from the iconic 1970s BBC sitcom *Fawlty Towers*, and far from the only one of these coming up). The *Dambusters March* also mentioned in this context is the theme from the 1954 film about the heroics of the Royal Air Force's 617 squadron, and their dashing assaults on the Ruhr dams in 1943: the tune is most often heard, these days, during the pre-match ceremonies of England vs. Germany football fixtures, when it is taken lustily up by the England faithful to drown out the playing of "Deutschland Über Alles."

China Drum split up in 2000, after three albums and around a million times that many road miles, most of them logged in vehicles even less sturdy and glamorous than the one we drove to Bosnia. According to an email from singer Adam Lee—announced with the Geordie salutation "Aalreet!"— it sounds like they're all doing well. Bill McQueen teaches guitar, drives a truck and raises four children. Dave McQueen is also married with two kids and has what sounds like some species of grown-up job. Adam has his own landscaping company, a wife and a couple of children and a new band called Sickhoose (this translates into English as "Sick House": www. myspace.com/sickhoose). Phil Barton, their former manager, is married with a baby daughter, and owns two excellent record shops—Sister Ray in Soho, London, and Rounder in Brighton. You should go to them, if you're ever in the vicinity, and spend money.

I occasionally bump into Max, The Serious Road Trip's photographer, while wandering the London Borough of Hackney, where we both live. He remains a decent chap, for a Kiwi (this wholly gratuitous barb inserted by way of demonstration that we peoples of the South Seas are as prone to the internecine conflict fuelled by the narcissism of minor difference as the denizens of the Balkans, and of Tyneside).

★ ★ ★

THE VAN PARKED outside the rental office in King's Cross is a battered white Iveco that appears to be held together by rust and gaffer tape. The legend "Midnight Flyer" is written in purple above the front passenger door, indicating either that this van cut rather more of a dash in its heyday, or that a previous owner possessed an overdeveloped sense of irony. My first thought is that we've got roughly as much chance of flying it to the moon as we have of getting it, and us, to Sarajevo and back in one piece. In fact, I'm prepared to offer decent odds against it getting around the next corner without losing a wheel.

There is a simple reason why we've had this four-wheeled cousin of the Raft of the Medusa foisted upon us.

"I told them where we were taking it," explains Phil Barton.

Phil is the manager of Newcastle rock group China Drum. When Phil first spoke to me about this trip his band were planning, some weeks ago now, there was no mention of decrepit rattletraps with cracked windows and—oh, this is reassuring—a side door that won't open from the inside. The idea was that China Drum were going to travel to the former Yugoslavia in style, in a Hercules cargo aircraft belonging to the Royal Air Force. The plan was that they would play one show for British troops stationed in the Croatian port of Split, another for the peacekeepers serving with the NATO-led United Nations Implementation Force (IFOR) in Sarajevo and, finally, one for Sarajevo's public. This sounded like great fun, a good story, and I asked to be counted in.

Days before lift-off, the Ministry of Defence contacted Barton, muttered something about "operational difficulties" and informed him that the trip was cancelled. China Drum, having announced their intentions, and having heard that people in Sarajevo were looking forward to it, and being men of their word, decided to go anyway. Feeling that I could hardly cry off just because I wasn't going to get a ride in a cool camouflage-coloured aeroplane, I said I'd go too. I have been soothing myself ever since with visions of a gleaming deluxe tour bus, replete with tinted windows, comfortable bunks, televisions, stereos, sofas and microwave ovens (I felt I could live without the jacuzzi, if necessary).

"It does have tinted windows," observes Barton. "Well, one tinted window. And a video."

The man is as incurably, ludicrously optimistic as a Somalian travel agent. Even if this thing gets us as far as the Bosnian border, which it won't, it's going to disintegrate as soon as it hits the first shell-hole. We might as well be trying to take Cape Horn on a windsurfer.

"Well, it's all we could get."

Still, I take it the driver knows the roads well.

"He's never been."

Jesus. The truck is split into two parts: the band's gear goes in the back, the people in the rest. There are seats for two in the front, and three rows of three seats in the back; the first of these faces backwards to allow space for a small table. It might be grudgingly conceded that half a dozen people could ride in relative comfort inside for a short distance. There are eleven of us labouring under the delusion that we're going to Sarajevo: myself, Phil, all three of China Drum, China Drum's tour manager, two crew, one driver and two photographers, on a round trip of about 2500 miles. This heap will be our home, more or less, for a week.

"You could stop whining and give us a hand with this amplifier," says Barton.

Further introductions are effected once we've loaded up and repaired to a nearby pub to await one of the photographers—Andy Willsher of the *NME*—who is marooned on a train somewhere outside Euston. China Drum are a heavily Hüsker Dü-influenced punk trio from Newcastle: Adam Lee (drums and vocals), Bill McQueen (guitar) and Dave McQueen (bass). At the end of their last European tour, they explain, they'd fetched up in the Italian city of Trieste. Scanning a map of the continent in search of interesting-sounding places to play next time out, they'd hit upon Bosnia. The war in that country had just been ended by NATO's airstrikes and the subsequent Dayton Peace Accord, and China Drum reckoned, if they were quick, they could be the first British band to play post-ceasefire Sarajevo.

Once the link with the MoD had broken down, China Drum had turned for help to London-based aid organisation The Serious Road Trip. The Serious Road Trip had become a minor legend during the Bosnian war, ferrying food and medicine through the worst of the fighting in garishly painted Land Rovers and yellow Bedford trucks decorated with murals of cartoon characters. They had also taken clowns and other circus performers on tour in Bosnia and run music and painting therapy courses for children; copiously dreadlocked New Zealander Max Reeves of this fine organisation is the other photographer joining us.

The twin entertainments in the Caledonian Road pub we've picked on are watching former Pogues singer Shane MacGowan subsiding into unconsciousness at the next table, and the domestic travails of two other customers, a married couple who alternate moody silences with eruptions of screaming, and occasionally stumble outside to continue the debate with their fists, before coming back in as if for the first time. It seems to be a regular performance; they are regarded with surreal indifference by the pub's other clientele.

"I like a spot of cabaret with dinner," says Adam.

We finally leave, with all aboard, two hours overdue, but we make a

late ferry from Dover to Calais, and are on the road in Europe by three
the next morning.

AS THE SUN comes up over Belgium, I'm sitting up front alongside Andy
Matthews, the driver who came with the truck. I have not yet spoken
to Andy, but I already suspect that he is the single most rock'n'roll man
on earth. The blond mohawk, the sunglasses and the earrings are a good
start, but where most veteran roadies will have tour t-shirts and caps,
Andy has tattoos: "Yazoo: Crew" engraved on his left upper arm, and
"Lenny Kravitz: Crew" on his ribs, visible beneath his torn t-shirt.

Heading towards the morning's first coffee stop, Andy reaches over
and takes a small leather case out of the glove compartment in front
of me. He opens it to reveal a syringe and some phials of clear liquid.
Keeping the wheel steady with his knees, he fills the syringe and injects
himself calmly in the stomach. Suddenly, I feel strangely very awake.

I realise, I tell him, that this seems a funny thing to say to someone
on first acquaintance, but I really hope that he's diabetic.

"No," he grins. "I'm a crack fiend."

Ask a silly question.

Dave peers into the front cabin from behind the curtain. "Can we,"
he asks, "stop at Mademoiselle Le Miggins' croissant shop?"

This is the journey's first deployment of authentic tour-ese, that
weird, reductive dialect spoken by otherwise intelligent people who
find themselves shut in a small moving space with a bunch of other
otherwise intelligent people and doing something fundamentally
stupid, like taking a rock'n'roll band on tour. Mrs. Miggins' Pie Shop
is a fixture of the popular television comedy *Blackadder*, and the popular
television comedy *Blackadder* is a fixture on every tour bus in the
world. No matter who the band, no matter where they travel, almost
all tour bus conversations consist of verbatim or bastardised quotes
from television sitcoms: Dave, accordingly, has cunningly regionalised
Mrs. Miggins to suit our surroundings.

"No problem," says Andy.

The drive across Belgium towards the Rhine is so transcendentally
tedious that I become almost nostalgic for those school holidays when
I'd travel by bus from Sydney to visit my grandparents in Adelaide,
across twenty-eight hours of untidy scrub-country and deserts as vast

and featureless as UB40's back catalogue. To a landscape as relentlessly, heart-breakingly boring as this, there can only be one response.

"Monners!" cries Adam, producing the travel *Monopoly* kit from his bag. "Who's in?"

This could end in tears. Mine, if I don't win. Theirs, if I do. With a mixture of skill, cunning and taking it far more seriously than anyone else, I win the first two games. After which everyone gangs up on me.

"We're in Germany," announces Phil, as I try to stage a comeback with assets totalling £20, Pentonville Road and a station. "Don't mention the war."

The inevitable collective hum-along of "The Dambusters March" follows.

"Can we stop at Frau von Miggins' sausage shop?" asks someone.

There are a great many beautiful and historic palaces along the road that joins Cologne, Frankfurt and Munich. "Look," someone will occasionally say, "there's another kraut castle." This rarely registers with the majority of the expedition, who are degenerating rapidly, engrossed in interminable travel *Monopoly* death matches ("Right, no buying on the first two laps, all fine money to be collected at Free Parking, no rent on a double, except triple rent if it's a double four, you can have more than one hotel on a property and you have to move backwards on a seven . . . who's in?") or in the *Carry On* films which are being loaded into the video player. In a lull between *Monopoly* and puerile movies, several exquisite architectural confections are ignored while China Drum, all card-carrying volunteers in Newcastle United's Toon Army, lead a stirring twenty-minute singalong of "Thank you very much for the six points, Sunderland, thank you very much, thank you very very very much."

A few hours short of Munich, we are pulled over by a motorcycle policeman. Andy, who is now nearly fifteen hours in the saddle, has apparently been overdoing it.

"Everyone in the back keep quiet," he hisses, as the cop approaches. "I can talk my way out of this."

It all goes terribly school excursion. The strain of keeping a straight face causes several of us to water at the eyes. Dave cracks first.

"For you, Englander," he says, quietly, "zer tour iz over."

The passenger compartment erupts.

"You vill pay for your inzolence."

We get a ticket.

Some miracle of record company largesse has provided rooms at the Hilton in Munich. Any flat surface would have done. A flat surface with a mattress and sheets and a neatly wrapped chocolate on the pillow is as welcome a sight as could be imagined.

THE CUSTOMS OFFICIAL at the Austrian border looks like all customs officials at all borders, which is to say he looks like his dog's died and he can't sell the kennel.

"Pliz ver are yoo goink?" he wants to know

Bosnia and Herzegovina, we tell him.

"Vot iz zer purpoz ov your vizeet?"

We tell him that, as well. He regards us with an expression that suggests he thinks we're probably taking the piss but he can't be bothered with us at this time of morning. He waves us through.

We pull in at Fraulein Migginsheim's sauerkraut shop. This is a motorway service station owned by someone with a serious garden gnome fetish. Dozens of the little ceramic chaps are congregated on the forecourt by the café. While we're taking pictures of each other sitting amid the tiny red-hatted elves, Adam appears from the gear storage area at the back of our truck with a triumphant expression.

"You can't take a team photograph without this," he says. He's found the football. I feel that this cannot be good news, and I am swiftly proved right. Adam hoofs the ball into the car park. "Right," he says. "I'll be Alan Shearer, like." Within minutes, we are re-enacting key moments from the 1996 European Championships for an audience of bewildered Austrian truck drivers. We stop only because nobody wants to be Scotland.

Back aboard, cabin fever is setting in. We have now watched every episode of *Blackadder* ever made, one series of *Absolutely Fabulous*, more than enough *Carry On*, and a bid to put *Fawlty Towers* on is shouted down when someone observes, correctly, that there's no point, so many times have all present seen it. Already, indeed, any mildly controversial opinion advanced by anyone, on any subject, is greeted with a rousing chorus of "No! I won't have that! There's a place in Eastbourne!" delivered in the style of Ballard Berkeley's doddering Major. By lunchtime, *A Place in Eastbourne* is an early contender for the title of China Drum's next album.

We stop for food in a small town in the hills. As we wander around the village delicatessen, an appalling sound rends the air, something like a misfiring tractor. It is China Drum's tour manager, Stealth, laughing. In the refrigerator cabinet, he has found a locally-made yoghurt with the unfortunate, if undeniably evocative, name of Dïchmïlch. All of us, at this stage, think this is not only funny, but the funniest thing any of us have ever seen, heard, or in any way experienced. The poor shopkeeper now has an aisle blocked by eleven allegedly grown men, most in tears, several unable to stand up, having what must appear to be some sort of collective seizure.

"Iz zer a problem?" he asks.

There's no answer to that.

Travelling does this: you reach a point at which it dawns on you with crystal clarity that you are a fool, that through your own choice, you are not at home, comfortable and content, but out in the middle of nowhere, miserable, exhausted, bored and annoyed, and you don't know whether to laugh or cry. Often, provoked by an amusingly-named foreign snack food, you will do both. Then, it's like yawning: one person starts, everyone else follows.

There's no stopping us now. Everything is hysterically, convulsingly funny. Trees. Roads. The Slovenian border. Hills. Rivers. *Monopoly*. The ritual that has developed for getting back onto the truck after getting off at a stop—on climbing aboard, you must now shout, "Morning, Fawlty!" to which everyone else on the bus replies, "Morning, Major!" to which you, in turn, enquire, "Have you seen my paper?" to which the bus choruses, "It's under your arm," whereupon you say, "Ah, so it is," and sit down, and await the next person, who climbs on and shouts, "Morning, Fawlty!" et cetera et cetera.

"The time has come," intones Dave as solemnly as a hopelessly giggling man can manage, "for . . . Billy Duffy! Ian Astbury! Ladies and gentlemen . . . The Cult!"

He loads the tape. The effect is devastating. The Cult's collected videos would probably provoke a fair degree of mirth at a toddler's funeral. In our current state, it's like pumping the truck full of nitrous oxide. As the screen fills with Astbury preening and prancing through

"Love Removal Machine" and "Wildflower" like some satin-wrapped heavy metal morris dancer, most of us can no longer breathe properly.

"LOVE REMOVAL!"

We sing along, punching the air on the downbeat.

"LOVE REMOVAL MACHEE-EEE-INE!"

Another running joke is born: at every stop from here on, someone will announce, unnecessarily, that they're "just going to buy a Coke from the drinks MACHEE-EEE-INE," or "getting some tabs from the cigarette MACHEE-EEE-INE." Random exclamatory shrieks of "LAWD have MERCY!" also become popular.

The guards at the Croatian border don't delay us much—a surprise, given that customs officers generally react to the approach of musicians much like hungry lions do to an elderly wildebeest that has lost its way home, and that Croatian customs officers are hard work even by the standards of their profession. We make Karlovac by dinnertime. Adam has been reading the "Welcome To Croatia" leaflet we've been given at the border.

"Can we stop at Mrs. Migginsovic's cevapcici shop?" he asks.

We find lodgings above a restaurant.

THE MORNING DRIVE through Karlovac takes place in near total silence. Of the eleven of us on the bus, only myself and Max have spent any time in the former Yugoslavia. The rest would only have seen things like this on the news, or in films. Karlovac has taken a bit of a caning.

The only things you can possibly say about the sight of a recently ruined neighbourhood, deserted by all life but weeds, are insufferably banal. A couple of people say them anyway, and nobody responds. I was in Karlovac about a year ago, and it looks now like it looked then, like it had just gone a dozen rounds with a much larger opponent. The sorry truth is that Karlovac, compared to many towns in the region, got off fairly lightly.

My flesh starts crawling properly when we get to Slunj. I've been here before, as well, but it couldn't look more different. A little less than a year ago, I came this way out of the Bosnian town of Cazin with two employees of Feed the Children—"Bill" and "Ted" from a previous visit, described elsewhere in this volume—with whom I'd just travelled to the Bihac Pocket in the days after Croatia's offensive against the Serbian population of Krajina. Bill and Ted were giving me a lift back to Zagreb.

Slunj was deserted that afternoon. Its largely ethnically Serb population had decamped about a week previously, rather than take their chances with the advancing Croatian army. There was some evidence of fighting—the occasional shot-away shopfront, the odd rocket-propelled-grenade hole punched through a wall, footpaths chewed up by tank tracks, buckled bridges on the outskirts of the city, blown by the fleeing inhabitants—but Slunj was mostly overwhelmingly silent. Our Landcruiser was the only traffic.

As we drove through Slunj, devilment seized Bill. "Bugger this creeping about," he said. "I'm going home." As we drove through side streets at crawling speed, watching for mines on the road, he explained that his organisation had a house in Slunj, in which Bill had lived for much of the last couple of years. We found the house, opened the front door—very, very slowly—walked in and found ourselves face to face with half a dozen Croatian soldiers in the process of looting the place.

Looking back, I have to say that Bill's command of the situation was admirable. My own instincts, on the grounds that the blokes in khaki had guns and were less than sober, would have been to say, "Sorry to bother you, chaps, carry on, and let me know if you need a hand shifting anything—I'll be outside chewing my fist and praying." Not Bill. He strode up to the soldier nearest us, indicated the box of books and clothes the hapless private was removing, and said, "That's all mine." He took the box from the astonished soldier and gave it to me. "Put this in the truck, then come and help me with the rest."

Upstairs, in what had been Bill's room, the windows were gone and there were bullets in the walls, one of which he souvenired with his pocketknife. We loaded more books, more clothes and other bits and pieces into more boxes and piled them into the Landcruiser. The soldiers, who regarded us throughout with a bafflement that suggested they thought we were some kind of slivovitz-induced mirage, said and did nothing to stop us.

"Right," Bill said, back in the car. "Let's get out of here before they change their minds."

Slunj today is unrecognisable.

"Seems quite a cheerful place," someone says, and they're right, it does. The streets bustle, the cafés are full, the bullet holes have been plastered over, the windows replaced. I just wonder how many of the people doing the bustling, coffee-drinking, plastering and glazing today lived here a year ago. Slunj, for centuries a mixed city of Serbs and Croats, is now liberally sprayed with Croat nationalist graffiti, and the Croatian checkerboard flies from every flagpole and many windows. Slunj has been ethnically cleansed to positively clinical standards.

The Bosnian border is no problem—we are, surely, going to pay for this luck somewhere down the line. We pause at a petrol station south of Bihac for a kickabout, which evolves into another attempt to recreate the key moment from the England vs. Scotland game of Euro '96. We get further this time, mostly because Max grudgingly agrees to be Garry MacAllister, and I decide I can cope with the Colin Hendry role, on the grounds that it only involves standing still and gawping up into the sky like some woad-smeared peasant terrified by an eclipse, as Paul Gascoigne (played by Stealth) flicks the ball over me.

It occurs to me to wonder why Stealth is called Stealth.

"He was in a band himself," explains Adam. "And it bombed."

Near Jajce, we pass a hill into which the word "TITO" has been mown in letters several storeys high. The homage is overgrown, but still readable. It was in Jajce, in 1943, that Josip Broz Tito was officially declared head of a new Yugoslavia according to a constitution drawn up by something grandly (and, all things since considered, ironically) called the Antifascist Council for the National Liberation of Yugoslavia. Part of this road through central Bosnia and Herzegovina passes through the entity known as Republika Srpska, the Serb-controlled portion of this effectively partitioned country. Under the terms of the Dayton Peace Accords, at least as we've been led to understand it, troops of the Bosnian Serb Army may stop vehicles and inspect passports, but no more. All the same, we're happy to get through this stretch without seeing any.

In the late afternoon, as we head through the hills towards Vitez, I'm sitting at the table in the rear, facing backwards, trying to read while keeping half an eye on the *Monopoly* game in progress. The mood on board has settled into wearied, silent torpor.

The truck is rumbling up a gentle hill when Andy, in the driver's seat behind me, yelps, "Jesus fucking Christ!" There's a squealing of tyres and deafening crash from somewhere to my right. I look up from my book: we've stopped very abruptly, but everything inside the truck—bags, bottles, suitcases, guitars, the *Monopoly* set—is still moving, and most of it towards me. It all seems to happen very slowly and very quietly, and then very quickly and very noisily.

"What the fuck was that? What's happened?"

Everyone is shouting at once.

"Are you okay? Is everyone all right?"

Everyone seems to be, aside from a few scrapes.

"Are you okay? I'm okay. He's okay. We're okay."

Shaken, adrenalised, we must sound like a support group for recovering caffeine addicts. We've had an accident, obviously, though I can guess what everyone's first thoughts had been, on stopping suddenly on a road in Bosnia after hearing a loud bang.

The roadie who was sitting in the passenger seat up front opens the side door and lets us all out.

"Stupid bitch," he says, gesturing at a red Renault sedan parked sideways across the road in front of us. It's not hard to figure out what's happened. The woman driving the car has tried to pass us going uphill on a blind corner—Bosnians have a tendency to drive like they're still being shot at—seen a truck coming the other way, and cut across in front of our truck, clipping the front left corner as she went. I feel suddenly quite ill as I realise what a close call we've had. That Andy, driving a right-hand-drive vehicle in a left-hand-drive country, even saw the Renault, is amazing. That he saw it in time to hit the anchors is miraculous. If he hadn't, and she'd clobbered us harder, there's nowhere we could have gone but off the road and down a steep incline before coming to rest, if we were lucky, in countryside which is as likely mined as not.

"No problems," grunts Andy, but he's gone very pale. The woman in the Renault, meanwhile, isn't happy.

"She's got a baby in the car," says Max, who understands some of the language. "So she's angry with us."

"She's angry with us?" snorts Andy. "She'd be well advised to get out of here before I show her what angry really bloody means."

"Should we wait for the police?" asks Phil.

"Christ, no," says Max. "We'll be filling in forms for days."

He's right: it's a rule of third world travel that bureaucracy grows in inverse proportion to functioning infrastructure—the less that works, the more things you have to sign and stamp to get it to happen. The woman in the Renault seems to appreciate this herself and, after letting fly with another torrent of invective, which Max declines to translate, drives off.

We have a problem, however. Our plunge from 80 kilometres an hour to standstill in two yards flat has seized the brakes. The truck will not move, forward or backward.

"It's Daffy Ducked," diagnoses Bill, in his doleful, treacle-thick Geordie accent. Our expedition has turned into a cross between *Auf Wiedersehen, Pet* and *Gilligan's Island.*

"It could be worse," offers Dave. "I mean, we could be broken down on a blind corner miles from anywhere in the middle of a mined battlefield just as it's starting to get dark."

Someone hits him, and a contemplative silence descends.

"I'll pay for the pizza if someone else goes," says Adam.

Someone hits him.

We do a fair bit of that thing blokes do when confronted by a malfunctioning motor vehicle, which is to say we stand around next to it scratching our chins and nodding sagely and discussing engine parts like we've got the first idea what any of them do. Someone rummages in the wreckage in the back and discovers an unbroached—and, amazingly, unbroken—crate of beer we've been carrying since Munich. It is warm but, in the circumstances, not unpleasant.

"So," says Phil, asking the unanswerable. "What are we going to do?"

The plan was to be in Sarajevo before nightfall. This is obviously not going to happen—the sun is beginning to set, and driving on Bosnian roads after dark is a pastime only for the heavily armoured or the sensationally stupid, though most of us would agree at this point that we qualify handsomely on the latter count.

"Mr. Fawlty," says Adam, addressing Phil in a Spanish accent, "I no want to work here no more. I go home to Barcelona to my mother and six aunts."

With the stage set for the cavalry to ride in and save the day, the next best thing appears: a truck belonging to the Queen's Lancashires regiment serving with IFOR. They are stationed about an hour down the road near Vitez. We explain our predicament, they respond with more sympathy than we deserve, and hitch up a tow rope. Our truck doesn't move.

"What the fuck have you done to this?" they ask.

They try again. They might as well be attempting to pull St. Paul's up Fleet Street.

"Wait there," says the sergeant. "We'll go and get a mechanic."

We wait there. Every ten minutes or so, Andy has another crack at getting the truck to move. At the fifth or sixth attempt, it lurches crankily forwards. We climb aboard and leave before it thinks better of it. We head off the soldiers coming back for us about half an hour up the road.

"You won't make Sarajevo tonight," they say. "Come and stay with us."

In a fit of *Partridge Family*-style hey-let's-do-the-show-right-here enthusiasm, China Drum offer to play in the barracks, but by the time we get in, it's decreed too late for such frivolity. We decide we'll settle for a cold beer.

"No you won't," grins a young officer with, I feel, unnecessary glee. Deep and real is our grief on discovering that we have been rescued by the only dry regiment in the British Army. The Queen's Lancashires, a corporal explains, have been forbidden alcohol since an incident involving a couple of drunk squaddies, a Saxon armoured personnel carrier and a few parked cars belonging to annoyed Bosnians. This corporal is never going to cut it as a spy; he further regales us with tales of the money he's made unloading army petrol on the local black market. He also essays the disgraceful lie that, during the siege of Sarajevo, Bosnian forces deliberately shelled their own city in a bid to elicit western sympathy (this argument collapses beneath the slightest weight of logic: the Bosnian government, given the circumstances at the time, had neither the ammunition to spare nor the need to manufacture supplementary atrocity).

Sensing our disappointment at the lack of freely-flowing lager, the soldiers take us on a tour of the barracks, letting us climb around inside their Saxon APCs and look up into the surrounding hills through the sights of their rifles. It's very sweet of them, but the novelty is lost on me: my father is in the army in Australia, and I grew up in military barracks. If I wanted to play with tanks, I'd have stayed at home, where I could at least have got a drink. Still, we can't complain: the Lancashires feed us in their canteen, buy us a round of Cokes in their bar, round up some mattresses for us to kip on in the guard room, and see us off with hot, sweet tea and handshakes just after dawn.

ONLY A DAY late, we're in Sarajevo for lunch. Our rendezvous is Kuk, the venerable Sarajevo club in which China Drum will play tonight and tomorrow night. A few people have gathered here, clearly wondering what's happened to us. I'm happy to catch up with several friends, including unfeasibly attractive translator Ida, to whom I present a photo of Robert Smith that I got him to sign for her last time I interviewed him; sadly, she doesn't seem any more disposed towards marrying an unshaven hack in a bad Hawaiian shirt than she was last time. I also see Jim, who'd shown me around the Sarajevo suburb of Grbavica a few months previously, on the day it was handed back to the Bosnian government by its departing Serb population. Jim has been saving a delightful snippet for me: in the three weeks after we'd been pratting about in the ruined district, IFOR mine clearance operatives had discovered and removed 11,000 devices.

Our day at Kuk begins with a press conference, at which reporters from Sarajevo radio stations and magazines ask China Drum what they're doing here. To China Drum's credit, their attitude is devoid of any righteous, crusading aspect. They happily admit to being hazy on the details of Balkan politics, and explain that their rationale was always less "Why?" and more "Why not?" They name their influences (The Police, Stiff Little Fingers, The Undertones, Hüsker Dü, not The Cult) and recite the band's history. "We used to play Wakefield snooker club for £12.50," mourns Bill, to general mystification.

China Drum are then interviewed for the television music programme *Channel 99* by the extravagantly permed-and-moustached apparition of Zelimar Altarac-Cicak, a sort of Bosnian John Peel figure. He asks China Drum what it was like touring with Ash and Supergrass, and what they think of the recent Sex Pistols reunion.

The next port of call is the studio of Radio Zid, where the band give an interview, I drop off a large swag of CDs I've blagged for them from various record companies and then get interviewed myself about the last time I came to Sarajevo, to meet the city's rock bands, and the piece I wrote about them. The people at Zid seem genuinely and humblingly pleased by the story, though it's peculiar to find myself explaining Sarajevo's rock scene to the people who told me everything I know about it in the first place.

Back at the venue, that fearful ennui that sets in between soundcheck and gig is proving as tempting an arena for foolishness as it would at any other venue anywhere else in the world.

Someone says that, actually, if you think about it, and forget the videos for a minute, The Cult did make some quite good singles.

"No!" comes the well-rehearsed response. "I won't have that! There's a place in Eastbourne!"

I shamefacedly mutter something about the descending guitar riff from the opening bars of "She Sells Sanctuary" being an oddly satisfying one to play.

"You can play it?" asks Stealth.

We all know what we're thinking. China Drum's instruments are all set up. There's nobody in the venue apart from a few Bosnian journalists.

Stealth, one of China Drum's roadies, and me bound onto the stage and seize, respectively, bass, drumsticks and guitar.

"Ladies and gentlemen," announces Stealth. "We are . . . Suck!"

We clatter through "She Sells Sanctuary" and, seeing as how we're here and they're practically the same song, "Love Removal Machine."

"Thank you!" announces Stealth, as I try to armwheel up a proper heavy metal ending. "Suck have left the building! Goodnight!"

China Drum's own set, and that of support band Z.O.C.H., are considerably more auspicious, and a capacity crowd energetically demonstrate that Bosnians dance like they drive.

There's still an 11:00 PM–5:00 AM curfew enforced in Sarajevo, so post-gig revelry is cut short. We retire to a variety of spare beds, couches and floors.

ON SATURDAY MORNING, at the behest of The Serious Road Trip, we make the drive about an hour west of Sarajevo to Pazaric, a run-down psychiatric hospital situated amid some of the most green and rolling of Bosnia's infinite resources of green, rolling hills. The Serious Road Trip have bought performers here before, and China Drum play the inmates as normal a set as they can manage with an acoustic guitar and a set of bongos.

The afternoon is given over to sightseeing in Sarajevo—a city which remains an attractive place to look at and a pleasant one to spend time in, despite the best efforts of the Bosnian Serb Army—and a six-a-side football match. This takes place on a concrete pitch behind a billiard club, and may be the first game in the history of the sport in which fluffed chances can be legitimately blamed on unlikely bounces caused by shrapnel craters. Much I care: my team wins 2–1, the winning goal put away by Stealth from my cross ("cross" in this case being a term denoting an attempt at goal sliced so badly it left my foot at a right angle).

At Kuk that evening, the second gig, supported this time by Protest, is just as mayhemic a success. Afterwards, China Drum head back to Radio Zid to co-host the night shift. If "There's a place in Eastbourne!" is not now a popular catchphrase in Sarajevo, it isn't China Drum's fault.

"MORNING, FAWLTY!"

Morning, Major.

"Have you seen my paper?"

Under your arm, Major.

"Ah, so it is."

Getting in the bus first is never a good idea.

"Morning, Fawlty!"

And so on.

After night and the curfew have lifted, we're on our way. Due to China Drum's commitments back in the real world, we're going to do Sarajevo to London in one go. This plan stays on track as far as a village on the southern outskirts of Vitez. There is an enormous bang, the truck bounces violently, and lurches to a stop.

"Shit! Is everyone okay? Are you okay? I'm okay! What the fuck was that?"

Everyone is shouting again because everyone, again, was thinking the first thing you think when you're driving along a Bosnian road and you hear a loud bang and your vehicle leaps into the air. It turns out to have been a speed bump that was bigger than it looked from a distance; for the effect it's had on the truck, it might as well have been an anti-tank mine. Smoke is pouring from the brake pads, front and rear. Adam reacts decisively.

"Right," he says, brandishing his video camera and carrying the football over to a vacant lot across the street. "Positions, everybody, please. We're going to get that Gascoigne goal right if it kills us."

Those guardian angels otherwise known as the Queen's Lancashires happen past again.

"We'll get you a mechanic," they say, sounding surprisingly jolly, as if they haven't yet done enough for us. "Wait here," they add, like we've got a choice.

An hour or so later, we're back under way; in the dust on the back of the van, one of our number has inscribed the words "Arses in transit, Bosnia and Herzegovina, summer 1996." Cresting a hill along the stretch of the road that passes through Republika Srpska, we find the route blocked by four armed men wearing purple camouflage. Whatever you believe about judging people by appearances, there are a few assumptions you can safely make about men wearing Bosnian Serb Army uniform in this part of the world, and none of those assumptions make us happy about having guns pointed at us by them. The one of the four who seems the least drunk and the most in charge—neither is much of a distinction—asks for our passports. Max, in the passenger seat, hands the stack over.

"What are you doing here?" asks the sentry.

"We're a rock'n'roll band from Newcastle," explains Max.

Not the answer he was expecting, to judge from his expression. His men lower their rifles and let us through.

In the hours it takes us to drive to the border, we manage to get menaced by both of Bosnia's other querulous factions. During a petrol and football stop approaching Bihac, Stealth gets an animated lecture from a Bosnian policeman with conspicuous scarring around one temple and a distracting way of waving his pistol about while he talks. We eventually deduce that he's displeased by Stealth's camouflage-print shorts. His point made, the cop gives us all patches and stickers bearing his unit's shoulder-flash. At the border, Croatian customs officers search everything bar the clothes we're wearing, but given the way we must all smell by now, I think they'd have left us alone even if we had all had suspiciously grenade-launcher-shaped bulges in our trousers.

ONCE CLEAR OF Bosnia, we settle into the ennui and *Monopoly* of the long road ahead. At the Slovenian border, it becomes apparent that we've relaxed too soon. They won't let us in. As far as we can understand, there's a problem with our paperwork. Phil, the veins in his forehead throbbing impressively, explains that the paperwork we have now is exactly the same as the paperwork we had when we were let into Slovenia coming the other way three days ago.

"You do not have permit," says the official. "You must return for permit to Zagreb."

He mutters something else about a green sticker we don't have in our windscreen. We've never had a green sticker. We've never heard of a green sticker. There was nothing about green stickers in the brochure. Getting one from Zagreb now would add another eight hours to what is already going to be at least a forty-four-hour drive, an enormously depressing prospect. It's like being told two songs into a Morrissey gig that he's going to do an encore.

We consider our options in a layby.

"There's another crossing 20 kilometres away," says Stealth, consulting a map.

"But what if they want this fucking green sticker thing there as well?" asks Phil.

It's hard to say who has the idea first; the attention of all seems to fall, as one, on Bill, who in the current *Monopoly* game ("No buying except on a double, all fines to be paid to the player on your left, every player immune from rent on one pre-named set of properties, er . . .") has Regent, Oxford and Bond streets in his portfolio. The green properties.

"Brilliant!" yelps Stealth. He seizes the deeds from an aggrieved Bill ("Fucking hell, man, this is the first one I've looked like winning") and affixes them to the inside of the windscreen with gaffer tape.

At the crossing up the road, we are waved through without question. The rest is easy.

9

HUNGRY HEARTLAND

Bruce Springsteen in America
NOVEMBER 2007

IN WHICH YOUR correspondent and *Uncut* magazine make a virtue of necessity. I'm fairly certain there was some pretty solid talk at one point that this piece was going to be my long-hankered-for, proper on-the-road-with-Bruce-Springsteen story. This plan fell through, for reasons I can no longer recall, possibly because my anguished subconscious has deleted them from memory, the better to prevent me from being caught muttering imprecations about the unfairness of the universe in queues, on buses, during dinner parties and so forth (I would, yes, quite like to interview Bruce Springsteen at some point).

It was Michael Bonner, *Uncut*'s associate editor, who suggested that we do it anyway. He observed, quite rightly, that Bruce Springsteen's ongoing efforts to embody something of the best of his country made it uniquely possible, in his case, to write a tour story which would be as much about the places Springsteen was going and the people he was playing to as it was about the artist in question. With this idea in mind—of, essentially, conjuring something of a road movie to which Springsteen would provide the soundtrack—we settled upon the least alluring stretch of the *Magic* tour: St. Paul, Minnesota; Cleveland, Ohio; Auburn Hills, Michigan.

For all the mild sport that I make of those locations in what follows—St. Paul in particular struck me as a plausible facsimile of what it might have been like to visit Leipzig in about 1974–there are no places I enjoy travelling more as a journalist than those that lie a way off the regularly trodden path in the United States. This is, admittedly, partly due to the way in which they compensate handily for my own awkwardness and laziness–which is to say that it's not like you even have to make an effort to ask questions of the people in these places, as once they perceive even a few hesitant syllables of a foreign accent, you can neither shut them up nor pay for your own drinks. But I'd admire and enjoy that openness and generosity even if I wasn't working.

So, I'd like to dedicate this chapter to all the people who shared a drink, their time, and their thoughts with me during this trip. I believe that there is much to be said for the theory that artists tend to attract the audiences they deserve, and on that score Bruce Springsteen has more to be proud of than most. Everyone I met, whatever their ideological inclinations, was astutely attuned to both the essential hope and the crucial melancholy at large in Springsteen's songs, whether they were songs about the political, the personal or both. They all understood what Springsteen has articulated with greater facility than any other songwriter I can think of: that a decent man, and a great country, are perpetual works in progress.

★ ★ ★

"IF ANYONE TELLS you," says Jon Landau, "that they saw the E Street Band in 1897 or whenever, and they were better than this, don't believe it."

Landau, Springsteen's long-time manager, producer and confidant, would say that, but he'd know better than most. In 1974, Landau, then a rock critic, went to see a promising New Jersey singer-songwriter, and filed a review declaring said troubador the future of rock'n'roll. Thirty-three years later, it ranks as one of the shrewder predictions committed to print by our erratically reliable trade. We're backstage at the Palace of Auburn Hills, a venue on the outskirts of Detroit.

"There's a spirit about them," continues Landau. "I think it's just that they're still here, still alive, still together—in more or less the same lineup since 1974. Every time out that seems a bigger blessing, I guess."

We're awaiting the start of the third Springsteen show I'll have seen on this tour, and I remark that it has all been very tight, almost devoid of Springsteen's trademark rambling between-song soliloquies.

"He's edited himself a lot," agrees Landau. "It's a really compressed show. I mean, it's two hours, ten minutes—we used to do a first set that long—but it's still twenty-two, twenty-three songs. He's tightened it up a lot. He just wants to play."

I explain that Springsteen's reticence on that front had surprised me, given that the new album, *Magic*, is as explicitly political a record as he's made, and also, I'd argue, his most confrontationally pessimistic.

"Those undercurrents are there, absolutely," says Landau. "But they work as rock'n'roll songs. And that's what he's concentrating on."

TWO SHOWS EARLIER, one song into the encore, Springsteen mumbles something about this next one being a request for someone, and exhales that instantly recognisable sigh of harmonica, that riff which really does resemble the sort of breeze capable of blowing a screen door shut. The rest of the introduction of "Thunder Road" disappears beneath a roar of incredulous bliss that could only previously have been equalled in this cavernous hockey rink in the event of a last-second winner. Springsteen smiles, settles down, sings the first verse straight, then approaches the best line he's ever going to write.

"So you're scared," he growls, "and you're thinking . . . that maybe . . . ," he leans back, tilts the microphone stand towards the crowd.

"We ain't that young anymore," 18,000 people chorus.

They're not, either. It briefly seems almost cruel of Springsteen to get the crowd to sing this line: it's safe to say that if you're in your forties or fifties, as most of those present appear to be, and living somewhere like St. Paul, Minnesota, then your current credentials for channeling the wild-eyed tearaway narrator of "Thunder Road" are questionable. But the moment works, as the barnstorming two-hour show that has preceded it works, because Springsteen has always been smart enough to know that the grandly romantic ideal of American rock'n'roll that he has embodied for more than thirty years has, despite outward appearances of exhilarating simplicity, nuances and quirks that justify the attention he has given it. And, as I'll discover over the next week or so, his audience are smart enough to know that, too.

Springsteen has said that the best line he's ever going to write wasn't just about him, but about America (his best lines are never just about him, and always about America). When Springsteen wrote the best line he's ever going to write in particular, and 1975's *Born to Run* album in general, he was evoking America's Vietnam hangover, the national unease born of having been led by a government of creeps and incompetents into a stupid war, for lousy reasons, and losing. His new album, *Magic*, musically resembles *Born to Run* more than any of the others in between, and is released in 2007, into an America which is uneasy about having been led by a government of creeps and incompetents into a stupid war, for lousy reasons, and losing, morally if not militarily.

So, following the *Magic* tour through the least glamorous leg of its first North American stretch—St. Paul, Minnesota; Cleveland, Ohio; Auburn Hills, Michigan—is more than just going to three rock concerts. It's seeing something of the country that Springsteen has been singing about for three and a half decades, the country whose people still fill arenas to sing those songs back at him. *Magic* debuted atop the Billboard album charts. The touts outside St. Paul's Xcel Energy Center are asking, and getting, US $200 a ticket. Thousands of people who've grown up with—or become less young with—Bruce Springsteen still want something from him: something that lives, perhaps, in the line after the best line he's ever going to write: "Show a little faith, there's magic in the night."

If Alexis de Tocqueville was alive today, he'd go to some Springsteen shows.

"IS HE BIG in Britain?" asks Pam.

God, yes, I tell her.

"Really?'

Huge. Vast. Could sellout a year of Tuesdays at Wembley if he felt like it.

"Wow," she says. "What do you think British people see in him?"

An excellent question. The romance, I think out loud, the possibility— that thrill of an open road and an uncharted, unconstrained future which you're not going to get anyplace where you know how far it is to Newport Pagnel services. We're at the Eagle Street Grille, across the road from the Xcel Energy Center, where Springsteen will be playing a few hours from now. It's a great bar, a glorious realisation of every American cliche: big windows letting in a perfect autumn afternoon, brewery logos in neon, bartenders who ask how you are in a manner that suggests they care, homages to local sports outfits lining the walls, especially the Minnesota Wild ice hockey team, whose rink Springsteen is borrowing. There are, also, bracing reminders that our American cliches aren't what they once were: graffitied farewells from a couple of regulars bound for Iraq, and one photograph of a uniformed American soldier in some foreign field, embraced in a black wooden frame. The staff play it safe with the music: the *Born to Run* album segues into *Born in the USA*.

The place is filling with Springsteen fans, of which Pam and her husband, Brian, from nearby Minneapolis, both in their mid-forties, are two. She's a social worker with a smile that could illuminate a coal shaft, he's a health clinic director with a greying goatee. Pam got into Springsteen when she heard him on the BBC World Service when her family lived in Sweden in 1975. Six years later, she was at college in Madison, Wisconsin, when Springsteen came to town with *The River*.

"I had my dad's Amex card," she remembers. "Strictly emergencies only. So I bought tickets for twenty of my friends—fifteen bucks each."

I get the impression that Brian's fondness for Springsteen began as a condition of marriage, but it's grown into something genuine enough. He saw Springsteen in St. Paul in 2004, when Springsteen appeared with Neil Young and R.E.M. on the Vote For Change tour—an attempt to excite people about voting for John Kerry, the baffled mannequin inexplicably fielded that year by the Democratic party as a presidential candidate. Brian is what's known in current American political parlance as a "liberal"; something he feels obliged to whisper somewhat guiltily. He frets about what America is turning into, and about what the rest of the world thinks it's turning into.

"But I still like what Bruce represents," he explains. "That great, optimistic naivety."

Which is the nigh universal appeal of America, right there. The country's history is essentially a series of sensational failures to be impeded by the question, "Gee, what could possibly go wrong?" No other country would have had the damnfool idea of planting democracy in Baghdad; no other country would have had the damnfool idea of parking men on the Moon.

"We've always been naive," says Brian, "and I think it's a good thing—well, mostly—but I think that's changing. I see it in our kids. They're cynical, weary about things."

And no other country, returning to Pam's original question, could have produced Springsteen. No British artist would presume to assume the same role—of conscience, of flame-keeper, of a kind of national uncle (*Magic* is, to a large extent, a gentle warning as to the consequences if its audience doesn't pull itself together). Any British artist who did tempt hubris thus would exit the stage beneath a barrage of unfresh fruit (the difference is discernible in other media, as well—imagine the reaction from British fans of *The West Wing* to a programme which attempted to imbue Downing Street with similarly noble tones).

"To me," says Brian, "he's just the best of what America could be. Should be."

ST. PAUL IS, at first glance, as completely un-Springstonian as might be imagined. All that might be said for its downtown in that respect is that if you did decide to go racing in the street, you could do so safe in the knowledge that you wouldn't hit anybody—and, if you did, they might well expend their dying breath on whispering "thank you." The buildings along the eerily empty sidewalks are devoid of advertising, because there's nobody on the streets to advertise to.

The citizenry are indoors, it turns out, plodding between muzak-haunted car parks and climate-controlled office blocks on a network of enclosed above-street bridges called the Skyway—the Minneapolis equivalent of which was immortalised in the eponymous ballad by The Replacements. In an instructive—if personally infuriating—illustration of the way in which inner cities all over America have outsourced themselves to circulating strip malls, doing something as prosaic as buying a two-dollar notepad in which to chronicle one's ennui necessitates thirty bucks' worth of taxi-rides to the nearest Wal-Mart.

Making St. Paul an epicentre of rock'n'roll fury is, then, going to be a task akin to applying defibrillators to a stuffed and moth-eaten moose, but it takes Springsteen and his E Street Band about ten seconds to make St. Paul feel like the only place you'd want to be right now. The first thing visible when the lights dip is a wheezing, spotlit steam organ rising from the rear of the stage. Under cover of this diversion, the black-clad E Street band emerge into darkness. "Is anybody," demands the centremost silhouette, "alive out there?" (if Springsteen had also been taking in the sights earlier, a fair question). The stage floods with light, and Springsteen unloads the garage-rattling riff of "Radio Nowhere," the song that has opened every night of this tour. It sounds hungry, feral, fantastic, and at its close there's barely a hammering heartbeat's pause before the band pile onto "No Surrender" like it's a home-run ball rattling around the bleachers. They pull it back for the last verse, letting the words echo: "There's a war outside still raging/ You say it ain't ours anymore to win/I want to sleep beneath peaceful skies in my lover's bed/With a wide open country in my eyes/And these romantic dreams in my head." Absolutely essential Springsteen: that total fearlessness about being obvious.

The E Street band are eight, tonight; saxophonist Clarence Clemons, keyboardists Roy Bittan and Danny Federici, guitarists Nils Lofgren and Steve Van Zandt, drummer Max Weinberg, bassplayer Garry Tallent, violinist/guitarist/singer Soozie Tyrell. Absent is guitarist/singer/ Springsteen's missus Patti Scialfa (she takes occasional nights off to spend time with their three children). The set is bare to the point of barely existing: an overhead lighting rig with video screens each side, and no backdrop, exposing the stage to the seats behind it, and lending the crowd in those seats the appearance of a white gospel choir (with exceptions in single figures, the only black people I see at three concerts are Clarence Clemons or venue staff, an indication of the bewildering way in which much American culture is divided by race—bookshops regularly have separate "African-American" shelves, as if skin colour is a literary genre).

Springsteen doesn't speak until five songs in, when he pauses to introduce the title track of *Magic*. It's a song, he says, about the last six years, about lies turned into truth, truth into lies. "It isn't really about magic," he concludes. "It's about tricks." It's also the bleakest vision he's ever committed to record: it's a mighty long way down from "We're gonna to get to that place where we really wanna go/And we'll walk in the sun" to "The sun is sinking low/There's bodies hanging in the trees." Later, before "Living In The Future," there's some muttering about rendition, illegal wiretapping, the demise of habeas corpus, the Constitution, and that's the last of the evening's chat. Either he thinks the songs say it all, or he's attuned to the possibility that not everybody here agrees with him (Minnesota is more relaxed with America's politico-entertainment complex than most, though—this is the state that elected Jesse Ventura governor, and from which Al Franken is seeking nomination as a Democratic candidate for the US Senate).

The setlist betrays Springsteen's determination to make *Magic* heard. Though he would know what people have really hired babysitters for, eight songs from *Magic* appear tonight. They're surrounded by capricious choices from the canon: "Incident On 57th Street," the Bo Diddley shimmy of "Working On The Highway," "Night," "She's The One," all delivered with that inimitable E Street Band wallop, that sound that feels something like being crushed by an avalanche of the collected works of Motown, The Beach Boys, Elvis Presley, Phil Spector, The Band and Bob Dylan. Best of all is "Reason To Believe," the spectral sign-off of 1982's crepuscular acoustic lament "Nebraska," rebuilt as a colossal Skynyrd-ish boogie, Springsteen distortedly declaiming its terminal throes into the harmonica microphone, like a radio preacher being tuned in through a thunderstorm. During the five-song encore, a woman down the front waves a sign announcing "I lost 100 pounds just to dance with the Boss," but the 2007 "Dancing In The Dark," subtly de-80sed by Tyrrel's violin, is uninterrupted by a solicitation for a partner from the floor, however svelte. The finale sees Bittan and Federici emerging from behind their keyboards and donning accordions for a raucous "American Land," the shout-out to America's waves of immigrants that sprouted from *The Seeger Sessions*. Lest anyone miss the point behind this glorious Pogues-ish tearup, the lyrics—"The hands that built this country we're always trying to keep out"—scroll up the video screens.

Afterwards, in a nearby sports bar, I get talking to John and Joel, who might have been dispatched as a neat personification of what this corridor of America I'm following Springsteen along once was, and what it now is: John, wearing a Minnesota Vikings top, drives a cement truck; his good friend Joel, in a golf shirt embroidered with a corporate logo, does something in IT, and John joshes him about the apparently impressive amounts of money he makes. I guess that John in particular was unbothered that Springsteen didn't labour his political themes overly.

"Yeah, I was pretty pleased about that," he says. "I paid a hundred bucks for a ticket, I want to see a rock'n'roll show, not the news."

"Redneck," says Joel.

"Liberal," retorts John.

Here's a thing, I ask John. If you do drive a truck—or, indeed, have any sort of proper job—how does it sound when a guy who is, if not necessarily through any fault of his own, uproariously rich, sings about you?

"Bruce wasn't always a millionaire," notes John. "And hell, he still puts everything into it. I mean, he's working up there."

CLEVELAND'S GORGEOUSLY MASTHEADED city newspaper, *The Plain Dealer*, calls it "Super Sunday." "For a single, shimmering day," declares the front page, "we are the centre of the (pop) cultural universe." Not only is Springsteen in town, but the Martha Graham Dance Company are doing a matinee at the Ohio Theatre, Australian child-amusers The Wiggles are playing the University and the local NFL team, the Browns, are at home to the Seattle Seahawks. The article goes on to suggest a schedule by which it might be possible to attend all four. "You," the front page continues, "a lover of high art, simplistic 90-second singalongs, working-man anthems and beer-soaked blood sport, want to experience each and every one . . . you'll need serpentine reflexes and a reliable car to pull it off, but it can be done."

Cleveland has had to grow a sense of humour: it's a town people joke about. The Cuyahoga river, which flows through the town, was once so polluted that on June 22, 1969, it caught fire. R.E.M. would amplify the shame with a song named after the congealed waterway, on which they regarded Cleveland and suggested, "Let's put our heads together/ And start a new country up." Ian Hunter wrote the anthem "Cleveland Rocks," and he may have been joking, but it earned him a hefty exhibit in the Rock & Roll Hall of Fame, a depressing mausoleum situated on Cleveland's Lake Erie shore (induction ceremonies are held in New York, because nobody wants to come here). And, since *This Is Spinal Tap*, Cleveland's name is reflexively invoked whenever a rock band, or anyone associated with one, gets lost backstage, anywhere in the world.

For a while, shivering outside the Quicken Loans Arena, usually home to the Cleveland Cavaliers basketball team, I wonder if Springsteen has fallen prey to precisely this mishap. The advertised opening time is 6:30. An hour past that, and everyone's still outside, subsiding towards hypothermia—but, as luck would have it, able to avail themselves of the warmth that can only be generated by unexpected communal ecstasy.

Plasma screens around the outside of the venue show the closing stages of the match taking place across town at Browns stadium. When I'd left at halftime, the Browns looked cooked—21-9 down, and if it had been a fight, the referee would have stopped it. The home team have clawed their way back, though, and the venue doors open just as an extra-time field goal seals a 33-30 Cleveland victory. When "Radio Nowhere" cranks into gear, the mass lowing of "Brooooooooce" is competing with chanted homages to the Browns.

Patti Scialfa returns tonight, with two effects. One on the sound—the doubling of the female backing vocal accentuates the simple classicist choruses for which Springsteen has always had such an extraordinary facility. The other on the spirit—there's a more relaxed feel about the E Street Band tonight, more smiling; Steve Van Zandt's perpetually jutting bottom lip has retracted a couple of inches. "It's Hard To Be A Saint In The City" is exhumed from Springsteen's 1973 debut album, and decorated with duelling solos by Springsteen and Van Zandt with the exuberance of kids silly-stringing the principal's car on the last day of term. It slams into "She's The One"; Springsteen catches a daisy thrown from the crowd and wears it in a hip pocket. Momentum dips slightly with the curious inclusion of husband-and-wife duet of "Town Called Heartbreak," from Patti Scialfa's last solo album, "Play It As It Lays"—a record there was little wrong with, but which is ill-served by the cinematic bombast of the E Street Band, who are trained to build the epic visions of their leader. Which is not to declare them incapable of subtlely. "Devil's Arcade," steadily establishing itself as a classic, is a study in restrained fury, dying away to a martial drum roll, the stage dark but for flickering neon beneath Max Weinberg's riser, an effective evocation of a spotlit airstrip, and the beat to which men carry caskets draped with flags.

Afterwards, I visit a bar rejoicing in the name of The Boneyard Beer Farm, its speakers pumping "Thunder Road," its chairs and sofas filled by patrons largely dressed in Cleveland brown, celebrating a memorable day. I find myself sitting next to Tim, a 40-something Springsteen fan of two decades' standing who has driven down from Detroit, where he works as a fundraiser for a Catholic high school. Tim identifies himself as "a conservative Republican" and has Springsteen figured for "a conservative Democrat," which is an astute call. Even Springsteen's most overtly folky album, 1995's *The Ghost Of Tom Joad*, offered no whiff of Guthrie/Seeger-ish revolution, beyond stumping for a fair day's pay for a fair day's work, and the dearest wish of even his most emblematically reckless figures (the narrators of "Thunder Road," "Born To Run") is, at the setting of the sun, to make an honest and happy woman of, respectively, Wendy and Mary.

"What his songs are about," says Tim, "isn't this politically correct welfare America we have now. They're about: do something. Go to work. Get it done. Take pride in what you have."

Tim is punctiliously polite, one of those Americans with the hopelessly endearing habit of inserting your name into every conversational foray.

"Now, Andrew," he grins. "I know what you're going to ask next." So I do.

"I may be a Republican," he says, "but I can tell when I'm being lied to. And we feel like we've been lied to. And that's what I like about Bruce, and that's what I like about the new album. He's a straight guy. He stands up, and he tells the truth as he sees it."

THREE SHOWS IN and I'm getting a sense of what Landau means when he talks about how Springsteen has edited these concerts. Nothing is tailored to the location, other than the odd bellow of the town's name—in Cleveland, Springsteen didn't take the free shot of the Browns' comeback, didn't drop "Youngstown" into the set just because it mentions Ohio. Tonight in Auburn Hills, Michigan, he says nothing of the travails besetting Chrysler, whose headquarters is here, and who have, just seventy-two hours previously, announced plans to lay off 12,000 workers, having already canned 13,000 in February (when the lights are up, though, he'd be able to see one economic indicator—the empty rear upper deck of the only non-sellout of the tour). The introduction to *Magic*, about how it's really about tricks, is the same, as is the brief list of Bush's malfeasances at the beginning of "Living In The Future," as is the audacious toss of one of his hard-ridden Telecasters to a nervous roadie at the end of "She's The One." In the old-fashioned sense of the phrase, he's putting on a show.

With due respect to Springsteen's home state, this is the most apposite place imaginable to see him do it. Auburn Hills is a suburban extremity of Detroit, the town whose industry once built the cars that drove the roads that crisscross Springsteen's creative landscape. Auburn Hills isn't auburn, and has no hills, but it is ostentatiously proud of its receding heritage. Tonight's venue, the Palace of Auburn Hills, is usually home to the Detroit Pistons, the basketball team whose home jersey is trimmed by, yes, a blue collar (team motto: "Goin' to work"). At the risk of tempting fate, Auburn Hills could serve as the setting should some agent of Beelzebub ever consider staging *Born To Run: the Bruce Springsteen Musical*.

Tonight, "Jackson Cage" makes its tour premiere, "I'll Work For Your Love" its first live outing. The segue from "Living In The Future" (from *Magic*) to "Promised Land" (of 1978's *Darkness On The Edge Of Town*) is, again, a jarring crash of experience against innocence. "Tunnel Of Love," the title track of the 1987 album which Springsteen recorded largely without the E Street Band, is reclaimed with a dazzling Lofgren solo coda. "Gypsy Biker," though its name might have been suggested by a computerised Springsteen song title generator, is a powerful reproach, eclipsed for righteous anger among the *Magic* material only by "Last To Die," whose key question remains John Kerry's only enduring political contribution, the one the young Vietnam veteran put to the Senate Foreign Relations Committee, and which should be above the desk of every head of government with armed forces at their disposal: "How do you ask a man to be the last to die for a mistake?"

The encore contains a moment of spontaneity. Springsteen mentions a kid in the front row, sitting on his dad's shoulders. "He can't be more than six," laughs Springsteen, "and he's been rocking hard all night." The infant has also been holding up a banner, reading "Ramrod please" (this request for the somewhat salacious cut from 1980's *The River* may have been ghostwritten by his father). "Okay," says Springsteen. "Unplayed in five years. Let's go." It ends with Springsteen and the kid making devil's horn salutes at each other, and a drum roll like a landing helicopter, until the lights come up and Weinberg ignites "Born To Run." It's one of those indisputable absolutes, like the Taj Mahal, or *Henry V* or something—a work that it is honestly difficult to imagine any half-sentient being quibbling with, and a product of definitively American audacity, of a young man who, thirty-odd years ago, decided that he was going to make the greatest rock'n'roll record of all time.

AT A BAR across the street, more people for whom Springsteen has served as a soundtrack to a life gather to swap stories. I fall in with Dan, a silver-haired advertising copywriter from Huntingdon Woods, who has seen Springsteen more than fifty times, including six on this tour, and one Dublin show with the Seeger Sessions band. Tonight, he reckons, was in "the upper third" of his all-time list.

"I just love his passion," says Dan. "He means what he's saying."

And we order some beers and talk about what that might be, and Dan raises the optimism that so many others I've met have also mentioned, and I say to him, as I've said to them, that that new album of his, though it's one of his very best, sounds almost crushingly pessimistic.

"These," says Dan, "are not optimistic times."

And Dan mentions "Long Walk Home," which has, at all three shows, taken on something of the quality of a singalong at a revival meeting. There's work to be done, it acknowledges, stuff to fix and a reason for doing it that only an American—and, in today's climate, possibly only Springsteen—would proffer with a straight face.

"That flag flying over the courthouse," roared nearly 60,000 people of more than 60,000 different opinions over three nights, "means certain things are set in stone/Who we are, what we'll do, and what we won't."

Corny as hell, of course. But the truth often is.

10

THE FIRST TIME EVER I SAW YOUR FEZ

Def Leppard in Morocco
OCTOBER 1995

IT SAYS MUCH about the vertiginous nature of the music industry's decline that as recently as 1995 I saw fit to bemoan the fact that major labels didn't charter private jets on wholly gratuitous junkets to North Africa very often. Nowadays, the operatives of those same labels tend to run a nervous finger around a sweaty collar when you turn up at a playback and ask for carbonated water. The mid-90s were, in retrospect, something of a last hurrah for the idea of a record company as a profligate subsidiser of demented entertainments for music business insiders. This was especially the case in Britain, where a commercial boom and a general giddy triumphalism were being fostered by the rise of a phalanx of new artists distinguished by their unmistakable and—unusually—unabashed Englishness. As is always the case during eras of plenty, everyone assumed that the good times would last forever. Which is to say that nobody imagined that the imminent unleashing of a new form of communication would have the interesting effect of subverting, subsuming or destroying all the others.

None of which has anything to do with Def Leppard—but then, what does? While the idea that anything can ever be so bad it's somehow good is the infuriating folly of the irrecoverable aesthetic retard, there are things in this life so overwhelmingly and guilelessly preposterous that they are weirdly endearing despite themselves: Def Leppard, like France, are among those things. Minutely though I have ransacked my memory, I have no recollection whatsoever as regards my assignment to this trip. It may have been that I was simply alone among *Melody Maker*'s roster of writers in never having committed to print any overt hostility towards the subject. It may have been that I was shanghaied by a cruel editor performing the common trick of dangling the destination in front of the journalist before revealing the band. It may have been a dare.

Whatever the reason, it was, as is always the case when the Fourth Estate descend en masse upon some location or event, excellent fun. An actor once told me, plausibly, that the worst thing about her job was the company of other actors. One of the very best things about my job is the company of other journalists. Given that the profession is—or should be—the last refuge of the otherwise unemployable, it attracts a disproportionate quantity of eccentrics, oddballs, flaneurs and freaks, people motivated in equal parts by a questing curiosity and a horror of having to work for a living. I believe I speak for all veterans of this particular escapade in expressing profound gratitude to the people and local authorities of the municipality of Tangiers that none of us were arrested, deported or chased to the city limits at pitchfork-point.

★ ★ ★

THEY DON'T THROW parties like this anymore. Record launches these days—if you're lucky—involve a free pint of watery lager, a dozen ballsachingly banal conversations with people you've been trying to avoid for months, and the album in question played back at a volume sufficient to render it utterly unlistenable, even assuming it wasn't utterly unlistenable in the first place, which it almost certainly was.

Occasionally, as closing time looms, old-timers will reminisce about the days when the dinosaurs roamed the earth, when a rock'n'roll party was a proper rock'n'roll party. Televisions rained from balconies. Swimming pools were for parking the Cadillac in. Cadillacs were for parking in the pool. A record launch was a tableau from *Days Of Sodom*, with dissolute celebrity helicoptered in from all over, chilled champagne flowing from golden bathroom taps, bald midget waiters proferring vases of rolled-up tenners, balancing crystal bowls of best Bolivian marching powder on their finely polished heads. Yes, the veterans recall, those were the days. All green fields round here. Still had all my own teeth.

So the excitement is palpable as the bus leaves Polygram's Hammersmith headquarters for Gatwick Airport. Def Leppard are releasing a Greatest Hits album for Christmas. The long-serving Sheffield heavy metal band have proved beyond doubt that global fame is a realistic dream even for those hampered by a total disregard for musical fashion, a drummer with one arm, and haircuts—to say nothing of one or two lyrics—that would embarass German football players. They are an inspiration to us all, and an inevitably chart-topping collection of their inimitable oeuvre is the least they deserve. To celebrate and, not incidentally, to draw attention to the record, Def Leppard asked their record company to think of something weird.

AS WE GENTLEFOLK of the press take our seats on the chartered jet—each with a customised Def Leppard napkin draped over the headrest—it just seems extravagant and silly, which is obviously no problem at all. The idea is that Def Leppard will play three shows on three continents in one day. Tonight, at one minute past midnight, they will start playing in the Moroccan port of Tangiers, on the edge of Africa. They will then head back to the airport, from where the chartered plane will fly them back to England for a lunchtime performance in London, fulfilling the European leg. From there, a bus will bear them to Heathrow, and a scheduled flight to Canada; the eight-hour time difference between London and Vancouver will allow all three gigs to be completed on the same calendar day. Def Leppard will then be able to claim a place in the "Guinness Book Of Records" for their endeavours, and hope that the attendant publicity will help sales of the new album do the same.

On the publicity front, at least, this absurd stunt was never going to fail. Myself and photographer Stephen Sweet are here, for a start, and Def Leppard have never really been *Melody Maker's* thing, their few appearances in our achingly hip journal generally restricted to the news pages, and then occuring only when one of them dies, or a bit of one of them comes off. So it's good of them to have us along, joining the hundred-plus other freeloading hacks, television crews, radio stringers and fan club competition winners on the flight. Excitingly, Sweet and

I find ourselves sitting directly behind Leppard frontman Joe Elliott—lest we forget, the man who wrote the line "I suppose a rock's out of the question"—and the bassplayer, whatever his name is. There is something about his round spectacles and perpetually anguished demeanour that strongly suggests hours of leisure time devoted to the painting of bloody awful watercolours.

The captain welcomes everybody aboard, and extends special greetings to his star cargo, "Deaf Leper". The members of the band, on whose career much of the movie "This Is Spinal Tap" was surely based, don't blink as the rest of the plane dissolves into delighted guffaws.

IT'S MY FIRST view of Africa: chocolate-brown beaches giving way to a few struggling tufts of nondescript scrub as the plane approaches the airport. The continent fires the imagination of the traveller like no other. For centuries, Africa has attracted adventurers, opportunists, glory-hunters and criminals. It's where people have gone to forge empires, build fortunes, hunt game or hide from the law. I have come to watch a rock group play in a cave.

A hotel on the outskirts of Tangiers has been booked as a temporary base, and we arrive as the sun sets, with a couple of hours to spare before the official nonsense commences. Most of the party demonstrate the intrepid, questing spirit that has made the British press what it is, and elect to spend the free time lounging around the hotel pool swigging free cocktails served by miserable-looking waiters in traditional dress ("traditional dress": a universally-recognised expression meaning "Silly outfit and daft hat nobody around here would normally be caught dead in"). A few of us get taxis into town, and the medina. The medina is Tangiers' vast, walled market, a biblical bazaar of hustlers, merchants, thieves and, it turns out, guides, who are something of a combination of the three. A phalanx of these determined, weirdly short, mostly-middle aged men blocks the medina's gate.

"I will be your guide," says one. "Very good price."

"No thanks," we tell him.

"I will be your guide," says another. "Good price."

"No, we're okay," we assure him, trying, without success, to push through them.

"I will be your guide," says yet another. "Very good price."

"Bugger off, the lot of you," we say.

"Very good price."

We're getting nowhere, literally and semantically. Several of us have travelled in the Middle East before, and have learnt the hard way what usually comes of hiring a guide in an Arab souk: a tour so quick you feel like you're watching a film about the place with the fast-forward button on, followed by several hours locked in his brother's rug shop.

"We are representatives of Her Majesty's press," says someone with a two-surname accent, who has brought two cocktails from the hotel with him, and is sipping alternately from each. "We can look after ourselves, and we have no need of carpets, camels or any of your sisters. Now fuck off."

It doesn't help.

"I will be your guide."

"Nooooo."

"Very good price."

"Go awaaaayyy."

The stand-off continues.

"Please, sirs," says a voice we haven't heard before. "It is better to have one mosquito working for you than to be fighting a swarm."

He's even shorter than the others, and is talking nonsense. But it's nonsense with a certain poetic, sage-of-the-orient charm. He also promises that he has no commercial or familial ties to any of the shops in the medina. We hire him. He marches us around the bazaar at double time and delivers us to a spice shop. The doors clang shut behind us. "Please meet my brother," he beams.

When we are allowed to leave, an hour later, we are heavily laden with vials of essential oils, sachets of scents and bags full of funny-smelling bark fragments alleged to cure piles, kidney stones, impotence and gout—a sales pitch I suspect has more to do with an astute reading of the customers than the truth. At a souvenir shop we pass on the way back, to the mortification of all present, the man from *The Daily Mirror* not only buys a fez, but insists on wearing it. He will live to regret this. For the rest of the night he will be plagued by claret-sodden hacks tottering up to him, announcing "I've forgotten your name, but your fez is familiar," and laughing until they weep.

BY WAY OF a warm-up for Def Leppard's midnight performance, a ceremonial dinner is held in a huge marquee tent in the hotel courtyard. The food is adequate, the wine appalling, the entertainment terrific. A variety of local artistes, all of whom look like they've recently returned from a raid on the wardrobe department of Eastbourne Amateur Dramatic Society's production of "Ali Baba & The Forty Thieves," eat fire, bellydance, twist themselves into improbable shapes and charm a snake. The snake-charming turn makes me think the same thing I always think when I see someone doing this: I wonder who the first bloke was who, when confronted by a rearing cobra, decided that the thing to do was not scream and run away, or whack it with a shovel, but sit down cross-legged four feet in front of it and play the bloody thing "The Sheik Of Araby."

As is the way of these things from here to Butlins, a few of the audience are embarassed into participating—though not, disappointingly, in the snake-charming act. Def Leppard guitarist Phil Collen volunteers to be carried around by a large bearded chap in a turban who walks barefoot on broken glass. Over dessert, we are treated to the rarely edifying spectacle of drunk European women trying to belly-dance: it gets uncomfortably reminiscent of the hippopotamus scene from "Fantasia." Outside, Moroccan soldiers put on a show for us, charging around on camels, firing guns into the air and shouting. At least, we assume they're putting on a show for us. It looks more like they're putting on a coup d'etat, until they dismount and ask if anyone else fancies a go.

The finale of the sideshows is a performance by four men with traditional instruments ("traditional instruments": universal euphemism for "unwieldy contraptions made of goat-bladders, horse tails and cat's whiskers, which sound like someone cutting rusty tin with a hacksaw, and which nobody around here would normally be caught dead playing") who play us some traditional music ("traditional music": "fearful, tuneless caterwauling about donkeys, dead kings and/ or God which nobody around here would normally be caught dead listening to").

Before we leave, a be-fezzed photographer wearily makes the rounds of the tables, offering for sale polaroid snapshots he's been taking of revellers during the evening. To his disappointment, nobody really wants a picture of themselves looking drunk in the presence of a camel.

He has only one item of in-demand merchandise: a beautifully lit and delightfully framed shot of the eye-wateringly gorgeous blonde woman who is here acting as producer with some cable television crew. "I'll have that one," says someone, daubing it with sticky rosé fingerprints. "No, I want it," says someone else. "I saw it first," objects another voice, not a million miles from Sweet. A scuffle ensues.

IT IS THE kind of statement that would normally cause people to back slowly away, trying to not to make any sudden movements, but Def Leppard's show comes, all things considered, as something of a relief. The press are poured into mini-buses and driven to the venue, deep inside a complex of beautiful caves near the seaside. As we duck between the stalactites, those of us who've grown tired of the fez joke are now giggling, "Hey, I suppose a rock's out of the question," and listening to our hoots echo off the stone.

On the stroke of midnight, Def Leppard appear on the stage that has been erected in one of the bigger caves, and we gentlefolk of the fourth estate are herded away from the punchbowls in the ante-cave in which we're gathered, and towards what we're supposed to be writing about. A few protests are made ("We'll be able to hear them perfectly well from here," says someone. "You won't be able to hear them at all," pleads an emissary from Def Leppard's record label. "That's what I mean," comes the reply). At least one broadsheet reporter tries to hide under a table.

Def Leppard's set is an acoustic-guitars-only unplugged kind of thing, consisting of stripped-down versions of a few of their hits and several entrancingly predictable cover versions: The Rolling Stones' "You Can't Always Get What You Want," T-Rex's "Get It On," David Bowie's "Ziggy Stardust," Jimi Hendrix's "Little Wing"—PJ Harvey's "Sheela-Na-Gig" has obviously been dropped due to time constraints. In fairness to the Lep—I feel I can call them this—there's a minor revelation in that those turbocharged vocal harmonies, Def Leppard's signature on every one of their utterly fatuous but irresistibly catchy choruses, are not just a product of Mutt Lange's Mission Control-sized mixing desk. Tonight, on "Animal" and on, er, others, they're absolutely spot on, sounding like several jet engines being revved at once.

Def Leppard depart to an ovation from the competition winners, polite applause from the media and, from somewhere up the back, a slurred rendition of "You'll Never Walk Alone" from one hack who has evidently been at sea too long. Buses arrive to take us back to the airport. Predictably, a head count reveals that we have less on board than we arrived with, and a couple of put-upon local guides are dispatched back into the caves with torches to locate those missing in action.

By the time we get back to the airport, it's three in the morning, with the flight not due to leave until five. The entertainment available at Tangiers airport is somewhat limited at this hour, so people make half-hearted attempts to sleep on any flat surface. It looks like an evacuation from some variety of disaster, and in some small way I suppose it is. Those who haven't lasted the bus ride conscious are deposited in sad little heaps on the floor by the departure gate.

WE ARRIVE AT The Bottom Line club in Shepherd's Bush, London, with three hours to kill before Def Leppard's second performance of the day. Mutiny is in the air, especially among the press not due to carry on to Canada in the afternoon. The two leitmotif phrases of the morning are "Do you know what time they're going to open the bar?" and "Bugger this for a game of soldiers, I've had my fun, I'm off." A full-scale rebellion is only narrowly averted by the serving of an immense buffet to we accredited scroungers.

A few of us nonetheless get bored enough to go and do our jobs, and head outside to talk to the punters waiting for the limited free tickets for the show. The people at the front have been queueing 24 hours, huddled in sleeping bags next to their camp stoves. "It's a privilege, man," one of them shouts. "It's history in the making." It must be wonderful, to be so easily pleased. He shakes a fist triumphantly and tries to give me a hug. Further along the line, a film crew from one of those insufferably bright and chirpy breakfast television programmes are encouraging some fans to sing their favourite Def Leppard songs for the camera. It isn't pretty. Those harmonies, like air traffic control and neurosurgery, should not be attempted by amateurs.

Shortly before the doors are opened, Def Leppard assemble behind the crush barriers at the front of the stage for a brief press conference.

They say that, gosh, wow, this whole thing is just so crazy and, hey, you don't have to be mad to work here but it helps, ha ha. I toy with the idea of adopting a stentorian Finnish accent and feigning outrage at the corporate decadence of it all ("Yes, Mr. Leppard, please. I am Sven Svennsenn, zer rocking and zer rolling correspondent of zer Daily Reindeer of Helsinki, yes, undt I am sinking zat perhapz you could haff been buildink zer hospital for zer unhappy children with this money, is? I am sinking zat perhaps zis means—ho!—zat your rock is out of my question, hey?") but I can't find a way through the rank of cameras. Besides which, the canapes are really rather good.

THE SECOND SHOW is much the same as the first, and after they finish, Def Leppard leave the building for Heathrow and their flight to Vancouver, along with the representatives of those press organisations deemed important enough to go to all three continents. *Melody Maker* is not among them, as they probably thought we'd only take the piss, so Sweet and I stuff our pockets full of caviar sandwiches and walk out into the sun, looking for a taxi.

11

EYE OF THE GEIGER

Chernobyl
APRIL 2004

THIS IS A declaration that may well prompt throbbing of veins and empurpling of complexions, but here goes: being a travel writer isn't as easy as it looks. I feel that this is something I should qualify hastily, i.e., in less time than it takes someone to load a gun and discover my address. I therefore urge you to understand that I'm not about to complain that the fold-down beds in business class don't quite accommodate all six feet of me (they do), or that staying, at someone else's expense, in hotel suites with bathrooms bigger than your entire apartment isn't marvellous (it is). The travel part of travel writing is a doddle. It's the writing that's tricky.

I'm talking specifically about what has come to be understood as travel writing as you generally see—or, I'm willing to bet, far more often ignore—in the travel sections of newspapers and magazines. To an even greater degree than other segments of an increasingly craven and uncritical mainstream media, these sections are hopelessly beholden to the idea that nothing that appears in their pages must be affronting or confronting to anybody whose eyes may happen to rest upon them, and especially not to their advertisers (who are, almost invariably, the people who actually pay for the writers' travel). So these outlets are, with a few honourable exceptions, difficult to write for on two counts. First, they're rarely willing to let you go anywhere interesting.

Second, they won't let you say anything interesting about the dull places to which they are prepared to send you.

This observation is like everything else in this book, rooted in a strictly personal preference—it may well be that millions of people enjoy consuming eye-glazing advertising copy phoned in by some junketing hack idly rearranging the lexicon of travel section clichés ("land of contrasts," and so forth). Such a revelation would, I confess, make no less sense to me than the way that millions of people choose to spend their own holidays—which is to spend them in the sort of places people take holidays. There is no body of people, not even the religiously devout or jazz fans, that baffle and boggle me more than the travelling public. I simply don't understand why they go the places they go—which is to say, the places everybody else has been already. And I don't understand why they do the things they do when they get to them—i.e., the things everybody else does. The defining absurdity of modern mass tourism is the crowd perpetually gathered in the Louvre, beneath the *Mona Lisa*, taking pictures of it. Assuming that few if any of these people are commendably ambitious art thieves, what are they doing with these photographs? How does that conversation proceed when they show their snaps around back home? "And that's the *Mona Lisa*." "Really? Is that what it looks like? I'll be damned."

This should not be construed as the lofty railings of a misanthropic snob with a rampaging ego who perceives himself as a capital-T Traveller as opposed to a mere tourist. I mean, I am a misanthropic snob with a rampaging ego, but I'm perfectly happy to acknowledge that, when I'm working abroad, I'm really just a tourist with a press card and a certain implicit license to ask people annoying questions and generally get in the way. I also appreciate—that is, am frequently briskly reminded by friends who work for a living—that if your professional life is an arduous and regimented one, then the traditional holiday of sunbaked idleness punctuated by various ritualised merriments provides welcome opportunity to lift weary eyes to a view other than the grindstone. The problem is that the vista isn't going to be all that interesting, and certainly not surprising.

Smart-aleck travel writers making fun of travellers is a tradition dating back to the 1869 publication of Mark Twain's *Innocents Abroad*, his account of touring Europe and the Holy Land with a gaggle of American pilgrims. It's a matchlessly funny book, but back then there actually was good reason to visit the obvious places, and see the obvious stuff. The tourist's world was still substantially mysterious, rather than a checklist of landmarks that look like the pictures (Stonehenge, if you hadn't seen a thousand images of it, would be impressive and moving; now, it's just smaller than you imagined). Most importantly, a century or more ago, such a trip would have been an adventure, a struggle, an accomplishment—three elements key to any worthwhile enterprise and three things missing from a sorry percentage of the modern jobs from which the modern tourist vacations.

Nobody needs to spend further time on a palm-fronded Balinese beach. Not one of the six billion human beings presently breathing wants to see another photograph of the Coliseum. Not even your closest friends and family—or, I reckon, you—are interested in a yarn about Disneyland, or the Tower of London, or the Taj Mahal. So I guess the travel feature that follows is a kind of plea to travellers, and to travel editors, to recognise that the world is bigger place than they might think, and that almost all of it is startling, fascinating and wonderful (apart, perhaps, from Lunderskov, Denmark, where in September 2008 a local innkeeper answered my enquiry as regards what a visiting reporter might do on his afternoon off by mournfully intoning, "We have a pond."). Even—or, perhaps, especially—when you decide to try taking a holiday in pretty much the last place anybody would.

★ ★ ★

A DOSIMETER IS a grey, rectangular device about the size of an early-90s mobile phone. On its LCD screen, numbers flicker. These measure the radiation to which the dosimeter is being exposed. Yuri, our guide, explains what the number means in merciless technical detail, but I don't really take it in. This is partly because I never really take in any technical detail, but mostly because the one technical detail I have taken in is concerning me a bit. Yuri has told me that in areas of normal background radiation, like any reasonably-sized city, the display on his beeping, whirring dosimeter would read 0.014. Maybe a bit more, maybe a bit less, but 0.014 or thereabouts.

While Yuri has been explaining this, I've been watching the numbers on the device in his hand climb past 0.014—quite a way past 0.014. I've watched them clear 0.020, 0.050, 0.100, and then carry on, like a space shuttle's speedometer at take-off: 0.200, 0.300, 0.400. At about 0.500 I start holding my breath, which I exhale at 0.700 when I admit to myself that holding my breath isn't going to make much difference. Up past 0.800 the display goes, flickers past 0.900 and then settles at 0.880: about sixty times normal background radiation.

"They're called microroentgens," says Yuri, as I write it down. "M-I-C-R-O-R-O-E-N-T-G-E-N-S. About 880. No, hang on, 900. Something like that. Don't worry. It won't do you any harm."

About 200 metres away stands what must be the least visited famous building in the world, the most ostracised member of the fraternity of distinguished landmarks, the one edifice doomed never to dine at the cool buildings' table with the Sydney Opera House and the Taj Mahal: the giant grey sarcophagus that shrouds Reactor No. 4 of the Chernobyl Nuclear Power Station, which exploded in the small hours of April 26, 1986, belching a colossal cloud of radioactive dust across Europe and wreaking damage which may not be comprehended for centuries. Photographer James Reeve and I have come to redress the balance. As we wave the dosimeter about in search of more spectacular readings, we're doing the equivalent of posing goofily in front of the Coliseum, or buying postcards of the Eiffel Tower.

We're tourists.

THE CHERNOBYL TOURIST business is the least developed part of Ukraine's undeveloped tourist business. There are no hotels inside Chernobyl's Exclusion Zone, the 4,300 square kilometres around the ruined plant, blocked off by military checkpoints. The authorities don't want anyone wandering around the Zone unsupervised, so Chernobyl is strictly a day trip from Ukraine's capital, Kiev, a two-hour drive to the south. You book through one of the companies in Kiev that organise the excursions. They fix the paperwork necessary to enter the Zone and provide a car, driver and guide. There are no restaurants in the Zone, either, though lunch is part of the deal (the food, you are solemnly assured, is trucked in from a very long way away). And neither has any provision been made for people who might wish to purchase souvenirs. A shame, as the possibilities are spectacular: glow-in-the-dark fridge magnets, gloves with six fingers on each hand, t-shirts saying "I visited Reactor No. 4 and all I got was sixty times the normal background radiation."

Our driver, Sergei, forty-seven, knows the Zone well. In the 1980s, he was a driver for Soviet news agency Tass, and he took reporters into Chernobyl after the accident. Later, he ferried the engineers who built the sarcophagus over the simmering reactor. After Sergei negotiates the checkpoint at Dytyatky, which marks the edge of the Zone, the most immediately surprising thing about the Exclusion Zone is how unexclusive it is. This is no incandescent moonscape bereft of life but for the occasional five-armed zombie. There are thick forests of fir and birch and many, many animals: deer, birds, stray dogs and cats.

The Zone is also startlingly busy with people: technicians, forest rangers, police, soldiers. The small town of Chernobyl—now offices and accommodation for the Zone's workers—is almost lively. The Zone may be toxic and dangerous, but it was never wholly abandoned. Bizarre though it seems, the nuclear plant continued to operate long after Reactor No. 4 erupted. Reactor No. 2 was closed in 1991 after a fire, albeit one that didn't release any radioactive material. Reactor No. 1 was switched off in 1996. Reactor No. 3, housed in the same building as the gutted Reactor No. 4, supplied power to Ukraine until December of 2000.

Sergei drives us to the office of the Ministry of Ukraine of Emergencies and Affairs of Population Protection from the Consequences of Chernobyl Catastrophe (their business cards must be the size of dinner trays). Here, we are introduced to Yuri, our guide for the day. Yuri, a thirty-one-year-old former English teacher, and once the drummer in a local speed metal group, has lived in the area all his life. His hometown, Chernigov, wasn't evacuated after the accident, but he remembers that when it rained the next day, there were yellow spots on Chernigov's pavement. Like all the 3,500 people who work inside the Zone, he operates according to rota to allow his body time to process the junk it soaks up: fifteen days in, fifteen days out. He says his wife was worried about him taking the job—"About the potence," he grins—but says he's already got two kids, and besides which, he makes three times doing PR here what he would teaching outside the Zone.

Chernobyl's only real concession to tourism is the visitor's centre across the road from Reactor No. 4. The centre features an excellent model of the interior of the devastated plant. The detailed diorama includes figurines of workers huddled round the shattered reactor core: the blast blew the 1,000-tonne lid clean off it. I tell Julia, who runs the centre, that I assume that this is what it looked like just after construction of the sarcophagus was finished, in late 1986.

"No," she says, "this is what it's like now."

But, I say, puzzled, there are models of people in there.

"Yes," she says. "About 400 personnel work in the shelter. They do maintenance and monitoring."

I contemplate, for a moment, what I'd want to be paid to set foot inside that thing for five minutes. I come up with a sum that would enable me to purchase Ukraine outright, and have it painted.

"They make maybe US $200 a month," says Julia. Julia wears a dosimeter around her neck, one that measures cumulative radiation and is checked every month to make sure she isn't over-exposed. Another dosimeter, mounted on the outside of the visitors' centre, reads 1.600—more than 100 times normal background radiation.

On the walls of the centre, alongside photos of famous visitors—Al Gore, Hans Blix—are photographs of what those workers in there can see: lava-like lumps of nuclear goo, cracking support beams, sagging scaffolding. Even under ideal circumstances, almost everything built by the Soviet Union was a jerry-rigged botch, and the circumstances under which the sarcophagus was constructed may have been the least ideal in engineering history. It isn't surprising that cracks have developed. In a brochure Julia gives me called "Shelter Object: Chronicle of Events and Facts," the preface warns that "Development of other emergency situations is not completely excluded."

"It's collapsing, really," says Julia. "There is work starting on it later this year."

After the creaking sarcophagus has been stabilised, Julia explains, it will itself be sheltered under a new edifice—a vast concrete arch, 108 metres tall, 250 metres wide, and 100 metres long. It seems incredible to me that this is the best we can do—responding to an atomic-age accident with such basic, primitive measures.

"There's nothing else possible," says Julia. "More than 75 percent of the reactor has always been inaccessible, due to radiation or structural damage."

So nobody really knows what's going on in there.

"Not really."

Other sights on the Chernobyl tourist trail include a lurid monument to the firefighters who fought the blaze—they comprised the majority of the thirty-one people who died of radiation exposure immediately after the explosion. There's the tank graveyard, containing the radioactive military vehicles that transported workers to the disaster zone, and the enormous, ungainly Mi-8 helicopters which flew more than 1,800 sorties above the fire, dropping lead and sand on the burning core. There's also the place that was once a village called Kopachi, and which is now scrub-covered hillocks planted with nuclear hazard warnings— the whole village, and substantial quantities of nuclear waste, was buried here, and all that remains are the road signs. In Ukraine, as in much of Eastern Europe, towns have signs informing you when you've passed their city limits. These consist of the name of the place you've just left, with a red line through it. Kopachi's still stands, an unintentionally prescient monument to a town that has been crossed off the map. It's a creepy place to be, but it's only a warm-up.

Pripyat's name should be better known, at least as well as those of Hiroshima and Nagasaki. They are the only three cities to have been destroyed by nuclear power, and Pripyat, four kilometres from Reactor No. 4, is the only one that didn't recover. On April 25, 1986, Pripyat was a model Soviet new town, purpose-built in the 1970s to house the best and brightest of the USSR's nuclear technicians. By April 28, 1986, Pripyat was abandoned, its 47,000 people evacuated in a hastily convened fleet of buses. They never came home, and they never will. Their town was fatally poisoned, and its corpse is still slowly decomposing.

Behind the main square is a funfair, which was due to open on May 1, 1986, as part of the May Day celebrations held annually throughout the communist bloc. Yuri tells me not to tread too close to the dodgem rink. When I ask why, he holds the dosimeter against green moss which has gathered around the rink: 1.080, our highest reading of the day, even more than we'd racked up standing right outside the reactor. "Just don't touch anything organic," says Yuri. A few decades from now, that moss may have enslaved the human population of Earth.

Pripyat was a nice place to live, apparently. Before the accident, Sergei wanted to move here.

"One of the best places in the USSR," he remembers. "Lots of young families—people who worked at the plant, and they earned good money. You could get imported things. Good clothes, good food."

Sergei is keen on clothes and food. He has reported for duty today in a dapper olive-coloured suit, and he credits his survival of the radiation he absorbed in 1986, and since, to Crimean red wine.

"Everyone who drank it was okay," he confirms.

The atomic Pompeii of Pripyat is a complete mismatch of sound and vision. To walk through a city and hear no sound at all, other than your own footsteps and the occasional tweets and buzzes of birds and insects, is as disorienting as, say, having your contemplation of a desert interrupted by a cacophony of police sirens, car stereos and Hare Krishna drums. Nothing, save for the slow reclamation of buildings by trees, has happened here for eighteen years. The hammer-and-sickle emblems still hang on the lampposts and perch astride the tallest apartment blocks—there was nobody here to discredit communism when the Berlin Wall fell in 1989, or celebrate Ukraine's independence from the USSR in 1991. In a dusty room at the back of the concert hall on the square, we find a room stacked with Soviet flags and banners acclaiming Lenin and placards bearing portraits of local Communist Party officials.

"Props for the 1986 May Day parade," explains Yuri. "Indefinitely postponed."

Away from Pripyat, some normal human life, of a sort, persists in the Zone. Though it is not permitted for newcomers to move into the Zone, a few of the people who lived here before April 1986, mostly elderly, have drifted back. Of the 130,000 people evacuated from the district after the accident, about 350 have returned. The village of Parishev boasts a population of eighteen, all of pensionable age. Yuri takes us to meet one of them.

Maria, seventy-five, is delighted to see us, which is understandable, as we may be the most exciting thing that has happened to her in months—a meeting with a local is a common feature of the Chernobyl day trip, but the outings are not over-subscribed. Maria lives alone in a three-room wooden house, decorated with family photos and her own tapestries. A small farmyard outside is home to chickens, geese and cats. The cats have just the one head each, and the chickens don't lay square eggs. The average background radiation here, according to Yuri's dosimeter, is 0.014, about normal.

Maria produces a generous spread—vegetables, goose lard, raw eggs—which I'm not sure about at all. Yuri reassures that the vegetables are from outside the Zone, sold by a mobile shop that comes through twice a week. The eggs?

"From Maria's chickens," he smiles, cutting a hole in the top of one and sucking back the contents. Anxious not to offend, I accept a glass each of Maria's excellent homemade moonshine, and birch juice—water tapped from the trunks of birch trees. This tastes like diluted furniture polish.

I ask Maria what she remembers of the accident. Yuri translates, between mouthfuls of egg.

"A sunny day, like this one," she says. "I had been swimming in the river. This village was part of a collective farm then, and the head of the collective farm told us we had seventy-two hours to get out. We were put on buses on May 5. A year later, I came back."

Why?

"It's my home. I'm happy here. I have my chickens and cats, and my grandchildren come to visit."

Weren't you concerned about what the government was telling you?

"Those lying communists?" she cackles. "They never told the truth to anyone."

IN THE CHERNOBYL Museum back in Kiev, there's a copy of the *New York Times*, dated April 29, 1986. The front page announces that the government of the USSR had issued the following statement: "An accident has occurred at the Chernobyl Nuclear Power Plant as one of the reactors was damaged. Measures are being taken to eliminate the consequences of the accident. A government commission has been set up." This communiqué could charitably be described as an understatement, and more accurately as a dishonest, belief-beggaringly cynical attempt to deflect publicity from a catastrophe with global consequences.

Reactor No. 4 at Chernobyl exploded at 1:23 AM on April 26, 1986. The accident occurred after a test of the cooling systems, during which safety procedures were ignored or overridden and, once things began to fizz out of control, panicked errors were committed by the Homer Simpsonovitches on duty. The USSR did their best to keep the story secret. The same *New York Times* story reports, chillingly, "A British reporter returning from Kiev reported seeing no activity in the Ukrainian capital that would suggest any alarm." The people of Kiev weren't told they had anything to be alarmed about—Kiev's May Day parade went ahead as scheduled. Sergei had told me that he'd been warned that if he spoke of what he'd seen in Chernobyl to anyone in Kiev, he'd be locked in the nuthatch. The Soviets were only shamed into their admission when abnormal radiation levels were detected in Scandinavia.

The scale of the disaster is so vast that it may never be precisely measured. What is known is dreadful enough. More than five million people, mostly in Russia, Ukraine and Belarus, suffered some detriment to their health. At least 2,000 cases of thyroid cancer have been attributed to Chernobyl, and the numbers of such cancers still being found in children in towns near the Exclusion Zone may mean that more evacuations, more Pripyats, are necessary. The only good news was that the betrayal of its own people perpetrated by the complacent USSR in the days after the accident helped speed the end of the entire dreary communist experiment. The rupture in Reactor No. 4 was the first crack in the Berlin Wall.

I do eventually find a souvenir of Chernobyl. On Kiev's famous market street Andriyivsky Uzviz, I stop at a stall specialising in the ephemera of both Ukraine's twentieth-century occupiers. After I've fossicked through the Lenin badges and swastika-spangled SS cigarette cases, I ask the stallholder if he has anything relating to the nuclear plant. He nods, and shows me a medal—a scarlet and gold cross hanging from a green and red ribbon. The design in the middle of the cross consists of a blood-coloured teardrop, and some atomic symbols.

"For the Liquidators," says the stallholder. "Twenty dollars."

The Liquidators were the people who cleaned up the mess, and who built the sarcophagus. They were drafted from the military and other government agencies, and there were somewhere between 400,000 and 600,000 of them—as is often the case where Chernobyl is concerned, nobody really knows for sure. There are both financial and social advantages to claiming Liquidator status, and it is believed that some have contrived to get themselves falsely added to the list—the Ukrainian equivalent of hanging around in New York bars after September 11 in a rented firefighter's costume.

"It was presented in the 1990s," says the stallholder, while I hold the medal up to the sun. "So no radiation. Don't worry."

That's not what I'm worried about. What I'm worried about is what happened to the bloke it was awarded to.

12

STRAIT TO HELL

Anzac Day at Gallipoli
APRIL 1998

WHEN PETER WEIR'S 1981 film *Gallipoli* was released in the United States, it was trailed with the slogan "From a place you've never heard of, comes a story you'll never forget." Had this sales pitch been more widely known about in my homeland, we'd have put your ambassador to sea in a longboat with a hunk of stale bread. The idea that anybody should know of Gallipoli only because it helped launch the career of Mel Gibson would be the sort of thing we'd take enormous offence at, if only we didn't find the idea so incredible.

If you grow up in Australia, not hearing of Gallipoli is approximately as likely as not hearing of Australia. American readers desiring some perspective as to Gallipoli's place in the Australian psyche could try imagining Valley Forge multiplied by Iwo Jima, but they'd still be struggling. Gallipoli became the most famous place in Australia, despite the apparent handicap of its situation in Turkey, when soldiers of the Australia & New Zealand Army Corps stormed Turkish defences on the peninsula on April 25, 1915; the date is a devoutly observed national holiday in both countries, known as Anzac Day.

I visited Gallipoli for the *Sunday Times* on the eighty-third anniversary of the landings, and left more bemused than ever by my country's relationship with this bleak stretch of shoreline. My feelings about the place have become no more resolved in the decade or so since. In the early years of the twenty-first century, the Australian government of Prime Minister John Howard swaddled itself ostentatiously in khaki—partly to shore up support for Australia's involvement in the War on Terror, mostly as a symptom of Howard's instinctively belligerent and defensive notions of patriotism. This sometimes made observing Anzac Day feel an act of collaboration with aspects of Australia that the country should—and can—rise above: parochialism, insularity, a certain suburban suspicion of the rest of the planet. In that same period, however, Gallipoli inspired the historian Les Carlyon's *Gallipoli*—not just magisterial military history, but a genuine literary masterpiece—and an interesting national soul-searching prompted by the death, in May 2002, of the last surviving veteran of the campaign.

He was Alec Campbell, and he was 103 years old when he died, just a few weeks after leading the 2002 Anzac Day parade in his native Hobart. He joined the fifteenth battalion of what was then called the Australian Imperial Force in 1915; he lied about his age, adding two years to the sixteen he had on the clock at that point. He arrived on Gallipoli six months into the eight months that the campaign lasted. He served as a rifleman and water carrier, was wounded, contracted a serious fever which partially paralysed his face and was invalided out of the army still a year too young to have joined it in the first place.

Campbell's remaining eighty-six years were eventful and industrious: he built railway carriages, sailed ocean-going racing boats, helped in the construction of Australia's first parliament house, organised and ran trades unions, married twice, and fathered nine children, the last of them at the age of sixty-nine. He disdained attempts at co-option into the role of mythical elder. "Gallipoli," he told one inquirer, "was Gallipoli."

This chapter is for him, and for all the others.

★ ★ ★

AS DAWN ASSERTS itself through unseasonal April clouds, the first Australians to make it off the beach have occupied the steep, flat-topped hill they call Plugge's Plateau; one of them wears his national flag draped around his shoulders like a cape. On the next row of ridges, a few bold pathfinders pick their way through the clinging scrub and the deep, treacherous trenches dug by the hills' defenders. Some of the

Australians break left, scrambling up to positions at Quinn's Post and Walker's Ridge. Others head right towards Lone Pine.

Back down on the beaches of Ari Burnu and Anzac Cove, chaos reigns. Confused and exhausted invaders search in the dim light for the people they landed with, and the people they were supposed to meet prior to pressing on up the cliffs. Thousands of dry, blunt, Antipodean accents call names and swear the sweet, misty air blue.

A lone bugler by the cenotaph at Ari Burnu signals the end of 1998's Anzac Day dawn service, and I wander off in my own hopeless hunt for the bus I arrived in, which is parked in the dark among dozens of others in a queue of headlights that winds along the beach road. Not for the first or last time, I wonder what it is with my countryfolk and this rugged, uninviting sliver of Turkey, trailing awkwardly into the Aegean. Eighty-three years, we've been coming ashore here, and we still can't get it right.

THE DARDANELLES CAMPAIGN of 1915 had all the core ingredients necessary for the staging of a really top-notch military catastrophe: a) a bad idea; b) the inept execution of same; and c) the total boneheaded refusal by those responsible for a) and b) to stare the truth in the face when it became apparent that the wheels were falling off.

The bad idea, largely that of a First Lord of the Admiralty called Winston Churchill, was the forcing of the Dardanelles, the narrow strait between the asiatic Turkish mainland and a dog-leg-shaped peninsula called Gallipoli. The view from whichever region of Cloud-Cuckoo Land that British high command were inhabiting was that such an expedition would lead to the swift capture of Constantinople and the removal of Turkey from World War I. So confident were they that simple, fearful Johnny Foreigner would fold his tent and flee at the first meaningful brandishing of British steel, that the initial attempt to take the Dardanelles, on March 18, 1915, was an exclusively naval operation. A British fleet, consisting of 18 battleships and many more cruisers and destroyers, sauntered up the straits—"an unforgettable picture of aloof grandeur," according to the historian Robert Rhodes James.

It didn't impress the gunners in the Turkish fortifications. They sank three of the British battleships and crippled three others. By the time this aloof, grand Imperial armada limped back whence it came, no doubt with hoots of Turkish derision pursuing it across the water, it had 700 fewer sailors than it arrived with. Turkish losses totaled forty men and four cannons. From a British point of view, the humiliation can barely be imagined: a nation which had defined itself so much for so long as the greatest of the world's naval powers had been dealt a rare old caning by a people still popularly regarded as backward peasants with daft tassled hats and a mania for selling carpets. It was as if Manchester United had been given a Cup draw away to Ed's Bar & Grill of the Runcorn & District Jumpers For Goalposts Sunday No-Hopers' League and gotten stuffed 6-0—except, of course, that the overwhelming majority of the British public didn't think it was hilarious. On April 25, 1915, allied troops went ashore on Gallipoli.

British troops of the twenty-ninth division landed at Cape Helles, on the tip of the peninsula. French troops took Kum Kale on the Asian side of the strait. The British encountered stiff resistance and incurred shocking casualties. The French captured their objective with minimal difficulty. Both groups of soldiers were instantly forgotten by posterity. To the north, on Gallipoli's Aegean shore, the first assault was made by the Australian & New Zealand Army Corps—the Anzacs.

Gallipoli has since been so completely appropriated into the mythologies of Australia and New Zealand that it's news to most of my British friends that anybody other than the Anzacs took part in the campaign. The truth is that French, Canadian and Indian troops also fought and died for the allied cause, and that of the 36,000 commonwealth servicemen whose names are listed in Gallipoli's thirty-one allied cemeteries, two-thirds are British. Regrettably, if they're remembered at all, it is mostly in the context in which they were portrayed in Peter Weir's 1981 film *Gallipoli*: ambling ashore at Suvla Bay, "drinking tea on the beach," while the eighth and tenth regiments of the Australian Light Horse were fed into Turkish machine-guns at a slim, rocky platform called The Nek in a series of absurd bayonet charges. While it's true enough that this criminally senseless slaughter occured, on August 7, 1915, the implicit suggestion that British, or French, or Turkish troops were having a relatively easy time of it is at best insensitive and at worst insulting.

What *Gallipoli* the film does depict accurately is Gallipoli the popular legend, a myth that is as much a part of growing up Australian as Vegemite toast for breakfast: our bravest and finest martyred by stupid, arrogant, brandy-swilling, upper-class pommy martinets with suspiciously camp lisps. True or not—and the officers who could have called off the carnage at The Nek, Colonel Jack Anthill and Brigadier Frederic Hughes, were both Australians—it's what we've been taking out on the English on the cricket pitch ever since. I suppose it could be worse. The only other nation to base so much of its self-image on a military shellacking by Turkey is Serbia, and the world would certainly be a happier place if they'd been able to placate their rage by whizzing a few bouncers around Michael Atherton's ears.

The Anzacs were put ashore a mile or so north of their intended landing site—the squabbling has continued ever since about whether this was due to drifting currents, inaccurate maps, misunderstandings on the ground or thundering incompetence at command level. "All of the above" seems as good a bet as any, though the latter option, naturally, is the received folk wisdom (In July 1993, I came to Gallipoli while backpacking around Turkey, and went to the battlefields with a group of Australians. When our guide introduced himself as an Englishman, we raced to make the same joke—"Make sure you take us to the right beach.") Instead of hitting the relatively gentle slopes just south of Hell Spit, the Anzacs found themselves staring up at serrated cliffs and ridges that rose almost vertically from the beach, hundreds of feet high, to a triangular pinnacle nicknamed The Sphinx.

Even discounting such obstacles as barbed wire, trenches, mines, mortars and raking machine-gun and sniper fire, the cliff face at Ari Burnu is daunting. I couldn't climb it in a day, not even with regular breaks for water and hyperventilation. The first Anzacs ashore on the first Anzac Day began their ascent at around 4:30 AM. By 8:00 AM, one group of Australians, led by Captain E.H. Tulloch and Captain J.P. Lalor, had not only scaled these towering heights, but fought their way inland as far as The Nek, a mile or more from where they'd landed.

The Gallipoli campaign—grotesque, murderous and futile even by the standards of World War I—was allowed to fester for eight more months before the peninsula was evacuated. In that time, the Anzacs got no further than they had on the first day, but they dug themselves immovably into the cherished memories of three nations—Australia, New Zealand and, altogether bizarrely, Turkey.

ACROSS THE DARDANELLES from Gallipoli, tucked into a bay at the narrowest point of the straits, is the town of Cannakalle. Cannakalle is the centre of the Gallipoli industry, and one of the strangest places on earth. Cannakalle, uniquely, is a city-sized shrine to a defeated invader.

In Australia, commercial exploitation of the Anzac name is prevented by law. In Cannakalle, there is an Anzac Hotel, an Anzac Bar and at least two Anzac grocery stores, both of which stock Vegemite and Violet Crumble bars. One restaurant posts the latest Australian Rules football scores in its windows, and another hangs a sign offering free glasses of the Australian chocolate drink Milo with every meal. The map of the peninsula I buy in Cannakalle confirms that Turks still call Gallipoli's desolate ridges and hills what the invading soldiers did: Quinn's Post, Monash Valley, Shrapnel Gully. Anzac Cove is known officially as Anzak Koyu. So far as I know, there is not an area of the Ardennes renamed Wehrmacht Wood—nor, more pertinently, a suburb of Darwin called Tojo. On April 24th, the day before Anzac Day, the barely distinguishable flags of Australia and New Zealand are flying from poles along the seafront and in the windows of every shop.

Granted, Cannakalle's status as a corner of a foreign field that is forever Australia is partly basic commercial sense, of which Turks are not generally short. Several companies based in Cannakalle run tours of the battlefields, and while Cannakalle is a pretty little town with a couple of nice places to eat, there's no other reason why you'd go out of your way to visit it. But the respect of the locals for the invaders of 1915 and the fondness they harbour for the visitors of 1998 are both unmistakably genuine. I have a cold glass of Victoria Bitter in the Anzac Pub and reflect that if I was to open a bar where I live now, in the East End of London, and call it The Luftwaffe, my only passing trade would be from local arsonists.

The Anzac Day embarkation begins just after midnight. Ponderous white ferries crowd Cannakalle's tiny dock area while tourist coaches, minibuses and bedraggled, bleary-eyed solo travellers with bedrolls and backpacks roll and shuffle aboard. Aboard the ferry, it's quieter than I ever imagined several hundred Australians in a confined space could be, though I suspect this is due less to a sense of occasion than it is to exhaustion. Most are in their 20s, though there's a smattering of older folk, some with service medals pinned to their cardigans and windcheaters, and a few here in uniform, taking breaks from peacekeeping operations in the Middle East and Bosnia.

In the interminable queue for the toilet on the car deck, I strike up a conversation with an Australian Air Force officer in desert camouflage. He has been serving in Kuwait.

"Fucking hot, fucking dusty, fucking full of fucking Americans who fucking think they fucking know fucking everything, and a complete fucking waste of our fucking time," he says, summing up his current posting. "Nothing to fucking drink, either." I ask him if he and his men are excited, or awed, or honoured, or what, by the thought of being on the beach at Gallipoli for Anzac Day. "Fucked if I know," he shrugs. "We'd have gone on holiday to fucking hell to get out of fucking Kuwait."

We are not, as a people, prone to rigorous self-analysis. I don't get much further elsewhere on the boat with my efforts to find an explanation for this pilgrimage (the term is appropriate: the Anzac Day crowd is not just backpackers who were passing through—my flight from London to Istanbul two days previously had been rammed full of Australians). Sample responses include "Dunno, mate," "Dunno, really," and "Dunno, mate, really, just wanted to see what the place felt like."

This is actually not a bad answer. It's certainly why I came to Gallipoli the first time. I've never known what to make of the whole thing—no rationalisation of its place in the Australian consciousness really holds up. True, a lot of Australians died here, but more died at Villers-Bretonneux three years to the day later, and we won that one. True as well that Australians fought here with extraordinary courage, but it's not like we remember their names—though most of us have heard of Private Simpson, killed while ferrying wounded soldiers to safety on his donkey, few Australians could name even one of the seven Anzacs who won Victoria Crosses during the battle for Lone Pine between August 7th and August 9th, 1915 (Keysor, Symons, Shout, Tubb, Burton, Dunstan and Hamilton, but I had to look them up).

When an Australian journalist called Jonathan King went in search of Gallipoli veterans in 1997, he found only seven still alive, aged between 99 and 104. These amazing old men all told life stories that made the Indiana Jones films look like "Five Go To The Seaside." One, Len Hall, had not only served at Gallipoli, but charged in history's last successful cavalry action with the Light Horse at Beersheeba, ridden into Damascus with Lawrence and then returned home and married the stranger to whom he'd given the emu feather plume from his hat when he'd embarked five years previously. However, these survivors are not half so individually revered in life as their less fortunate comrades are revered collectively in death.

There's not even consensus on the symbolic value of Gallipoli. There are some who claim that the fiasco was "the birth of the nation," that the blood spilt was a belated consecration of Australia's federation in 1901; those who push this line are generally the sort of people who are perfectly happy that Australia's head of state is decided by an accident of birth in a foreign castle owned by the most dysfunctional family on earth not called Jackson, and that a quarter of our flag is taken up by somebody else's. Gallipoli has also been used as a cornerstone of the Australian republican position—as a signifier of the trouble blind loyalty to some other mug's empire can get you into, it's difficult to beat.

For whatever reason, Gallipoli is hallowed ground—Anglo-Saxon Australia's only sacred site. It occurs to me, as the ferry draws up to the peninsula, and buses and people start puttering and stumbling ashore in the dark, that those back home who continue to strew obstacles in the path of land rights for Australia's indigenous people could do worse than to ponder how they'd feel if a Turkish government told us we couldn't come to Gallipoli anymore and, furthermore, that they were going to dig the place up to look for uranium.

NOT THAT TURKEY is likely to do anything quite so crass.

"Those heroes that shed their blood and lost their lives," begins the dedication, "you are now lying in the soil of a friendly country, therefore rest in peace. There is no difference between the Johnnies and the Mehmets to us where they lie side by side here in this country of ours. You, the mothers, who sent their sons from far away countries, wipe away your tears. Your sons are now lying in our bosom and are in peace. After having lost their lives on this land they have become our sons as well."

These generous words are embossed on a sort of stone billboard near the Anzac landing position at Ari Burnu. They were spoken in 1934 by Mustafa Kemal Atatürk, the founder and first President of modern Turkey. As a 34-year-old Lieutenant-Colonel serving in the peninsula's defences in 1915, Atatürk led from the front in halting the Anzac advance. His exploits won him a popularity which, after the war, he exploited and expanded to allow himself to reinvent Turkey in his own image. His zest for modernisation gave Turks a roman alphabet, a semblance of secular democracy, a largely western outlook and surnames—Atatürk, the name he chose for himself, means "Father Turk." His attention to detail was as admirable as his fashion sense: he passed laws abolishing baggy trousers and fezzes because he thought they looked silly.

Turks venerate Gallipoli with concrete reason: if Atatürk's gold pocketwatch had not, in true Boys' Own Adventure style, stopped the fragment of British shrapnel that struck him in the chest near Chunuk Bair, Turkey today would be an utterly different place, and Turks need only look over their borders to Syria, Iran and Iraq to see how different. Atatürk's portrait hangs in every public building in Turkey. His statue stands in every empty space, and he smirks raffishly from the 100,000 lire note, looking undeniably like Peter Cushing after a few sherries.

There must be more Australians and Kiwis on the beach this morning than there were in 1915—seven or eight thousand at least, I reckon. The Anzac Day dawn service is conducted from a temporary platform mounted just above the beach. It includes some stomping and shouting by a Maori warrior, a speech by the Governor-General of New Zealand and another speech by an Australian minister for something. These are followed by the spoken lament that starts "They shall not grow old," and ends with "Lest we forget," a one-minute silence and a communal mumbling of our national anthems.

As the day progresses, more ceremonies take place at the other cemeteries on the peninsula. There's a memorial for the Turkish 57th regiment, wiped out on the first day of the campaign. Those who have travelled from New Zealand mourn their dead at Chunuk Bair. A few—very few—attend ceremonies at the British and French graveyards. The Australian service takes place at Lone Pine.

The terrible thing about Lone Pine is how small it is. The entire battlefield is perhaps the size of three football pitches. In two days in August 1915, 2,200 Australians and 5,000 Turks died here. Here, there are more speeches, more silence and another hopelessly indecisive stab at "Advance Australia Fair." It's a common assumption, though a debatable one, that Australians aren't much use at expressing emotion on a personal level. It is indisputable fact that when it comes to expressing emotion in a group, we're completely bloody hopeless—though, this morning, some inventive souls do find an appropriate vent for their feelings.

On the carefully manicured lawn behind the Lone Pine cenotaph, in what is clearly a well-rehearsed rite, three young men remove their windcheaters to reveal Australian Rules Football jumpers—the navy blue of Carlton, the black and white of Collingwood, the gold and brown of Hawthorn. As a lifelong Geelong man, I initially find the spectacle rather distressing, but what follows is, in its way, lovely. The bloke in the Carlton jumper produces a weatherbeaten red Australian Rules ball from his backpack. To general approval from onlookers, a solemn kickabout ensues.

The last official ceremony takes place at the Turkish memorial at Morto Bay, towards the tip of the peninsula. The road to this giant grey brick henge is lined by Turkish solidiers, all nervously polishing and buffing hidden nooks of their kits while they await the limousine carrying their President. Eight flagpoles stand at the front of the Turkish memorial, on which the banners of Gallipoli's Australian, New Zealander, French, Canadian, Indian and British invaders are flown just as high as those of its Turkish and German defenders.

A comically inept Turkish army bugler honks mercilessly through all eight anthems, making "Advance Australia Fair" sound indistinguishable from "La Marsellaise," and "God Save The Queen" indistinguishable from "Cum On Feel The Noize." Another thing Australians aren't good at is stifling giggles. If the bloke with the trumpet wanted a ten-year posting to an isolated sentry post out in the militarised Kurdish badlands of the southeast, surely he only had to ask.

The service is conducted in Turkish and English, and concluded with a massed rifle volley that scatters the hundreds of starlings nesting in the top of the memorial, an instant constellation of tiny black stars.

THE REST OF Anzac Day is given over to aimless wandering around the battlefields. There's a desultory museum of the campaign at Gaba Tepe, but there's little in it that can't be found with minimal effort in the trenches that still scar Gallipoli's hills. The smallest amount of scratching in the dirt will disinter rusted splinters of tin can, congealed knots of melted shrapnel or a few of the countless millions of bullets that were expended. For decades, Turkish authorities tried to cultivate an atmosphere of serenity on the peninsula by planting pine forests, but they all burnt down a few years ago in a fire widely blamed on Kurdish terrorists. It's better this way, though. It looks like a battlefield, bleak and barren and lonely.

I never really understood what Australians were doing here in 1915—how many of them had even heard of Turkey?—and I still don't know what any of us are doing here now. Sometimes, as I wander through the overgrown trenches and across the immaculate graveyards, I think, on the whole, that our veneration of Gallipoli and the men who died here is a good thing, that the demonstrated sense of history and the concurrent lack of any kind of nationalistic bitterness is admirable. Then I notice that the Australia represented here today isn't an Australia I recognise: there is barely a trace, among the pilgrims, of Asian, or Mediterranean, or Baltic, or Middle Eastern ancestry. And I wonder if there isn't, somewhere at the depths of the Gallipoli myth—which inspires more and more people to come here every year—something unhealthy, reactionary and frightened.

Then I think that I'm trying too hard. Still, it's my job. I guess more than anything it's a nagging, subliminal sense of loss. Even if we don't realise it or won't admit to it, we come here in a quest for clues of what might have been, had a country only 14 years old, with a population of less than five million, not buried 8,702 remarkable young men here—to say nothing of the 52,000 more who perished on other World War I battlefields—along with everything they might have gone on to achieve, build, discover, create or solve.

On Baby 700, the forlorn hillock with a name like a bad mid-80s pop group, I stop by the grave of Captain Joseph Patrick Lalor, the officer who'd led his men as far as The Nek in those three unimaginable hours on April 25, 1915. Lalor didn't survive the first Anzac Day. He was killed here during the frenetic fighting for this dismal little lump of land, which changed hands five times on that afternoon.

Lalor's name was already famous when he arrived on Gallipoli. His grandfather, Peter Lalor, lost an arm leading the 1854 Eureka Stockade miners' rebellion on the Ballarat goldfields, before going on to become a distinguished parliamentarian. Captain Lalor's own CV was scarcely less picturesque. Before wading onto the beach at Anzac Cove that morning, clutching his cutlass and whiskey flask, Joseph Lalor had joined and deserted the British Navy, served with the French Foreign Legion and fought in a South American revolution. He was 30 years old.

Joseph Lalor might have become any combination of brilliant, inspirational, eccentric or dangerous. A man like that, you can imagine, might have ended up figuring, on the scale of great Australians, anywhere between Errol Flynn and Ned Kelly, and I'd like to have found out. So would we all.

13

IF YOU WANT MUD (YOU'VE GOT IT)

Woodstock II
AUGUST 1994

I DON'T GO TO festivals anymore. It would be neatly piquant to be able to report here that the unmitigated calamity that was Woodstock II was the last festival I attended, but it wasn't; one or two further straws still needed to flutter down atop the hefty log dropped, that dreadful weekend in 1994, upon the camel of my enthusiasm for outdoor rock'n'roll. The precise moment at which I understood that my days as a festival-goer were over was, in fact, the opening night of the 1996 Reading Festival. I was, that evening, in a position which, I am certain, would have been envied by most of the tens of thousands in attendance: I was backstage, festooned with the wristbands, stickers and laminated access passes which can serve to make the better-connected festival attendee resemble a commanding officer in some hastily convened guerilla military. In my immediate vicinity were liberal quantities of drink, numerous people willing to buy me same and the aristocracy of contemporary rock'n'roll. On top of all that, I was being paid for my attendance, covering events for a national newspaper. I thought: this is pretty much the supreme realisation of all the wildest dreams I ever harboured as a teenager bent on becoming a rock journalist. And then I thought: if I push off now, I can be back at the hotel in time for *Frasier*.

At the time, I felt burdened by the commission of this monumental heresy, much as Spinoza and Julian the Apostate must have upon rejecting all that they had grown up believing—though my recantation prompted neither formal process of excommunication nor Persian arrow in the gizzard. Eventually, however, the truth proved as liberating as the truth always does, and the truth is this: festivals suck. Like the religious faiths foresworn by the enlightened, festivals are organised dementias, collective determinations to ignore logic. The entire prospectus is a monstrous falsehood.

If you set out to design an environment hostile to the enjoyment of music, you could construct nothing more diabolical than a festival field: an acoustically moribund arena in which the minority actively interested in whichever hapless troupe are occupying the stage struggle to hear anything over the din of herds of idiots yammering into phones, yelling after their friends and blowing whistles (any adult who blows a whistle in public for purposes other than officiating in a sporting fixture is—and it behooves us to be very clear on this—an irredeemable simpleton who genuinely deserves to be kicked to death). And the idea—which lurks, still, in the advertising and marketing of all festivals—that these ghastly events are a manifestation of a counterculture is plain risible. Even the annoyingly mythologised free festivals of the 60s and 70s, held when rock'n'roll was comparatively innocent, and before Glastonbury grew as sponsor-spangled as a Formula One meeting, accomplished nothing beyond the only demonstrable good that festivals accomplish today: luring battalions of morons away from the cities for the weekend, thereby making the comforts of civilisation that much more agreeable for the rest of us.

The festival cult is not merely grotesque, but actually faintly unsavoury. Broadly speaking, two sorts of people attend rock festivals. The first sort is under the age of 24, and charged with the giddy exuberance of youth. Given the likelihood that they will, as I did, grow out of it, there is nothing wrong with their attendance at such things—indeed, any regular user of public transport will concur that there's a reasonable argument for incarcerating them in such remote encampments on a full-time basis. The second sort is everybody else, who urgently need to take a fairly withering look at themselves. In disdaining, even just for the weekend, the everyday technological miracles of modern urban existence—indoor plumbing, paved thoroughfares—they also implicitly reject the moral advances that our urban centres have encouraged to flourish. For all the flowery feel-nice rhetoric that inevitably accompanies festivals, the reality is utterly reactionary. A rock festival is a total monoculture: beneath the stupid hats lurks less diversity of thought, culture and race than you'd find at a Ku Klux Klan picnic.

A rock festival also represents, for all its pretensions to equality and brotherhood, a brutally stratified class system. Try the stuff about how we're all one, man, on the bouncer keeping the riffraff out of the backstage enclosures (where, I can assure you, nobody expects the corporate freeloaders to endure the indignity of non-flushing toilets; those are strictly for paying customers). A person who spends money on festival tickets is contributing their small but infuriating bit towards hauling us back to an age of sun-worship and witch-burning. If you think I exaggerate, read on. Woodstock II was the nearest thing to a post-apocalyptic society I ever wish to visit.

When I try to be charitable about festivals, I wonder if maybe they subconsciously represent a pure, if misguided, attempt to expiate the guilt about the comfort and security that we enjoy on a harsh, chaotic, unforgiving planet. Maybe, much like the Filipino Jesus freaks who volunteer to be nailed to crosses at Easter that they may feel the pain of Christ, millions of privileged citizens of the first world spend money to endure weekends in conditions that, if foisted on ragged-trousered, soggy-socked foreigners, would instead see them buying charity records and/or demanding that the UN send soldiers to do something about it. Perhaps festivals are, at a subliminal level, a message of solidarity and hope to the wretched of the world: to the refugee who may happen across coverage of such an event on his dung-powered satellite dish, and think, "Wow. Well, I also live in a tent, subsist on awful food, suffer oppressive proximity to hordes of malodorous crackpots, and have to crap in a pit. But at least I can't hear The Stereophonics."

The simplest explanation that fits the facts, of course, is that every person who voluntarily attends a rock festival is completely off their trolley. On that front, any reader who gets as far as the first paragraph of the ensuing dispatch may find themselves wondering if the author hasn't a case to answer as regards his own sanity, with specific regard to his apparent bonhomie vis-à-vis The Cranberries. It does require a degree of contextualising. I had followed them to Woodstock at the behest of long-expired British music monthly *Vox*, on the grounds that I'd been faintly partial, at this early stage in their career, to The Cranberries' pastoral folk-pop noodlings. I had been a quarter of the crowd at their first London show, and once travelled to the Scottish town of Wick to watch them play in front of of 27 people at an arts and poetry festival.

Back then, however, their music possessed a certain winsome charm and Dolores O'Riordan actually sang—which she was very good at—as opposed to squawking like a territorially aggrieved corncrake, which is what she has largely done in the years since. Granted, by the time of Woodstock '94, The Cranberries had released "Zombie"–their ham-fisted, if well-meaning, analysis of the Northern Irish question, with its TANKS and its BOMBS and its BOMBS and its GONNS–but they were still a way off perpetrating the truly fearful *To The Faithful Departed* album, which is without much doubt one of the very worst records ever made. Seriously, look the lyrics up online, after first disabling your browser's bad rhyme blocker. Scan through "I Just Shot John Lennon," or any of the songs about Bosnia, and just try to imagine how the earlier drafts must have read.

Anyway. Woodstock II. The horror. The horror.

★ ★ ★

THE RAIN STARTS gently, pattering on the roof of The Cranberries' dressing trailer like polite applause. There are a few half-guilty glances and giggles as Dolores O'Riordan and her band realise how perfectly they've timed things. They were the first band to play on this ominously overcast Saturday, and now they're free to make their escape. As they congratulate themselves and commiserate with us, the rain builds to a thunderous ovation.

"Here," says Fergal Lawler, proffering a leftover bottle of red wine. "You're going to need it."

THERE HAVE BEEN better-organised car accidents and less self-important Soviet funerals. We've only been at Woodstock '94 a matter of hours when it dawns on us that we may be witnessing—nay, actually participating in—the greatest American fiasco since the Bay of Pigs.

Back down in New York City the previous day, the usually mercilessly cheerful television weather forecasters could not have appeared more grim if they'd delivered their reports dressed in hooded robes and carrying scythes. So apocalyptic were their predictions for the Woodstock weekend that I'd been apprehensive about venturing upstate without several cubits of oak, and manuals on elementary boat construction and animal husbandry.

I had tried to reason with my travelling companions, Vicki Bruce of Island records and *Vox* photographer Ed Sirrs. I pointed out that we were comfortably ensconced in a fine hotel on Park Avenue, that Woodstock '94 was going to be broadcast live on pay-per-view television, that we could cover the event just as thoroughly while staying dry, clean and within walking distance of the bars and restaurants of Manhattan and if they didn't tell anyone, neither would I. They didn't listen. They thought I was joking.

And so we join the 300,000 befuddled souls gathered in these New York state paddocks. We are being rained on, pissed about, ripped off, spattered with slime and generally tormented like no other assembly in human history, with the arguable exception of General Haig's 4th Army, and at least the footsoldiers freezing in the trenches of the Somme had been able to get a drink, and hadn't had to listen to Del Amitri.

For no, we cannot get a drink. There is no alcohol available on site. Indeed, in the backstage press tent, we cannot even get a cup of coffee. Americans, while admittedly useful to have around if you're trying to liberate a continent, are the last people you should call if you're trying to organise a party. I've had more fun in Sweden. It would take a leaky press tent full of mutinously muddy, bored, annoyed and sober journalists three days to list everything that is wrong with Woodstock '94, and speaking as one of those journalists, I can report that our deliberations are exhaustive. In fact, the only area in which Woodstock '94 lives up to its declared ambitions of, like, bringing people together as one, man, is the manner in which scores of personal and professional British media rivalries are forgotten in the cause of a good self-pitying whinge. "This is hell, isn't it?" announces one damp British writer to the assembled hackery, huddled in the press tent, our chairs sinking slowly but inexorably into the mud. "Utter fucking hell."

There are jails which permit their inmates to get away with more than organisers allow the punters at this crazy, zany homage to the anarchic, devil-may-care, do-what-thou-wilt spirit of the original Woodstock. We are not allowed take our own food onto the site (well, the concession-holders jacking their prices a hundred percent and more over the odds are only trying to make a living). We may not spend US dollars (greenbacks have to be converted for festival scrip, the reason for which is a mystery to everyone). We are strictly forbidden tent pegs. At a festival at which tens of thousands have arrived expecting to camp out, this last edict verges on genius.

It's only Saturday afternoon. It's going to get so much worse. We can tell. The rain is now hammering against the tent with all the ferocity of a vengeful God and, it has to be said, he'd have every excuse. Out in the fields in front of the stages, humanity is returning, literally and spiritually, to the primeval ooze.

THE MUSIC ON the Saturday commences with a set by Joe Cocker, a veteran of the original Woodstock. He's touting the same act that he has been for thirty years, which is to say he still looks and sounds like he's shat himself and it's running down one leg. The crowd go mad, but Americans will clap at anything. Baseball, for example. As Cocker delivers "With A Little Help From My Friends" like it's being forced out of him with thumbscrews, I traverse the swamp to Woodstock's other stage.

Things here are, if anything, worse. I hadn't been expecting great things from Woodstock on a musical level, but nothing had prepared me for the horror of Zucchero in full flight. Zucchero is Italy's idea of a pop star, which explains why Italy, over the years, has been to rock'n'roll roughly what Rwanda has to package holidays. Zucchero resembles nothing so much as a drunk Albanian taxi driver in the process of emptying a karaoke bar. He is followed by Youssou N'Dour, today's token world music artiste, who is something of a stranger to Mr. Tune, and then The Band, or part thereof. They play for a week, then bring on someone from The Grateful Dead, and play for another month.

With blood beginning to collect on my palms and visions of St. Francis dancing in my eyes, I strike out for the press tent, hoping to reach sanctuary before night falls and jackals begin emerging from their lairs to pick off the fallen and unwary. By now, the walk from the South Stage to the backstage area is at best ankle deep, and at worst capable of swallowing troops, horses and cannons. On the liquefying hills and slopes along the way, those who have surrendered to the conditions hold mud toboggan races on stretchers stolen from the medical tents. Gangs of mud-covered vigilantes roam the site looking for clean newcomers to haul forcibly into the slime.

One forlorn form, naked but for a pair of shorts and an all-over suit of steaming slime, totters around in the downpour clutching a smudging, hand-written sign that reads "I Want Drugs." Alone in the middle of a vast mud lake, a drenched youth sits in a half-submerged deckchair, cradling a sodden hardback book, having clearly plumbed Colonel Kurtz-like depths of dementia. Woodstock now looks like the set of one of those nuclear armageddon films that were so big in the 80s, and I am walking through a crowd scene from the day after the bomb.

In the press tent, the atmosphere is souring further. Two distinct, mutually hostile camps have formed: i) the British media; ii) everyone else. The festival organisers think we're being a bit hard to please. "You have things like this in England, don't you?" asks one. "Yes," replies the journalist, without lifting his head out of his hands. "But with the one crucial difference that ours are, in some respects, any fun at all." The American media, meanwhile, charge around us foreign types, waving television cameras and tape recorders, asking us What We Think It All Means. "It's a bunch of bands playing in a field, it happens all the time in Europe, it doesn't mean anything," is one common response. "Piss off," is another.

Almost excitingly, from an Australian perspective, among the visiting press is Ian "Molly" Meldrum. Meldrum spent the 70s and 80s hosting a television rock programme called *Countdown*, on which he mumbled a great deal, crawled like a millipede cowering from sniper fire to anybody foreign or famous who deigned to turn up, and promoted a succession of desperately witless local acts. *Countdown* is often recalled with fondness by people who grew up in Australia during this time, in much the same way that people will, a few years down the road, laugh about a night in the cells. Call me humourless, but I don't think the man who delivered fame, however fleeting and local, to (for example) Kids In The Kitchen, Pseudo Echo, The Uncanny X-Men and Indecent Obsession at the expense of (say) The Go-Betweens, The Triffids, Ed Kuepper and The Hummingbirds should get off quite so lightly. The thought of seizing his trademark cowboy hat and tramping it into the mud occurs to me, as does the idea of kicking away the crutches with which he's walking today. But no. He's here, and he's him, and between them that's punishment enough.

Outside, the music is degenerating as fast as the weather. The North Stage hosts tedious crusties Blind Melon, tedious weightlifter Henry Rollins and tedious nobody Melissa Etheridge. These acts are introduced by a ridiculous bullshitter in a tie-dyed t-shirt who spouts interminable cosmic drivel about how we're all "beautiful" and "making history, man." History is what he'll be if he comes within chair-throwing range of the press tent. I realise that, all things considered, I'm quite looking forward to Crosby, Stills & Nash, which is a new experience.

The only act to properly sum up the squalor of the weekend are Nine Inch Nails, who address the crowd, with commendable accuracy, as "miserable, muddy fuckheads." Reznor and company are plastered from head to foot in brown goo after a pre-show punch-up, and are a welcome torrent of cleansing venom. Their triumphantly misanthropic set ends with "Head Like A Hole" and a comprehensive demolition of their equipment. After that, Metallica's gruff barking, pointless widdly-widdly soloing and dim macho posing is only ever going to look a bit daft, and does. We beat a retreat to the strains of redoubtable heavy metal pantomime queens Aerosmith. How we chuckle at "Walk This Way" as we blunder through the dark, damp undergrowth in search of our car.

IT RAINS ALL night. The swimming pool in the middle of Pollace's Crystal Palace Resort in Catskill bursts its banks at about two. Me, Ed and Vicki sit on the porch behind one of our villas and drink too much. Pollace's Crystal Palace Resort is a kind of Italian-American Butlin's, a couple of dozen white weatherboard villas clustered around a tatty mermaid's grotto constructed of theatrical maché rocks and artificial waterfalls. The clientele, aside from us, consists of Italian-American families who each have a dozen wheelchair-bound grandparents and a thousand screaming children. The decor of the reception area resembles the plunder of inept archaeologists who've excavated a Bulgarian discotheque.

Still, the staff are friendly, and excited beyond reason that they have "you British press guys" staying with them.

"WOULD ANDREW MUELLER . . ."

It's six o'clock in the morning. Christ.

". . . PLEASE COME TO RECEPTION IMMEDIATELY . . ."

It's booming from the loudspeakers that sit on poles around the resort compound. It's some consolation that everyone else is being woken up by this.

"WE HAVE AUSTRALIA ON THE LINE."

What are they talking about? I stand unsteadily up and get hurriedly dressed; it's only by great good luck that I don't get my trousers over my head and my shirt around my knees. I squelch barefoot through the pouring rain in the dawn half-light to reception.

"There's this radio guy on the phone for you," beams the bloke at reception. "He's calling all the way from Australia!" He's beside himself. "Are you, like, famous or something?"

Not that I'm aware of. I exploit my celebrity as far as asking for a cup of black coffee, which the reception bloke positively sprints off to organise, and pick up the phone. It turns out to be a researcher from Radio National back in the old country, who's got my name and contact number from someone in London, and wants to know if I'd be okay to be interviewed about the Woodstock catastrophe by Philip Adams. Adams is a reliably amusing and acerbic commentator and columnist, and something of a childhood hero. On one hand, the idea of bantering on air with the great man is no problem at all. On the other, I'd prefer not to do it on the strength of two hours' sleep while sweating tequila through my palms.

"How's it going, Andrew?" comes Adams' unmistakable, sonorous drawl. And so, after years spent dreaming of just such a moment, the first word I speak to the distinguished broadcaster is, "Shithouse." "I can imagine," he laughs. "I've seen the pictures on television. Though if you could give us a slightly more tactful perspective once we start, I'd be grateful."

I get through it okay, suffused by the coffee provided by the receptionist, who smiles ecstatically and hops from foot to foot while the interview takes place. At the conclusion of an epically self-pitying rant wishing all the miseries of the pit upon Woodstock's organisers, Adams says, "Well, Andrew, you've acquired a most engaging mix of Australian cynicism and English detachment," which, until I get a better offer, will do as an epitaph.

Back at my villa, after two more hours' sleep, I am woken again, this time by a knock on the door. It's Ed Sirrs.

"I don't care," he announces, "if it means I never work in London again. But I am not going back to that terrible fucking place today."

Ed is no lightweight. He has braved the most violent of moshpits, the most inadequate of stagefront security, the most temperamental of musicians. He is probably the best live rock photographer working, and does not baulk at much. But his mind is made up, and I for one will not hold it against him.

Indeed, a few miles up the road, Vicki and I wish we'd had the same resolve. The entire Woodstock site now has the consistency and colour of French onion soup, but smells a good deal worse. You'd get further in a punt that you would in car. All the roads into the festival area are closed. We try to reason with a security guard, using the time-honoured means of waving our laminates and trying to sound as foreign and as important as possible. We claim to be Peter Gabriel's management, Bob Dylan's children and the Red Hot Chili Peppers' trombone section. "I don't care who you're here with," he tells us. "You can't drive a car where there ain't no road."

We're still seven miles from the gate when we abandon the car in a ditch by the road. A bit further along, some enterprising yokels from nearby farms are running a tractor shuttle from the point at which the road is closed. We pay a man with no front teeth and eyebrows on his cheeks ten dollars each for a lift as far as he can take us, which is to a roadblock four miles from the entrance. We walk the rest of the way, proceeding against a steady human tide—an exodus of filthy early leavers, refugees from the disaster occuring over the ridge. The only good news is that by the time we squelch into camp, we've missed The Allman Brothers and Traffic. I hadn't realised they were still alive.

"I'm not sure they are," says someone who saw them.

Surveying the now half-submerged press tent, it's clear that we've actually been quite lucky. There were some whose devotion to duty was such that they stayed until the end of Aerosmith's set, with the result that they weren't able to get out of the site at all, and had been forced to sleep here on whichever tables and chairs hadn't sunk down to the mesozoic layer. There is a Woodstock poster still clinging to one wall of the tent, bearing the festival slogan "3 Days of Peace and Music" in stars-and-stripes-coloured writing. Over the "3 Days," "Peace" and "Music," some sleepless soul has written, with feeling, in red marker pen, the words "FUCK," "RIGHT" and "OFF."

Today's bill is no less dismal than yesterday's, featuring sets by The

Neville Brothers, who I forget while I'm listening to them, Santana, during whose performance I swear I grow a beard, and Jimmy Cliff's All-Star Reggae Jam. There are few more frightening phrases in the language than "All-Star Reggae Jam." All three acts, though atrocious, play to large crowds, and I have to wonder how many of these people are so mired by the sludge that engulfs everything that they can't move even if they want to.

Cometh the hour, though, cometh some unlikely heroes. In the late afternoon, Green Day appear. Their daft Buzzcock-ish pop romps are perfectly agreeable in and of themselves, but their singer, Billie Joe Armstrong, displays an instinctive understanding of what the weekend is about, or at least what the weekend has degenerated into. He goads two sections of the audience into a mudfight. This, inevitably, leads to an avalanche of earth landing on the stage itself, and the weekend's only stage invasion. Green Day's set is abruptly curtailed by venue security, but Billie Joe frees himself of their grip, runs back onto the stage and begins heaving great handfuls of mud back into the crowd, before being removed again by the bouncers who are supposedly protecting him. It's a fine, fine performance and one which, when replayed on the television monitors in the press tent, draws a heartfelt standing ovation from the by now almost hysterically irritated media.

It's on the North Stage today that Woodstock II achieves some sort of redemption—ironically, through a figure who famously snubbed the original Woodstock. Bob Dylan appears just as the clouds break, for the first time in forty-eight hours, to reveal an appropriately apocalyptic sunset. Behind the stage, it looks like the sky is on fire, and Dylan and his band rise to the backdrop. He delivers "It Ain't Me Babe," "It's All Over Now, Baby Blue" and "Masters Of War" with chilling conviction; where his voice these days often resembles an asthma sufferer blowing into a kazoo, tonight it's as startling and forceful as it must have sounded when he first imposed it on an unsuspecting rock'n'roll landscape. During "I Shall Be Released," his face, up on the giant stage-side monitors, looks transported and tear-struck, as if looking for escape from his myth in the raging red sky above us. The expression stays with him during "Highway 61 Revisited"; he now looks like a man with nowhere to run but the endless road ahead, and it's just about been worth coming here and putting up with all this nonsense to discover that Dylan, of all people, can still sing it like he means it.

THE ONLY WAY to get out afterwards is pay two inbred solvent-abusers a hundred dollars each for a lift in their van. I sit between them in the front, trying not to think too hard about the possibility of our ride ending in shallow graves in the surrounding forest. Our mercenary rescuers bicker about my directions to our stranded car.

"Hey," says one. "I think that's, like, near the titty bar."

"Yeah," says the other. "We could like, drop these guys off, and go to the titty bar, and spend all their money."

"Yeah," agrees the first. "That'd be, like, cool."

They have their radio tuned to Woodstock's on-site station, which is now playing highlights of Dylan's set. When "I Shall Be Released" comes on, I hum along, quietly.

14

BASTILLE CRAZY AFTER ALL THESE YEARS

1968 revisited, Paris
MARCH 1998

IT'S INCREDIBLY EASY to make fun of the French, which is why so many people do. However, those who amuse themselves by deriding France's weird food, silly language, baffling cinema, interminable literature, tawdry politics and erratic military record, among other hilarious defects, rarely pause, amid their mirth, to consider a yet wider virtue of mocking the snail-chewers. Which is that deriding the French as a breed of shiftless, unhygienic, duplicitous, cheese-scoffing, white-flag-hoisting, stripy-shirted, beret-wearing, bicycling onion retailers is not merely amusing in and of itself. It is also, in a way that cannot be claimed of the ritualised insulting of any other identifiable ethnic grouping or nationality, utterly righteous.

This is because the French just don't give a crap. They are completely, loftily, almost magnificently unupsettable—and on those rare occasions they give the impression that someone has succeeded in offending them, they're just pretending, as they know that this is even more annoying. In a truly logical world, France's national anthem would be—indisputably splendid though "La Marseillaise" is—Travis Tritt's "Here's A Quarter (Call Someone Who Cares)," perhaps arranged for the accordion. The slogan "Liberté, Égalité, Fraternité" would actually translate as "Talk to the hand." The French are, to use the lovely word they surely coined just to describe themselves, insouciant. As such, they nobly and generously serve as a global safety valve, a means by which all the world's chronically fractious and querulous peoples can let off steam without seriously scalding anybody. Mixed gatherings of different nationalities can be edgy affairs, everybody treading carefully around imagined or perceived sensitivities and resentments. It usually only takes one person to tell the joke about the difference between Frenchmen and toast, and before you can sing a bar of "It's a Small World After All," even the most previously tense of international soirees becomes a cacophony of hearty backslaps and insistent protestations that no, old chap, it's my round.

All of which is by way of buying time before confessing that the journey into France's revolutionary heritage recounted here, commissioned by *The Face* on the occasion of the thirtieth anniversary of the student revolt of 1968, stirred in your correspondent the budding of an understated, but unmistakable, Francophilic tendency. Vive, you infuriating contrarians.

★ ★ ★

WERE THE POLLSTERS of *Family Fortunes* to ask a hundred randomly selected riffraff what they most associate with Paris, the odds are the *Mona Lisa* to a 2CV that the greatest percentage would imagine a scene like this. In a hysterically baroque theatre near the Arc de Triomphe, a fashion show: next year's clothes hung on young women built like broomsticks, so excruciatingly thin they must have to move around in the shower to get wet, and on the brieze-block shoulders of swaggering, flawless young men with unfeasible jawlines, punchably smug. At the end of the catwalk, a battery of photographers, firing flashguns into the whites of eyes that never blink.

The clothes are by Jean Colonna, the occasion one of the umpteen catwalk shows of Paris Fashion Week. Colonna is not as big a name as Gaultier, and he hasn't attracted as many riot police to his opening as Armani did, nor is he as big a deal as McQueen, McCartney or any of the young British designers who have recently taken the helms at some of France's biggest labels, but he's pulled a decent enough crowd, some of whom are wearing their sunglasses inside with a shamelessness sufficient to suggest that they're in some way important or famous. I wouldn't know—what I know, or care, about fashion, could be carved onto foie gras with a chisel. But I think the knee-length tartan coat is quite smart, and I'm as gratified as anyone would be to see the Paris of popular imagination made flesh, however in need of a decent feed some of that flesh looks.

Outside, in the grey chill of an early spring morning, another Paris is sleeping off another day of living up to another sort of magnificent cliché.

"Revolution is the ecstasy of history."
—GRAFFITI, PARIS, MAY 1968

AT THE BOTTOM of the Boulevard Richard Lenoir, not far from my hotel, a huge digital clock is counting down the 56-and-a-half-or-so-million seconds that remain between now and the end of the millenium. It seems right that people will gather here, in the vast square over which the clock presides, to watch an era end. Six-and-a-half-or-so-billion seconds ago, people gathered here to watch an era begin, though they wouldn't have known it at the time. The storming of a prison called the Bastille on July 14, 1789 was, in itself, more than slightly quixotic, delivering the release of four forgers, two lunatics and one drunk, syphilitic, aristocratic idiot who had been locked up at the request of his own father. Louis XVI recorded the day in his diary with the terse entry "Rien," which goes to show how wrong a chap can be—as Louis himself doubtless reflected as he mounted the guillotine four years later.

The mob who razed the Bastille did more than burn down an old and ugly building. They instituted a municipal tradition of revolt that would dominate their city for the next two centuries—and counting— and which would ensure that Paris dominated the imagination of the planet. The reason that Paris is so often and so lyrically celebrated in film, theatre, fashion, music, holiday brochures and all our received wisdoms about romance is the lingering sense that in Paris, as nowhere else, the world can be turned upside down.

"Open the nurseries, the universities and all the other prisons."
—GRAFFITI, PARIS, MAY 1968

AFTER GETTING OFF the train at Gare Du Nord and dumping my bags, I get a taxi to the Sorbonne, Paris's 750-year-old university. In 1998, of all years, these tatty beige halls will get used to visitors. Thirty years ago, the Sorbonne was the epicentre of a rebellion remarkable even by the standards of 1968—a year, like 1989 or 1917 or 1871 or 1848, in which the prevailing institutions of the world suddenly looked less like rigid structures and more like a spaghetti-western film set: facades held up by wires, hooks, pulleys and the crossed fingers of those who'd erected them. In 1968, in Vietnam, the United States, Czechoslovakia, Pakistan and Great Britain, from the LSE to the Élysées, things stopped making sense.

On May 2nd, 1968, following weeks of protest by students outraged both by events in Vietnam and a rule that prohibited cohabitation between male and female students—the debate over their priorities has never been entirely resolved—the university in Nanterre, in the western suburbs of Paris, was closed by the Ministry of the Interior, acting under the orders of President Charles de Gaulle. The evicted students, led by ginger-haired German agitator Daniel Cohn-Bendit, marched into the centre of Paris and occupied the Sorbonne. Barricades were erected. Slogans were painted. Flags were waved. Speeches were made. Fists were shaken.

Given time, the students might all have got bored and hungry and gone home, but De Gaulle didn't wait to find out. On May 3, police were dispatched to clear the Sorbonne, a task they carried out with what might tactfully be described as excessive enthusiasm. As the students took control of Paris's Latin Quarter, the public mood shifted from bemusement to anger at the heavy-handedness of the government—few things are more sacred to Parisians than the right to protest. On May 10, the "Night Of The Barricades," 100,000 students and sympathisers rioted. There were 500 arrests and 370 injuries—though it has recently emerged that a student who died two weeks later did so as a result of wounds inflicted by a police stun grenade, and that his Gaullist parents were persuaded to comply in a cover-up for fear that a martyr could have ignited full-scale revolution.

France's trade unions, under pressure from their members, and sensing an opportunity to bend the government over a barrel, took the side of the students. A general strike on May 13 brought 250,000 workers onto the streets. De Gaulle, the most colossal figure of the French twentieth century, was rattled. He embarked on a bafflingly-timed state visit to Romania—where, just over twenty-one years later, his host, Nicolae Ceausescu, would demonstrate that he'd taken on board several unhelpful lessons from the De Gaulle technique of charming a restive public.

When De Gaulle returned to his collapsing capital, he delivered an ineffectual address to the nation, sulked for a bit and then vanished. While his government wondered where he'd got to, De Gaulle was staging another eerie preview of his friend Ceausescu's demise, making a farcical flight by helicopter to assure himself of the support of his military. The differences were that De Gaulle flew to Baden-Baden in Germany, not Tirgoviste in Romania, and that De Gaulle's generals encouraged him to return to Paris and assert his authority, rather than dragging him to a barracks wall and shooting him. On May 30, half a million pro-government demonstrators marched down the Champs Élysées and reclaimed Paris. The ghosts of the Paris Commune, and of the French Revolution, had been vanquished, but only just.

"Down with the spectator commodity society!"
—GRAFFITI, PARIS, MAY 1968

THE SORBONNE TODAY does not look a hotbed of revolutionary fervour, unless you count a few dog-eared posters grouching about how hard it is for students to find accommodation or pay for public transport. The kids I harass in the hall seem resolutely unexcited about the impending anniversary of the 1968 rising, reciting more workaday concerns like passing their exams, finding a job after passing said exams and getting away from another foreign journalist with a "Whither 1968?" angle before he makes them any later for their lectures. The only graffiti to be seen is on the wall of a building across the road from the Sorbonne: a racist slogan daubed by some—surprisingly literate—devotee of elderly buffoon Jean-Marie Le Pen and his crypto-fascist National Front.

It is difficult to find, among memoirs of the period, a clear statement of what the rioters of 1968 were fighting for. There's not even a lot of agreement about what they were fighting against, and this is perfect. The reason that May 1968 still looms so large in the popular consciousness is precisely that it was so completely, gloriously unreasonable, a splendid and petulant revolt against everything, a delirious reaction against the comforts of a capitalist society where—as René Viénet puts it in his snappily-titled *Enragés and Situationists in the Occupation Movement, France, May '68*—"we pay to consume, in boredom, commodities we produce in the weariness that makes leisure desirable."

The Athena-print ubiquity of the graffiti of the period ("I take my desires for reality because I believe in the reality of my desires"; "Underneath the paving stones, the beach!") suggests that, at best, May '68 remains a resilient bridgehead of dissent with modern life and, at worst, that it was a whole lot of fun. Much of the music and images of the counter-culture prevalent at the same time in America dated quickly because they were pitched against the contemporary cause of the war in Vietnam. What happened in Paris in May 1968 continues to inspire and intrigue because it was about nothing in particular and, therefore, about anything you like. What were they rebelling against? What have you got? May '68 was rock'n'roll without the music.

Indeed, each of the preeminent British rock'n'roll bands of the three decades since '68 have subscribed rigorously to this creed of defiant, unexplained rejectionism, as if the greatest solace lies in the refusal to offer a constructive argument. The Sex Pistols in the 70s ("I don't know what I want but I know how to get it"), The Smiths in the 80s ("We may be hidden by rags but we have something they'll never have") and Radiohead in the 90s ("We hope your rules and wisdom choke you") were all, in this sense, French.

> "We won't ask for anything. We won't demand anything.
> We'll just take and occupy."
> —GRAFFITI, PARIS, MAY 1968

THE IRONY IS that for as long as there has been rock'n'roll, the world has been running screaming from French attempts to make it, and generally with good reason. Listening to the French make rock music has the same morbidly compelling appeal as watching pensioners negotiate stone staircases after a frost. No government appointment since Caligula named his horse a senator has provoked as much merriment as the one the French made in the mid-90s, when they created a cabinet post with responsibility for French rock music. David Stubbs, a colleague of mine at *Melody Maker* at the time, ventured into print with the suggestion that the holder of such a portfolio would be kept about as busy as the Squadron Leader of the Royal Dutch Mountain Rescue Service, and we didn't get many letters arguing with him.

I put this to Emmanuel Tellier, who writes for the redoubtable Parisian rock magazine *Les Inrockuptibles*. He also plays in a band called Melville, who really aren't bad at all, and buys me lunch despite my assault on his nation's honour, which he defends with good humour.

"Our cultural interests are more diverse than Britain's," he argues over the soup. "Here, we think theatre, film, fashion and art are as important as music and football are in Britain. People here have more options for expressing themselves, so they don't care that our rock music gets laughed at in Britain. And we can get a drink after 11 o'clock."

Touché. I also drop in on DJ Dmitri from Paris, who lives off the Boulevard de Sebastopol in an apartment crammed with his immense collection of toy robots. He seems less impressed by Paris's civilised licensing laws, tells me Parisian clubs are terrible, and says he'd rather play in London or Tokyo.

"Music has never been important here," he shrugs—and it's true that May '68 didn't have a "Blowin' In The Wind" to call its own. "People here don't want to be in bands the way they do in Britain. Kids here use the music, but they don't want to live it."

Dmitri concedes that the recent international success of French electro-melancholists Air and Daft Punk might change this, but doesn't sound optimistic. "People here don't go out to hear music," he says, glumly. "They go out to talk."

At the moment, they—which is to say Paris's wide circle of self-conscious bohemians—are going out to talk in Menilmontant, a neighbourhood a few blocks north of Père Lachaise cemetery, where the tombs are embellished by impressionable Smiths fans inscribing neatly-lettered homage to Oscar Wilde and gormless American college kids daubing fatuous dedications to Jim Morrison, arguably the most overrated person who ever lived.

As tourists and professionals have started moving into the once-hip area around Place de la Bastille, the artists and students have decamped east to Menilmontant, a hilly suburb of cement and immigrants. Rue Oberkampf, the curiously German-sounding street which runs through the area, now houses Café Charbon, Café Mercerie, Le Scherkhan, Le Meccano and any number of other quiet, dimly lit, decorously decorated and altogether agreeable places to get drunk in. Except that the stylishly disheveled Parisians in these places don't drink, at least not in that race-you-to-nausea way that people do in British pubs. Again, Paris lives up to its clichés: they really do sip at tiny cups of espresso and argue about philosophy. In fact, there are philosophy cafés, where punters are encouraged to stand up and pontificate on the eternal, and which are every bit as ghastly as they sound.

There are also people who clearly are in need of a stiff drink, like the solemn youth in Le Meccano who earnestly informs me that it's wrong for me to be writing about May '68 in a magazine that is sold for money.

So when you finish reading this, go out and burn down a bank.

"Be realistic—demand the impossible."
—GRAFFITI, PARIS, MAY 1968

IN AN EFFORT to get closer to the revolutionary soul of Paris, I spend a day revolting, myself. This isn't difficult—in an average week, Paris hosts around 200 demonstrations. One morning tabloid, *La Parisien*, carries a daily map of streets likely to be blocked by protests. A short walk from Place de la Bastille, a run-down office block hosts the bases of two of Paris's uncountable pressure groups, SUD (Solidarity Unity Democracy) and CNT (some species of anarchist, judging by the red and black flags fluttering from the windows). This gloomy Sunday, the rest of France is voting in regional elections. SUD and CNT are staging what they have described to me on the phone as a "manifestation."

I speak to Pierre of SUD, who claims a national support of some 20,000 for his organisation. Pierre was fourteen years old in 1968, and remembers enjoying the time off when his teachers walked off the job. He explains that SUD wants to help the homeless and the unemployed.

"We want," he says, "to organise a movement with all who are excluded, and make a junction with the workers." Next to him, a younger man called Vincent, of a syndicate called Droits Devant, adds that "The government is making one law for the rich and one law for the poor," and then, in a whisper, "there are lots of police here," though I can't see any. He gives me a blue sticker which reads "Plan de relogement pour touts les personnes entrant dans du foyer!" I have no idea what this means, but it sounds damn exciting.

After a bit of milling around, a crowd of maybe a hundred demonstrators and half as many media walk to the Metro station at Gare de Lyon, where we commit the first insurrectionary act of the day by swarming in through the exit gates, thus skipping the fare. We are, it seems, going to commute to the revolution. As the train proceeds to wherever it is we're going, someone explains that we're off to stage an "occupation" as part of a bid to obtain housing for twenty homeless families.

We get off the train at a Metro station somewhere south of the Seine, and are led at a jog up a street past a church, which has already been occupied by illegal immigrants who are demonstrating about something else entirely. They cheer us as we run past, and we cheer them. The few dozen police standing outside the church look bored and annoyed.

Our brisk trot ends a few blocks later, outside an apartment building in the final stages of construction. The demonstrators leading the charge remove the sheet-metal and wooden hoardings and usher everybody in. It's dark and dusty inside, but there's a couple of people at the front with torches, so I follow them as far as the first floor landing, watch as the rest of the protestors push past me to the upper floors and onto the roof and decide to leave them to it and go back outside to take the broader view.

The paranoid whispers about police were not the delusions of self-important armchair rebels: a couple of the people who'd been running and shouting alongside us since we left the SUD/CNT offices are now barking into walkie-talkies. Their colleagues are not long in arriving: around a hundred of Paris's finest, the Compagnies Republicanes de Securité, or CRS. They trot out of three buses and seal the streets around the occupied building. The CRS are the legal response to Paris's culture of protest, a paramilitary police force equipped with shields, batons, tear-gas, sidearms, rifles and bullets both rubber and metal. Their body armour makes them look like the android bounty hunters that chased Harrison Ford through three *Star Wars* films, they wear no identifying serial numbers on their uniforms and have a reputation as fearful as their appearance. From the roof, the demonstrators take up the popular May '68 chant of "CRS—SS!"

A briefly tense and interesting but eventually calm and tedious stand-off ensues. Terms are negotiated. Women and children leave the building. Threats are made. The chief cop on the spot is a young plainclothes officer who looks like he cabbed it here straight from a Paris Fashion Week show. He's immaculately dressed, in a style best thought of as Suavely Thuggish Chic, and looks like an elongated Jean-Claude Van Damme. I try, with the help of French-speaking *Face* photographer Franck, to talk to him, but he regards us as if we were stains on his crisply pressed overcoat and continues listening intently to whatever he's hearing in his earpiece. In front of the rank of CRS troops, one luxuriantly bearded protestor, dressed as a biblical shepherd and carrying a life-size toy donkey over one shoulder, waltzes back and forth with a ghetto blaster playing "If I Were A Rich Man." The CRS troops ignore him. When I try to speak to him, he ignores me. Someone else explains that he's just an itinerant fruitcake who turns up at these things, and nobody really knows what he's on about.

While we wait around to see what, if anything, is going to happen, activists for other causes wander along, distributing leaflets advertising other demonstrations. People who pass by the besieged building react with benign disinterest, apart from those trying to reach their homes on the sealed-off streets. The CRS refuse entry to a young black man who's trying to get home with his shopping. A few minutes later, to the amusement of all non-CRS parties on the ground, a frail old white couple try to pass the same way. The embarrassed CRS have no real choice but to let them through, along with the young black man, who pauses to express his opinion of the CRS with a passion that transcends any linguistic barriers.

"He said . . ." says Franck.

I got the idea.

Another woman in a car has her path blocked. She erupts in a spectacular fury of honking and swearing for some minutes, before handing over her identification card for inspection.

A few hours later, with occupiers and police having apparently decided to bore each other into submission, I follow the directions on one of the leaflets I've been given, and end up at Charonne Metro in the early evening. A crowd of terribly angry young people assembles, and the pattern established earlier is repeated: we pour into the station through the exit doors—the Parisian authorities might think about spending less on riot police and more on ticket inspectors—and are given further instructions as we travel. I talk to Germinal, a twenty-five-year-old philosophy student from the Sorbonne, who explains that we are participating in another "manifestation," this time organised by AC! (Agir Contre le Chomage, or Action Against Unemployment).

"This is similar to May '68 in spirit," he tells me, "but it's more real. This time, it's about survival."

His reply when I ask him what he means by that is less concise.

We emerge alongside the silly, inside-out Pompidou Centre, and sprint a few blocks to the side door of a building, which is kicked open and entered with a great deal of joyful shouting. I walk around to the front of the place to see what they've stormed, and can't help but laugh—it's the hall in which the Green-Socialist-Communist coalition are planning to hold their post-election piss-up. The occupiers hang from the windows a huge banner demanding a fairer shake for the homeless and unemployed. A blizzard of leaflets is tossed over the street, and a couple of doubtless deserving cases from the Greens have their bewildered gazes up at their ransacked party venue rewarded with mercilessly accurate water bombs.

When the CRS arrive, I notice that a lot of them have come from the occupation I was at earlier, which is only fair enough, as so have a lot of the protestors in the building. Inspector Suavely Thuggish is with them again, still in thrall to his earpiece. There's a bit of a scuffle when the occupiers try to admit film crews and press through the front door. A few enterprising cops pile in with them and remove several demonstrators, who are—no pun intended, really—frogmarched to a waiting paddy wagon. They paste stickers of anti-government slogans to the insides of the van windows as they are driven away.

"Humanity will be happy the day the last bureaucrat is hung
with the guts of the last capitalist."
—GRAFFITI, PARIS, MAY 1968

BACK AT MY hotel, I call Rome to speak Angelo Quattrocchi, the
Italian author whose lovely, if somewhat florid, memoir of May '68,
The Beginning of the End, is being republished this year as part of the
minor boom in situationist nostalgia. Quattrocchi is an excitable sort
of indeterminate age ("I refuse to be quantified," he explains, like a
good anarchist) and maintains that 1968 was not an isolated event, but
part of a process, and thoroughly, uniquely, French.

"You follow the French revolutions," he sputters. "Liberté, égalité,
fraternité . . . France is aware of what those terms mean, and tries to
do something about it. The rest of Europe is becoming more and more
inconclusive and consensual, but the French revolution continues."

France, it's true, has developed a culture where taking to the streets
is not a last resort, but a first response. French governments, in turn,
have learnt to fear the streets, and with good reason, as the spectres of
many former kings and mayors would attest, if they still had heads to
attest with.

"In 1968, we liberated Paris," Quattrocchi enthuses, "from the banks
and the cops—same thing, to me—and we controlled it for fifteen days.
To be there, to start a new life without money, was such an exhilarating
feeling. People today don't think. They are told the present is the only
possible present. This last generation, patrolled by the media, this cop
of the mind, has not had a single original thought."

Kids today, tch. Before leaving London, I'd met with Tariq Ali, the
writer who was banned from several countries for his writings about
and involvement in 1968 risings in Britain, Czechoslovakia, Pakistan
and America. He is also publishing a book about the momentous year,
and also despairs of the generation born since 1968, blaming "television
and rave culture." Nobody so conservative as an old hippy.

Myself, I'm starting to think that maybe the French are just
attracted to drama for its own sake. This isn't necessarily a bad thing:
as Europe drifts towards a complacent, centre-right consensus, at least
the French are still trying, still clinging to the same wilful belief in the
perfectibility of human society that drove them to revolt in 1789 and

at regular intervals since. And maybe whatever it is that drives them to bounce bricks off riot police is the same force which has bequeathed us all those exquisitely overwrought films, heroically prima donna footballers and the eternal idea of Paris as a city of possibilities as wide as its boulevards, as grand as its monuments, as provocative as its fist-sized paving stones. We need Paris. We mightn't be able to live up to living in it, but it's nice to know it's there.

> "The tears of a philistine are the nectar of the Gods."
> —GRAFFITI, PARIS, MAY 1968

IN ANOTHER OVER-DECORATED venue near the Arc de Triomphe, more people gather to fiddle, or at least rap, while Paris burns, or at least while a few of its citizens smoulder with righteous umbrage. I'm at a party in honour of some new record by some new French hip hop group, clutching a glass of watery punch in one hand and a raffle ticket (first prize, tickets to the World Cup final) in the other. The homegrown strain of hip hop is enormous business in France, aided by the 40 percent quota of local product that radio stations must play, and by the fact that the mellifluous cadences of the French language are oddly suited to the genre. Tonight, the extent to which the French have coopted hip hop is obvious: the people in here are wearing the latest American street gear, but there's only one place in the world where a rap group would furnish a party with vases of fresh flowers and bowls of wax fruit.

> "Those who go halfway down the path of revolution dig their
> own graves."
> —GRAFFITI, PARIS, MAY 1968

MY PATH TO Gare du Nord station on my last day in Paris is blocked by a demonstration. I don't know what it's about, and by now I wonder if the demonstrators do themselves. There are people from SUD, AC! and CNT present—one or two of them wave—and though I can't see the bloke with the donkey, I imagine he's on his way.

15

WHOLE LOTTA FAKE KING GOIN' ON

Tupelo, Mississippi
AUGUST 1999

THIS TRIP WAS undertaken for *The Independent*, who sent me to Mississippi to cover the first-ever Elvis Presley festival to be held in the King's birthplace. In 1999. I recall spending quite a lot of the flight to Memphis, and the drive to Mississippi wondering what had, in previous decades, been discussed at the strategy meetings of Tupelo's Tourist Office. "Well, let's see. We need think of ways to attract visitors to our otherwise largely unremarkable little town, in and around which, frankly, very little of interest has ever happened. Goshdarn it, but this is tricky. If only the most famous entertainer who ever lived had been born here, or something."

While writing this introduction, I discovered that Janelle McComb, whom you'll meet shortly, died in 2005, aged eighty-four. This caused me minor, momentary angst about the disobliging assessment of her poetry that appeared in the original piece. I've left it as it was, however, on the grounds that while she seemed nice enough and (as her obituaries properly noted) worked hard and selflessly on worthwhile community projects, her poetry really was dreadful. I also looked up Paul McLeod, the tireless proprietor of Graceland Too. According to any amount of startled, bemused, baffled and/ or somewhat alarmed online reminiscence, he's still there—and, according to his own MySpace page, ready and willing to give guided tours twenty-four hours a day, 365 days a year. I have no plans to return.

There were three or four other British-based journalists covering the festival. The sense of humour among collective hackery on the road being what it is, you may rest assured that at no point did anyone tire of asking for directions to the hotel, in anticipation of the reply, "Down at the end of Lonely Street."

★ ★ ★

FOR THE OPENING track of his 1985 album *The First Born Is Dead*, the Australian singer Nick Cave and his band, The Bad Seeds, chose to enshrine the Mississippi town of Tupelo in song. It's a good song, as well, a fine start to a much under-rated record. While the Bad Seeds rumble and clatter with their customary power and menace, like a troop train emerging from fog, Cave appropriates a tone of gothic portent that might have pleased Mississippi's second-most famous son, William Faulkner: "In a clap-board shack with a roof of tin," Cave snarls, "Where the rain came down and leaked within/A young mother frozen on a concrete floor/With a bottle and a box and a cradle of straw . . . with a bundle and a box and a cradle of straw."

It's not a new idea, recasting Tupelo as a twentieth-century Bethlehem—Greil Marcus, for one, is especially fond of it—but it has rarely been expressed so well. "Tupelo" the song, with its echoes of Delta blues and language of deranged prophecy, paints a vivid picture of Tupelo the place: a storm-lashed huddle of lamp-lit shacks housing an itinerant population of dirt-poor factory workers and sharecroppers; a town too windy for birds to fly, too wet for fish to swim, a place forsaken by a clearly disinterested Almighty until a winter's night in 1935, when a young woman called Gladys Presley, who lived with her husband Vernon along Old Saltillo Road, gave birth to twin boys.

"Distant thunder rumble," sings Cave, "Rumble hungry like the beast/The beast it cometh, cometh down/The beast it cometh, Tupelo bound."

The eldest, Jesse Garon, never drew breath in this world, and was buried in an unmarked grave. His younger sibling by thirty-five minutes, Elvis Aron, did rather better for himself.

"Why the hen won't lay no egg," Cave continues, "Cain't get that cock to crow/The nag is spooked and crazy/O God help Tupelo! O God help Tupelo!"

Nick Cave, to the best of my knowledge, has never been to Tupelo. His heartfelt prayer remains largely unanswered.

THERE ARE THOUSANDS of towns like Tupelo, scattered like carelessly flung wheat across the expanses of the United States. Too small to be cities, too big to be villages (Tupelo claims a population of 30,000), these places subsist on some startling yet strangely dull freak of economics (Tupelo is the second or third largest manufacturer of upholstered furniture in either the world or the United States, or something like that).

Places such as these generally boast a wide, dust-blown and deserted main street, punctuated by the boarded-up fronts of recently-bankrupted family businesses, and are generally orbited by self-contained metropolises of immense shopping malls, owned by the global corporate monoliths that bankrupted the family businesses, and Tupelo does and is. These towns also generally offer, for the amusement and edification of passing tourists, a site of desperately minor historical import—the termite-chewed remains of a fencepost to which J.E.B. Stuart briefly tied his horse, perhaps—or something more up-to-the-minute, like a giant fibreglass prairie dog.

Tupelo has one natural advantage in the tourism department, though the town makes astonishingly little use of it. Whether out of abashed deference to the Presleyian riches of Memphis, two-and-half hours' drive to the northwest, or due to chronic modesty, Tupelovians seem disinclined to make much fuss. I have come here for Tupelo's first Elvis Presley festival—Tupelo's first concerted effort, forty-three years since *Heartbreak Hotel*, to make capital from the fact that one of the dozen most famous people who ever lived spent his first thirteen years within its limits.

Some of the weekend's scheduled events make sense: a performance by Vegas-based Elvis impersonator Trent Carlini, an exhibition of posters, screenings of Presley's still arrestingly awful films at Tupelo's pleasingly bedraggled pink cinema. Others have a certain tangential relevance: a vintage car show in Main Street, a gospel singing competition on the temporary open-air stage. Yet others make me feel like I'm spending three days in an episode of *The Simpsons*—like the "celebrity" bicycle race, which features the local equivalents of Mayor Quimby, Troy McClure and Kent Brockman, and is watched by nobody at all. On Sunday morning, a front-page report in the *Northeast Mississippi Daily Journal* rather halfheartedly suggests that "Sizzling heat kept daytime crowds to a minimum Saturday during day two of Tupelo's inaugural Elvis Presley festival."

Still, even if the locals can't be bothered, I try to enter into the spirit of things, such as they are, and it seems logical to start where Elvis Presley did. The street he was born on is now called Elvis Presley Drive, and the tiny, two-room house that Vernon Presley built in 1934 in anticipation of his imminent family is immaculately maintained, and filled with authentic furniture of the period. It is part of a humble complex of buildings devoted to Elvis—there is also a museum, a chapel and a souvenir shop—which is overseen by the Elvis Presley Memorial Foundation of Tupelo, which in turn is overseen by Elvis fan and friend of the Presley family Janelle McComb. "Elvis was born on a Tuesday and died on a Tuesday," she says, at one point. "His life was full of coincidences."

Ms. McComb's enthusiasm is commendable, though she often seems keener to stress her own connections to her hero than she is to impart anything about Elvis himself. The small museum does contain some genuinely fascinating memorabilia but affords undue prominence to the artworks and verse Ms. McComb has created in Presley's honour; the latter, which she reads tearfully aloud, offers little but the awesome possibility that the North American continent contains a worse poet than Maya Angelou.

Tupelo's other Elvis-related sites sulk unsignposted and unlinked by anything so self-aggrandising as a bus tour. At 114 West Main Street, Tupelo Hardware—where Gladys Presley bought her eleven-year-old son an eight-dollar guitar—survives the discounting of the mega-barns on the outskirts. At Lawhon Elementary School, where Elvis attended grades one to five, a peeling artwork on a corridor wall reads "Elvis Was Here" and a photocopied sign in the window observes that guns are prohibited on school premises. Milam Junior High, where Elvis completed sixth and seventh grades before the Presleys moved to Memphis, is a nondescript brown brick bunch of blocks making no outward boast of its famous alumnus. Tupelo Fairgrounds, where Presley played legendary concerts to riotous audiences of hysterical teens in 1956 and 1957, is a ruin.

By far the most interesting relics on view this weekend are those that are only in town for the occasion: Joe Esposito and George Klein, friends and associates of Elvis, perform compering duties on the open-air stage. More excitingly, Scotty Moore and D.J. Fontana, guitarist and drummer on Elvis's early hits and constant touring companions during the unimaginable years in the 1950s when their employer was inventing rock'n'roll stardom and modern celebrity as he went along, take the open-air stage on the final day.

In sight of the remains of the fairground where, a little over forty-three years ago, they played before a crowd so wild that reporters and photographers were forced out of the front row to seek safety behind the police guards on the stage, Moore and Fontana smile amiably at the few dozen people crumpled in deckchairs in the street, and fall in behind cabaret singer Ronnie McDowell.

McDowell is a capable crooner, who has ghosted Elvis's voice in films, but he knows who's in charge this afternoon, and cedes centre stage as he should. Moore, as venerable and hefty an antique as his Gibson guitar, and Fontana, an extravagantly quiffed vision of rock'n'roll aristocracy, rattle off their parts of songs that can hardly be more familiar to them than they are to anybody who has ever been touched by western popular culture; this muggy afternoon, Moore's exquisitely mournful solo on "Heartbreak Hotel" still rings as true as six strings ever have.

"I can't believe it's forty-three years since you recorded that," says McDowell. "Does it feel like that long?"

"Yep," says Moore.

Over the weekend, there are one or two minor outbreaks of Elvis impersonation on the street corners of Tupelo, but otherwise the festival is devoid of the sort of unselfconscious fanaticism generally held to characterise hardcore Elvis fans. For that, I have to go to Holly Springs, a pretty, well-kept town on the road to Memphis. Here, Paul McLeod and his son Elvis Aaron Presley McLeod operate Graceland Too, a two-storey warren of rooms crammed with testaments to an obsession that might be charitably described as impressively thorough:

in the gloomy lounge, six televisions and video recorders run twenty-four hours a day, scanning broadcasts for mentions of Elvis, all of which are diligently noted and filed.

McLeod Sr. personally conducts tours of his home and its immense collection of pointless ephemera. Unfortunately, his unruly top false teeth and congenital inability to construct a coherent sentence prevent him from communicating anything beyond an aura of demented devotion that discourages any questions along the lines of "Why?" or "Who cares?" McLeod, like most people who have sublimated every aspect of their lives to a cause ("I only sleep three hours a day, keeping up with all this stuff"), is initially dimly amusing, eventually extremely tedious and ultimately downright worrying. The reek of formaldehyde that permeates the building is not encouraging.

"My wife told me twenty-two years ago to choose between her and Elvis," McLeod splutters, in a rare burst of lucidity, "so she had to go, 'cos you have to do what makes you happy," and on he goes, a man whose Elvis—in clinical terms, at least—has well and truly left the building.

AT ONE OF the press conferences on the first day of the festival, I speak briefly with D.J. Fontana, all raffish middle-aged affability, a comb protruding from the pocket of his pink bowling shirt. I ask him what he recalls of the sessions that yielded "Don't Be Cruel," "All Shook Up," "Hound Dog," "Any Way You Want Me" and any number of other sounds for which, and with which, this century will be remembered. I wonder whether D.J., Scotty Moore, bass player Bill Black and Elvis had any inkling at all of what they were wreaking at the time, or whether they just walked out of the studios at dawn shrugging off another average night at the office.

"We were only ever thinking of the next record," says D.J. "We didn't understand what was going on, and to be honest I'm still not sure I do. Elvis never got it. He took one record at a time, one show at a time, always worried that it was going to end. He remembered how he grew up. He didn't want to be poor again."

Rock'n'roll is, still, more than anything else about the desire and the struggle to escape—circumstances, upbringing, boredom, routine, whatever. Rock'n'roll is also, still, defined by the template established by the high-cheekboned, half-smiling kid from Tupelo, and if his hometown today suggests little else of him, it's very recognisably a place such a driven and restless young man wouldn't want to be. At midday on the Saturday of the festival, Tupelo Hardware closes as usual.

16

TAKE THE VEDDER WITH YOU

Lollapalooza in America
JUNE 1992

IT IS EXTREMELY weird reading things that you wrote nearly half a lifetime ago, and even weirder to prepare them for repeated public exhibition, especially when your every instinct is to bury them under tonnes of reinforced, lead-lined concrete, around which you then propose to establish a total exclusion zone ringed with razor wire and minefields, punctuated by watchtowers staffed by armed sentries issued with exceedingly relaxed rules of engagement. Such ambivalence is the inevitable consequence of the excruciating experience of encountering a much younger version of oneself, and being uncertain whether to pat him on the head, or slap him upside it.

At the time I wrote what follows, I clearly believed that Lollapalooza and events like it mattered, were important, could change things—despite being informed bracingly otherwise by at least two of the acts on the bill. I seem to have believed that quacking, attention-seeking clowns like the (no longer extant, so far as I can tell) Parents' Music Resource Centre—and other similar simpletons whose sole claim on public attention is how dreadfully offended they have decided to be about something or other—should be either engaged with, or rebelled against. Whereas what I believe now is that querulous buffoons of this ilk should be ignored. And/or, should the opportunity present itself, teased.

I'm at least pleased to detect a note of sour cynicism in my dispatch about the prospect of a Bill Clinton presidency. If I'm honest, I doubt that I'd really picked the then Governor of Arkansas from that distance as a duplicitous, insincere, ruthless, ego-crazed thug who would establish a record for foreign policy incompetence which would have been regarded with baffled and appalled awe down the aeons, had he not been succeeded by someone who made him look like a diplomatic genius to rival Bismarck and Metternich—a successor who would, indeed, have conferred similar honour by comparison upon any given inhabitant of the macaque enclosure at the National Zoo. I was probably just trying to sound wise, knowing and cool—meet the new boss, same as the old boss, and so on.

Most of the artists encountered below are still active enough, in one way or another, that anyone sufficiently interested can find out what they're doing fairly easily. I saw a few of these people again over subsequent years. At some point in the mid-90s, charged with interviewing The Jesus & Mary Chain about their single "I Hate Rock'n'Roll," I took them to dinner at Bill Wyman's theme restaurant in London to annoy them; it worked. Around the same time, I spent a few careful days on tour in Britain with the Jim Rose Circus Sideshow, making sure I was nowhere in the ringmaster's sightline when the show reached the point at which Matt "The Tube" Crowley sought volunteers to sup the cocktail he brewed in his own stomach. At time of writing, Kevin Westenberg is yet to be troubled by much in the way of peer as a photographer, as may be confirmed at www.kevinwestenberg.com.

Readers overly sensitive on the subject of premature departures from this mortal coil by vibrant and amusing souls are advised to skip ahead at this point, while I furnish the dedication of this chapter. It's to the memory of Lush's drummer, Chris Acland, 1966-96.

★ ★ ★

"**THEY'VE TURNED DOWN** the cover of *Time* magazine today, you know."

So he keeps telling me. The Red Hot Chili Peppers' tour manager, after enduring two days of my nagging, has secured me an interview with the band's singer, Anthony Keidis.

"This is Anthony," says the tour manager, and I shake the hand of the tiny, chunky singer. "Anthony will talk for three minutes exactly, starting . . . from . . . NOW."

Having fun, mate?

"Yeah. Hopefully, we're bringing a slightly diverse collection of musical cultures together. It's a big, fun, wreck-it-up summertime package. It's for everybody. In terms of the political aspirations of Lollapalooza, what you have to understand is that so many of the right wing are such boring people that they have nothing better to do with their time than sit around organising themselves. And what this thing here today does is to help people that are maybe more interested in having fun to broadcast their views to America. And to the world."

The press release couldn't have put it better.

REWIND THIRTY-SIX HOURS or so.

"Sir, I'm calling from the United States customs office at the Canadian border, and . . ."

This, I take it, is not the wake-up call I've ordered.

"Sir, I have a man here who claims you can vouch for him."

This guy really must have the wrong number. I can barely vouch for myself most of the time. I wonder what . . .

"Mr. Mueller?"

Mmm? Vancouver, that's it. I'm in Vancouver. This whole American-Canadian thing is making a bit more sense, now. Some coffee would be nice.

"Hello?"

Right. The customs officer gives me the name of the person he's detaining, which, as it turns out, I do recognise. We are going to do a story together. I'm pretty sure that was the idea. He's taking the pictures. It's all coming back to me now. Bit cloudy outside.

"I'll send him on his way then, sir."

You do that.

Only after I've put the phone down do I think to wonder why he's calling an Australian representative of a British magazine to ask if it's okay for a Canadian-born American photographer to drive from Seattle to Vancouver. A slow morning, I guess.

WE'RE LATE. SO late, in fact, that we have missed Lush and Pearl Jam, the two bands I was most looking forward to seeing. We park behind the stage in a vacant lot, which is, in traditional rock festival fashion, rapidly liquefying beneath a steady patter of rain.

Bearded genius photographer Kevin Westenberg and I have come to cover the third and fourth shows of the 1992 incarnation of Lollapalooza. Lollapalooza started life in 1991, as travelling farewell party for the mighty Jane's Addiction, and had been so rousing a success that Jane's Addiction singer and Lollapalooza organiser Perry Farrell had decided to turn it into an annual event. This year's lineup—Red Hot Chili Peppers, Ministry, Ice Cube, Soundgarden, The Jesus & Mary Chain, Pearl Jam and Lush—will play thirty dates in outdoor arenas across the United States and, today, Canada.

The festival has become an immense commercial success, a major talking point and possibly even an election issue. Last year, the Rock the Vote booths that form part of Lollapalooza's accompanying ideological freakshow registered more than 100,000 new voters from one of America's most disenchanted electorates: the young. This year, Lollapalooza is taking place at the same time as a presidential election campaign which, for the most part, is of a sufficient banality to make the custard pie scene of any *Keystone Kops* film look like the zenith of scalpel-sharp rhetoric. Come polling day, voter turnout is anticipated to be the lowest ever recorded. Rock the Vote will be looking to register another 100,000 this year, and then some. This may not make much difference to either of the chaps after the top job, but it could make a hell of a difference to would-be mayors, judges, sheriffs and dog-catchers all over the country, wherever Farrell's circus wanders.

Watching CNN over the past few days, four sequences of images recur. One, George Bush and Bill Clinton—reverse faces of the same wooden nickel. Two, Slobodan Milosevic and Franjo Tudjman, who still appear sadly unlikely to be chained together and pitched off a high bridge anytime soon. Three, Tom Cruise and Nicole Kidman, who seem determined that every television viewer on earth is going to hear about what private and retiring people they are. Four, Ice-T.

Ice-T was part of the lineup of last year's inaugural Lollapalooza, and was this year's opening night compere. He is now America's favourite scapegoat, since some or other meddlesome wowser noticed that he'd written a song called "Cop Killer" and recorded it with a band called Body Count. There are few things, if I'm to believe half of what I hear and read, that are not currently his fault. Every time I turn on a television, a concerned news programme is parading one of an astonishing assortment of mendacious buffoons and blithering jackasses suggesting, in all seriousness, that Ice-T's faintly amusing but rather silly record is directly responsible for crime, drugs, teenage pregnancy, the fact that kids today don't got no respect, etcetera.

It'd be funny if it wasn't so serious—across America, state congresses are trying to turn themselves into everyone's babysitter. A law recently passed in Washington State makes it illegal to sell recordings containing "erotic content" to minors. It is just about likely that this will apply more to the works of Nine Inch Nails and 2 Live Crew than it will to those of Giuseppe Verdi. One of the agitators behind this and similarly dimwitted legislation passed elsewhere in the United States is the Parents' Music Resource Centre (the PMRC is also responsible for those cute little stickers that now festoon CD cases in American stores: "Warning: Adult Content," and so forth, though the irony inherent in accusing an Aerosmith album of containing any such thing seems to have eluded them).

One of the PMRC's founders, and its major driving force, is one Tipper Gore, a woman who gives every impression of being so comprehensively repressed that it can be imagined she eats bananas sideways. Her husband is a certain Al Gore. So if America goes out and votes for cool, hip, draft-dodging, dope-smoking, saxophone-playing Bill Clinton, the country will be one lucky shot away from having, effectively, Mary Whitehouse in the White House.

If Lollapalooza this year feels less like a rock'n'roll tour than it does a crusade, it may have its reasons. And astonishingly, though I've listened to the entire Body Count album at least twice and own several other recordings by Ice-T, I haven't killed a single policeman yet. All that crack must be keeping me calm.

LOLLAPALOOZA'S HEADLINE ACTS play on a large stage in front of the main arena. A smaller stage in a tent just out of earshot of the large stage hosts useless local rock groups from whichever region Lollapalooza finds itself in, and The Jim Rose Circus Sideshow. The Jim Rose Circus Sideshow are already getting more press than any other act on the tour, and it isn't surprising. The troupe's performers include Mr. Lifto, who lifts heavy objects with the portions of his anatomy that the rest of us would be least likely to use for the purpose; Matt "The Tube" Crowley, who pumps ingredients into his own stomach down a nasal feedline and then retrieves the result to be poured into glasses and served to the audience; and The Torture King, who walks on swords and sticks skewers through his face. Though this is only what any sane person would rather do than listen to any of the bands on the second stage, it is undeniably fascinating. At frequent intervals, gaps appear in the standing crowd where someone has fainted.

Lollapalooza's spirit seeks to manifest itself on the concourse area between the two stages. This concourse, squelchy and slippery underfoot, but just about navigable, recalls Glastonbury's bubbling bazaar of ideas idiotic and intriguing, of merchandise erratic and essential. There's a large metal sculpture that people are invited to hit with sticks. There's a cage in which people are encouraged to take sledgehammers to television sets—sadly, it isn't possible to tune them to MTV first. There's also a gyroscope, in which people can be spun through all sorts of angles and contortions, and food stalls peddling the usual festival fare, in case anyone feels like being ill and queasy but doesn't want to stand in line for the gyroscope.

At a raffle wheel, punters can donate a dollar to AIDS charities in return for a chance to win a backstage pass—though, having sampled the food in the artists' catering tent, I feel this is no bargain. Other things to spend money on include paintings and sculptures that look like they've either been backed over by a tractor or ought to be, and stickers and badges from the barely countable stalls which are here representing almost every cause on earth. With an admirable sense of fair play, Lollapalooza's organisers invited various anti-abortion groups and the National Rifle Association to come along and set up shop, but none appear to have taken up the offer. Lightweights. At least the NRA could have defended themselves.

I'm back in the main arena in time to see The Jesus & Mary Chain, and the weird thing is that I can actually see The Jesus & Mary Chain. After years of watching the perpetually scowling Reid brothers in dismal, dank clubs where they were barely visible through the billowing fogs of dry ice and iridescent crosshatches of laser, this afternoon matinee appearance takes some getting used to. It's not like I seriously suspected that Jim and William usually spent their daylight hours hanging upside down in caves, but the outdoor life really doesn't suit them. All things considered, they're on good form: "Head On" is emphatically reclaimed from The Pixies, and "Happy When It Rains" is, as usual, life-affirmingly upbeat yet ineffably melancholy, which is something of an ironic double-bluff with a one-and-a-half twist, given the conditions (pissing down, by now).

Soundgarden have tattoos, and guitars that go, "Skreee! Widdly widdly widdly!" Not a problem if you like that kind of thing, and most people here seem to. The enormous, threshing moshpit in front of the stage is by now giving rise to impenetrable clouds of steam, as the cold rain fizzes against acres of hot skin. Ice Cube gets everyone to shout "Yo-oo" and "Motherfucker," which is quite good fun the first half dozen times, but eventually starts to sound like bingo evening down the Tourette's Syndrome support group. I've got no problem with swearing loudly in public, but I prefer to do it as and when I see fit, rather than on demand. Ice Cube asks that everyone "Wave your hands in the air like you just don't care." I don't get involved with this, because I don't really understand the request. I don't understand the request because I am not normally given to expressing indifference by waving my hands in the air. I reach a compromise, and wander off to pay attention to something more interesting like I just don't care.

Backstage, a harassed-looking little chap is scuttling about muttering in some species of euro-accent. He looks as haunted as the Somme, and almost as muddy, though by this stage the latter is something we have in common. He recognises me from somewhere, though I don't recall where.

"I am tour managing Ministry," he says, as if that explains his panic, and it probably does.

"Alain Jourgensen is saying he will not play the show unless I get him a limousine to take him from the tour bus to the stage."

Well, it is all of forty yards.

"He wants one with horns on the front."

I don't imagine anyone's going to get in his way.

"No, like a cow's."

He drifts off, carrying my sympathy with him. The job of the rock'n'roll tour manager combines all the least savoury aspects of baby-sitting and zoo-keeping, and I wouldn't wish it on anyone. While I sit in the catering tent nursing a coffee, Ice Cube walks in, entourage in tow. He's finished his set and is after some water to take back to his bus. If I were a proper journalist, I'd go over and pester him. But I don't have to. Because somebody who clearly is a proper journalist does go over and pester him.

"Hey, Ice . . . "

The reporter is wearing a khaki overcoat and a red woollen bobble hat and is carrying a radio microphone.

"Could you tell me who your favourite homeboys are?"

He is not, after all, a proper journalist. He is either the bravest man in the world, or a moron with a fanzine and a death wish. So far, my money's on the latter.

"Are you missing your 'hood?"

This really is sensational stuff, though, as breathtakingly tactless as heckling at a funeral. There's surely nowhere further this bloke can take this, unless he's going to black himself up with boot polish, get down on one knee and start doing "Swanee River." Ice Cube regards his interrogator with the bemused contempt of a rhinoceros who has just been witlessly satirised by a ferret.

"Get a job, asshole," he grunts, and stalks past.

A tough act to follow, but Ministry manage. Jourgensen is delivered to the stage by the requested limousine, and leads Ministry's set of deranged electronic rockabilly from behind a microphone stand festooned with the skulls, spines and other skeletal remains of goats, rodents and sundry roadkill. Ministry, uniquely in rock'n'roll history, have a full-time bone roadie on tour with them, whose sole job is the augmentation and maintenance of this grisly prop. From where I'm standing, next to the stage by the entrance to the photo pit, I can see the medics under the stage dealing with the evening's first casualties. They wheel one kid past me on a stretcher, unconscious and covered in blood—there have been actual riots less worthy of the description "riotous" than what's going on in the arena now, although, the steady stream of wounded aside, it all looks bizarrely amiable. Red Hot Chili Peppers are fantastic for about the first fifteen minutes, which is as long as it takes for them to demonstrate that they are yet to have the second idea of their career.

There's not much going on after the show, as most of the tour buses have long since started hauling their star cargo south to the border.

Westenberg and I determine to suck the very marrow from the nightlife of Vancouver, and are back at the hotel by eleven.

"I'M AFRAID WE can't offer you gentlemen a full menu this morning."

We left Vancouver earlier than we probably needed to, and got across the border with no trouble, mostly because, when the guard asked if we were carrying any concealed weapons, we resisted the temptation to ask, "Why, what do you need?"

"The chef is late, you see."

We've stopped for breakfast somewhere just inside Washington State.

"But I can cook eggs, hash browns, sausages, that kind of thing."

Whatever.

She brings the food, and it smells great, and we eat it, and it tastes better. When we go to pay for it, one of those things happens that only happens in America.

"Oh no," she says, waving our money away. "The chef will be buying your breakfasts when he gets here."

We don't want to cause any trouble. Maybe the guy's car broke down. Perhaps he's ill. The food was delicious anyway. We're on expenses. It doesn't matter.

"Look," she says. "It's the only way he'll learn. You fellers have a good day."

True to our established form, Westenberg and I are late for the festival again. While the pine trees around the Washington State town of Bremerton are lovely, Kitsap County Fairground seems an otherwise uninspired choice of venue. Access to the site involves negotiating erratic ferries from Seattle, useless access roads, endless traffic jams and utterly incomprehensible road signs. After hours of blundering about what we believe to be the general vicinity of the venue, we find an important-looking gate.

"Artists only," says the guard.

Well, it's all a question of perspective. We wave every item of Lollapalooza accreditation we can find and affect the most convincing English accents an Australian and an American can muster. Amazingly, we are ushered through. We have managed to park ourselves directly backstage. We have missed Lush, again.

"Just make it up," says Emma Anderson, one of Lush's singer-guitarists. "You usually do."

Trying to gain journalistic access to bands who are not Lush at an American festival is not easy. At British festivals, it is perfectly possible, once you've got backstage, to find yourself queueing for lentil stew alongside Tom Jones and Blur. American bands, in contrast, surround themselves with people whose job consists largely of stopping other people from doing theirs. They say things like "We cannot comply with your request for an interview at this time" and have lots of keys hanging off their belts.

I ask someone with lots of keys hanging off his belt about the possibility of speaking to one or more members of Pearl Jam. "We cannot comply with your request for an interview at this time," he says. We are arguing next to Pearl Jam's astonishing tour bus, which is painted from front to rear in a mural replicating the cover art for The Eagles' *Hotel California* album. "It used to belong to Gene Simmons from Kiss," explains Mr. Keys, sounding suddenly less commanding. On cue, Eddie Vedder climbs off the bus. To the evident irritation of Mr Keys, Eddie recognises me and gives every indication of remembering me fondly.

Eddie looks a wreck even by his standards, but we have a bit of a chat about what we've both been up to since I'd accompanied Pearl Jam on a memorably mayhemic Scandinavian tour six months previously (me: editing a music paper reviews section; him: rapidly becoming one of the most famous rock stars on earth). He says he hadn't realised till he'd read my piece that he'd had the same surname as me at one point in his multi-family childhood, and we agree that it's nonetheless unlikely that we're related. This is as far as we get, before Mr. Keys comes back with someone with even more keys, who hustles Eddie back onto the bus and gives me a look that could curdle milk.

"I'll talk to you later, when everyone's gone home," says Eddie. "Nice to see you, anyway."

There are, of course, official channels through which all media requests for access should be directed. Lollapalooza includes in its retinue a Minister for Information, whose job includes deciding who can talk to who, and when, and for how long. Happily, this almighty personage was, until a few months ago, a colleague at *Melody Maker*.

"Have you seen my golfcart?" asks Ted.

The production office have brought along a fleet of these nippy little vehicles for getting around Lollapalooza's vast venues. They are already

proving an irresistible temptation to bored musicians. Last time I saw
Ted's, Emma was chasing a cow in it.

"Fuck."

I was wondering if there was any chance of talking to the Mary
Chain.

"What? Oh, yeah, they're in that dressing room over there, just go
and knock, though I think they're in a bit of a strop. Did you see which
way she went?"

It's not been the best of days to be in The Jesus & Mary Chain. At
what is effectively the Seattle date on the tour, they've been little more
than a convenient portaloo break between local heroes Pearl Jam and
Soundgarden. I knock on the door just as Soundgarden are starting.
Jim answers, lets me in, and apologises for the mess.

"Um . . . yeah. William knocked a few things over and then went off
somewhere. I'm a bit pissed, Andrew. Actually, I'm quite a lot pissed.
You'd better have a beer as well."

Jim's laconic East Kilbride drawl sounds like someone twanging
a loose rubber band; it would make Martin Luther King's "I Have A
Dream" speech sound witheringly deadpan. Jim's really not happy.

"The thing that's wrong with this," he begins, "is that musically,
at least, there's not enough variation. They ought to have had Nirvana
headlining. And more than just a token rap band. There's too much
heavy metal ideals and rap tokenism, man . . . it should have been more
50-50, with Public Enemy and De La Soul or whoever. And if that
would have meant there was no room for us, so be it."

I don't know. I've been enjoying myself.

"Why, for fuck's sake? You can't call this alternative, surely? The
headliners have been Number One for about five thousand fucking
years. No, I'm not enjoying myself. I enjoy it when we're out there,
playing, but all the rest of the bullshit, all this . . . this fucking
vegetarian food backstage . . . there's something too organised about
this, too pinstripe-suity, too un-rock'n'roll."

I am genuinely saddened that I have to decline Jim's kind offer to
"stick around and get bladdered," as I have go and find out why Ice
Cube hasn't arrived yet. By the time I get outside, just as Soundgarden's
finale is shaking the Mary Chain's trailer, he has.

"Shit, man," Ice Cube says. I've figured that if he didn't throttle that ghastly twerp in Vancouver when he had the opportunity and every excuse, he can't be that scary. "They found a little fuckin' residue from one motherfuckin' joint and busted us, the motherfuckers. Fuck 'em, man. They jack off to that shit."

No Christmas card for United States Customs & Excise from Ice Cube this year, I fear. Ice glowers impressively from the lounge of his bus. Someone, somewhere, is working on a short-notice lineup compromise that will involve Ministry going on early and Ice doing a shortened appearance by way of ushering on the Chili Peppers.

"Aw, shit," he continues. "It pisses me off, man, because I got fans out there that have never seen me before, fans who've been buying my records for years but wouldn't come to a rap concert because of all the bad press rap concerts get."

It must be a hard thing for the kind of kid who buys Ice Cube records to admit, that he's scared to go to a gig.

"Shit, man," says Ice, suddenly cheering up. "Did you see them down the front last night? These kids don't seem like they'd be scared to go anywhere, man. They're crazy! Never seen anything like it. But that's what this is about, you know? These kids are down with me, just like they're down with Ministry, and Soundgarden and Lush, you know what I'm saying? Music has a way of doing that. If musicians were politicians, we'd have no problems."

No different problems, anyway.

"This kind of stuff can change things, if only a bit, you know? A bit. It's a small dent. But it's a dent worth making."

Around some trucks and up a hill and across the catering tent and picking gingerly at broccoli that smells like it has been boiled in roadies' socks, Paul Barker of Ministry isn't so sure.

"Politically," he says, "to join this kind of thing rubs us up the wrong way. There are too many compromises we have to make, as a touring band. But, four days in, so far so good, I have to say."

Barker, half the creative core of Ministry, is a funny bloke. He leaps like a schoolteacher on any loose arguments or doubtful propositions, can't be bothered about projecting a united front and is refreshingly honest about his band's motivations.

"Money," he smiles. "Basically, six weeks of this pays for a studio for us. And we want a studio so bad. That's not entirely it, but it is 90 percent of it. We're not in this for Lollapalooza's benefit. That is, we are because we deigned to do it, but it's not the kind of thing we like doing."

Nor is Barker taken with Lollapalooza's ideological subtext, offering the admirably arrogant argument that people enlightened enough to like Ministry are already enlightened enough to be aware of the festival's pet causes.

"The next generation of politicians," he says, "are going to have grown up on punk rock. What does that tell you?"

That America is in real trouble. Americans think punk rock happened in 1989 and had something to do with The Sisters of Mercy. And besides which, the next generation of politicians is married to a woman who believes that rock'n'roll is turning our children into serial killers.

"Well, that's the only good that's going to come out of this. Tipper Gore is going to have a fuckin' muzzle put on her, because she can't be allowed to embarass the presidency."

Two words: Dan Quayle.

"Well, Jesus. Who runs that White House? I think it's . . . what's the name of the dog who writes the books? Millie. She's making all the money."

I'm attempting to find my way back through the dark to see Ice Cube's truncated set when I hear a rustling in the trees next to me, followed by the shriek of a tortured engine, a squelch of rubber on mud and a familiar voice squealing, "Shit! Look out!"

It's Emma, in Ted's hijacked executive conveyance. I swiftly realise that the cart's passenger seat is the only place on the site where I'm unlikely to be run over by it, and climb aboard.

"HEY, THERE YOU are. I thought you'd gone."

No . . . at least, only to hell on a golf cart.

"Come with me. We can talk now."

Eddie Vedder looks even more of a mess than he did this afternoon, and walks like he's trying to hide his head between his shoulders. I wonder, guiltily, how long he's been waiting here, sitting in the rain on a step outside a deserted dressing trailer. I know he said we'd talk later, but I'd have forgiven him if he'd got a lift back to Seattle with the rest of his band. We find a dressing trailer that hasn't been locked and sit on wooden benches.

Eddie still looks like the guy I met in Oslo in February, but has changed completely in every other respect. He was so infectiously energetic that talking to him for an hour was like drinking six espressos. He's as listless tonight as a flag on a calm day. He was unabashedly, recklessly romantic about the possibilities of rock'n'roll. Now, he sounds like he's been broken on a wheel.

"It's nice to see a friendly face, anyway . . ."

No end of crap has rained down on Eddie since we last spoke. As Pearl Jam have grown from a promising new addition to the Seattle lineage to one of the biggest bands on earth, they've suffered a vicious backlash from the press and from their contemporaries, derided as careerist chancers and bandwagon-jumping fakers (the fact that two of Pearl Jam, Jeff Ament and Stone Gossard, had been members of Seattle punk pathfinders Green River—pretty much the template on which every bunch of goateed northwestern grungeniks have based themselves—has been conveniently forgotten).

The record-buying public, however, have continued to snap up Pearl Jam's debut album, *Ten*, as fast as the world's CD plants can press it. As sales have cleared seven figures, the band have been toured into the dust, rolling out their uniquely punishing live show night after night, city after city. Everyone wants a piece of them and, most of all, of Eddie. Eddie, being Eddie, has tried to give all comers their minute of his time—he has a Boy Scout-ish belief in answering what he perceives to be the demands of his position. Six weeks ago, while Pearl Jam played in Stockholm, a souvenir-hunter broke into their dressing room and took Eddie's book of lyrics and stories, collected over the last two years. Eddie freaked out, cracked up and broke down. The European tour was cancelled the following day, amid a blizzard of press releases repeating that catch-all euphemism for every variety of road fever: "exhaustion."

"I hate to get sentimental," says Eddie now, hunched over in his chair, "but to write while you're travelling, with no solitude, is a lot harder than when you've got a bit of time to think about things, you know. And these words and passages were really hard to come by, much more work than usual. And they were gone, and some bastard had them. I felt totally raped, I lost my mind. And then I got home and found one my friends—Stephanie, from Seven Year Bitch—had died of a heroin overdose. And that . . . well, it kind of put me in a tailspin."

It's amazing, and not a little sad, what five months and a million album sales have done to Eddie. But he's enjoying Lollapalooza, surely.

"Should be."

But.

"Parts of it I am. But today . . . you know, if there's a moment where things should be better, then I want to go and make them better. It's probably going to kill me, because if it doesn't happen, then I get really upset. Today's example was that Ice Cube was stuck at the border, so there was this . . . dead space, and we should have been up there with Soundgarden doing those *Temple of the Dog* songs, especially seeing we are where we're are. Everyone was up for it, a perfect opportunity in the only place we'd do it. But trying to get everyone in the same place . . . it's impossible."

Outside, the Chili Peppers are cranking up "Suck My Kiss." Earlier, during Pearl Jam's predictably hysterically-received set, Eddie announced that he'd be taking a personal stand against Washington State's risible "anti-erotica" law, to the extent of hanging around Tower Records in Seattle and volunteering to buy warning-stickered records for anyone under sixteen who asked him. It's the sort of thing musicians say all the time, but I can imagine Eddie doing it. I can also imagine him being genuinely surprised when it starts a riot.

"Yeah, I know. I can't keep my mouth shut, I guess, and that's what gets me into trouble. I mean, you know me, I think it's great seeing youth get out and come together and think they can change things, which they can, but . . . whatever."

I wish Eddie luck. I suspect he's going to need it. He's still coming to terms with his job, and hasn't quite figured out where the line is that divides what he can actually do and what people think he's capable of, between good intentions and delusions of grandeur. He still seems a fundamentally decent human being—he's waited here for hours to see me, just because he said he would—and I hope he doesn't lose that, or give it away without a struggle.

"If it's something important," he mutters, "I'll use my voice to speak for a bunch of people, but only if the issue is hardcore and heavy. But don't come to me about a backstage pass, or . . . if I did all that, I'd have no time left for the important shit. Some people think singers can do anything, I know that . . . but leave us to the big miracles."

"WANKER! RUBBISH! GET off! Booooo!"

We are in a hotel in Bremerton.

"Bollocks! Booooooo! Go home!"

In the hotel is a karaoke lounge. At the karaoke machine is a large man in a pastel golf shirt and interestingly-patterned trousers who is taking it very seriously indeed. "Purple rain . . . purple rain," he groans, like a man in the tempestuous throes of a grand, passionate agony, or complete renal failure.

"Rubbish! Get off!"

Lush are heckling from a cocktail-glass-covered table up the back. Westenberg and I are joining in because some genius has booked us into a hotel in Seattle, miles and miles away over Puget Sound, and Lush have kindly agreed to find space for us on floors and spare beds.

"Booooooo!"

We are, any second now, going to get beaten to a whimpering pulp, of this I feel sure. At the bar, Al Jourgensen is flicking fifty-dollar notes at the barkeeper and barking "Margaritas for all my friends!" As his friends, for the moment, include anyone standing anywhere near him, I stick about. The barkeeper goes about his work with a terrified diligence, like a man defusing an unexploded bomb.

I don't think they get many people who look like Jourgensen in the karaoke bars of Bremerton. Jourgensen is clad entirely in sunglasses-at-midnight black, topped off with a ten-gallon hat decorated with the polished craniums of unfortunate rodents, and is clutching a wooden staff, taller than he is, on which is mounted the skull of a goat.

17

24 HOURS FROM TUZLA

The Bihac Pocket
AUGUST 1995

IN WHICH YOUR correspondent goes to war for the first time, more or less by accident.

Every reporter who finds themselves out of their depth in a war zone feels, upon their thrashing limbs, the hand of the ghost of Evelyn Waugh's William Boot, attempting to drag them irrecoverably into the murky brine. (For the purposes of sustaining this metaphor, please assume that the spectre of the hapless ingenue mistakenly dispatched to an obscure African frontline in *Scoop* is, for some peculiar reason, a seaborne phantasm). At best, I reckon I managed to stay but a few strokes ahead of said spook. That said, there is something to be said for leaping into a situation you don't understand, in anticipation that afterwards you'll have to write something about it with your name attached. With little in the way of received wisdoms to fall back on, you've no choice but to keep asking people the really crucial and elemental questions: When? Where? Who? Why? What the fuck is going on here?

The latter of these, where Bosnia in the mid-1990s was concerned, was always especially pertinent.

★ ★ ★

THE DAY CROATIA re-joins the war is the day the music dies.

The annual A&M (Art & Music) festival in the pretty Istrian town of Pula has been running for one day of its scheduled three when we start hearing reports that the Croatian army has launched an enormous offensive. More than a hundred thousand troops have poured into Krajina, the nominally ethnically Serbian enclave which occupies about a third of Croatia's territory along the border with Bosnia and Herzegovina, and which has been operating as a self-declared, if unrecognised, independent state since 1991. To nobody's great surprise, the remainder of the festival is cancelled, under state of emergency laws that forbid public gatherings in open spaces.

Photographer Phil Nicholls and I had arrived in Pula a few days previously, to cover the A&M festival for *Ikon* magazine. It had been going pretty well. We were billeted in an agreeable resort complex with easy access to quiet beaches. We'd spent a lot of time loafing around the bars and cafes of Pula's fairy-lit old city square. We'd even been quite enjoying the festival.

There had been an interesting exhibition of cartoon art, of which the recurring motifs were bitter lampoons of the United Nations Protection Force (UNPROFOR) operating, with minimal success, in the former Yugoslavia, gothic demonisations of Yugoslav President Slobodan Milosevic, and laments to Kurt Cobain. There had been some slightly less interesting performance art—exactly the kind of the thing, ironically, that usually provokes critics to call fervently for a swift reintroduction of conscription.

There had also been music, performed on a stage in a courtyard in the old city. I had been prevailed upon to help judge the A&M band competition, due to the sudden absence of one of the adjudicating panel, a writer for satirical Croatian paper *The Feral Tribune*. He'd vanished, either—depending on which rumour you believed—because he'd been mobilised, or because he was trying to avoid being mobilised. So I'd attempted tact about the dreary, gruff speed metal of Blockade Runner, A Je To and the promisingly named Megabitch. I'd managed to muster some enthusiasm for Leave, a skittish, Banshees-type concern from Osijek. I'd tried not to look too despondent during the set by whichever dismal headbangers had followed them, and I'd downright enjoyed The Holy Joes, the festival's guest stars from London.

I just wasn't too sure what to make of the rumours sweeping the site that Croatian army units were driving around town hauling fighting-age men out of their beds, that the border had been sealed, and that the Yugoslav Air Force were preparing to come to the aid of their ethnic brethren in Krajina.

ON WHAT WAS supposed to have been the second night of the festival, Nicholls and I head down to the site anyway. The roads are full of cars honking their horns while their occupants raise noisy toasts to the prowess of the Croatian army, and wave the Croatian flag, at its centre the sahovnica—the red-and-white checkerboard emblem of loony fascist Ante Pavelic's World War II Nazi puppet state. News reports from the front suggest that it's a rout: the Krajina Serbs have fled their centuries-old homeland with hardly a shot fired in return, and there is no sign of the Yugoslav or Bosnian Serb military coming to help them.

At the festival site, a few dozen people are sitting around with acoustic guitars, drinking and singing mournfully. The songs are all local, or local-ish, favourites, many by still-popular Serbian band Party Breakers. This is a subtle protest—Serbian songs were banned from Croatian radio in 1990. Since then, the Serb variant of the language which used to be called Serbo-Croatian, but which is now called Serbian, Croatian or Bosnian depending on where you're standing or who you're talking to, has gained some currency around Pula as code of dissent. There's one especially bohemian squat in Pula whose residents make a point of speaking nothing else, even if this does seem a little like aggrieved Londoners trying to make a political point by affecting Yorkshire accents.

By now, the speakers and tannoys that have been hoisted all over Pula are playing nothing but Croatian radio, which in turn is playing nothing but patriotic music. This, while it is thoughtfully provided in every genre imaginable, from country to techno to powerpop, all sounds worse than the news that Bauhaus are getting back together.

The logic of this approach to programming during wartime is apparent, however: after three days of hearing it blaring from every stereo in every bar, I want to kill somebody, as well.

• • •

IT'S NOT JUST a desire to escape these infinite annoying variations on the "Y Viva Croatia" theme that drives Nicholls and me out of Pula, though they're a factor in our decision. We get a bus to Rijeka, and from there an overnight ferry down the coast to Split. We're both struck, on the way, by how normal everything looks. The beaches we pass are full of holidaying Slovenes and Czechs. The other passengers on the boat sit up on the top deck and sip beer while the sun disappears behind the horizon. Nothing looks at all warlike until we get to Split, and to our villa in a resort complex near Trogir. These implausibly beautiful Roman cities—Split is built around the vast ruins of Emperor Diocletian's third century retirement palace—are full of German and English visitors, which is what you'd expect, but the former aren't staking out deckchairs, the latter aren't taunting them with chants of "Two world wars and one world cup, doodah, doodah," and they're all wearing uniforms. It's from here and hereabouts that UNPROFOR is directing its peacekeeping operations, such as they are.

It rapidly becomes clear to us that our decision to understand the former Yugoslavia by going to the former Yugoslavia makes as much sense as trying to assess the efficiency of a pasta factory from inside a vat of tagliatelle. If—and this is an "if" big enough to block out the sun and plunge the world into a new ice age—two people in the whole ex-country agree on why the war started and how it will end, we only meet one of them. While we spend a few days in Trogir phoning round to see if we can get a lift somewhere more interesting, my map of the Balkans gets covered in arrows, dotted lines, crosshatches, circles, squares, one sort of lopsided trapezium arrangement—in fact, everything but snakes and ladders—drawn by Croatian soldiers, Bosnian refugees, Italian journalists, Bangladeshi peacekeepers, American aid workers and the hotel telephone operator.

By the time Feed the Children offer us a lift on a convoy they're running into Bihac, I have heard, and dutifully noted, more batty and preposterous opinions than Lyndon LaRouche's secretary. I have met Croats who claim that the Bosnian government is a clique of Koran-waving fundamentalist fanatics intent on establishing a European branch of Iran, which is probably to be expected. I have met Bosnian Muslims who think the same, which isn't. I have met Croats who say their fat thug of a President, Dr. Franjo Tudjman, is a Balkan Churchill, which isn't surprising. I have met Croats who call Tudjman a bully and a war criminal, which, while it has the virtue of accuracy, is surprising. I've met aid workers who think NATO should bomb the Bosnian Serb Army, and aid workers who think the UN should pack up and go home. And I've met UN troops who think the whole thing is a total waste of everybody's time, and UN troops who don't want to leave.

I thought I knew my stuff. I'd been here before, hauling a backpack around the then-Yugoslavia in 1990, when the place was like a bad party at midnight, the six republics eyeing each other testily to see who'd be bold enough to be first to leave, though the whole thing still seemed a bit unlikely ("Where are you going to hold this war?" I remember asking a drunk barman in a hotel near Plitvice. "Your whole country is the size of the second-smallest state of mine. You haven't got room, you fool." He'd smiled at me, said, "Aha, but . . ." and fallen over). I'd tried to follow the story since. I even knew the history. Battle of Kosovo Field? 1389. Death of Tito? 1980. Red Star Belgrade's European Cup win? 1991. Didn't even have to look them up. I could even spell "Izetbegovic" nine times out of ten.

But by the time we get to the convoy's assembly point in Karlovac, after an overnight drive via Senj, I can feel myself turning into Lisa Simpson: "Why? Why must people fight? Why can't everyone live together? In peace, and stuff?"

I'D LIKE TO meet some Serbs, as well, to see what they make of it all, but they haven't stuck around to be met. Croatian television carries pictures from the Krajina offensive, accompanied by reports whose gloating tone transcends any linguistic barrier, of an entire population on the march, trudging back across Bosnia towards Serbia with whatever of their possessions they can carry.

In Karlovac, we wait. Nicholls and I have ridden here up the coast in a Feed the Children Landcruiser with two Feed the Children employees, whom I'll call Bill and Ted. Bill is a long-haired, softly-spoken young Englishman with an admirable facility for spotting the worst pun in any given situation ("Is that a school?" I'd asked on the way, pointing at a building on top of a hill. "Yes," Bill had replied. "It's what they call higher education.") Ted is a robust New Zealander whose speech is a bizarre mixture of obscure kiwi colloquialisms, convoluted acronyms of his own invention and swearing. Bill and Ted both seem to have a fair bit of time for the vanquished Republic of Krajina—Ted shows me the pages in his passport where he's encouraged Krajina checkpoint guards to put their stamps on top of his Croatian visas ("Really pisses the fuckin' cabbages off," he chuckles, deploying the standard aid worker euphemism for Croats).

There are forty or fifty vehicles in the convoy: trucks, vans and 4WDS from dozens of different organisations, and one white armoured car full of German journalists ("Silly bastards," snorts Ted. "If some fuckin' cabbage-eating dickhead does open up on us, you know which vehicle he's going to go for.") Nonetheless, Ted rearranges the luggage in our truck so the helmets and flak jackets are where we can reach them.

When we're finally given permission to move, a lone Croatian police motorcycle escort leads us on an unnecessarily circuitous route through the northern part of the newly former Krajina. "This isn't the usual way," explains Bill. "There must be something on the other road they don't want anyone to see." What we do see is unpleasant enough. The towns we pass through were, until seventy-two hours ago, bustling villages. They're ghost towns now, though it can be imagined that most ghosts would find them too spooky for habitation. In Plaski, the domestic details bear mute testament to the terrified speed of the Serbian exodus: livestock wandering the streets, washing billowing on lines behind deserted houses, a half-full bottle and two full glasses on a table outside an empty cafe.

President Tudjman had been promising to any reporter who would listen that property would not be gratuitously damaged, and the human rights of all Krajina Serbs who stayed put would be respected. It doesn't look like anyone was too keen on testing his word, and it does look like that might have been a good call. The houses that have got off lightly look like mine did the morning after my twenty-first birthday party. Others tilt at some point between that and smouldering ruin. Outside one two-storey villa, a television set lies smashed on the drive, as if the place has been captured and looted by Led Zeppelin.

On the outskirts of Plitvice National Park, the convoy slows and stops before we head for the border, to make sure we've still got as many vehicles as we started with. Up and down the long line of trucks, people piss against the wheels of their vehicles—they've obviously seen the same mine awareness map I have, in which the whole region is shaded yellow (medium risk) or red (high risk).

Along the road from the opposite direction come several commandeered trucks and hijacked tractor trailers carrying Croat soldiers back from the fighting. All adrenalised, mostly drunk, they greet us by waving, singing, and firing burst after burst of automatic fire into the air. It looks like something out of a b-movie matinee, and sounds like it—Kalashnikovs emit a dull, relatively quiet bark. The trouble is that those bullets, having gone up a couple of miles, are going to come down, and at lethal speed. Most of us retreat behind or into our vehicles. A bolder spirit emerges from one of the trucks belonging to the Catholic aid agency, Caritas: a nun gets out of the cab, accosts the shambling, unshaven, sodden Croatian officer ostensibly in charge of these camouflaged clowns, and gives him a bollocking that drowns out the last discharges of gunfire. The embarrassed soldiers apologise, and start trying to shake everyone's hand. One of them speaks English. I ask him about the burnt houses in Plaski.

"Muslims," he says, with the straightest face he can manage. "We opened the road into Bihac, and they came out and attacked the Serbs. Or perhaps the Serbs burnt their own houses when the attack started."

When we reach the border crossing, thick grey smoke is billowing from behind a small wood a few hundred metres away to the right, just inside Krajina.

"It was a village," shrugs a Bosnian Army soldier at the checkpoint.

THE BIHAC POCKET is the modern equivalent of the torturous diplomatic conundrums of bygone eras, the Alsace-Lorraines and Schleswig-Holsteins that still strike terror in the hearts of fifth-form history students.

The Bihac Pocket, the northwestern corner of Bosnia and Herzegovina, has a history as impressive and bloody as its impressively bloody present. During World War II, Bihac was the base for the partisans of Josip Broz Tito, the man whose political skill, populist cunning and monstrous violence (in the first year of his reign alone,

250,000 people died in massacres, forced marches and concentration camps) is widely, if dubiously, credited with keeping Yugoslavia intact. In the spring of 1954, the Pocket town of Cazin, where I stay for a few days, was the scene of the only peasant rebellion in the history of Cold War Eastern Europe: Bosnian Muslims, Serbian Orthodox Christians and Croatian Catholics all fought on the same side.

When Yugoslavia was still Yugoslavia, it was the most beautiful country in Europe, and the Bihac Pocket one of its most under-rated treasures. The region could have been created to adorn the lids of chocolate boxes: lush green hills trundle gently to every horizon, horse-drawn carts stacked high with hay and picturesquely ragged farmworkers compete for road space with backfiring cars. The Una River is a rich, sparkling blue that would embarrass sapphires. The place looks an agrarian utopia. The hospital in Bihac has recorded cases of malnutrition. The majority of the cargo of the convoy I come in with is food.

Bihac and Cazin have elegant elderly buildings that wear shell damage with the dignity of parading veterans, and footpaths teeming with people enjoying the sun and idle chatter. Electricity is supplied to every house for one day out of every ten, and the siege that the Croatian army has just lifted has inflated prices to the absurd levels of the Weimar Republic. A 12-kilogram sack of flour doesn't leave much change from £500. When I go to the market in Cazin with some people from Feed the Children to buy some plastic bags to bundle food supplies in, we're charged the Deutschmark equivalent of £23 for fifty. And most people in the area haven't seen a paycheck for the better part of a year.

The Bihac Pocket has spent four years being strangled half to death. Before Croatia's assault on Krajina had, with the help of the 5th Corps of the Bosnian army, reopened the roads into the Pocket, the region had been besieged by Bosnian Serbs to the south, and by a renegade Bosnian militia to the north. The latter was essentially the private army of a local businessman (Agrokomerc chairman Fikret Abdic) who had a grievance with the Croatian government, and had thrown in his lot with the Serbs after the Bosnian army had tried to bring him into line.

In Cazin, people tell me that things have improved dramatically even in the last few days. The Bosnian army now controls the entire

Pocket—a fact they celebrate all night, every night, periodically interrupting the drone of cicadas with more skyward volleys of automatic fire. Abdic has gone, various rumours placing him in gaol in Zagreb, in exile in Serbia or doubtless, given the Balkan mania for conspiracy theories, running a haberdashery in Toledo with Elvis Presley. Everyone in the pocket is terribly pleased about all this, except those who'd lived in the region Abdic had controlled. In accordance with the Balkan custom of petty retribution, they are now paying for their loyalties—in Pecigrad, north of Cazin, I see groups of people bussed in from Velika Kladusa, the capital of Abdic's self-proclaimed Republic of West Bosnia, being made to sweep the streets.

The Krajina Serbs have gone, and the retreating Bosnian Serbs are contenting themselves with half-heartedly shelling Bihac, attracting no more attention from the locals than the intermittent summer drizzle. There is a pervading sense of smoke lifting and dust settling. Certainly, it's all smiles at Cazin's radio and television station, which operates out of a shrapnel-pocked and sandbagged building that used to be a bank when people around here had money to put in one.

Cazin is a small town, with a news beat that probably once consisted, as it properly should, of school fetes, cats up trees and the fortunes of a useless local football team. In 1991, the staff of the station found themselves training on the job as war correspondents. Indira Topcagic and Nihada Seferagic, two of the station's seven journalists, have worked eighteen-to twenty-four-hour days since following the local brigade, the 503rd. Their resources total one tape recorder, three typewriters and an assemblage of antique broadcasting equipment that looks like Heath Robinson drew it. In the field, they travel by foot. They're paid fifty Deutschmarks a month, when they're paid at all, which isn't often. "It's our way of showing that we're with our army," they say.

We chat for a bit through an interpreter. They show me the remains of the rocket that came through one of their windows last year. I tell them I think they're very brave and clever, because they are, and they ask me what everyone in the Pocket asks eventually: what do people out there think about what's going on in here?

It's a tough question, doubly so through an interpreter, but I have a go. I tell them that when people I know think of the war in Bosnia, they think it's terribly sad, but that's it. Nobody has really kept track of how it started. There was no moustachioed dictator with a big army whacking a little country with no army but a lot of oil wells, no jackboots goosestepping across Poland, and while there are many dead in the streets of Sarajevo, none of them are Austrian Archdukes. I mean, everyone's vaguely grasped that Slobodan Milosevic is never going to make a convincing Santa Claus, and nor have the revolting Bosnian Serb President Radovan Karadzic and his attack dog, General Ratko Mladic, won many fans, but western politicians too cowardly, too stupid, or with too many vested interests to involve themselves in the conflict have done all too effective a job of persuading the media and public that what's going on in Bosnia and Herzegovina is unfathomably complicated, locally contained and Not Our Problem.

"But we're dying."

I know that. But if you believe most of what you read in the papers, tribalism and violence are just what you ex-Yugoslavs do, they've become two more of those universally accepted, wacky, inexplicable European character traits. The general feeling, however misinformed, is that the west can no more intervene to enforce peace among the Yugoslavs than it can to make the Italians organised, the English friendly or the Germans funny.

Indira and Nihada have heard all this before, but they listen to it again, and then say what every Bosnian says at this point.

"You could give us guns."

THIS IS GENERALLY the point at which the west stops giving and sharing and starts washing its hands. We'll give people in trouble food, clothes, medicines and other things that make us feel good about ourselves, and while those people are usually happy enough to have them, the people of Bosnia would, on the whole, prefer the means to defend themselves. As Indira and Nihada, among many others, point out, if they were properly armed, they wouldn't be besieged, and if they weren't besieged, they wouldn't need anyone's help in the first place. It's a fair point, but it's hard to imagine anyone organising a benefit album to raise money to buy artillery.

If there's one thing that spending time in Bosnia will clarify, it's the arrant stupidity of the international arms embargo on the former

Yugoslavia, which has only hindered the friendless, landlocked Bosnians. It never troubled the Serbs, who had access to the formidable resources of the Yugoslav Army. As for the Croats, ask a Croat.

Back in Pula, I speak to Major Oriano Bulic, thirty-three, a doctor serving with the Istrian-based 119th brigade of the Croatian army. When he isn't curing or killing people, he writes poetry, and claims to have successfully treated himself for bone marrow cancer as a young man. He comes to the flat I'm staying in clad in battle fatigues with red and yellow ribbons hanging from the tunic (the Croat and Serb armies use identical ex-Yugoslav kit, so they festoon themselves with these colours so they know who's who, making the war look like paintball played for keeps).

Major Bulic blinks an awful lot less than the rest of us. He is proud of the fact that his unit were the first into Plitvice—it's a national park set around sixteen lakes connected by waterfalls, and one of the most gorgeous places on earth. I tell him that I've been there, not just last week, but in the middle of the winter of 1990, when the lakes had frozen and the falls turned to stalactities, and it looked like Eden on ice. I remark that he must be terribly pleased to have it back.

"He is," translates Lara, our endlessly helpful host.

Then I say something about the amount of suspiciously shopfloor-shiny military hardware I'd seen driving and flying up and down the coast road between Split and Karlovac.

"It's German," he says, without hesitating. "I think they ship it via Ukraine. Or American. Or Israeli."

Germany and America would certainly deny this, and I can't prove it either way, though the alleged Israeli connection is one for the true conspiracy connoisseur. Germany has a historic (and, for neighbouring republics, frequently unfortunate) alliance with Croatia. America may have an interest in seeing the Bosnian Serbs shut down. What Israel would be doing, arming a state with a Nazi-blackened past, governed by a belligerent buffoon who has said that the Holocaust was "overstated," and which is currently fighting alongside a nominally Muslim army, is anyone's guess. I've heard this story elsewhere, though. There again, I've also heard, and more than once, the one about how Britain started another of the ex-Yugoslav wars by dressing MI6 agents up as Croatian paramilitaries and shelling Bosnian villages (though when you ask why Britain would do such a thing, you tend to get fairly imprecise answers).

"Oh, the stuff's all German," another Croat soldier tells me. Nenad Vrbanic, twenty-seven, is known to all as Charlie, thanks to a childhood bout of meningitis that left him with one leg shorter than the other and a stilted, Chaplinesque walk. Charlie is also of the Istrian 119th, but a little less ebullient than Major Bulic about their triumphal march into Plitvice. "We got lost," he says, "and that's where we ended up."

I tell Charlie I went through some of the same towns he did, and mention the throngs of wandering livestock. He tells me that these hapless animals came in handy, as Croat soldiers herded them across paddocks to clear mines. Unforgiveably, but unavoidably, this Pythonesque visual image provokes giggles in both of us. Charlie also tells me that one house he "captured" himself had been fled in such a hurry that there was a meal cooking on the stove.

Charlie has extraordinary silver-blue eyes, wispy sideburns and looks like he should be playing bass in Supergrass. When he's not fighting for Croatia, he spends his time "at home, listening to rock'n'roll—Lynyrd Skynyrd, Hendrix, Jefferson Airplane and The Allman Brothers." He volunteered in 1990, "because I love Croatia." Charlie also says he's a pacifist, and solemnly informs me that "one human life is more important than politics or nation."

Yet he keeps risking his own.

"It's under my skin," he shrugs. "It's a drug."

He says something else to the interpreter.

"He wants to know," she says, "if you do not love your country as well. Would you not fight if you were attacked?"

It's not a question I'd presume to answer. The lack of plausible military threats to most western nations at this end of this century allows most of us to love our homelands like we love distant relatives—glad they're there, and all that, but we don't give them a lot of thought, except during World Cups. I suppose if Australia was invaded by New Zealand or menaced by militant Tasmanian secessionists, then I'd do what I usefully could—even if this would most likely amount to keeping out of the way—but the possibility doesn't keep me awake nights.

Charlie takes the point, and I ask him whether or not he thinks that when the war ends, ex-Yugoslavs will be able to live together again.

"No," he says. "People have suffered, and they can't forget."

But none of them are going to go anywhere. The people of Western Europe get on with each other, more or less, despite two terrible wars this century. What's so special about this place?

"This," says Charlie, with exasperation and, I think, a certain defiant pride, "is the Balkans."

IT'S PROBABLY AS good an answer as any. But there's a bottom line beneath the rhetoric and chauvinism, and I find it in a chicken shed near the Bihac Pocket village of Bajrici, not far from Cazin. This flimsy tin structure has been home for four years to thirteen gypsy families, all refugees from Bosanska Krupa. Among them is Sudic Hasib, a twenty-one-year-old with a firm handshake, a wintry, unshaven smile and a horrible, horrible mess where he should have a left leg.

Sudic's story, by Bosnian standards, is no big deal. Sudic wasn't killed in a headline-stealing massacre and shovelled into a satellite-detected mass grave. He wasn't interned behind wire, or tortured and starved in a sickeningly evocative detention camp. He wasn't a civilian evicted from his home for having the wrong surname, wrong accent or wrong ideas about God, and he wasn't forced to walk hundreds of miles to refuge.

Sudic was a soldier, and he fought, as soldiers do, and he got hurt, as soldiers will. On June 22, 1995, he was serving with the 511th brigade of the Army of Bosnia and Herzegovina near Vrnograc, when he was injured by shrapnel. He doesn't know who fired the shell—the 511th were in the thick of Bihac's multi-player fighting, and it could have been the Bosnian Serbs, or it could have been Abdic's militia. "It doesn't really matter," he says, and lights another cigarette.

The lower half of his left leg caught the worst of it, and is now held together by an unwieldy metal contraption, screwed into both ends of his shin and strapped in place by a bandage. Beneath the bandage, as Sudic cheerfully insists on showing me, is a yawning wound that exposes the bone pretty much from knee to ankle, as wide as it is deep. A nurse from a nearby hospital dabs at it with antiseptic pads, and trades banter with Sudic, but it's the kind of joking people do to keep each other going when they've been assigned to a task they know is futile. Gangrene has already claimed three of the toes on Sudic's left foot. He lives in a room built from wooden crates in a tin chicken shed, and winter is approaching.

And he's no big deal. Jasmina, also twenty-one, an interpreter from Cazin, can't understand why I want to know so much about him. "This is nothing," she says, and Sudic's resolutely unperturbed expression suggests that he agrees with her. People get used to the strangest things—I suppose I'd feel the same about a visitor to London taking an appalled interest in someone sleeping in a shop doorway. Jasmina's own brother suffered a head wound in the fighting for Bihac. "But he'll be okay," she'd said, earlier, rapping herself on the forehead. "He has a Bosnian head—very hard."

But it's this very banality of Sudic's story, his little tragedy lost in the enormous one around him, that's bothering me. While the alleged leaders of western civilisation continue to regard the war in Bosnia with the baffled distaste of Etonian prefects who have been asked to sort out the brawl happening in the playground of the borstal down the road, Sudic's story will be retold countless times, adding further ugly grist to the Balkan mill of guilt and revenge.

Two days later, as our train out of Zagreb rolls out through the deep lime valleys of the Sava River and heads towards Llubljana, the song playing on my Walkman is Neil Young's electrified, outraged version of Dylan's "Blowin' In The Wind."

You know the words.

18

BORNE TEHRAN

By IranAir to Caracas
MARCH 2007

THIS ONE WAS spotted by Andrew Tuck, editor of *Monocle*, who has
a rare and treasurable knack for finding a way into a story that few others
would even begin to think of. We had talked vaguely about doing something
by way of illustrating the alliance that appeared to be flourishing between
Iran's president, Mahmoud Ahmadinejad, and his Venezuelan counterpart,
Hugo Chavez. A lesser publication would have contented itself with getting
some hack to cobble together something from the news cuttings; Andrew,
reading around the subject, noticed that IranAir was opening a route to
Caracas, and called to ask if I fancied trying it out. At the risk of giving away
the ending, I answered in the affirmative.

I'd never been to Iran before, and at time of writing I haven't returned, and
though the couple of days I spent in Tehran on this trip scarcely qualify me
as an authority on the Islamic Republic, it is one of the joys of travelling as a
journalist that you can learn a lot quite quickly, especially if it registers with
people that you might serve as a conduit for their feelings. In Iran especially,
it is not easy to be unobstrusive and independent as a visiting journalist:
the Department of Foreign Affairs issues you with (and charges you for, and
wastes half a day of your life wrangling) an escort, who translates for you,
possibly even reliably, and brandishes the appropriate pieces of rubber-
stamped official stationery every time some interfering yahoo in uniform tries

to arrest you for behaving like a foreign journalist. Annoying though this is, it does mean that people talk to you, and I thought some of what they said was interesting, especially given that they appeared to have no compunction about saying it in front of our government minder. One afternoon, as we photographed the totalitarian concrete origami of the Azadi monument, a besuited commuter paused to ask, in English, "Why do you photograph this? This country is turning to shit." Several other people were insistent that I record their dissatisfactions, which were largely to do with lack of economic opportunity and surfeit of Koranic strictures upon everyday existence.

As became clear a couple of years later, when Iran was convulsed by violent protest about the results of its presidential election—or, to employ the correct technical term, "election"—these people were not alone in their frustrations. Nor, I'm sure, were the Iranian women on the flights I took, whose reaction to the lights and beeps that denote imminent landing or the achievement of cruising altitude also struck me as significant (and hopeful) straws in the wind. On being informed that the first IranAir flight I caught, from London's Heathrow, would shortly, Insh'allah, be landing in Tehran, they rummaged resignedly in their carry-on luggage for the scarves and shawls that would shroud them in accordance with the dress code that Iran enforces upon its female population under threat of violence (writing or reading it as clearly as that helps, I find, in reaching the appropriate pitch of anger at this idiocy). On the outbound journey, upon hearing that we'd cleared Iranian airspace, the drab, observant garb was immediately stashed. I remember thinking that IranAir should add a second light next to the seatbelt indicator, perhaps in the shape of a ranting cleric, and/or alter their takeoff and landing announcements ("We will shortly be landing in Tehran. Please raise your seats to the upright positions, stow your tray tables, switch off all electronic equipment—and, if you're female, enact acquiescence to the institutional misogyny of our homeland, a country where grown men, paid by the government, in the twenty-first century, are licensed to threaten, arrest or hit women for flashing an untoward quantity of hair").

For reasons surpassing my understanding, we remain, as a species, bewilderingly content to excuse all manner of nonsense so long as someone asserts divine sanction for it. I don't claim to know all that—much one of the benefits of doing a job that involves finding stuff out is that you are constantly reminded of the unfathomable expanses of your ignorance. But I've been around a bit, by now, and I hold at least a couple of truths to be self-evident.

Any government that rules by fear is illegitimate. And anybody who claims to speak or act on God's behalf is insane.

★ ★ ★

TEHRAN AND CARACAS appear, to understate matters recklessly, curious candidates for an air link. Tehran is the capital of a Central Asian Islamic republic. Caracas is the capital of a South American "Bolivarian"—in honour of Simon Bolivar, serial vanquisher of South America's Spanish imperial overlords—republic. Tehran is a drab, joyless, religiously straitened hovel whose people make what merry they dare behind the closed doors of private homes, and where alcohol is illegal (although available, we've been pleased to discover, if you fall in with the wrong crowd). Caracas, or so I've been reading, is a colourful, lively, unbuttoned sort of place whose people are cheerful even when they're not out drinking until sunrise. Tehran's women use more material restraining their hair than many Caraqueno females apparently do covering their entire bodies. Iran is probably the only country in the world not plagued by Venezuelan buskers.

The reason for the establishment of this route—the flight I'm sitting on, alongside *Monocle* photographer Christopher Sturman, is only the third of what is intended to be a weekly service—is the one thing that does unite Iran and Venezuela: brash, populist, ambitious presidents radiating a disdain of the United States, an erratic respect for human rights and a streak of what might be charitably described as eccentricity. Iran's Mahmoud Ahmadinejad threatens the destruction of a fellow member of the UN and convenes covens of Holocaust-deniers. Venezuela's Hugo Chavez, more amiably if no less oddly, has, for much of his eight-year reign, hosted a weekly four-hour television programme, *Alo Presidente*, a good deal of which is devoted to the spirited abuse of his opponents.

Ahmadinejad and Chavez have become friends of the enemy-of-my-enemy variety. They have visited each other's countries, embraced each other as revolutionaries, supported each other diplomatically, and IranAir's ludicrous Caracas route is an emblem of this alliance. During my brief stay in Tehran, I have been soliciting the opinions of the people I've encountered: every response has included some, if not all, of the words "crazy," "political" and "bullshit." In fairness to the two leaders, while their relationship may have begun as instinctive solidarity against a common, larger foe, this odd couple do have some other overlapping concerns. Iran has the third largest oil reserves on Earth, Venezuela the seventh. Iran owns the world's second-biggest natural gas stores, Venezuela the ninth.

From the perspective of a window seat in economy class, it's clear that little of this wealth has flowed to IranAir. Before the Ayatollah Khomeini's Islamic revolution in 1979, the state-owned airline possessed a prestigious cachet similar to that enjoyed by Emirates today. However, IranAir's American routes were an inevitable early casualty of Khomeini's seizure of power, and the sanctions imposed upon Iran since have restricted the purchase of new aircraft. For the passenger, this isn't all bad. IranAir's small fleet of ageing planes have an air of charming retro gentility, their cabins decorated with silver and blue geometric shapes only otherwise seen on the shower curtains of midwestern American motels. And despite the strictures under which it operates, the airline has a superb safety record—it cannot be blamed for its worst disaster of modern times, the 1988 downing of an Airbus A300 over the Persian Gulf by the USS Vincennes, with the loss of all 290 aboard.

It's just as well that there is so much consideration that can be made of the political context of our journey, and the state of repair of our transport, as it turns out that we've some time to kill. Indeed, in the interregnum between boarding the elderly 747 and liftoff, Christopher and I would have had time to read, memorise and recite to each other the entire umpty-thousand-verse Iranian national epic *The Shahnameh* in the original Persian, a language neither of us speak. At 8:00 AM, our 5:00 AM departure still looks no closer to occurring. These hours pass without a word of explanation from the crew, nor the merest murmur of complaint from any of the passengers. Not for the first time in my travels in the Islamic world, I'm torn between admiration for the general stoic disdain for the insistent ticking of any nearby clock, and wanting to command a mutiny.

Another thought that occurs, as we wonder at what point our technical designation will change from "passengers" to "hostages," is that, despite the scoffing we'd heard in Tehran, it does look like the Caracas route has made some purchase on the local imagination. The plane is nearly full, though few aboard look dressed for the South American sun: most of the passengers are elderly women in religiously observant costumes and men in traditional Arab garb, a noticeable proportion of them blind and otherwise disabled. It does not take us long to discern that few, if any, of these people have sombreros in their checked-in luggage: they're Syrian pilgrims, who've been visiting Shi'a shrines in Iran, and they're only going as far as Damascus. As the 747's engines come alive, and the cabin loudspeakers quote sonorously from the Koran, and the cabin screens fill with pictures of Mecca, Caracas seems even further away than it is.

We reach our first stop still having spent less time in the air than we have on the ground, even allowing for a circuitous route around the somewhat unpredictable airspace of Iraq. The couple of hours we wait in the transit lounge of Damascus International Airport are enlivened by the lesson in prevailing political realities offered by the souvenir stalls: alongside the t-shirts and keyrings emblazoned with the image of Syrian president Bashar-al-Assad are trinkets bearing the green and gold, clenched-fist-and-Kalashnikov logo of Hezbollah. Tempting though these are, the purchase is made resistible by the thought of the number of airport security procedures (Caracas, Frankfurt, Heathrow) still separating me from my home in London.

Our mood, as we brace ourselves to return to a much less populated aircraft, could not be characterised as optimistic. The interminable and unexplained delay in departing Tehran, though annoying, had hardly been surprising. Even prior to that, absolutely every stage of our booking, confirmation and check-in had been handled with truly fabulous incompetence—IranAir could only have got things more profoundly wrong if they'd checked me and Christopher in as cargo and issued boarding passes to our bags. By now, I am of the opinion that if Iran's nuclear programme is run like Iran's state airline, the day that Ahmadinejad fulfils his threat to wipe Israel off the map could be a bad one for Poland. However, upon reaching the aircraft's door, something finally goes right—and wondrously so. A uniformed vision at the top of the stairs, perhaps recognising myself and Christopher as men whose will to live is ebbing perilously, ushers us into business class in the nose of the plane. Our saviour is the Senior Flight Purser, Aryana Malekpour, and agreeably spacious though it is up forward, there's plenty of room in the back, as well—Ms. Malekpour explains that there are only sixty passengers aboard, and that at any rate this flight, given the fuel load necessary for the fourteen-hour haul to Caracas, could carry no more than a hundred. There is only one other passenger in business class, a silver-haired cove of distinguished mien who turns out, when introductions are effected, to be Lebanon's Consul to Venezuela.

After we reach cruising altitude, Ms. Malekpour dispenses a potted history of the aircraft along with our coffee. This 747 is called A4 Delta, and at thirty-two years it's the oldest aircraft in IranAir's fleet, though a recent overhaul is evident in the new pale blue, purple and pink paisley upholstery embracing the seats. Doubtless figuring that we'll be spending a bunch of time together, she also introduces us to the crew—several of whom, the saintly Ms. Malekpour included, have been with IranAir as long as the plane, and can remember when New York and Los Angeles were all in a week's work. In polar contrast to the ground-based contingent of IranAir, their in-flight staff are courteous, efficient, friendly, touchingly proud of their airline and their country and cheerfully talkative. All, that is, except one—he wears a brown suit, black sunglasses at all times, and reacts to my attempts at friendliness like he'd much rather be regarding me from the other end of a pair of toenail pliers. Like most undercover Middle Eastern intelligence operatives, he could scarcely be more obvious if he was wearing a t-shirt spangled with his agency's logo, and this is perfectly deliberate—a police state must ensure that its subjects know they're being policed (and they do know—a few crew members whisper requests not to report anything "political" they may have said, though not one of them utters a word that could be interpreted as disloyal to their airline, or their country).

When, to my considerable surprise, I'm led upstairs and onto the flight deck, I sit next to Flight Engineer Mohammed Reza Rafat. I ask him to outline difference between the pre-revolutionary IranAir of the Shah's Iran, and the IranAir of the post-1979 Islamic Republic.

"Well, we don't serve alcohol anymore," he grins. "And, of course, the female crew had to cover up."

While IranAir's male staff sport generic, vaguely military, black and white uniforms, IranAir's women are shrouded in an elaborate, but not ungraceful, dark blue and gold headdress.

"Also," says Rafat, "the men had to stop wearing ties."

I'd read that Khomeini objected to these on the grounds that they were offensively western.

"I don't know if that's true," says Rafat, adjusting the folded newspaper blocking the sunlight beaming into the cockpit's port window. "That's just what we were told."

At any rate, all the male aircrew maintain dutifully naked necks aside from the captain, James Farrahi—who is, as we swiftly learn, a man of firmly held beliefs. He initially refuses to be photographed for *Monocle* on the grounds that "I don't like the English." My efforts to make common cause with him on the grounds that I'm Australian fall upon stony ground. "There is no difference," he harumphs. When I ask him to elaborate, he accuses England of "screwing the world up with their conspiracies." (The UK ranks second to the US in Iran's official menagerie of bêtes noir—sort of the Great Satan's Little Helper; specifically, Iranians blame Britain, quite rightly, for its role in the 1953 coup d'etat which, with CIA connivance, removed secular nationalist prime minister Mohammed Mosaddeq and paved the way for the succession of dictatorial thuggery and theocratic foolishness which has misruled Iran ever since.) After a few cups of coffee, Christopher and I are able to persuade him a) that neither of us bear much, if any, personal responsibility for overthrowing Iran's last vaguely sane government, and b) more importantly, for our purposes, to pose for a picture.

Back in economy class, I meet a few Syrian contract labourers emigrating for building jobs in South America, but most of the passengers are middle-class Iranian professionals, hoping to take advantage of the tax concessions offered by Ahmadinejad to encourage business links with Venezuela. They ask me what I thought of Tehran, which is a potentially tricky moment, as what I think is that Tehran is about the least pleasant big city I can recall visiting, containing as it does everything that is bad about urban living (crowds, noise, traffic, filth) and redeemed by absolutely nothing that is good about it (freedom, opportunity, diversity, tolerance). However, I rarely lie, for the reason that I'm no good at it—I'm terrible at making things up, and even worse at delivering the falsehood convincingly—and so I tell them a version of the truth, which is that I hadn't much cared for it, but was sure it had hidden charms that take a while to flower, and so forth.

"No," says someone. "It is a terrible place. Next time you come to Iran, you must visit Shiraz."

"And Esfahan," says another. "My family are from Esfahan. You can stay with them."

"And Qom," offers another, suggesting the Iranian holy city and spiritual heart of Khomeini's revolution. "The religious guys are a bit weird, but it's very interesting."

I mention that during my brief stay in Tehran, our compulsory minder had taken us to visit Khomeini's vast and still unfinished mausoleum. This elicits the sort of patronising chuckles that a Londoner might make at hearing some rube's wide-eyed tales of visiting Madame Tussaud's. I ask one of my new friends—a grave, sharply suited management type—why he thinks IranAir have launched this new route.

"You ask," he retorts, in perfect English and a stentorian baritone, "why this flight is happening?"

Yes, I reiterate.

"This flight is happening," he declares, "because of something very important that our two great countries have in common."

Sensing a punchline in need of a set-up, I ask him what, exactly.

"Crazy presidents," he replies.

I ink this quote gratefully into my notebook with a promise that I won't attach his name.

"I didn't," he reminds me, returning to his newspaper, "say anything at all."

The return fare for the Tehran-Caracas route, another passenger tells me, is US$1500. He adds that there is a Lufthansa option via Frankfurt, which is only a little bit more expensive, so I ask whether his choice is informed at all by patriotic ardour.

"No," he says. "I like the space on board this one. And there's a really nice atmosphere."

And he's right. With so few aboard, and so much space, people—passengers and underemployed crew alike—meander and chat. Some visit the onboard prayer room, in which a screen displays a computerised graphic indicating the direction of Mecca. There is little else available in the way of distraction. IranAir offers none of the fripperies of modern air travel—no in-flight games, no seat-back movies, and only a couple of (entirely ignored) Iranian family comedies on the big screens, alternating with the SkyMap chronicling our progress across the Atlantic. There is an inflight magazine, *Homa*—named for the griffin-like creature of Persian mythology that also serves as IranAir's tailfin motif—but it's a drab melange of travel guide hackery unriveting even by the standards of inflight magazines. The halal food is pretty good, though—buttery rice with meat and vegetables.

Surprisingly, but rather delightfully, this lack of the usual amusements proves an unalloyed blessing as our unlikely journey around half the globe unfurls. The absence of the usual vacuous distractions—and the lack of any mood-altering agent stronger than Iran's Coca-Cola substitute Zam Zam—promotes an unusual focus on what a glorious thing air travel really is. We live in a world in which any middle-class wage earner can skip across the planet in less than a day, and we contrive to take this miracle for granted. Worse still, we actually complain about it (I mean, I did myself, only a few paragraphs ago). We whine about the food, moan about the queues, bitch about the legroom, sulk about being compelled to perform the dance of seven veils—or, rather, the dance of jacket, belt and shoes—at security. We've become so settled into a default position of reacting to flying like it's detention that we've forgotten that roaring across the sky at 1,000 kilometres an hour is about the coolest thing we ever get to do, the moment at which we are in closest contact with the possibilities of human imagination. It is astonishing, really, that we as a breed have reached a point where, given a choice, we'd rather watch *Friends* than the tops of clouds, or take Richard Curtis movies over the sun dipping behind the Cordillera de la Costa mountains that shield Caracas from the sea. The relationship between Iran and Venezuela may strike many as worrisome, but it has produced one of the great romantic, quixotic, travel-for-the-silly-sake-of-it experiences presently available.

Caracas's airport, like Venezuela's currency and any number of Venezuelan locations, is named after Simon Bolivar. It is, in every respect, a long way from Tehran: new, clean, spacious, as much like a mall with a runway attached as any major airport in Europe, and the large numbers of armed, uniformed men are at least friendly.

For flight IR744's pair of infidel passengers, Caracas also offers the welcome prospect of a restorative beer or several. Mighty forces appear determined to torment us further, however. The bars and bright lights of Caracas, in theory just thirteen miles over the hills, are in fact two and a half hours away, at the end of a traffic jam of such hilarious length that it could almost have been imported from Tehran.

19

(GET YOUR KICKS ON) BEIRUT 66

The Road to Damascus
AUGUST 2007

ANOTHER ADVENTURE PROMPTED by a phone call from Andrew Tuck at *Monocle.* "The road to Damascus," he declared. "Everybody knows what it means, but nobody knows what it's like. Go and find out."

I was happy to do this, because I'm always happy for a reason to visit Beirut in particular, and the Middle East in general—not necessarily for any rugged, righteous, bullet-chewing, seeker-of-truth-in-valley-of-death foreign correspondent reasons, but because the weather is lovely, the food fantastic, the scenery magnificent, the wine delectable, the women beautiful and the people in general supremely courteous and hospitable. If the Arabs could collectively grasp the wisdom of putting their lunatics and criminals in asylums and prisons, instead of installing them in their parliaments and palaces, they'd be the envy of all humanity.

As it happened, my peregrination along the Road to Damascus did prompt an epiphany of sorts, and it went like this. There are few things that the professionally opinionated enjoy more than a few hundred words' fulminating at the ignorance of the general public. My, how we love a good fulminate. We spend hours anxiously scanning news wires, searching for the latest poll which reveals that x percent of the population can't name their own president, that y percent think Afghanistan is where Gandalf lived, or that $

percent don't know the letters of the alphabet. From this raw material, we sculpt the prose equivalent of an accusingly pointing finger.

The assumption underlying these self-righteous tirades (and I should know; I've written a few) is that it's A Bad Thing that so many people know and care so little about politics. Mostly, this is an assumption to which I subscribe. However, the great thing about travelling is that one's assumptions are continually being prodded in the sternum and asked who they think they are, and in this excursion to Lebanon and Syria I found myself wondering whether the bovine complacency often demonstrated by large swathes of first-world electorates is really a problem—and whether, instead, popular indifference to politics should rank alongside literacy and child health as measures of national prosperity.

In Lebanon and Syria, as in all police states, war zones and sundry basket-cases, everybody knows their politics, because everybody has too. Not knowing your politics—not knowing who holds power, and where the limits of that power lie—can leave you dead, or ruined, or receiving a brisk education in prevailing realities as you hang by your ankles. Next time I read a lament that I live among people who, despite unparalleled opportunity for learning and participation, substantially choose not to give a crap, I plan to hum a happy tune.

★ ★ ★

"AND as he journeyed, he came near Damascus, and suddenly there shined about him a light from Heaven. And he fell to the Earth, and heard a voice saying unto him 'Saul, Saul, why persecutest me thou?'"
— ACTS 9:3-4

WELL, THE SUN is certainly bright out here, but nothing my Ray-Bans can't overcome. The only voices saying anything unto me are my translator keeping up a steady commentary on the view and, on the car's radio, the wearisomely inescapable purveyors of the global mall's muzak: Nelly Furtado, James Blunt, Christine Aguilera. As for persecutions, we hope to ward them off with a bagful of bureaucratic talismans: accreditation from Lebanon's Ministry of Information, a number for a contact at the Syrian equivalent. The Road to Damascus isn't what it used to be.

We are, it should be conceded, fudging slightly. It is simply impossible, today, to retrace exactly the journey that made the Road to Damascus a universally understood allegory for conversion. When the first-century Jewish vigilante Saul of Tarsus set off for Damascus around AD 36, intending to deal some uppity Christians an exemplary smiting, he did so from Jerusalem. Somewhere en route, Saul perceived a dazzling beam from the sky and heard the voice of Christ asking him what, in his father's name, he thought he was doing, or words to that effect. Saul swiftly got with the programme, and is remembered as St. Paul the Apostle. Thanks in no small part to the reluctance of Paul and other earnest types with beards to keep their revelations to themselves, his route between what are now the capitals of Israel and Syria is now blocked by barbed wire, fences, sandbags, minefields, history, blind fury and bad faith; the single border crossing between the two countries, at Quneitra, is only grudgingly open to Druze from the Golan Heights. So we're leaving from Beirut.

Not that this is a straightforward undertaking. In recent years, this version of the road to Damascus has hosted its share of upheaval. In 2005, Syrian troops withdrew along it, having been forced by massive popular protests to end their twenty-nine-year occupation of Lebanon following the immense bomb blast in Beirut that killed Lebanese Prime Minister Rafik Hariri. His assassination was widely blamed on Syria. In 2006, a year or so ago, this road teemed with Lebanese refugees from Israel's onslaught of that summer in response to the seizure of two Israeli soldiers by the Lebanese-based Hezbollah. Israeli aircraft struck several targets along the route.

What with one thing and another, we've been told, the Road to Damascus isn't as busy as it once was. At our hotel in Beirut, staff who help us wrangle a car and driver tell us that the road once thronged with Lebanese pilgrims visiting holy sites in Syria, and less devout voyagers seeking designer bargains (Benetton and other prized brands are apparently much cheaper in Syria). Now, with relations between the two countries at a sulky nadir—despite Syria's withdrawal, a steady tick of Lebanese politicians and journalists espousing anti-Syrian stances continue to meet spectacular ends—fewer Lebanese are visiting the neighbours.

Myself and photographer Cristobal Palma have persuaded two locals to join us: a driver, whom I'll call Peter, and a translator, whom I'll call Sheila. When we start out on the Damascus Road—that's what it's called—in Beirut, it's immediately noticeable that most of the traffic is coming the other way. It's quite early, and these are commuters descending from the hills for a day's work. The first significant landmark en route, past a district called Hazmi, is outside the Lebanese Ministry of Defence, the entrance of which is graced by one of the weirdest works of public art anywhere in the world: a ten-storey pillar of concrete, embedded with decommissioned trucks, tanks and artillery pieces. The work of the French sculptor Arman, it was unveiled in 1996 as a monument to the Lebanese Civil War of 1975-90.

The soldiers standing guard are used to bemused tourists photographing the thing—I've done it myself before—but they're a bit edgy. Not all that far away—in tiny Lebanon, nothing is all that far away—their comrades are at war, fighting the militants of the Fatah al-Islam sect, who are mounting a prolonged last stand in the wreckage of a Palestinian refugee camp near Tripoli. More than a hundred Lebanese soldiers have died in three months of fighting. The soldiers outside the MoD allow Cris to photograph the monument, but only from a few prescribed angles, to avoid capturing any images of nearby buildings. Though I suspect that the chances of us learning anything the Israeli Air Force don't already know are remote, we cooperate.

From there, we detour through a verdant hill suburb called Yarze—the sort of place which boasts its own country club and a villa belonging to the billionaire Saudi arms dealer Adnan Khashoggi (which, Sheila laughingly notes, was commandeered by the Syrians for use as a headquarters, and is now in the possession of the Lebanese army). We rejoin the road in a queue of belching trucks, groaning up the hill towards a suburb called Araya. The climb is now steep enough to make a difference in the speeds of the opposing lanes. Coming downhill, Lebanese traffic looks like a demented cavalry charge, the sleek stallions branded with the logos of Audi and Mercedes-Benz whipping through the ponderous high-sided carthorses trucking freight into Beirut. Going uphill, wheezing, groaning and grinding gears, the same array of vehicles resembles a depressed, weary retreat after a regrettable result at the point of contact. By the roadside, billboards maladriotly translated into the snappy gibberish of advertising mark our path: Shhhh Silent Parquet;

Sexy Hot Summer Shower Gel; Loke International Hair Transplant Centre; Burger King—Welcome To Aley.

Aley, like its succeeding suburb, the resort of Bhamdoun, boasts glorious views across the barren uplands (the cool hills around Beirut, at least when not hosting invading armies or wars, are popular holiday destinations—in summer, Arabs vacation away from the heat). By this point, Peter has begun concentrating ostentatiously, hunched over the steering wheel, scanning the way ahead with the nervous intensity of a sniper. His concerns, however, are not to do with anything so glamorous as militia activity or enemy aircraft, but with his fellow Lebanese motorists.

"Very dangerous road from here," he mutters.

Proof is not long in coming. We pass a three-car tangle of metal, sprinkled with shattered glass, surrounded by soldiers and drivers sorting out who hit whom and how. Further along, an olive Range Rover, shortened the length of its engine block by what must have been an emphatic shunt, is being loaded onto a recovery truck. Beyond that, a crowd of laughing bystanders help rescue a four-wheel-drive whose careless owner has planted a front wheel in an open gutter.

Aside from the cool haven of St. George's church, still beautiful despite the Civil War-era shrapnel damage, and a children's funfair, whose depressed owner offers to sell me the business for US$200,000, the buildings along the road are functional, modern and ugly. The industrial squalor is only interrupted by the surreally serene appearance of a Bedouin encampment, the nomads' goats gathered beneath a canvas canopy. It may be that in this region there's little point in dallying too long on attractively crenellated columns—you never know how long your building is going to stay up. A few years ago, a mighty bridge was built linking the suburbs of Sawfar and Daher el Baydar, shaving a decent lump off the journey time. Last year, an Israeli bomb punched the middle out of the bridge, returning the traffic to the winding slog through the valley it traversed. The span is being repaired now. By the valley road, a billboard erected by Hezbollah calls last summer's war "A Victory From God." I've barely been in Lebanon forty-eight hours on this trip, and this must be at least the hundredth giant Hezbollah poster I've seen: the road in from Beirut's airport is lined with grinning portraits of Hezbollah Secretary-General Sayyed Hassan Nasrallah, and the whole city is upholstered with gloating images of wrecked Israeli military hardware (in the southern suburbs, Hezbollah have even established a temporary museum chronicling the war, which we'd visited the previous day: the highlight was an audio-visual display featuring a captured Merkava tank, surrounded by mangled dummies dressed in IDF uniform and splashed with red paint).

The political billboards increase in number as the road unfurls, Lebanon's uncountable rival factions seeking to outdo each other for volume and position. A few honour one of the country's survivors— Nabih Berri, former Amal warlord, now speaker of Lebanon's parliament. Many more are shrines to Berri's less fortunate rivals and colleagues, graphic reminders that Lebanese politics is, as a pastime, at least as hazardous as driving on Lebanese roads: Rafik Hariri, blasted all over Beirut's seafront; George Hawi, the communist party leader killed by a car bomb in June 2005; Gebran Tueni, the journalist and MP killed by a car bomb in December 2005; Pierre Gemayel, Minister for Industry—and nephew of an assassinated Lebanese president—gunned down in November 2006; Walid Eido, the member of parliament blown up in June 2007. "Martyrs for Justice," says the slogan beneath the portrait of Eido, and his son, who died in the same blast.

We get our first glimpse of the Bekaa Valley from the top of a vertiginous winding road. The flat green sward of the Bekaa is infamous for secreting the camps of organisations unbeloved by the United States, and better liked for its fabulous wines and dairy produce. When we reach Chtaura, it's time for lunch, and Sheila, unlike bemusing numbers of Lebanese, disdains the options of Kentucky Fried Chicken and McDonald's, instead directing us to the Jarjoura laiterie—a purveyor of the Bekaa's local specialties of yoghurt and cheese. The proprietor, Antoine, a forty-seven-year veteran of the store, labours beneath a black and white portrait of his utterly identical father, who founded the shop in 1922. As he tots up the bill for our lunch of (fantastic) haloumi cheese wrapped in rolls of salty flat bread, I ask him how business has been.

"Not great," he says. "But, thank God, better than last year."

Apparently, people fleeing bombardment tend not to stop for sandwiches.

In downtown Chtaura, we ask Peter to pull his air-conditioned Volvo into the taxi station, so we can see how the locals travel. The cars that ply the route between here and Damascus, for around US$5 per person each way, are yellow-painted, battered, rusty, backfiring American sedans, mostly Dodges and Pontiacs dating from the 1970s. Given that they are, by definition, being driven by Arabs who don't speak much English, Chtaura is at least this evocative of New York. Stalls around the garages sell cheap watches, dodgy electronica, dubious cosmetics, including "breast-firming cream" and "sex appeal gel," and Saddam Hussein lighters. Sheila picks up some jasmine oil for her hair.

Chtaura offers little but the practicalities of travel—food, transport, repairs. For this reason, I'm attracted to a shop whose window is stacked with rainbows of multi-coloured glass hookah pipes. The young proprietor is reluctant to give his name but happy enough to chat. He says he sells to Lebanese, but not to locals—rather, to the diaspora when they return for brief visits to the old country. Since last summer, though, they're staying put, and if business doesn't pick up soon, he's going to join them, in Canada or Paraguay.

"The Israelis bombed a bridge 300 metres away," he says, gesturing back up the street. "I was scared they'd hit that one," he continues, pointing directly out his window at the canal covering we've just driven across. "I don't want to live like this."

I ask if he fears another war.

"Who knows?" he shrugs. "It's nothing to do with Lebanon. It's all between Israel and Hezbollah."

On one wall of the shop hangs a portrait of Saddam Hussein, superimposed on a view of Jerusalem.

THE LEBANESE BORDER crossing is an astonishing, infuriating shambles, the failure of which to escalate into riotous violence is unbeatable testament to the extraordinary patience and courtesy that define day-to-day interactions in the Middle East. Unless, of course, the chaos is a consequence of the same philosophical good humour—after a few hours' wait in the crowd and heat and noise and exhaust fumes, I can't help feeling that the surly, slothful soldiers running the place would buck their ideas up considerably under the threat of spontaneous lynchings. Cris asks someone in uniform if he can photograph the mess, and Peter brandishes our Lebanese press credentials. This elicits mirthless laughter, and the promise that, if we're contemplating trying our luck anyway, plainclothes spotters are lurking. I pass the time by calling the Syrian Ministry of Information in Damascus, seeking assurance that we'll be allowed to take pictures once across the border, if we ever get across the border. A typically circular Middle Eastern conversation ensues.

"You will need accreditation from us."

It's the kind of thing the Syrian embassy in London might have mentioned when we applied for press visas. How do we get that?

"From here in Damascus."

A bit late now, but out of academic interest, is there any other way?

"No."

But we want to take pictures on the way. It's kind of the point.

"Yes, you will need accreditation from us."

In Damascus.

"Yes."

Sensing that this discussion could occupy us both until the sun collapses on itself, extinguishing all human life and reducing our planet to a dead ball of frozen carbon, I ask how the functionary how he rates our chances of making it to Damascus unarrested so long as we don't photograph anything that looks military.

"You will need accreditation from us here in Damascus."

I'm gnawing gaily on my phone when Peter tugs on my sleeve, having somehow negotiated the impenetrable queue on our behalf.

"I have found some friends here," he grins, "we can go."

For two countries so close together, and with so intertwined a history, Lebanon and Syria do their best to keep their distance. Between the two frontiers is seven kilometres of black asphalt ribbon winding through rocky red jebels, lined with trucks awaiting permission to cross. There's one immense—and startling—landmark in this no-man's land: a huge, gleaming duty free mall, like an extension to Singapore's Changi airport that got delivered to the wrong address, complete with a Dunkin' Donuts franchise. The Syrian border itself is marked by faded stone arches bearing the portraits of Hafez al-Assad, who ruled Syria for thirty years from 1970, and Bashar al-Assad, the young British-educated ophthalmologist who inherited the family business upon his father's death in 2000. Bashar was never supposed to become president—the heir was always his elder brother Basel, who forfeited his place in the succession when he crashed his Mercedes-Benz in Damascus in 1994, with fatal consequences. As if to banish any doubts about who is in charge now, the road beyond the border is punctuated at approximately ten-metre intervals with images of Bashar overlaid with a fingerprint in the colours of the Syrian flag, above the dedication, "We love you." With only a few gaps, these continue all the way into Damascus.

Peter pulls into a petrol station, the forecourt of which is plastered with posters of Assad Jr. and Nasrallah (since last summer's war, perceived throughout the Arab world as a victory for Hezbollah and a humiliation for Israel, Hezbollah's clenched-fist-and-Kalashnikov logo has also begun to appear in Syria with a frequency that can only be officially encouraged). The petrol is cheaper here, Peter explains—twenty litres costs US$15 in Lebanon, $11 in Syria. Once on the road, he slams his foot down, the identical Assads lining the central reservation whipping by in a blur like an extremely low budget animation. I ask him if he's just taking advantage of the better road.

"Partly that," translates Sheila. "But also because here you can fix anything with money."

(A couple of days later, we'll see the truth of this when Peter, having collected us from Damascus, eases our surprisingly unharassed progress back into Lebanon by palming a quantity of notes to Syrian border guards).

It gradually becomes clear that there's another, more fundamental reason for Peter's haste: he doesn't really want to be in Syria, especially not with a journalist and a photographer who still don't have the proper credentials from Damascus. Most of Cris's requests to stop the car so he can take pictures meet a flat, "No. Not here," and when Peter does pull up by some roadside fruit stalls, near the town of Dimas, the extravagant greetings of the fourteen-year-old proprietor, Bilal—"Welcome in Syria!"—do little to calm him. Peter's agitation is initially a little difficult to take seriously. I've travelled in many police states, and it's no exaggeration to say that the fear can seem part of the weather, as tangible as sunshine or rain. Syria doesn't feel like that to me—the only soldier we see in the short rush from the border to Damascus waves to us—but it certainly does to Peter.

"You have to understand," Peter says, "they won't just take the cameras. They will take you to the police station."

He's also asking me to understand that while the probable worst that could befall myself and Cris would be a recital of the Riot Act and deportation, matters might be much less amusing for a Lebanese citizen accused of ferrying foreign spies. Back in the car, even though Cris resigns himself to photographing on the move, his every click of the shutter provokes winces from Peter and exclamations of, "Oh my God. Forget about it," from Sheila, especially as we pass through the area that harbours the now closed but still fearful Mezze prison.

The geography has become less hospitable, as well. Lebanon is green, fertile and hilly, much more reminiscent of Italy or Greece than of any preconceptions of Arabia. Syria is desert, a beige sea of sand, and while the view as we hurtle to Damascus has a certain rugged grandeur, it's hard to enjoy it properly for the inescapable gaze of the president, staring peevishly from hundreds of posters. Peter and Sheila only cheer up once, upon noticing that one silver Mercedes, which briefly pulls up alongside us before disappearing at hilarious speed, contains Nancy Ajram, the Lebanese pop starlet, whom we've already seen, back on the other side of the border, pouting from dozens of Coca-Cola billboards.

SAUL OF TARSUS'S journey to Damascus ended at an address on the Street which is called Straight (Acts 9:11), and so does ours—at least after a diversion via Syria's Ministry of Information where, with the aid of a wall-sized panoramic photograph of Damascus, the press officer who issues our accreditation outlines which parts of the city we are permitted to take pictures of.

In Damascus, the world's oldest continually inhabited city, the New Testament is almost a street directory, and the Street which is called Straight is now the main artery of the Old City's bustling souk. Somewhere along here, at the home of a man named Judas, Saul received baptism and salvation from a disciple called Ananias. All I got was a scoop of the fabulous local ice cream from the famous Bakdash cafe, and a camel-hair rug for the hall (still, as Saul/Paul would later write to Timothy: "And having food and raiment, let us be therewith content" —1 Timothy 6:8). The deal for the carpet is sealed after the traditional hour's worth of tea, amiable bickering over the price, and survey of Middle Eastern politics.

"We're actually pretty busy," says the young shopkeeper, in impeccable English. "It's still a surprise to me. After 9/11, we started getting more Americans coming here—they seem to want to find out more about the Middle East."

Angling for a neat validation of the Road to Damascus metaphor, I ask if he thinks any of them have left his shop, or his country, with their minds changed about anything.

"I don't think so," he grins. "They still don't understand us, and we still don't understand them. But it's nice that they try."

20

CALIFORNIA SCREAMING

Courtney Love in Los Angeles
OCTOBER 1991

THIS IS *THE* oldest story in this book, and very arguably the proverbial oldest story in the book: of a determined young woman with a dream descending upon Hollywood. Courtney Love—for it is she—is a name that will now be known to most readers, which is, I suppose, in the way of these things, what she would have desired when she first determined to fling herself upon the mercy of Tinseltown. While revisiting this piece, I spent some time perusing Courtney's audaciously punctuated postings on various websites, attempting to determine whether she sounded like someone who'd got what she wanted or—and this is always the more difficult trick—wanted what she'd got. Given that Courtney now chooses to communicate in a dialect similar to that of a relative newcomer to the English language on mushrooms undertaking an elementary typing module on a trawler adrift in a typhoon while a stoned kitten staggers back and forth across her keyboard, gleaning definitive insights proved difficult.

That said, I'd still advise skimming through this story until you get to the bits in quotation marks. My first-timer's observations of Los Angeles are trying rather too hard—though I've not warmed to the place overmuch on subsequent visits—but Courtney's thoughts, when laid out correctly spelled and punctuated, are interesting and perceptive. I think she already understood that the notoriety she craved was likely to prove more a poisoned chalice than a holy grail—and this, remember, was at a time when her "fame" barely extended further than two clubs in Hollywood and one pub in Camden Town, and pretty much the only publication taking much interest in Courtney was the one that had sent me to interview her.

That publication was *Melody Maker*, which had been first aboard the Courtney Love bandwagon thanks to my predecessor as the paper's reviews editor, Everett True. I'm dedicating this chapter to ET, now virtually resident at everetttrue.wordpress.com, and actually resident in Brisbane, Australia, for two reasons. First and foremost, by way of gratitude for printing in *Melody Maker* an unsolicited review of Straitjacket Fits at Sydney's Lansdowne Hotel in 1989, which I posted to him on spec from the old country when the idea of writing for *Melody Maker* was, for me, what the idea of being a globally famous rock star was for Courtney at around the time I met her. Had Everett not approved my scribblings for print, the last twenty years of my life would, I suspect, have been altogether less entertaining (it's also possible that, somewhere back home, there's some girl I never met who'll never know what a debt she owes him). Second, and more pertinently to this story, I'd like to thank Everett for offering what is still the wisest advice I've ever been given before embarking on an assignment. "For the love of all that is wonderful," counseled the great man, the day before I left, "do not give that woman your home phone number."

★　★　★

"PEOPLE WANT ME to be evil," shrugs Courtney Love. She yawns, again. Her blonde hair is so intricately and exuberantly tangled that it almost looks like the rest of her is but a life support system for the extravagant thatch on top. "People want me to be evil because of how I come across on stage and on record. People really, really do want me to be evil. And I'm really kind of not."

She doesn't seem especially evil so far. She's been making sure my glass is full, worrying that the noise of Nirvana soundchecking upstairs is going to sod up the interview tape, harassing someone from Nirvana's crew about getting a friend of mine on the guest list for tonight's show and telling me that we can do all this later if I'd rather go back to my hotel and have a nap, because I really do look very tired. I've come to

Los Angeles to meet rock'n'roll's new screaming witch vixen harpy she-devil, and I feel like I'm having tea with someone's aunt.

We're in a dressing room backstage at the Palace Theatre in Hollywood. Tonight, Courtney Love's band, Hole, will open here for Nirvana. Somewhere above and behind us, Nirvana's soundcheck continues, the usual formless racket of clonking drums, squawking guitars and amplified mumbling about monitors. The other three members of Hole are also in the room, sitting on plastic chairs or the floor. Jill Emery, who never says anything at all, plays bass. Eric Erlandson, who is the least assuming lead guitarist—and possibly the least assuming human being—I've ever met, doesn't say anything either. Carolyn Rue, who has a stud in her chin and plays drums, says things only when Courtney's mouth is otherwise occupied drinking or eating, and then mostly says things about Courtney.

"She's not evil, no," says Carolyn. "She's . . . not impossible, but she's difficult. Difficult because she's got something in her mind that's going this fast, and for someone else to pick it up, they've got to be thinking just as fast, because then she's onto the next thing, and if you're not keeping up, you get lost really quickly."

I'm beginning to get the idea. Courtney has a knack of answering questions before they're asked, accepting compliments before they're offered, spotting every gambit from six moves away.

"Don't jaywalk on Hollywood Boulevard," says Courtney, apropos of nothing. "The cops hang around on the corners busting tourists to make up their quotas. I'm serious."

LOS ANGELES—BASICALLY Tehran with film studios—is horrible. It's ugly and it smells bad and contains a greater density of humourless and desperately stupid people than anywhere on earth. When the big earthquake finally comes, it will cause billions of dollars' worth of improvements.

Los Angeles is annoying in all the ways you knew it was going to be annoying, and that's kind of annoying in itself. People really do tell you to have a nice day. Restaurant staff do actually say, "Hi, I'm Wayne, and I'll be your waiter." And they still smile pleasantly and vapidly at you if you respond, "G'day, I'm Andrew, and I'll be your customer," or, "Cool! Can I meet the bloke who washes the dishes, as well?" or even, "Mate, I don't care what your name is, as long as you keep your thumb out of my soup."

But Los Angeles is, as advertised, a city where miracles happen. On my first afternoon in Hollywood, as I'm walking, jetlagged and blinking, along Sunset Strip, a car screeches to a tyre-scorching halt on the road next to me. For a second, I wonder if I've just been discovered or if I'm about to get shot. Then Barry gets out of the car. Barry is a friend of mine from Sydney who was staying with me in London three months ago before going off to drive round America. He is possibly the only person in the entire North American continent who'd recognise me. When he left my flat, he forgot his leather jacket, which I have been borrowing regularly since. In fact, I realise, as he walks towards me looking like someone who's just found a pterodactyl in his broom closet, I'm wearing it right now.

"There you are," I say, handing him the jacket. "You forgot this."

It is, yes, just like a movie.

"We'll always have Paris," says Barry.

COURTNEY SAYS THAT her band couldn't have come from any city but Los Angeles, though she knows that Hole are not a Los Angelean band, at least not a proper one. Courtney seems to be one of those people who need to define themselves against what they're not, and if she's trying to define herself as against shallowness, complacency and inexorable idiocy, then she's come to the right place.

"When I first moved here and started this band," she explains, "I lived a block away from Hollywood Boulevard."

On Hollywood Boulevard, there are shops that sell "Rock Star Accessories." They are not joking. Nobody in Los Angeles ever is. I bought a new leather jacket in one of these shops, because Barry wanted his back. The man in the shop told me that the jacket I'd bought would "look real cool with maybe one of these portraits of Axl Rose or the dude from Skid Row airbrushed on the back." He wasn't joking either, though I definitely laughed.

"Yeah," continues Courtney. "Right near those shops. Anyway, the building my apartment was in was near this thing called the Guitar Institute of Technology. It's this school, a college, it's really expensive, and it's full of kids with trust funds from all over America learning how to play heavy metal guitar like Steve Vai. So, in every other fucking apartment in my building, there was a guy from G.I.T."

I maintain that this is the only city in the world where nobody among the school's founders would have noticed the initials.

"And so all day and all night it was like freeeeeeeowwww bwam bwam bwam widdly widdly skreeeeee widdly widdly, like really fucking loud. Anyway. We, I mean, Hole, my band, we had a couple of practices in my room, and in seconds, all these heavy metal kids would be banging on the door yelling 'Hey! What the fuck are you doing?'"

This can only be a recommendation.

The first song Courtney ever learned to play was Iggy Pop's "I Wanna Be Your Dog." Eric's was "Rock'N'Roll All Nite" by Kiss. Jill first made her parents wince with the riff from The Sex Pistols' "God Save The Queen," and Carolyn first hit things along to The Psychedelic Furs' "Sister Europe." Hole's debut album, *Pretty On The Inside*, sounds a bit like all of these without sounding quite like any of them.

"What do you mean?"

I have no idea. Actually, Hole remind me mostly of The Go-Go's, whom they sound nothing like at all. Something to do with being Californian but not taking it seriously.

"We used to play 'This Town' live."

That was always my favourite Go-Go's song. It was about being Californian but not taking it seriously.

"I'm pleased you mentioned them," says Courtney. "I like it when people say we do good pop songs. I'm really getting into songwriting as a craft, so maybe our next album will be more like a tribute to The Beach Boys. Or maybe not. But I do know that we are still evolving, and that there's a pop consciousness out there that I really don't know anything about. But it's nice of you to say that."

I didn't. She did. We'll let it go. I wonder if I should pursue The Go-Go's analogy further, through the fame and the drugs and the split-ups and breakdowns, and tell Courtney that I think it'd be just great if, in ten years from now, she was all respectable and designer-clothed and married to a besuited Republican party drone and plaguing the world's airwaves with anodyne radio ballads.

"I know this record is really bilious and black-hearted in a lot of ways, but there's a lot of other shit in us . . ."

Courtney gets up and goes outside to get some more coffee. A slight blonde bloke with red eyes and black and grey stubble comes in, says something to Eric, then nods at me and asks after another writer at *Melody Maker*. I have half an idea that I know this guy from somewhere, but I can't place him, so I just assure him that our mutual friend is fine, or at least was last time I saw him.

"Well, tell him hello," he says, and leaves.

Courtney reappears.

"Was that Kurt?" she says.

ON HOLLYWOOD BOULEVARD, next to that stupid Chinese theatre thing that looks like a suburban Chinese takeaway that has been at the Chinese swimming team's medical kit, sad little men in sun visors sell maps of where the stars live. Barry and I buy one, determined that we cannot live another day without seeing Zsa Zsa Gabor's letterbox or the front gate of that bloke in *Star Wars* who wasn't Harrison Ford, whatever his name was. Mark something, we think.

We spend an afternoon driving through pristine private suburbs with their own fences and police forces, filled with houses so big we wonder if the front and back porches have different postcodes or, in a couple of cases, if they're even in the same time zone.

Mostly, we wonder why anyone with enough money to buy one of these places would choose to live in Los Angeles.

COURTNEY CHOSE TO live in Los Angeles. It was convenient. It seemed like a good idea at the time. And anyway, to judge by her thus far modest but already riotously entertaining press file, she'd already lived everywhere else. The details vary according to Courtney's mood at the time and the imagination of whoever's writing it all down, but there're a few things we can be reasonably sure of.

She moved around a lot as a kid, even being dragged as far afield as Australia and New Zealand. She was the singer in an early lineup of Faith No More. She lived in England for a bit, where she appears to have done or said something to annoy Julian Cope, which is another entry on the credit side of her ledger. She has almost been a famous actress, having been considered for the starring roles in *Sid And Nancy* and *Last Exit To Brooklyn*, though how seriously she was considered is open to argument. She very definitely made a brief appearance in Alex Cox's point-free spaghetti-western farce *Straight To Hell*, about which she says, "Yeah, well."

Courtney Love, already, is a lot better known than what Courtney Love does.

"It's really weird," she says. "I mean, it's your life, and your life is being used to sell papers, or records, or . . ."

And that's just the stuff that's actually happened. Perhaps calling a song "Teenage Whore" was asking for trouble.

"A lot of that is fictionalised. I mean, no offence to Everett, but . . ."

Everett True, the journalist that Kurt Cobain was asking about earlier, was the first to write about Courtney—or Kurt, for that matter—for a British paper. He may well have gotten a little carried away, but then he does.

"Well, you know, he just decided he was bored and that England needed a new American character. There's things he wrote that were true and things that were absolutely not true. Some of the quotes he attributed to me were just amazing."

Anything in particular?

"Well, like that I had a profession based on a song I wrote, you know, a noble and ancient profession, but not one that I ever went to school for. I mean, when I read the last piece, I hit him."

She did, as well. Poor old ET was eating junket through a straw for a week. People get the songwriter mixed up with the song, though. It happens.

"But it's . . . narrative. Neil Young writes narrative, and nobody thinks . . . you know what I mean. The songs still feel like catharsis, still feel like exorcism, still feel really good to sing, but on the other hand, a lot of it is narrative. I'm not a character actress. I'm a songwriter."

It's only going to get worse.

"Oh, I know," she sighs. "I mean, I went to lunch with this corporate weasel from some major record company the other day, and he just said 'Courtney, what do you want to do?' Well, I told him I wanted to go and see Nirvana in Chicago, so he gave me a thousand dollars. I keep telling the other three they should be going out to lunch as well . . . I mean, we're talking here about restaurants I've never even seen the outside of. It's great. They buy me martinis and talk to me about money and it's, like, totally interesting . . ."

This is the first sarcasm I've heard since I arrived in California.

"We're just not ready," she decides. "For a band like us, with our ideology, the only reason to have a corporate label is better distribution. So if we sell enough records that we need that, then I'll think about it. They just want to buy something that they think is honest. But it's my life, you know?"

LATER THAT NIGHT, Hole open for Nirvana at the Palace. The crowd looks like a casting call for the next series of that MTV real-life soap where they stick six attractive young people in a house and see how long it takes for them all to wish each other dead. Axl Rose and Slash from Guns N' Roses are here, as is Perry Farrell of Jane's Addiction. Everybody else here looks like they either want to be them, or be very good friends indeed with them. There are at least half a dozen women in here wearing bikinis.

When Hole take the stage, Perry Farrell charges down the front, and stands still in the middle of the moshpit, head and shoulders above the melee. "Hey, bitch!" he calls between songs. "Suck my fuckin' dick!" Courtney, who appears to be in on whatever the joke is, smiles back. Perry's date for the evening has a disarming habit of unzipping the front of her dress at anyone she suspects of staring at them. Needless to say, she ends up doing quite a bit of this. Hole, meanwhile, are great, as noisy and chaotic as a train wreck but considerably more tuneful, and Courtney looks and plays like the lost lovechild of Angus Young and Kim Gordon.

After Hole have played, and after Nirvana have played, I experience the rare pleasure of strolling backstage past a purpling Axl Rose, who is getting the your-name's-not-down-you're-not-coming-in routine from bouncers. As I head for Hole's dressing room, I can hear his multi-platinum squawk squawking, "Well, why has that motherfucker got a laminate?" after me.

Courtney gives me a glass of wine, introduces me to someone to talk to and apologises, but she has to go and find another of her corporate weasels, to buy her drinks.

"The thing to remember," she says before she vanishes, "and this is important, is that I'm driven. I really am. I'm driven, for some reason. But I don't know where I'm going."

21

YEN WILL I BE FAMOUS?

Alisha's Attic in Japan
OCTOBER 1996

THE IDEA ANIMATING this story, originally written for *The Independent*, was to illuminate the reality of making a budding British pop group big in Japan. The group in question, Alisha's Attic—a pair of genial sisters from Essex—ended up doing okay, in Japan and elsewhere, without quite broaching the stratospheres. Which is to say they ended up doing a street better than 99 percent of pop groups ever founded. They packed it in shortly after the turn of the century and embarked on separate careers, Karen writing for The Sugababes and Kylie Minogue, among others, Shellie—who seems to have changed her name to Shelly—making solo records under her own name.

I can only hope now, as I could only hope then, that this story does, in some way, illuminate the reality of making a budding British pop group, etc., etc. Because I'm as certain as I can be that it illuminates absolutely nothing—beyond one hungover, food-poisoned hack's total bewilderment at his surroundings—about the nation in which it is set. I have, in the course of my journalistic peregrinations, dropped in on more than seventy countries. Japan is the only one that I have left feeling absolutely none the wiser about for having visited it. Everywhere else I've been, however briefly, I've flown home feeling like I've acquired some idea of what gets the people there laughing, crying and generally out of bed in the morning. I spent a week and a bit in Japan on this story, went to four cities, and met, I'm sure, dozens of local people. However, when I collected my thoughts as the homebound flight prepared for takeoff at Tokyo's Narita airport, I realised that they could, pretty much, be summarised thus: "Huh?"

★ ★ ★

THE PROMOTIONAL TOUR is a peculiar ritual, in which rock'n'roll performers are coerced into performing in as un-rock'n'roll a manner as can be imagined. On a promotional tour, the workaday touring creeds of riotous excess, grand debauchery and glamorous disdain are sacrificed in favour of restraint, modesty and affability. To participant and witness alike, the process is scarcely less disorienting than the prospect of senior members of the British royal family embarking on a vice-regal visit that saw them obliged to drive Rolls-Royces into swimming pools, cavort with ladies-in-waiting in baked-bean-filled gold bathtubs and heave bejewelled television sets out of palace windows.

Details of the promotional tour vary subtly according to local conditions, but the essential format is constant. The musicians are as pleasant as possible to as many as possible of the record company staff, disc jockeys and journalists upon whose favour future success may ultimately depend. The musicians will shake hands until they cramp, nod to the point of rheumatism and smile themselves halfway to permanent twitches. They must forgo the luxury of even the slightest lapse into sarcasm at what feels like the millionth introduction to someone called Hank Bucket of Plughole Records, apparently your licensee in Alaska, and his ugly, boring wife. They may not scream when asked, for the billionth time, where they got the name of their group from. Give any musician the option of going on a promotional tour or spending a week at home driving rivets into the roof of their mouth, and they will stride grimly but purposefully to the toolshed.

So it's a bit of a surprise to find the two members of Alisha's Attic in a highly chipper mood when we catch up with them in Polygram's offices in Osaka. Dagenham-born sisters Shellie and Karen Poole are new to all this—their debut album, *Alisha Rules the World*, has only been out in Britain a few weeks—and the excitement of visiting Japan for the first time is having an obvious buoying effect, though they can't have seen much of it. They've only been in the country three days, but Shellie and Karen have already nodded and smiled their way through a heavy schedule in Tokyo and Fukuoka, and so far today they've met the staff at the Polygram sales office in Nagoya, visited the studios of ZIP-FM in the same city, caught the Hikari bullet train to Osaka, been interviewed by a local pop magazine and introduced themselves to the Polygram office. It's about three in the afternoon.

I'VE BEEN IN Japan ever since this morning, arriving on an overnight flight from London with Alisha's Attic's press officer from Mercury Records, Susie Roberts. Even allowing for exhaustion and jetlag, it has been a strange day. It started at the hotel, with a series of hopeless, foggy-headed calculations with a pencil and beermat, trying to figure out if it was really possible that we'd just paid £120 for a taxi and £35 for four cups of coffee and a cake. We had. Even more disturbingly, we hadn't been ripped off. Those were the going rates. "I hope," said Susie, contemplating the wreckage of her expenses advance, "you like living on noodles and water."

It had gotten still stranger once they'd made our rooms up. My television wasn't capable of receiving anything but locally-produced hardcore pornography, the fellatio scenes in which made extensive use of an interesting cinematic innovation best described as Knob-Cam—all too literally, a Jap's eye view. There may be circumstances in which you want your television screen filled by a shot of the inside of someone's mouth going back and forth, but I can report that it's not just after you've got off a sleepless twelve-hour flight. She wants that filling looked at, I'd thought, trying to blink away ants-under-eyelids post-flight fatigue.

The bathroom didn't work, either. At least, I couldn't get it to work. After spending some minutes prodding uselessly at a console above the sink—it is possible to fly faster than sound in machines with less complex control panels—I rang reception. Someone came up, smiled and bowed a lot, and explained it all to me. I still couldn't see what was wrong with the hot tap/cold tap system. He smiled and bowed a bit more.

The digital bathroom is but one of thousands of symptoms of the technological psychosis that now grips Japan. Since 1945, the Japanese have invented everything humanity is ever going to need, and so the admirably restless Japanese creative impulse now finds itself with nowhere left to go but haywire. Hence alternately frozen and scalded hotel guests jabbing keypads and swearing while they learn the hard way that 17 degrees is too bloody cold and 44 is too bloody hot. Hence the machine outside the hotel doors into which you shove your umbrella upon entering, to have it instantly and tightly wrapped in a drip-preventing clingfilm prophylactic. Hence the presence, in the cubicles in the public toilet in the hotel bar, of buttons that produce a purely cosmetic flush, an ineffectual sloshing of water designed to spare the occupant of the next throne along the distress of listening to the splashes you're making for real. Hence, I guess, Knob-Cam.

Traumatised and confused, Susie and I headed for the aquarium. The Osaka aquarium is one of the best things in Japan, and very possibly the world. It's eight storeys high, and is structured so that you walk in at the top, representing the surface of the ocean, and proceed in a descending spiral to the bottom, passing as you go the various finned things that exist at different depths. So as you enter, you see lots of furry little otters cavorting cutely in the shallows, and just before you walk out, you are confronted with a tank full of giant spider crabs which are, indeed, enormous and do, indeed, combine all the most objectionable qualities of the two beasts they're named after—it's difficult to warm to a creature whose stomach is below its knees.

The real attraction is the central tank, as tall as the aquarium itself, and wide enough to comfortably accommodate dozens of sting rays, white pointers and hammerheads, schools of less excitingly dangerous fish and, most incredibly, two whale sharks. They swim slow laps of the tank, as vast and improbable and ridiculous yet strangely graceful as 747s circling a runway.

Back outside in the sun, we got mobbed. A shrieking posse of uniformed schoolgirls bore down on us, a white-socked lynch mob with instamatics, and took dozens of photos of each other standing next to me and Susie. The penny dropped on the train on the way back to the hotel: Susie has striped blonde and red hair. The Spice Girls were, or had just been, in Osaka. They thought she was Ginger Spice.

What worried me—though it should worry the relevant Spice Girl more—was which one they thought I was.

SOMEONE FROM POLYGRAM Osaka produces their business card from a little silver business card holder, hands it over, smiles and bows. So does somebody else. And somebody else. I get my cards out of my wallet, hand them back, find myself involuntarily smiling and bowing, and suddenly wish I'd thought to have some cards printed especially for this trip, if only to find out whether or not anybody actually reads them ("Andrew Mueller, fully qualified bat-wrangler and moose surgeon: no job too small, childrens' parties a specialty, early closing Tuesdays and Hannukah").

Alisha's Attic's debut single will be released in Japan in a few months' time. They're here now to meet the people who will be running the campaign when they return to formally seek the office of Pop Star. Polygram's view is that Shellie and Karen could find a lucrative niche somewhere in the middle ground between The Spice Girls (popular, but perceived as a touch strident) and Shampoo (two squawking adolescents from Plumstead who remain the biggest-selling British act in Japanese history). This is why the people at Polygram listen, beaming rapturously, to Shellie and Karen's earnest, self-conscious speeches about their hopes for a harmonious working relationship and an exciting future. It's why they burst into thunderous applause when the pair trot out the few halting Japanese phrases they've picked up. It's why they queue up to pose for photographs, and proffer CD booklets for autographs. They're laying on the superstar treatment for two relative unknowns in the hope that it will prove a self-fulfilling prophecy.

After a bit more bowing, smiling and distribution of business cards, a small swarm of Polygram employees, each wearing bomber jackets embossed with the company logo, organise us across town to the studios of FM802 and FM Osaka. At both stations, Shellie and Karen wander about introducing themselves to everyone, while the Polygram entourage scuttle around them with a ghetto blaster playing the first Alisha's Attic single, "I Am, I Feel," on an endless loop, and a cardboard sign bearing the Japanese for "I swear to support Alisha's Attic" to use as a prop in yet more souvenir photographs. Tottering a few steps behind, feeling my way through another blizzard of business cards, I think I can see where this particular jape is heading: "What do you mean, you won't play it? You swore that you would. We have the negatives."

Another logo-spangled Polygram minion is toting several plastic carrier bags full of sponge cakes in pretty purple boxes. The cakes, each decorated with another pro-Alisha's Attic diktat, are an expression of the ancient and noble Japanese custom of gift-giving. Whenever someone sufficiently ancient or noble hands over their business card, a cake is silently, anciently and nobly produced from one of the bags and handed to either Shellie or Karen, who pass it anciently and nobly onto the recipient, who responds with perfectly genuine-looking expressions of surprise and delight (and who then, doubtless, picks all the writing off the top, takes it home to his wife and says, "Darling! I've got a surprise for you!" To which she replies, "It's not another bloody cake, is it?").

"Everyone's really nice," says Shellie, or Karen, though most likely both. They're right. Everyone is really nice. What do they want?

ANYONE WHO GOES to any major Asian city for the first time always says it looks like the city in which Ridley Scott set *Blade Runner*, his long film about robots. Osaka actually is that city. We leave it for the airport in a train which, suitably, looks like what people in 1980 thought trains would look like in 2000. Our destination is Sapporo, the major city of Japan's northern island, Hokkaido. We get in late. I open my minibar and wonder which marketing genius decided to call a soft drink Pocari Sweat, and what sort of idiot is ever going to drink it. I wonder if a pocari is some kind of veldt-dwelling scavenger dog, or if I've got it mixed up with something else. There's nothing else in the minibar. I drink it. It tastes like the sweat of a veldt-dwelling scavenger dog. I turn the television on. More Knob-Cam. I'm sure that filling is coming loose.

We're back in business early the following morning. More bomber-jacketed Polygram folk take us to do the cakes'n'cards thing at the local Polygram office, and at Sapporo radio stations AIR-G FM and NorthWave FM. At both places, Karen and Shellie deliver their increasingly familiar address about harmony and an exciting future to assembled staff, and in both places are cajoled, bowed and smiled into singing a bit. They knock out one perfectly harmonised a capella verse of "I Am, I Feel," which is a decent little pop song by any reasonable standards, and everyone claps and whoops with such expressions of awe that you'd think they'd never heard music before.

At NorthWave, Shellie and Karen are press-ganged into an impromptu live interview with the DJ who is evidently NorthWave's resident "personality." Which is to say he's a complete, total, all-the-medals, copper-bottomed, chateau-bottled, ocean-going, four-wheel-drive, armour-plated, uranium-tipped, olympic-standard, now-with-wings dickhead. He has some sort of alter ego called "The Fly." You can tell when he's being "The Fly" because he yammers drivel into a distorted microphone instead of a clean one. He asks Karen and Shellie to engage "The Fly" in conversation. Karen and Shellie are far, far too polite.

All we see of Sapporo is what we drive through. By late afternoon, we're back in the airport, where most of the departures concourse is taken up by a vast fresh seafood market. Rows of tanks bustle with fish, lobster and infinite examples of the bizarre, unclassifiable ocean-dwellers that only exist in the novels of Jules Verne and Japanese restaurant menus. It would be an extraordinary enough spectacle if it were down by the docks. Here, it feels like wandering into a rodeo in the middle of a shopping mall. I don't even have time to wonder what kind of person buys live seafood before getting onto a plane: everybody is. I like to try to fit in. I order a sushi salad. I will live to regret this.

Our flight down the east coast to Sendai touches down after a lurching, storm-tossed approach that causes more than one of our party to wonder if the pilot hadn't learnt his trade crashing into American frigates. It's the kind of flight where you notice, as the aircraft pulls into the terminal that, up and down the plane, complete strangers are holding hands. It's early evening in Sendai, and we only stay long enough to distribute more tapes, goodwill and cakes to local Polygram staff and Sendai FM. I am feeling a hitherto unknown affinity with the Easter Bunny. The Shinkansen bullet train takes us to Tokyo.

The bar at Tokyo's Roppongi Prince Hotel appears to have been decorated by Ridley Scott's less clever kid brother. The walls are covered with a gold and black lunar landscape, and the arches holding up the ceiling have been painted to look like ancient Roman columns. The combined effect almost obviates the need for alcohol, but the evening proves even stranger than the decor. The occupants of the bar are myself, Susie, Shellie, Karen, their manager (a former Page Three model), a drunk Japanese businessman, an embarrassed-looking woman whom the drunk Japanese businessman keeps loudly introducing as his "cousin" while roaring with laughter, several members of the Harlem Globetrotters, who are also staying here, two seventeen-year-old actresses from a teen soap called *Byker Grove*, who are in Japan trying to sell themselves as a pop duo called Crush, and their manager, who someone tells me is the mother of the singer from Saint Etienne, though by this point I'm prepared to believe anything.

The drunk Japanese businessman keeps gesturing at Susie and asking me, in what he probably believes is a conspiratorial whisper but is actually a deafening, slobbering bellow that all but moves the furniture around, where I got her. Actually, I tell him, she's paying for me, which is true enough as far as it goes, but makes him laugh so much I briefly wonder if I'm going to have to call for assistance. His "cousin" gets up, smiles, bows and leaves.

THE THREE DAYS we've been allotted in Tokyo are given over to the print media. I miss the first of these—the Sapporo airport sushi comes back, and brings a load of its mates. I haven't felt worse since a dodgy moussaka somewhere in Turkish Kurdistan reduced me to a week-long all-banana diet. Feverish and verging on the delirious, I spend the day shivering and damp on the futon in my room, watching coverage of the US presidential elections. CNN's informed talking head is a Democrat congressman from New Hampshire called Dick Swett. Thus the hours of purging luridly coloured emissions through every orifice bar my ears are interrupted, every half hour on the half hour, by pauses to weep with laughter. Every so often, a hotel employee comes and knocks on my door, bows, smiles and asks if there's anything I need, and every time I answer, there's less of me.

The next day, still feeling like someone's set me on fire and beaten it out with a railway sleeper, I sit in the interview suite at the hotel while representatives of various fashion, music and style magazines file in at half-hourly intervals to ask Shellie and Karen the following questions:

What was it like working with Dave Stewart? What's it like being sisters in a band? Is the fact that their father is Brian Poole, once of The Tremeloes, in any way significant? Who is Alisha? What do they think of Japan? So, at half-hourly intervals, Karen and Shellie say "Great," "Fine, no problem," "No," "Sort of an alter ego," and "Not as weird as East 17 told us it would be."

I interview one Tokyo journalist about the interview she's just done. I ask her if she's aware that Japan is talked about by third-division English pop groups as a veritable rock'n'roll Shangri-La, that the general perception is that Japanese pop consumers are at once the most enthusiastic and ignorant on earth, happy to scream at, spend money on, and sleep with, any clump of British clowns who can hold a guitar the right way up.

"People do think we're easy," she agrees. "But everyone comes here now, and we can afford to be picky."

But they're not. "Big in Japan" is the defiant boast of every bunch of tuneless timewasters who couldn't get arrested in Britain if they ran through Downing Street naked but for an Irish tricolour and a grenade-launcher, and it's usually true. I know of musicians back in London who couldn't give away their records at home if they came with a £20 note stapled to the sleeve, but who've come to Japan and had to be smuggled in and out of the back entrances of hotels for their own safety.

"We just like music," she smiles. "And maybe we are not so cynical as you."

And maybe she's right. That evening, we are mini-bussed across town to Harajuku, the Tokyo suburb famous as the spot where Japan's somewhat demented yet oddly demure fascination with western pop culture is given its fullest expression. It's just like Camden Market, except that everything's three times as expensive and there are marginally fewer Japanese people here. Karen and Shellie pose for photographs in a fashion boutique where, I cannot help but notice, one set of shelves is decorated in clippings from old issues of *Melody Maker*. Taking this homage to a frankly disturbing level of fastidiousness, each shelf is upholstered with cuttings by a different writer. Mine is the fourth shelf from the top. I hope they're not arranged in descending order of preference. The bloke who's got the shelf above mine is a sub-literate plodder with the aesthetic sensibilities of a chair leg.

AT THE HOTEL that evening, there's a small cluster of giggling teenagers waiting in the lobby with autograph books, photos of Alisha's Attic and pens. They squeal delightedly while Shellie and Karen sign their stuff, though I can see that Shellie and Karen are thinking what I'm thinking: nobody in Japan has heard of them—who are these people?

"Yeah," says a friend of mine, back in London, whose own band had been through the same thing a few years previously. "The record company pays them."

22

WHAT TIME IS LOUVRE?

To France with Radiohead
JULY 2003

LIKE MOST PEOPLE—AND even, if they're honest, most rock critics—I arrived in my thirties aware of, and not much bothered about, the truth that my musical tastes were unlikely to expand much further, if at all. I knew what I liked—and, by and large, liked what I knew. It remains, I suppose, theoretically possible that some or other brainstorm will bestir a hitherto utterly dormant affection for techno or reggae, but it also remains theoretically possible, and about as plausible, that a long and complex sequence of early deaths and tenuous genealogical links will lead to me being crowned King of Tonga. And if that happens, I hereby promise that my first decree will order the adoption, as national anthem, of a Derrick May remix of Bob Marley's "Jammin."

The older I've gotten, the more likely it has become that my reply to the question of what kind of music I like will be: "Both kinds: country and western." The longer the road rolls beneath whichever conveyance is bearing me, the more my ears hunger for the truth—as Harlan Howard had it—set to three chords, with tears-in-the-beer vocals, crying violins, twanging guitars, lonesome lap steels, duelling banjos and the sort of piano you can imagine being played by some gold-hearted hussy in crinolines and fishnets while Gary Cooper and John Wayne hurl barstools at each other.

But I still listen to Radiohead, arguably the least country and western white band in the world. They seem one of few bands left even interested in trying to attempt something as ambitious as a soundtrack for the times—and one of very, very few bands left capable of creating such a thing. The album they'd just made when I climbed aboard their bus for this trip in 2003, *Hail to the Thief*, was—and is—a masterpiece, a superb articulation of the angst felt not just by Radiohead, but by the people rather like Radiohead who constitute much of Radiohead's audience: that vast global constituency of youngish, fundamentally decent, middle-class liberals born into a fortunate life which presents no real impediment to their happiness bar the nagging suspicion that their comfort is related to the fact that someone else, somewhere else, is being paid ten cents a week to sew stripes onto their training shoes.

For such a crowd, Radiohead's singer and principal songwriter, Thom Yorke, is the ideal everyman: an aggrieved, affronted figure whose rage was borne of impotence, who was nevertheless willing to rebel against whatever you'd got, but didn't quite know where to start.

★ ★ ★

"WELCOME ABOARD," SAYS Thom Yorke. "Coffee? Instant okay? I think there's a cafetierre here somewhere, but I'm not sure where . . ."

Thom rummages noisily in a drawer in the kitchen at the back of the bus. Radiohead have just taken delivery of this imposing, midnight-black vehicle, which will be their home for a couple of weeks of European festivals. Today, we're doing London to Paris with a complement of Thom, Radiohead guitarist Ed O'Brien, Radiohead producer Nigel Godrich, Radiohead tour manager Hilda, a crew member whose name I don't catch and me (I'm assuming there's a driver, as well). We're meeting the rest of the band in Paris, at the howlingly fashionable Costes Hotel.

"Have you stayed there before?" asks Thom, as he continues his search.

I haven't. What's it like?

"Unbelievably expensive, full of the most awful wankers, and decorated like a brothel."

You've stayed there before, then.

"We always stay there. It's brilliant."

The downstairs area of the bus, where we are now, contains the kitchen, the toilet, four blue and gold leather seats around a table, a sofa-cum-bed, a vast television hooked up to a PlayStation and DVD player and a stereo. Upstairs there's a lounge area, eight bunks, two more vast televisions, at least one more stereo, and, up the back, a separate room with a double bed and a mirrored wall.

"Maybe I should take that," says Ed. "I have trouble fitting into bunks."

This seems fair enough. Ed is six and a half feet tall, and tour bus bunks are, generally, less roomy than jockeys' coffins.

"Exactly," he nods. "Made for shortarses."

"Hmmm?" says Thom. Thom, even when he stands up following his efforts to locate the cafetierre is, it might charitably be said, bunk-sized. He regards Ed quizzically, something like a jaguar deciding whether or not to pounce on a faintly annoying rodent.

"I mean," giggles Ed, "for completely normally proportioned people much like you, Thom. As opposed to grotesque freaks like myself."

Good catch, Ed.

IF THOM YORKE the human being was anything like the Thom Yorke of received wisdom, his reaction to Ed's mild dig might have encompassed any or all of the following: i) Ed's instant dismissal from Radiohead; ii) the total destruction of every inanimate object on both decks of the bus; iii) Thom's relocation to a tin shack deep in the woods, there to perch atop a stack of tinned food and argue with the clamorous voices in his head. However, today as in several meetings going back over eight years, Thom Yorke the human being and the Thom Yorke of received wisdom seem nothing more than a coincidence of names. Thom is unstoppably talkative, laughs frequently and is only reluctant to submit to a proper interview because he and Nigel and I get too absorbed too early in a discussion of the world at large. Thom is vexed about Iraq, especially his own early views on the conflict. "I bought it," he admits, glumly. "I thought, okay, if he has these weapons, they should be taken off him. You'd think I'd know better."

This is a good place to start. Radiohead's current album, *Hail to the Thief*, is a distillation of the static that was buzzing in Thom's head at the end of 2001. If all you'd heard of it was the title, you'd be forgiven for expecting an explicitly political tract. As is always the case with Radiohead at their best, though, it is and it isn't.

"It's not an America-baiting thing," says Thom, as we watch Kent go by. "That's not the point at all. And the title keeps coming from different places, anyway. First, it's about that coup there, but look, there's another one here, and another one over there. And you could also think of it in terms of access and influence. It sets me off in different directions depending on what day of the week it is."

Hail to the Thief has an alternative name, *The Gloaming*. This is more in keeping with the obtuse titles that have graced previous Radiohead albums: 1993's *Pablo Honey* (a reference to a sketch by phone pranksters The Jerky Boys), 1995's *The Bends* (what Radiohead felt about their sudden rise to prominence in the early 90s), 1997's *OK Computer* (an approval of, or submission to, the technology that runs our lives), 2000's *Kid A* (possibly borrowed from Carl Steadman's novel *Kid A in Alphabet Land*), 2001's *Amnesiac* (answers on a postcard).

"I was unhappy about the potential consequences of calling it *Hail to the Thief*. Personal attacks, threats . . . people can get quite upset. So I wasn't wild about that. But it's more jubilant, and deranged, and doublespeak, like 'collateral damage,' or 'regime change.' *The Gloaming* was much too . . . aaah AAAAHH ahh."

Thom delivers these last three syllables in a passable impression of a church organ.

"And that wasn't the point either. The record definitely enters a dark place in the middle, but it isn't the whole thing. When we were doing *Kid A* and *Amnesiac*, I had this thing that we were entering a very dark phase. I mean, you know me, I've made a career out of saying things like that. But it did strike me that things were going to kick off one way or another, and at the same time there was a rise, politically anyway, in ignorance and stupidity, and all that lovely euphoria after the Berlin Wall came down had disintegrated into this global political and economic anarchy."

I'd wondered about the alternative titles also given to the songs on *Hail to the Thief*. They suggest a much gloomier record—the *Hail to the Thief* tracks "Backdrifts," "Go to Sleep," Where I End and You Begin," "We Suck Young Blood," "Scatterbrain" and "A Punchup at a Wedding" become, respectively, "Honeymoon Is Over," "Little Man Being Erased," "The Sky Is Falling In," "Your Time Is Up," "As Dead as Leaves" and "No No No No No No No."

"I like that one. That would have been a good name for the record. Here it is, the new album by—guess who—Radiohead, and it's called *No No No No No No No*."

Little Man Being Erased would have been a very Radiohead title, as well.

"That," beams Thom, "is my absolute favourite."

THE SLEEVE ARTWORK of *Hail to the Thief*, created by Stanley Donwood, is a series of maps of major cities in which the streets have been replaced by coloured blocks, emblazoned with malevolent phrases. London, for example, has districts renamed Spiked, Take You Down, Quango, Skinned Alive and Shareholders. It could be an aerial view of the London of George Orwell's *1984*: the dystopian capital of Airstrip One, with Thom Yorke, his voice a lonely cry of aggrieved, affronted humanity, in the role of Winston Smith. "2+2=5," the title of the opening track on *Hail to the Thief*, was the formula with which Orwell's party invigilator O'Brien demonstrated to Winston his utter powerlessness before the malign forces that ran his life.

Now, stop me if I'm trying too hard, but . . .

"I did re-read *1984* a while before we did this record," confirms Thom, "but I'd forgotten where 2+2=5 came from. The other bit in the book I thought about a lot was the fake war—we're at war with Eurasia, we've always been at war with Eurasia."

Did that hopelessness of Winston's position strike a chord with you? There's a line in "Scatterbrain"—"A moving target on a firing range"—that seems to sum up your view of most of humanity.

"It goes back to the Jubilee 2000 thing for me," says Thom. Thom was, for a while, involved with Jubilee's lobbying to get first world governments to write off the crippling, unrepayable debts owed them by third world governments. "I realised how out of control the disintegration was. When I started with Jubilee 2000, I thought it was the most exciting thing I'd ever got involved with. Potentially, we could show what's been going on for what it is. But it never happened, because the G8 were very smart, and they and the IMF and the World

Bank kept passing it to each other, and eventually I found myself thinking, 'Now I get it. It's never going to happen.'"

Did it put you off trying to accomplish anything outside music?

"No. I'd like to be involved, but it's difficult to know where to go with it. There were so many disheartening things about it, the fact that so much lip service was given, and you still end up with the reality that the IMF and the World Bank are there to keep everyone under their thumb, as they have in Argentina. They affect millions of people, yet they're completely unaccountable. I'd like to get involved again, but I find it difficult not to say that we should disband the IMF and the World Bank, to put it politely. Because that's what I believe. Some people say you have to work within the structures, which is fair enough, because they're the ones with the money. But if you do that, they're just going to spin you a line. You get some money, but it's money to make you go away."

Was that experience reflected in the songs on *Hail to the Thief*?

"Oh, completely. I guess the whole record was a response to those experiences. Becoming a dad amplified it as well, because you start thinking not only am I powerless, but there's an extremely dangerous set of things being set up for my son's future that I can't sort out for him. That's quite a simple thing that's very, very difficult to deal with."

In "Sail To The Moon," there's that line "Maybe you'll be president/ But know right from wrong/Or in the flood you'll build an ark/And sail us to the moon." Feel free to tell me it's none of my business, but seeing as your son is called Noah . . .

"It wasn't intended," Thom smiles, "but it ended up being a song for him, yeah."

While we're up this way, why Noah?

"That's what he looked like. That's what you do. Bugger the consequences."

I suppose he'll get used to the ark jokes. And the "It's up to you, Noah Yorke," ones.

"Oh, yeah," grins his father, who has lived down worse taunts. "He'll be fine."

IN THOM'S LIST of thank-yous on the sleeve of *Hail to the Thief*, after friends and family, there's a nod to Spike Milligan. Radiohead dedicated *The Bends* to the late American comedian Bill Hicks, another funny, outraged iconoclast. Hicks and Radiohead seem a congruent fit. Both are intelligent, informed, acutely sensitive to hypocrisy—as Thom says, "Bill Hicks was able to make things that were incredibly frightening funny, and by doing that make them seem okay." Milligan, whose best-known work was hyperactively absurd, seems a less obvious choice of hero for Thom.

Why him?

"He did a TV series called *Q*, which someone bought for me at a car boot sale, and I watched that a few times. There's this one about a dalek coming home for its tea . . ."

The Pakistani dalek?

"Yeah. The Pakistani dalek family. And every time I watched it, I thought, fucking hell, this is a person on the edge. There was another one where they wheeled in a staircase, and he just walked up and down it wearing costumes. He was so inconsistent, so incredibly spontaneous, and at the same time really fragile. There was also this book, *Depression and How to Survive It*, which he wrote with Anthony Clare. That had a really big effect on me."

In what way?

"There's one amazing bit where they're talking to people about whether there's a positive side to depression. These aren't people who are chronic, where it's really out of control, but a lot of them say yes, there are positive sides. You see things in a way that other people don't, and you feel things a lot harder than other people, and that's good, it's almost okay. It was good to hear people say it like that."

Has this been a constant thing with you, or has there been one particular period when it got really bad?

"On the *OK Computer* tour, we were in a situation where people were trying to persuade us to carry on touring for another six months, we should have said no but we didn't and I went bonkers."

When you say bonkers . . .

"Oh, bonkers. Not violent, but . . . enormously, uncontrollably depressed, delusional."

In what way?

"All sorts. Seeing things."

That's usually a sign that you should take some time off . . .

"No, actually. It was quite interesting. Sort of everywhere. Corner of the eye stuff."

Would it be crass to suggest that this is similar to what you're getting at with the idea of "The Gloaming"? You know, this twilight netherworld that you can't quite see, but which you know is out there somewhere?

"No, I guess not. I guess not. You know that film *Ghost*? Terrible film, but there's this bit where all these shadows come down and take that kid away who gets hit by a car. That's what it was like. We lost contact with reality, and got to feel like everything that wasn't related to what we were doing was annoying or irrelevant. We'll never do that again."

Have you read Spike Milligan's World War II memoirs? They're very good on people being yanked about by forces they can't control. And they're incredibly funny.

"No, I haven't."

Jonny had one in his suitcase at the Edinburgh show the other month. Borrow it from him.

"I will. You know, I think the appeal of Milligan is that he didn't suffer fools, at all. Some people really hated him for that. But why should anyone bother? Life is short, and people are stupid. That's definitely a depressive thing. You see the holes in things very quickly. Too quickly."

THE COSTES HOTEL in Paris is everything Thom promised. The price of a room would leave some change from the Earth, but not much. The food is great, and all the better if you derive some perverse thrill from paying twenty quid for scrambled eggs. As for the staff, it is possible that at least eight of the dozen most beautiful women alive are currently waiting the Costes's tables.

Those of us who came by bus park ourselves in the bar with a bottle of champagne. A woman in a peculiar dress comes over to tell Thom how much she liked the new album; Thom accepts the compliment graciously, and tells her, correctly, that she looks like Alice in Wonderland, and this goes over well. Neil Tennant drops briefly by the table, and when Colin Greenwood shows up—the only member of Radiohead who dresses at all like a millionaire rock star, or indeed at all like anything other than a dishevelled student—he's disappointed to learn that he missed Yves St. Laurent. It's that kind of hotel.

Thom's one of the last to retire. He's an even better talker with a few glasses of fizz inside him, and he's funny, very funny, with his own failings the punchline to most of his anecdotes. Of Radiohead's legendary appearance at Glastonbury in 1997, he remembers, "That show was a disaster. Everything that could have gone wrong did. I thundered off stage, really ready to kill, and my girlfriend grabbed me, made me stop, and said, 'Listen.' And the crowd were just going wild. It was amazing."

A few hours earlier on the bus, Thom and Ed had sat down to write the setlists for their festival appearances, and for the performance for French television that Thom and Jonny would be recording in Paris. In between lobbying as forcefully as I dared on behalf of my favourites—I believe I may have saved "Exit Music" for some lucky festival-goers—I'd asked Thom if his position made it more or less difficult to articulate Radiohead's hymns to humanity's impotence. He's a millionaire rock star, after all, and gets to run his life more on his own terms than most of us.

"It's easier," he decides. "It's easier, because you have more time to think about these things, more time to listen to Radio 4 and worry. But it's sort of my job. Just like you've got your job, mine is to be the Ides of March type person, and some poor fucker has to do it. Somebody has to put the jester's hat on and make a tit of himself. 'We're all fucking doomed.' It might as well be me."

23

IF YOU'RE LOOKING FOR ROUBLE

Ambulance chasing with *Highway Patrol*, Moscow
MARCH 1996

THIS DISPATCH DATES from a distant—yet startlingly recent—age in which foreign television was a novelty, rather than something you could ingest about as much of as you could stand whenever you felt like it. Indeed, I only happened across this story, about a Russian show called *Highway Patrol*, because I saw something about it on a British television programme about how weird and remote and exotic foreign television was. My preparations for the story were quaintly pre-internet. I made a note of the production company as the British programme's credits rolled, got their number out of the Yellow Pages, called and asked them for details of their contacts in Moscow—which they happily gave up, as journalists always should to a fellow hack—and sent some faxes to the pertinent numbers. I was planning to visit Moscow anyway, under my own steam, and thought that if I could sell this story somewhere, it would at least cover the hotel bills.

This was my first visit to Russia, which itself seemed a fairly otherwordly proposition at that time. Less than five years previously, Russia had been the principal constituent of a seemingly invincible leviathan called the Union of Soviet Socialist Republics. By 1996, it was the Wild West, with the horses, Colt revolvers and ten-gallons swapped for black Mercedes-Benzes, AK-47s and furry hats, and that's what *Highway Patrol* had been established to report on and profit from. Lurid and ratings-worthy though the content of *Highway*

Patrol certainly was, the real story was being missed. While the attention of most Russians was consumed by the relatively petty crime running rampant on the streets and television screens, arguably the greatest theft in human history was taking place elsewhere, as a small clique of instant billionaires made off with the former superpower's awesome natural resources. I've been back to Russia a few times since and have always been struck by the acutely personal disappointment and grief expressed by many Russians–that the unspeakable horror show that was their twentieth century should have no redeeming climax, that the whole ghastly grand guignol only ended, in effect, with someone stealing the set.

An infinitesimal proportion of Russia's twentieth-century agony is chronicled below, and I should issue the caveat that readers especially sensitive to the suffering of children in particular should probably avoid the next few pages. I'm sure that I'd wondered, as all young reporters must, how I'd feel when I first saw death up close. This was when I found out, and what I discovered was an indifference that, initially at least, surprised me. I mean, I didn't enjoy the spectacle, and I turned away as soon as I felt I'd seen enough to get the idea, but neither of the violently deceased corpses I encountered here–nor any of the (really not that many) others I've seen since–have since troubled my sleep or my waking hours. It took me a while to figure that out, but what it came down to, I think, was that it was already too late for them: there was simply nothing to be done. If–okay, when–the recollections rear up and start clawing, the ones that leave a mark are always those memories of living people, the outwardly unremarkable but essentially decent and kind ones, whose ambitions and hopes have been needlessly curtailed by avoidably stupid and cruel political or economic circumstances. For most of Russia's history, that would serve as a description of most Russians.

★ ★ ★

IN MOSCOW AS everywhere else, midnight is where bad television goes to die. Freezing on a spring night in a cheap hotel, I'm keeping warm by getting up every few minutes and walking across the room to change channels. On channel one, capitalist pornography—a low-rent game show tottering on a set that wobbles perceptibly every time one of the contestants leans on their buzzer. On channel two, a dismal documentary involving a surely unnecessary number of pictures of tractors. On channels three and four, music videos in a proportion of roughly four parts ballsachingly awful Russian ballad singers to one part the only thing worse: Phil Collins. On channel five, grainy highlights of an ice hockey game, apparently filmed on an ageing Super-8 camera by someone who had one or two drinks before reporting to work.

And over on channel six, a ghostly pale face leers from the screen, its bloodshot eyes divided by a ragged gash running from forehead to nose. A trickle of dark blood dribbles from the cut into a froth-encrusted, furiously yammering mouth which emits a frantic, babbled commentary as the camera pans dispassionately around the room in which this apparition is sitting, amid the detritus of a quiet night in that has clearly gone badly, badly wrong: pizza crusts of various vintages in cardboard trays, empty bottles strewn across the mildewed carpet, two spent syringes in a vase full of dirty water and, slumped in the far corner, the scene's other protagonist. His left eye has been neatly replaced by a bullethole, and the contents of his head splashed across the wallpaper behind him.

The camera dwells on the corpse just that little bit too long, the way you do when you can't quite believe what you're seeing, then pulls suddenly away, just like a human eye flinching from something unsightly. It rests again on the hysterical narrator, as he's handcuffed by police and hustled from view. A date—today's—appears along the bottom of the screen in type, followed by a time, about six hours ago. The picture fades to a shot of a sponsor-spangled white BMW estate leaving the site, and credits roll. So ends another episode of *Highway Patrol*, the most popular television programme in Russia, and one of the most watched in the world.

HIGHWAY PATROL IS a bona fide broadcasting phenomenon, boasting seventy million viewers in Russia, Belarus, Estonia, Latvia, Lithuania, Kazakhstan and, through some unfathomable miracle of syndication, Israel. The idea is hardly unique: most countries with sufficient noteworthy crime entertain and appall themselves with footage retrieved by ambulance-chasing camera crews (*Cops* in America, *Blues and Twos* in Britain).

Highway Patrol is different, however. It has an inescapable frequency,

producing a daily fifteen-minute show which is shown at midnight
every night and repeated twice the following day, as well an irregular
round-up of mafia activity—all too literally, a Greatest Hits. *Highway
Patrol* also has a pitiless attitude to broadcasting the grisliest of
material, though they do have their limits, as I eventually find out the
hard way.

Most importantly, *Highway Patrol* has a firm grip on the pulse of
its home city. Post-communist Moscow is a 1990s production of Al
Capone's Chicago—a city where the gangsters don't bother to conceal
their weapons, and where the police don't bother to change out of
uniform when they go to their other jobs as doormen at Moscow's mafia-
controlled nightclubs. Muscovites talk about crime the way Londoners
talk about weather, muttering and nodding wearily to each other that
it's bad, it's going to get worse and nobody's doing anything about it.

Highway Patrol began broadcasting in January 1995, the bright idea
of television producer Kirill Legat and businessman Dmitri Koriavov.
Koriavov, an amiable sort somewhere in his late thirties, is the essence
of what is often sneeringly referred to as a New Russian, one who has
been clever and/or cunning enough to ride out the uncertainties of
the post-communist years, to manufacture cash from chaos. When
Mikhail Gorbachev started talking about glasnost and perestroika in
1985, Koriavov was a mathematician at a Soviet scientific institute,
where his job was constructing climactic models intended to predict
the effects of nuclear winter. In one sense or another, he knew which
way the wind was blowing—by 1989, he'd gone into private business,
selling computers and importing luxury cars, before branching into
television. His production company, Aladdin, makes *Highway Patrol*.

When I meet Koriavov at Aladdin's offices, he is predictably
unrepentant about the view his programme presents of Moscow ("A
city of opportunity," he calls it) and the relentless frequency with
which it does it—it's not like he's making this stuff up, after all.

"This is real information about our lives in this city," he says. "It
does good, as well, for sure. Two years ago, I used to, you know, drive
home after I'd been drinking. But now, never. Because, three times a
day, five times a week, I see what results when people do that."

Koriavov recalls that the first few weeks of *Highway Patrol* were
characterised by mutual antipathy and suspicion between his film crews

and Moscow's emergency services, but says relations have improved: Aladdin's offices are abundantly decorated with certificates and awards presented by the city's police and fire departments in recognition of the illustrations that *Highway Patrol* has provided of the dangers of smoking while drunk in bed, its stark depictions of the consequences of drunk driving and its role in provoking public response to police enquiries. The relationship is now so close that a lot of the programme's information about new crimes comes from contacts within the police force. Otherwise, *Highway Patrol* relies on calls from viewers or their own monitoring of police radio frequencies.

"We don't judge," says Koriavov. "We don't criticise. We don't praise. We just show what happens."

Koriavov leads me out of his office and up the hall to meet the crew who've agreed to take me out for the night. The three of them sit around a table in a small, smoke-filled room, pouring the occasional slug from an unlabelled vodka bottle into shot-sized paper cups. This is what they do until something interesting comes in on the radio or telephone. I'm extended the welcome usually granted to the itinerant angler or visiting surfer: "You should have been here yesterday."

It had been, at least from the journalistic point of view, a good one—a black Volvo, driving up a busy road around the corner from the American embassy, had been cut off by a Jeep charging out of a side alley. According to a street full of eyewitnesses, the occupants of the Jeep had fired thirty or forty shots from two automatic rifles into the windscreen of the Volvo, killing both occupants, before driving off and disappearing into the traffic. A classic mafia hit.

I'm shown the unedited footage by the crew's reporter/presenter, Vladimir Yemelyanov, a ruddy-cheeked twenty-five-year-old.

"I wonder who did it," he muses, to nobody in particular.

Without thinking, I suggest that it won't be too hard for the police to find the perpetrators of a murder carried out in broad daylight on a busy street in rush hour. Vladimir laughs a mirthless laugh, and I try to cover my tracks by smiling the sort of smile you smile when you've just said something idiotic and you're trying to make it look like you were joking. The average Moscow police officer gets paid about £100 a month. Moscow is not much cheaper a place to live than most European capitals. So Moscow policemen have to find other work, and a moonlighting cop will find the easiest and steadiest employment from the kind of person who not only wants armed muscle, but a reasonable guarantee that nobody's going to look too closely at his own day job. A month before I arrived in Russia, a Scottish lawyer was killed by crossfire in a St. Petersburg cafe when two balaclava-clad hitmen attempted to assassinate a local crime boss. Two other men died in the attack, both St. Petersburg policemen working at their after-hours gig—bodyguards to the gangster.

I talk more to Vladimir while we sit and await the call to action. He gets one of Aladdin's receptionists to help his halting English through the more complicated questions. He happily confirms that he gets paid considerably better than any of the police officers, firemen and paramedics he follows around, and says he enjoys his job, though he gets rattled and "has some trouble sleeping" on nights after they've done a story in which a child has been on the receiving end. He wears a pistol on his belt, and I wonder if that's because *Highway Patrol* crews often arrive at crime scenes before the police—their new BMW is quicker than a rusty Lada patrol car.

"No, the job is not dangerous," Vladimir says. "But none of us have our own cars, and sometimes we have to walk home late at night."

I run a few standard knee-jerk reactions to his job past Vladimir: that he's a vulture with a camera crew, that he's making gruesome violence look like an acceptable part of everyday life, that he's encouraging the weak-willed to emulate what they see on the screen, that he's profiting from the misfortune of others. I don't believe much of this myself—*Highway Patrol*, like other such amoral cultural signifiers as tabloid newspapers, slasher films, gangsta rap and heavy metal, exists because people like it and are willing to pay for it—except maybe for the part about profiting from the misfortune of others, but as that's a fair, if cynical, definition of journalism, I'm in no position to criticise.

Vladimir's heard it all before, anyway.

"Our programme doesn't do any of that," he says. "There are lots of stupid action movies shown on television every day that are much, much worse. It's just that whenever people see death—I mean, real death, of real people—they are surprised. Nothing more than that. Death happens every day, but people are surprised when they see it. I was surprised the first time I saw Lenin in the mausoleum."

THE CREW'S DRIVER, Sacha, puts down his mobile phone and announces that we're off—he's heard something from one of his contacts. Vladimir throws me a spare *Highway Patrol* parka jacket, and while I struggle into it, he draws his pistol from its holster and points it at the temple of Leon, the cameraman. Leon looks up, briefly, finishes his coffee with exaggerated serenity and walks down to the carpark with us.

Sacha weaves the BMW through Moscow's comically potholed streets with the bravado of one who believes that the rules of the road were written for lesser mortals. Perhaps they were—policemen on point duty wave as the famous car passes, and one holds up traffic at an intersection to allow us through against the lights. We fetch up at a police station amid the crumbling tower blocks of Moscow's southern suburbs. Like every other public building I've visited in Moscow, including the office block that houses Aladdin, the cop shop is a dank, musty shambles that gives the impression of having been recently abandoned by a previous owner and hurriedly occupied by squatters.

The police trot out a singularly gormless-looking youth who has, they explain, been apprehended at the unpromising beginning of his criminal career—he was caught burgling a flat on the same block where his family lives. Vladimir interviews the kid, and then the station chief, but his heart's obviously not really in it, and his thoughts easy to read on his face: this is no big deal, a dull little morality play, strictly filler stuff, of use only if this turns out to be an especially desperate shift. Whether his disappointment is normal, or whether he was hoping for something a bit more hair-raising to show the visitor, Vladimir descends into a gale force sulk, fidgeting irritably with the car radio all the way back to base. He only cheers up when a motorcycle policeman, evidently no fan of *Highway Patrol*, pulls us over in front of the White House—the former home of the Russian parliament, which was shattered during the attempted coup of 1991—and books Sacha for speeding.

The next day means a new shift, and a renewed optimism among the crew that they'll come up with something really horrible to show me. They explain that they average one call to a proper underworld execution every day, so it's only going to be a matter of time. Nevertheless, we have to start somewhere, and so we start in what remains of the flat above a Hyundai spares shop, not far from the Aladdin offices. The resident of the flat obviously wasn't watching last time *Highway Patrol* warned of the perils of falling asleep drunk while smoking—he's fallen asleep drunk while smoking and incinerated himself. It looks bad, and smells worse, but there's a strange calm about proceedings. Firemen quietly lay down planks so that we can walk through the water they've sprayed into the place without getting our shoes muddy. A policeman pours me coffee from a thermos while Leon and Vladimir set up for Vladimir's piece-to-camera. Sacha tuts at me for getting paint on the *Highway Patrol* jacket I'm wearing, and wipes me down with turpentine—a scene which will baffle Moscow's viewing public later this evening.

AS IT TURNS out, this shift yields no decapitated hitmen, kneecapped stool pigeons, cement-flippered informers or horse's heads in anyone's beds. There aren't even any more workaday domestic catastrophes—no road smashes, clumsy drinkers, metro-jumpers or overdoses. We only get called to one more story, and it's something much worse than any of these, at least insofar as one fatal tragedy can be said to be much worse than any other.

In a courtyard between three dung-coloured tower blocks, in the snow next to a rubbish skip, somebody has left a baby boy. I get close enough to see how blue the naked form is, and how purple the vestige of umbilical cord trailing from its midriff, before I work out exactly what it is I'm looking at, and then I don't believe it, and then when I do believe it I don't want to. The *Highway Patrol* crew and a forensic scientist in a white fur coat hunch over the dead child; the scene looks like some grotesque parody of the Nativity.

Vladimir shoots me a look; he's not enjoying this one, and neither am I: I wander off and stare very determinedly at anything else at all. He and I seem to be the only people here who are remotely perturbed. Leon and Sacha fiddle about with the camera cables. The scientist discusses with someone else whether or not the boy was alive when he was left here, or if perhaps he was thrown from one of the balconies overlooking the square. There's one policeman in attendance, and he sits in his car, reading a paper, smoking, keeping warm, doing nothing to shy away passers-by—but this is exactly what they do: they pass by. This is a busy pedestrian route, and though people look over, and raise an eyebrow or two beneath their fur hats, they don't seem any more startled than I might be if someone parked an expensive sports car in my street. Despite what Vladimir had said about death being a surprise, these people are behaving as if a dead child on the footpath is about as surprising as the sun coming up. Nobody weeps or wails. No teeth are gnashed, no garments rent.

That said, I don't know the neighbourhood. Maybe people leave dead kids lying around here every day of the week; maybe it isn't that interesting. Or maybe it's just that Russia has never been an easy place to live, and maybe Muscovites have an attitude to death hardened by centuries of proximity to it.

"Don't know," says Vladimir, as we drive off. In the end, it doesn't matter anyway. Tomorrow is Women's Day, the Russian equivalent of Mother's Day, and a story like this is hardly going to make for suitable family holiday viewing. So Sacha drives us to a nearby flower market and we take some pictures of that, instead.

24

MID-LIFE STRAIN TO GEORGIA

Drive-By Truckers and The Hold Steady on the *Rock'n'Roll Means Well* tour

NOVEMBER 2008

WHEN *UNCUT* **MAGAZINE** called and asked if I fancied this one, I was initially hesitant. It wasn't because I had any reservations about either of the groups I'd be spending time with. I admire The Hold Steady hugely, and as for Drive-By Truckers, well, sometimes, when a cut from "Decoration Day," "The Dirty South" or "Brighter than Creation's Dark" pops up on my iPod at an apposite moment, I think they might well be the best band in the world. It wasn't even because I already had a trip to the US planned at around this time—to Philadelphia, to write an afterword for another book amid (or so I anticipated and hoped) the first days of the Obama era (I'd chosen Philadelphia partly because of its stature as the birthplace of America's glorious democratic experiment, mostly just because I like the place). What gave me pause was the prospect of being, for the first time in years, properly on tour—as in sleeping on the bus, massaging throbbing and hungover temples while someone's drummer soundchecks—even if only for a couple of days.

Because it's awful, it really is. Even the bits which aren't awful—the laughter, the in-jokes, the camaraderie, the odd surreal surprises that touring scatters in your path—only seem like they're not awful because they represent a fleeting respite from the awfulness of it all. Touring is—well, okay, was—not such a bad way to spend one's early twenties, when the average male human, certainly, is barely distinguishable from the average male baboon, and is therefore abundantly pleased by the trivial, mindless gratifications offered by this way of life. For grownups, however—for people, that is, like Drive-By Truckers and The Hold Steady, who have hinterlands, families, friends, lives, interests, the habit of reading unillustrated books—it's a wretched, detached, deranging and lonely vocation.

These are, of course, the views of the author, not necessarily of Drive-By Truckers or The Hold Steady, hardcore road monsters all—people absolutely driven to be driven, and a good thing too, as the more people get to see both groups live, the happier our world will be. The fact remains, however, that the piece that follows amounts to a snapshot of intelligent and sensitive adults voluntarily submitting themselves to weeks at a time of a daily regime of twenty-three hours of boredom, irritation, humiliation, drunkenness and fitful sleep erratically redeemed by a sixty-minute (give or take the encores) hit of adrenalised excitement. To which the obvious retort is that it still beats working, and I'm sure that's true, but not by as comprehensive a knockout as the uninitiated might imagine. It requires truly extraordinary commitment, and an acceptance of ennui verging on the Zen, to resign yourself to a day waiting in a car park to play to a half-full venue.

All that said—or, rather, all that whined—I'm glad I went (for one reason or another, whatever the story, wherever the location, I'm always glad I went). I got to go to two cities I'd never been to before. In Atlanta, I saw the Coca-Cola museum, which is as brilliant as it is strange. In Tallahassee, I met the single fattest person I've ever encountered, the driver of a taxi I hailed (his girth was such that the lower third of the steering wheel was completely enfolded by his surfeit of stomach, and he wasn't wearing a seatbelt because he couldn't, though as he was essentially his own airbag, I don't suppose it mattered, much). And I saw two great shows by two great bands, which works out at four great shows.

★ ★ ★

"THIS SHIT IS so good," declares Patterson Hood, brandishing the bottle meaningfully, "that they . . . they put a cork in it."

One senses that this is praise indeed for whiskey, where Hood is concerned. He waves dismissively at the lesser screw-capped bourbons huddled on the tour bus kitchenette, and passes the eight-year-old Basil Hayden's across the aisle. One swig confirms his judgement: high octane honey. Hood, a man gripped by ungovernable enthusiasms even at his most relaxed, has not long ago taken his last bows after a triumphant, riotous performance by Drive-By Truckers and The Hold Steady at Atlanta's Tabernacle, and is somewhat amped. Meet the wife (hello). Here's a picture of my daughter (she's lovely). You gotta hear the new Jenny Lewis (I have, but carry on). Next to Hood, Drive-By Truckers' tour manager, Matt DeFelippis, demonstrates the importance of modern communications technology in coordinating the modern rock tour. The Truckers' other primary songwriter, Mike Cooley, has phoned in lost while attempting to return from a post-show drink. He's muttering menacing imprecations about the tramp he paid four dollars for erroneous directions, and going so far as to suggest that General Sherman had the right idea when he burnt Atlanta to the ground in 1864: a spectacular heresy from a son of Alabama. Matt sighs, flips open his laptop, calls up Google Maps, and talks the guitarist in. It's already nearly 3:00 AM, and we still have a six-hour drive to Florida ahead of us, just as soon as all are aboard.

Tonight has been the third of the twenty-three-date *Rock'n'Roll Means Well* tour. Drive-By Truckers and The Hold Steady are taking turns to headline, and in Atlanta, in deference to the Truckers' local roots—most of the band live in nearby Athens—The Hold Steady had taken the early slot, and demonstrated that they had friends of their own in the building: the signature shout-along refrains of "Stay Positive," "Constructive Summer" and "Massive Nights" had all but drowned out the band. Even by his own hyperactive standards, Hold Steady frontman Craig Finn had been animated, whirling and twitching and conveying the impression that his guitar strap was all that was holding the constituent—and apparently unrelated—parts of his body together (he dances about as much like a late-thirtysomething white guy from Minnesota as might be imagined). It's a jarring, compelling spectacle, these wordy, coolly literate songs, soundtracked by the supercharged bar blues of The Hold Steady, delivered by this seething, bespectacled, anxious apparition: Bruce Springsteen trapped in the body of Elvis Costello.

It was always going to be Drive-By Truckers' night, though—most of the audience had looked like one or other member of the band, many men sporting beards rivalling those of drummer Brad Morgan, women favouring the high-piled hair of bassplayer Shonna Tucker despite the style's recent disgracing by Sarah Palin. Patterson had lumbered on ahead of his group looking, in silhouette under the spotlight, like a grizzly stalked by hunters. He'd beamed out at the crowd, just beamed, until Cooley had cranked up "Three Dimes Down." From there, the Truckers had unleashed a stellar selection of their bleary boogie, culminating in a furious version of Neil Young's "Rockin' in the Free World," Finn joining in on backing vocals, followed by a barrel through Jim Carroll's "All the People Who Died," involving a certain amount of instrument-swapping between the Truckers, The Hold Steady, road crew and friends of the bands.

Tonight's show has also, like this tour as a whole, functioned as a heartening national unity ticket, set as it is against the backdrop of the final stages of a sensationally rancorous presidential election. Drive-By Truckers and The Hold Steady appear, at first glance, a positively cartoonish illustration of America's enduring North-South divide. The Truckers seem almost an archetype of Southern rock—thick of facial hair, heavy of riff, lyrically interested in drink, despair and defiance. The Hold Steady seem an hysterically stereotypical exemplar of Northern college indie—wordy, nerdy, bespectacled. What can be said of both bands is that, in both cases, there's far more going on than the passing observer might conclude. The Truckers, Hood in particular, have omnivorous musical interests (over dinner before the show, Hood had launched, quite unprompted, into an impassioned and detailed soliloquy on the genius of Squeeze) and a lyrical outlook that is curious, compassionate and really not terribly philosophically congruent with much of the writings of Lynryd Skynyrd. The Hold Steady, for their part, rock as hard as any old-school bar-room rattlers, the unreconstructed fretboard-wringing of lead guitarist Tad Kubler suggesting what might have resulted had Steve Gaines survived the 1977 plane crash which wiped out Skynyrd, then—in an admittedly unlikely career move—successfully auditioned for The Attractions (Kubler has also impressed the heck out of me, at least, with what must be the first unironic live deployment of a twin-necked Gibson since the release of *Hotel California*).

Another thing the two groups have in common, for the next twenty shows at least, is a hell of a tough act to follow.

THE ATLANTA TABERNACLE is the kind of place that bands tell themselves they'll play in one day, as they toil to make the endurance of lesser dives and dumps feel worthwhile. The room itself is spectacular enough—a former Baptist church and hospital, built in 1910, now a 2,600-capacity venue with three layers of seating beneath a soaring ceiling. However, it's the separate backstage annexe that has all present grinning involuntarily as they wander the corridors. The catering is terrific, the toilets are clean, the dressing rooms sufficiently plentiful that a visiting journalist and photographer get one to ourselves and— these things really do matter much more to the itinerant musician than the colour-sorted M&Ms of popular legend—there's a washing machine and tumble dryer. As Drive-By Truckers' soundcheck thuds through the walls, The Hold Steady's bassplayer, Galen Polivka, sorts piles of socks, shirts and boxer shorts. "Living the dream," he smiles, and he's not entirely joking.

In between soundchecks, with the accordion practice of The Hold Steady's Franz Nicolay providing a soundtrack from an adjacent dressing room, Hood and Finn gather to survey the road ahead. *Rock'n'Roll Means Well*: discuss.

"I came up with the name for the tour," says Finn, "but it's based on one of Mike Cooley's lyrics [in the song 'Marry Me,' from the Truckers' *Decoration Day*]. I thought there was something in that was kind of what people who understood rock'n'roll would . . . well, we're both kind of older, as bands, and we have a pretty good take on what's cool about rock'n'roll. And, you know, there's a humour in there."

Finn is thirty-seven, Hood forty-four. For Finn, success has come late, and quickly. He first took the stage with The Hold Steady in his adopted New York in 2003—partly inspired into action, he wants it noted, by seeing Drive-By Truckers live—and has already led them through four albums even as they discharged a relentless touring schedule. For Hood, this is all he has ever wanted to do, ever since he saw Bruce Springsteen on *The River* tour, having spun his disapproving parents a sensationally elaborate web of deceit to explain his night away from home. Rock'n'roll was founded as a youth cult, and perhaps for that reason there remains a reflexive tendency to snigger at those who insist on practising past the point of that first fervid flush. Both men acknowledge this, but insist that they are (at least slightly) wiser, as well as older.

"It's that middle era of touring where I think the problems are," says Hood. "In the early days, you're in the van and you're just glad to be there, and you go and you go and you go. The middle is where it's getting better, but it's still really rough, and it's nothing like you think it's gonna be when it gets better—you're riding in a bus for the first time, but it's a shitty bus, and breaking down all the time, and the aircon don't work, you get a record deal, and it turns out it sucks."

"That's also when the partying can kind of get a little weird for a while," says Finn, "before you think, 'I don't wanna feel this way all the time.' Now, I can go on tour like a normal human being, whereas two or three years ago, I was just on tour."

The formalising of the Drive-By Truckers/Hold Steady mutual admiration society into this tour took place by email between Hood and Kubler after the two met in New York last summer. Hood loves The Hold Steady: the line "I'm trying to hold steady" in a newish Truckers song, "The Righteous Path," is a deliberate homage.

"And I just thought," says Hood, "this tour might be the best chance I ever have to see them play."

Hood's favourite Hold Steady song is "Chill Out Tent."

"That's the one that made me fall in love," he declares. "I heard it a couple of times before I really listened to it, and the first time I got it, it was like . . . wow. Let me hear that again. But I've been on such a big kick with the new album lately, and I'm really loving 'Lord, I'm Discouraged.' Y'all have got the best titles."

"I stole that from Charley Patton," admits Finn, acknowledging the legendary Delta bluesman. "Well, that and the fact that whenever I upset my mother, she'd shake her head and sigh 'Discouraging.' My favourite Truckers song changes daily, but I was thinking about two. One is 'Zip City,' which is Cooley's song, and one is 'Heathens,' which is Patterson's. They both feature cars that have gone into ditches. I was thinking there should be another song, and it should be the ditch trilogy."

"'Zip City' is my favourite Drive-By Truckers song," agrees Hood.

"Yeah," nods Finn. "There's something tender, in a weird way, about that song."

Hood laughs incredulously, as well he might. "Zip City," from the Truckers' 2001 epic *Southern Rock Opera*—a hugely ambitious concept album studying what Hood calls "the duality of the Southern thing" as expressed in the lives and works of such Alabama totems as Skynyrd, Bear Bryant and George Wallace—is a typically mordant Cooley lyric, recalling thwarted teenage lust for an underage girl resident in the titular Alabama hamlet. The song is, it's fair to say, somewhat unkind to her family ("Your brother was the first-born, got ten fingers and ten toes/And it's a damn good thing 'cos he needs all twenty to keep the closet door closed").

"Tender meaning wounded," insists Finn. "Painful to the touch."

"Man," hoots Hood. "You should have been there the day the girl turned up at the show."

In other respects, the two groups are very different. Drive-By Truckers hold open house backstage more or less until showtime, and arrive onstage with nothing planned beyond the first song—the set from thereon is improvised according to the mood of the room and the band. The Hold Steady take turns by alphabetical order to write a setlist, and prefer to be left alone before the show, listening to music—including, in Atlanta, The Cars' "Let's Go" and Boz Scagg's "Lido Shuffle." They engage in a clearly ritiualised circle of high fives just before taking stage. Then, of course, there's that North-South thing . . .

"I know we had to cancel those UK dates when Tad got sick," says Finn (Kubler had been hospitalised with pancreatitis a few months previously). "But my plan was to buy one of those Newcastle United shirts with [Newcastle's sponsors, a building society] 'Northern Rock' on it. But really, you can't say Northern rock and have people understand what you mean the way you can with Southern rock."

"I'm envious about that," says Hood, "because I fuckin' hate the phrase Southern rock. But I always loved music that had a real sense of place—Springsteen's Jersey Shore, The Ramones' Queens, The Replacements being so obviously from Minneapolis. When I was in high school, I didn't know what any of the stuff they were singing about was, but I wanted to."

"When I watch a movie," nods Finn, "I get really obsessed with the location, almost to the point where I can't concentrate on the film. When I get to spots on tour, I need to walk around for a while, just to understand where I'm at. I think that's very much part of writing, just being rooted, figuring out where you are."

Are there worries, putting together a tour like this, that there'll be locations where one band gets called back for three encores, while the other gets showered in empties?

"We broke up North first," says Hood. "The South and the Midwest were difficult for us. Actually, the South was brutal for us. All our songs are about small, fucked-up little hick towns, and in the South the only places where there are venues to play tend to be college towns which are full of kids who just got the fuck out of some small, fucked-up little hick town. The last thing they want to hear is someone singing about where they came from. They want to hear someone singing about somewhere exotic. Like Minneapolis, or Brooklyn. And I love that. I also like the fact that both our new records end with songs that namedrop directors, and they're almost representative polar points— John Cassavetes [in The Hold Steady's *Slapped Actress*] and John Ford [in the Truckers' *Monument Valley*]."

"We were on this tour this summer," says Craig, "and we hadn't really done the Southeast much at all, and we went to Baton Rouge, Oxford, Charleston—roadhouses, you know, putting 400 people where 300 people should be, and it was great."

"The lines in this country now," says Hood, "are more red state/ blue state, rather than North and South, because so many Southerners moved up North in the hundred years after the war."

There is laughter all round at this reminder that Hood is the only one in the room who comes from a place where "the war" is shorthand for the US Civil War, rather than World War II.

The collective regard for each other notwithstanding, is there a sense of competition between the bands?

"It's not super-competitive," says Finn, "but if someone goes on before you and plays really well, you want to do at least as well."

"It's the good kind of competition," says Hood. "I wouldn't respect 'em if they didn't go up there and absolutely try to wipe the stage with us every night. That's good for the rock."

This last line is delivered utterly absent of irony. Something else the two bands have in common: an unswerving belief in rock'n'roll as a means and expression of redemption and succour. Even on nights it feels like neither of those things.

"MAN," SAYS COOLEY, leaning on the bus, in the parking lot behind a Tallahassee nightclub called The Moon. "That was like fucking your sister. I mean, respond, goddammit."

It's one night and another Drive-By Truckers set later. Cooley's gift for deadpan coinages is no surprise: his songs heave with glorious zingers. It is clearly his view, however, that these have been insufficiently appreciated this evening: the Truckers went on first, playing to a room barely half-full, and barely half-full at that of Sunday drinkers who seemed to be coming down off a big weekend.

"The one time of day I don't want to be alone," he continues, "and where is everybody? This is Florida, dammit. Holler. Show me some titties."

Today has been a study in the unglamorous reality of the touring life: overnight on the tour bus, all day hanging around a venue in the kind of town in which there's nothing much to do but hang around the venue. At one point in the afternoon, Cooley had discovered i) a golf cart, and ii) the interesting fact that you can start one by jamming a bottle opener into the ignition, but there are only so many piles of empty beer cartons a grown man can satisfyingly drive through in a day. The only thing which has distinguished today from hundreds of others like it that Cooley has had, and hundreds more he is yet to have, has been the quite startling manifestation in the backstage parking lot of rooster-haired funk god George Clinton (he lives up the road, for reasons surpassing understanding, and is apparently a friend of the venue's owner).

And the show, at least in the Truckers' view, hasn't gone all that brilliantly. They're back in the bus, consuming the superb roast dinner that bassist Shonna Tucker has concocted on the onboard kitchenette from locally sourced organic meat and vegetables. Hood, as ever, is talking eight beats to the bar about music—about his father's recent induction into the Alabama Music Hall of Fame (David Hood played bass in the legendary Muscle Shoals rhythm section) and about the album the Truckers have just made as a pick-up band for Booker T, with Neil Young contributing guitar (Hood plays me some rough mixes: the version of Outkast's "Hey Ya" is astounding).

By common consent, tonight belongs to The Hold Steady. From the moment they bound on to their intro tape, David Lee Roth's "Yankee Rose," they're focused, furious, determined to wring what gold there is from the base metal of a smallish, diffident audience. The group's enthusiasm swiftly proves overwhelming, and the screams—actual screams, by the end—for an encore are rewarded with the biggest convening yet of The Drive Hold By Steady Truckers supergroup. Hood appears in a Barack Obama t-shirt to help out on The Hold Steady's creeping, malevolent take on AC/DC's "Ride On," and further Truckers wander on for Blue Oyster Cult's "Burning For You," The Band's "Look Out Cleveland"—Cooley has not deigned to change back out of his after-show apparel of sweatshirt, pyjama bottoms and slippers—and The Hold Steady's "Killer Parties."

In normal circumstances, all that both groups would now have to look forward to is another interminable bus ride. However, the schedule is disrupted by one of those strange, surreal surprises that makes the bumpy bunks and boredom of touring worth enduring: would we, someone asks, care to drop by Clinton's studio, where he is not only awaiting us, but has apparently switched on the Mothership—the famous flying saucer stage prop in which Clinton would descend stageward in his 70s heyday. And so, at two in the morning, two vast tour buses follow a car through the outskirts of Tallahassee, to a house distinguished only by a poetically apposite address—1300 Hendrix Road—and by colourful flashing lights in the windows. The bemused groups troop inside, through a couple of recording studios, past walls of gold and platinum albums won by Parliament and Funkadelic, to the source of the illuminations: the Clinton mothership, now parked permanently in one room in the complex. The craft's pilot duly appears, poses for photos, offers handshakes, bestows blessings and exits without betraying the vaguest hint that he knows or cares who any of these people are, or why they're in his house at this hour. Patterson leans unsteadily on my shoulder.

"Andrew," he says, "It's been a long day, and I'm tired, and I've had quite a lot to drink, but . . ."

Yes, I reassure him. That's a spaceship. And that was George Clinton.

THE LINE AFTER "Rock'n'roll means well" in "Marry Me" is ". . . but it can't help telling young boys lies." I bid farewell to Drive-By Truckers and The Hold Steady outside Clinton's studio, and commiserate with them on the sixteen-hour drive between here and their next assignation in Raleigh, North Carolina.

Both these bands are, as they freely admit, old enough to know better, but both are full of people still driven to scratch furiously at that itch caused by that first brush with Bruce Springsteen, The Replacements or whatever you're having yourself. And somewhere in America, though that person may not know it yet themselves, is someone who was in the crowd at the four shows played or the nineteen still to go, and who is, twenty or even thirty years hence, going to struggle for sleep on a bus, curse a flat crowd, be introduced in bewildering circumstances to a legend of popular music and his flying saucer and wonder whether to thank or blame Drive-By Truckers and The Hold Steady.

25

CRAZY NORSES

Iceland

FEBRUARY 1997, JULY 1997, JUNE 1998

I **HAVEN'T BEEN TO** Iceland since I wrote what appears below, stitched together from three assignments—one for *The Independent*, one for *The Sunday Times* and one, as it turned out, for reasons explained shortly, for nobody. What happened, essentially, was this. For the first time ever, Iceland exported a famous pop group, The Sugarcubes, from which emerged an even more famous pop singer, Björk. The inevitable result was that everybody in Iceland, more or less, then formed a pop group of their own. Most of these, as is the way of such opportunist clusterfucks—see Manchester circa 1990, Seattle circa 1993—were neither use nor ornament, but this did not deter the pertinent departments of Iceland's government from displaying the blithe largesse with public money characteristic of Scandinavian societies. Frequent flights and generous accommodations were laid on for foreign music, arts and travel journalists interested in visiting Reykjavik—and the aeroplane seats and hotel rooms filled briskly as word spread of Iceland's aptitude for sodden revelry, and (not incidentally) of the frostbitten island's womenfolk, whose poleaxing beauty was secondary, as an attraction, only to their cheerful, enthusiastic and altogether refreshing lack of discrimination where visiting males were concerned.

There were two severe, and eventually terminal, problems with this otherwise splendid arrangement. One was that commissioning editors rapidly grew bored with—and suspicious about—story pitches involving Iceland: one began to run up against responses like "What, again? Won't this be the fifth new Bjork and/or Sigur Ros you've interviewed this year?" The other was that we serial junketers failed to organise ourselves—somebody, on one of the flights back, should have struggled to their feet and reminded the whimperingly hungover and hopelessly lovelorn passenger manifest that if at least one of us didn't get something into print sometime soon, our hosts would wise up and we would be reduced, once again, to spending our weekends in places which didn't seem like some alien planet where everything was just like it was on Earth, but weirder and better.

So I haven't been back to Iceland. The spirit has been willing, but the bank balance weak—even by the uproarious standards of Scandinavia, Iceland was always very much a place you want to visit on expenses. I therefore missed riding along on any part of the up-as-a-rocket, down-as-a-stick economic trajectory that Iceland pursued over the subsequent decade. So I wasn't there as Iceland's financial services industry boomed, bequeathing every citizen with (one prefers to assume) their own platinum-plated snowmobile, and I wasn't there when the undignified implosion of that same banking sector, which has (or so one reads) reduced Iceland to a subsistence economy under which everyone is forced to dine on thin soup made from puffin beaks, and the currency is now the herring.

★ ★ ★

THEY DO THINGS differently in Reykjavik. This much can be gleaned, on this long, northern-lights-illuminated winter's night, from the polite, apologetic demeanour of the young chap who has been dispatched upstairs by his superiors at the Loftleidir Hotel's reception desk.

The scene before him would test the humour, and the credulity, of any hotel employee. In the corridor, three people lie unconscious, the worse for the evening's hilarity. The plate glass window on the landing is rent by a large, suspiciously foot-shaped hole. At the end of the hall, a half-dressed blond man with a length of blue rope tied around his waist is crawling on all fours and barking like a dog; at the other end of the blue rope is an unfeasibly tall red-haired woman dressed in black rubber, who appears to be taking him for a walk. There are parties occuring in at least five rooms, involving a volatile mix of musicians, local scenesters, foreign media and two pizza delivery boys who thought it all looked like more fun than going back to work. Leaning against one wall is a decent-sized tree that someone has liberated from its pot in the lobby.

Most hotels would have sent for the police, or possibly the army, some hours ago. The bloke from reception knocks on one open door, barely audible above the music blasting out of the room's television set. Unheard, he steps over the shattered form of Baldur Steffanson, the manager of Gus Gus, the Reykjavik band everyone's come to spend the weekend with. Baldur is dozing peacefully, a bottle of vodka cradled in one arm and the words "Love Me" printed on his forehead in black ink by some prankster.

"Excuse me," the bloke from reception says, dimming the volume on the television. "Could you all possibly please keep it down a little bit?"

It's just gone eight in the morning. So, they won't let you bring your cocktail into the breakfast room, but that aside, Reykjavik's credentials as a the kind of place you'd want to spend more time in seem, on first acquaintance, impeccable.

IN ICELAND IN the summertime, the sun doesn't set, it bounces. Just after midnight, it dips below the horizon before emerging minutes later, like some vast celestial digit that has been dipped gingerly into the North Atlantic and found the water too cold. It doesn't really get dark at all. I spend days feeling jetlagged—my body clock, deprived of its day/night mechanisms, demands hot dinners at four in the morning and plunges me into deep sleeps at five in the afternoon. There are few feelings as appalling as staggering out of a dark nightclub at three in the morning to get a face full of blazing mid-afternoon sunshine.

The acclimatised locals regard the relentless daylight of June and July as a fine excuse for staying up all night, getting uproariously drunk and staggering around Reykjavik until dawn trying to find someone to get into a fight or bed with. Though, given that Icelanders seem to feel pretty much the same about the other ten months of the year, not too much should be read into this.

For most of its thousand-odd years of human settlement, Iceland has been a wallflower at the dance of nations. On the rare occasions that the toadfish-shaped island has made the nine o'clock news, it's generally been due to forces beyond its control. These have originated either outside Iceland (the Cod War with Britain in the 70s, the Reagan/Gorbachev summit in 1986) or under it (the sudden appearance of the island of Surtsey in 1963, the volcanic eruption that forced the evacuation of the island of Heimaey in 1973, 1996's spectacular meltdown of the mighty Vatnajökull icecap).

In the last couple of years, though, Iceland's stock has risen dramatically. At last count, every magazine in the world has packed a feature writer off to knock up a piece titled "The Coolest Place On Earth." These pieces invariably mention that Björk lives here, that Damon Albarn of Blur lives here sometimes, that Icelanders drink a lot and eat puffins, and that the drink, like the puffin, and like everything else for that matter, is terribly expensive.

This is all true enough. Björk has become only the third internationally famous Icelander in history, after Leif Eiríksson and Magnus Magnússon.

Eiríksson achieved his fame by discovering America nearly five centuries before Columbus, even if he did keep getting chased out of it by the natives; Magnússon by spending years and years on television asking mad old librarians and retired colonels arcane questions about P.G. Wodehouse and steam trains.

Björk has done it by dressing up as an assortment of Christmas tree decorations and warbling, to periodically beguiling effect, in a voice which sounds like an angel with hiccups; I always kind of preferred the records she made with The Sugarcubes, myself. Her success has invigorated Iceland, encouraging Reykjavik's large subclass of bohemian dilettantes to entertain ambition as well as delusions of artistic grandeur. Everybody under the age of forty that I meet in Reykjavik gives their occupation as singer, poet, actor, novelist, photographer, director or sculptor. I have no idea who, if anyone, is doing Iceland's actual work. If this generation ever decides to replace Iceland's national anthem, the only realistic title for the new one will be "I Have a Number of Projects in Development."

It's not surprising that a few British artists have been tempted to find out if there's something stimulating in Iceland's sulphurous tap water. Blur recorded much of their fifth, and best, album in a Reykjavik studio. Several other celebrities of various description have been spotted beneath the tables of the city's nightspots. It's been enough to prompt Albarn to worry out loud that Iceland will turn into "the new Ibiza," but he shouldn't concern himself overmuch—Iceland's prices will continue to prove the most effective deterrent to package tour invasion a country could possibly muster, short of staging a civil war or ebola epidemic. A modest round of drinks for four leaves little change from thirty quid. The McDonald's takes credit cards.

REYKJAVIK IS HOME to half of Iceland's population of 260,000. It's a cosy, low-rise town almost completely lacking in such traditional signifiers of municipal stature as pollution, crime and poverty. The poor parts of town—the colourful new pre-fab flats that sit along the road in from Keflavik airport—don't look all that poor. The rich parts—the colourful old wooden houses that cluster around the body of water in the city centre that is either a small lake or a big pond—don't look all that rich.

Reykjavik has only two landmarks. One, Hallgrímskirkja, is a large basalt church that presides over the centre of the city; built from unblemished, monotone grey stone, it look like it was assembled last week from a kit. The other is Perlan, an excellent but riotously expensive revolving restaurant which sits atop four silver water tanks, and looks like something that might have been inhabited by the bad guy in the black jumpsuit in a Jon Pertwee-era episode of *Doctor Who*.

By day, Reykjavik has the forlorn, deserted feel of a theme park closed for repairs. The only times I see crowds are on the Tuesday, when they're out celebrating Iceland's national day—the birthday of nineteenth-century nationalist hero Jon Sigurdsson—and on the Friday and Saturday nights, when they're out celebrating Friday and Saturday night. Nothing happens in Reykjavik until midnight, and after midnight everything that does happen in Reykjavik looks and sounds like a crowd scene from *Caligula*.

The frenetic wassailing centres on a few clubs based on and around Laugavegur and Bankastraeti, all a short stumble apart in the middle of town. Places like Kaffibarrin, Cafe au Lait and Rosenborg begin to fill up properly at about 1:00 AM—due to the frightening expense of drinking in clubs, people tend to warm up by drinking at home.

By chucking-out time at 3:00 AM, all of them are full of Icelanders enjoying themselves, which is to say all these clubs look like they are hosting a match of some Nordic variant of indoor rugby played with 200 on each side and no ball.

The natives, while occasionally terrifyingly exuberant, are friendly. It's not difficult, on nights like these, to find people willing to talk to someone from out of town (that said, it's not difficult, on nights like these, to find people happy to talk to mailboxes, streetlamps, potted plants and themselves). And when the people of Reykjavik address you, after a few drinks, it's like nothing you've ever heard, especially if you're male and not used to women so beautiful they could have put Helen out of the ship-launching racket for good saying the kind of things that women who look like that usually only say to you when you're dreaming. Their technique stops only just short of a club over the head, a hoist over one shoulder and a drag back to their cave.

"Icelandic men," explains one such vision, one night, "are no good. That's why we like it when foreign men come here. Fresh meat."

Right.

"Icelandic men drink too much and never speak of their feelings."

I've heard this complaint about other nationalities of my gender, funnily enough, but I don't have time to elaborate. She grabs me by the hand and leads me at a brisk march through the crowd to a table at the other end of the club, where two morose young men sit silently contemplating their drinks.

"You see these two shitbags?"

Evening, chaps.

"My ex-husbands. I have a son with that one and a daughter with that one."

God, but I wish she'd let go of me. Neither of the fathers of her children look that far descended from the Vikings. Happily, they don't seem to object to her, or her tirade, or me, much. In fact, I get the impression they're used to it—it does seem that everyone in Reykjavik has been married to everyone else at least once.

"Now," she announces. "I have never slept with an Australian."

I return to my hotel alone, convinced that there must be a catch to this somewhere.

ASIDE FROM REYKJAVIK'S lately acquired, and thoroughly warranted, reputation as the world's finest night out, Iceland's major appeal is its unique geological volatility. Everywhere else on the planet, the ground is what things happen to, or on, or above. In Iceland, the ground is what happens. On this vast, spherical bottle of agitated, bubbling rock that humanity calls home, Iceland is the twitching cork.

There are numerous sites around Reykjavik that confirm this, strung together on a route called "The Golden Circle." The Golden Circle isn't circular, and nothing in the bleak, rugged Icelandic countryside is golden, but tourist brochures have to call their excursions something, and nobody's going to sell many tickets for a coach trip around The Gloomy Ellipse.

The first stop is enchantingly pointless: a large greenhouse where the principal "attraction" is a collection of South American banana plants. I wonder if, under some reciprocal agreement organised in the name of Icelandic-Colombian friendship, there's a museum full of horned helmets and longboats on the outskirts of Bogota.

We are then driven to a large, geographically significant hole in the ground, which I have difficulty distinguishing from the many large, geographically insignificant holes in the ground I have seen in my time. Things improve dramatically when the bus disgorges its cargo of German pensioners and me at the Gullfoss falls. Gullfoss, the most spectacular of Iceland's umpty-hundred waterfalls, is where the glacial waters of the Hyvítá River tumble down two thirty-metre cascades at right angles to each other. The result is a rainbow-necklaced fountain of vapour that goes up as high as the falls go down. As is the case with most of Iceland's natural attractions, there is little in the way of fences or ropes to stop you from getting too close. It's possible to creep along one muddy ledge far enough to reach out and touch the fall, which is both a startling lesson in the fall's power and a sad reminder of how many of the world's natural wonders are as fenced off and inaccessible as zoo exhibits.

At Geysir—the field of bubbling, sneezing puddles that has given its name to similar phenomena everywhere—there are only desultory ropes and signs gently reminding visitors that falling into boiling volcanic mud can be bad for you. The actual Great Geysir packed it in some decades back, so the main reason for being here now is the

Strokkur spout, which blasts water twenty metres into the air every five minutes or so. This is mildy entertaining the first time, and after that amusing only in proportion to the number of unwary German camcorder enthusiasts it drenches in hot sulphuric spume.

The final stop on the Golden Circle is Thingvellir, the lava plain that was the site of Iceland's—and the world's—first national assembly, the Althing, first convened in 930. The significance of the place is acknowledged only by an Icelandic flag flapping on the spot where chieftains would address this early experiment in democracy, but Thingvellir bears a much more imposing natural gravitas. The site is rent by a huge gash in the black rock that marks the boundary where the American and European continental plates grind together. The fissure in between the two cliffs is muddy, and carpeted with pale green moss. Climbing down to stand on it, I feel that with a big enough lever, I could prise the whole world apart.

ALL OF ICELAND is apt to engender a sense of humanity's impotence before the forces commanded by nature, but Heimaey, more than anywhere else, is an eloquent confirmation of our status as barely tolerated parasites. Heimaey is the largest of the Westmann Islands, a cluster of small-to-medium-sized lumps of rock off Iceland's south coast, a twenty-five-minute flight from Reykjavik.

The Westmann Islands are a reminder that, before the disintegration of the Soviet Union, it was only Iceland that kept the world's mapmakers in steady business. Contemplating the geology of the Westmanns, and comparing it with the stately pace at which the rest of the planet erodes and erupts, is as disorientating as listening to a 33rpm record at 78. One of the Westmanns, Surtsey, appeared out of the sea between 1963 and 1967. In 1973, Heimaey, the largest and the only inhabited Westmann island, was enlarged twenty percent by an eruption beneath the ocean that buried much of the town and forced the population to leave for six months—it can be imagined that Heimaey's insurance underwriters were the first aboard the fleeing trawler boats and its real estate agents the last.

This recently arrived portion of Heimaey still belches grumpy clouds of steam, and the ground below the top layer of dirt is hot enough to burn skin, which is something I discover the hard way. If you can be bothered, it is apparently possible to bake bread in it, by digging a hole and burying your dough overnight. It's a sobering idea to take on board, the notion of the ground as a living thing, capable of such fury. When I get aboard one of the cruise boats that sail around the island, it's striking how much the charred mountain spewed up in 1973 resembles an immense clenched fist in the process of snatching lush, placid Heimaey back into the sea.

The inert, lunar landscape of the new Heimaey is a total contrast to the life that teems around the rest of the island. On Heimaey's cliffs nest uncountable thousands of puffins, terns and gulls, and in the water beneath the boat lurk otherwordly fugitives from Neptune's nightmares. These creatures are on display in Heimaey's small aquarium, and are almost enough to put me off lunch. The Icelandic catfish is, beyond any doubt, the single ugliest creature on earth. They look like diseased lungs with faces.

AT THE OTHER end of Iceland, Grimsey Island feels like the last stop before the end of the world. This tiny tumour of rock, home to eighty or so hardy, self-contained souls, would be disregarded by the world at large were it not for a fluke of cartography: Grimsey perches neatly atop latitude 66°33' N—the Arctic Circle. A road sign embedded in a cement block set exactly on the Circle displays the immense distances between Grimsey and anywhere else—16317 kilometres to where I grew up, for want of a better phrase, in Sydney; 4445 kilometres to my last assignment, in New York; 1949 kilometres to my home in London.

Despite Grimsey's windswept remoteness, I'm not keen to leave, for two reasons. One is that Grimsey's windswept remoteness is rather beguiling: its subtle colours are delicately enriched by the late-night sunshine, and the clouds of arctic tern that eddy and swirl around the cliffs have a hypnotic compulsion about them, at least until they realise I'm standing within a mile of their nests and start going for my eyes—I suddenly understand why all the children on the island are wearing bicycle helmets. The other reason I don't want to leave is that leaving is going to involve getting back aboard the plane I arrived on.

Flying at the best of times—by which I mean sitting in a posh seat up the front with movies and video games in a nice big jet-engined aircraft on a calm, clear day—is about my least favourite thing in the world, comprised as it is of long periods of extremity-numbing boredom interspersed with moments of pure, sweaty-palmed terror. This is not the best of times. The daily flight between Grimsey and Iceland's northern regional capital of Akureyri is a dice with the crosswinds that ensnare the island and befoul the Eyjafjördur fjord into which Akureyri airport's runway juts. Yesterday, the pilot tells me, the twin-propeller, twelve-seater winged lawnmower that plies the twenty-minute route had been forced to turn back halfway. Our flight here had inspired in me an unprecedented interest in prayer, and had ended with an almost vertical dive onto Grimsey's runway, which is carved out of the side of a hill. Since then, the wind has, if anything, picked up.

"You know," says the pilot, who has either been driven insane by the job or was born mad enough to apply for it, "sometimes we have to wait for the weather. Haha! Once, we couldn't leave for two weeks! Haha!"

Hilarious.

"Haha! Yes! One of the passengers was supposed to be getting married! In Akureyri! You can imagine! Haha!"

Perhaps you had to be there. Half a dozen of Grimsey's cycle-helmet-encumbered children gambol up and down the runway, waving sticks and yelping, to clear the birds sitting along it.

"Yes! Haha! They can get into the propellers! Cause big mess! Maybe even crash! Haha!"

The children or the seagulls?

"Haha! You are funny guy! Haha!"

The flight back to Akureyri is the longest twenty minutes of my life; the only other occasion I can remember time limping by quite so agonisingly slowly, I was reviewing The Eagles' reunion concert at Wembley Stadium. The tiny aeroplane pitches and lurches like a drunk man on a wonky footpath. The hoots and whines of the engine struggle to be heard over the hooting, whining wind, and the tormented creaks of the aircraft's structure compete with periodic shrieks of "Haha!" that emanate from the cockpit. Approaching the runway, the plane bounces in mid-air with such violence that, my circulation-threateningly tight seatbelt notwithstanding, I crack my head against the ceiling, drawing blood. "Haha!" says the pilot.

Five quid a pint or not, I've earnt a drink, and I head into town to see what Akureyrians do for fun of an evening. Unbelievably, what they do is drive their cars in slow, nose-to-tail laps of the tiny main street and the two car parks at each end of it. The waitress in the bar I'm watching this nonsense from explains that the ritual is called the *runtur*—a wheeled version of the Spanish corso, a sort of ritualised showing off. Unfortunately, only three of Akureyri's young blades have got the kind of motors necessary for doing this kind of adolescent preening properly—the owners of the Dodge GTS, the Ford Mustang and the Corvette. Everyone else here is starring in their own private *Icelandic Graffiti* in Saabs, Hondas and Renaults.

A LITTLE LESS than twelve months later, I'm back in Reykjavik, where it could not be said that Iceland's geologic majesty is high on anyone's list of priorities. A planeload of British press has been flown here by the Icelandic Arts Council, or someone, to experience an Icelandic Pop Festival, or something.

It strikes me sometime after midnight on the Friday that this is probably the most confused, exhausted and disoriented I've ever been, at least since that Eagles gig at Wembley. Four days ago, on Monday morning, I woke up in Jalalabad, Afghanistan. I'd got back to London, via Islamabad, on the Tuesday afternoon. On Thursday night I was on a plane to Reykjavik. Friday morning, I'd woken up in a park near the hotel.

And now I'm in a bar flooded with dazzling midnight sunlight, surrounded by Reykjavik's improbably perfectly-formed populace and several rather less exquisite fellow journalists, all behaving like Russian submariners on shore leave. The music is deafening and dizzying, and the vodka cocktails are not helping. I keep thinking that a week ago I was urging a Kabuli taxi driver to step on it a bit, lest we be caught blundering through the powercut-darkened streets after curfew, and I keep wishing that I could have brought my Afghan translator here with me tonight, so he could get some idea of how completely his city had perplexed me. If I'd told him what it was like to be right here, right now, where literally everything happening would, in his home town, be punishable by public flogging, he'd have thought I was winding him up, again.

"I have sent my boyfriend to the bar for some drinks," she's saying.

Well . . . okay. Though it must be my round by now.

"We have probably five minutes before he comes back. Let's get out of here."

Outside, there are no taxis, just the amiable affray that is closing time in downtown Reykjavik. Still, she's a woman as resourceful as she is determined. She flags down a passing car.

"Where are you staying?"

The kid behind the wheel thought he was taking his mates home, but he resigns himself to events as quickly as I have. I tell him where the hotel is, and she writes him a cheque for his trouble while he drives.

We've made it as far as my room when something occurs to her.

"The babysitter!" she says, retrieving her shoes. "My God! I must go home at once and pay her."

Okay . . .

"In three weeks I will be in London. I have your number. I will come to stay with you." She never rang.

26

MAGICAL MISSOURI TOUR

Branson
NOVEMBER 2008

I WROTE SOMETHING elsewhere in this volume about my bafflement regarding, and/or horror of, holiday destinations. So it may seem nearly as peculiar to the passing reader as it did to me that when I visited a place that exists for no other reason than to be a destination in which people take holidays, I had about as fine a weekend as I can imagine enjoying.

This was, granted, substantially to do with the company. A lot of the travelling I've done has been solo, and there is much to be said for that. Alone in an unfamiliar place, your perceptions are raw and immediate. Liberated from having to care overmuch what anyone else thinks of you, you're more open to allowing yourself to be led even further astray than you already are: there is a wondrously whimsical aspect to sauntering along a city street secure in the certain knowledge that you are not going to bump into anybody you know. You could be anyone, and so could everyone else.

That much acknowledged, an astute choice of travelling companion can make anywhere the only place you'd want to be—even, yes, Branson, Missouri (though possibly not Ashford, England—there are limits). Sartre was entirely correct when he observed that hell is other people, but he'd have been just as accurate—if much less appealing to subsequent generations of moody students in maladroitly applied eyeliner—if he'd observed that heaven is constructed of precisely the same material.

And counter-intuitive though it may seem, Branson was probably as pure a travel experience as I've had. The place is, yes, a tourist trap of elephantine proportions. However, Branson is unusual among tourist traps in that it is only being what it is, rather than trying to be what it thinks visitors might want. Most tourist destinations, whether Caribbean resorts, Spanish hotel complexes, paradisical tropical islands the world over, labour to make their guests feel, essentially, like they're still at home but someone has turned the weather up—encounters with the reality of the locality, if they must be endured, tend to be restricted to picturesque ruins and waiters in silly waistcoats. Branson, by contrast, is everything the self-conscious travel snob who ostentatiously abjures such places generally claims to seek—an unadulterated and authentic expression of a living native culture. Honestly, the only thing I'd change about the place is the volume of the thunderstorm sound effects at the indoor jungle-themed mini-golf course—Branson is a justly popular destination for veterans' reunions, and I'm not sure the combination of dense foliage and sudden loud noises is a congenial one for all its visitors.

The editor who commissioned this assignment, Rahul Jacob at The *Financial Times*' travel section, instructed that I refrain from sneering at my subject, and quite rightly so. Branson, for all its indisputable—and utterly undisguised—foibles, and its breezy brashness, is an altogether unassuming place, and I didn't meet a single person who wasn't courteous, chatty, and hospitable. I would be appalled to learn that anyone who had read my dispatch was inspired to visit Branson in order to laugh at it. Laughing with Branson, of course, is fine—especially once you realize how wise, warm, and refreshingly lacking in malice the joke is. This one's for my Huckleberry friend, without whom it would very likely have soared over my head.

★ ★ ★

IN A SOUVENIR shop in Branson's downtown district, I am given, with the most purehearted of intent, the least helpful directions I have ever received. "The post office?" says the woman behind the counter. "Go around the corner, walk three blocks, it's the building with the big American flag out front." In Branson, Missouri, this is approximately as helpful as saying "It's the building": everything has a big American flag out front.

TO FOREIGNERS WHO'VE heard of it, and to many Americans, Branson is a punchline: a chintzy, cheesy, corny, hopelessly downmarket destination, an above-ground cemetery for has-been and never-will-be entertainers and those visitors whose critical faculties are sufficiently derailed by old age to appreciate them. It represents an America generally disdained and/or misunderstood by foreign tourists, who tend to gravitate to big cities on the coasts—and it's the very definition of what metropolitan Americans mean when they snort, "flyover country." Branson is a place altogether unburdened by the ironic, a place where one may— as someone has—open a theatre bar called God & Country, knowing that nobody will think this gauche, a place where all the applause is sincere. It's also great fun, so long as your idea of fun includes jungle-themed indoor mini-golf, four-storey go-kart tracks and listening to lesser Osmond brothers singing Christmas carols on a Friday morning in November.

Even if all those things are your idea of fun—and they are mine, or can be, given the right company and blood alcohol level—you still really have to want to go to Branson. The sole irony available in Branson is its location: though Branson exists almost exclusively for tourists, it is situated almost exactly in the middle of nowhere, tucked into the Ozark mountains along Missouri's border with Arkansas. It has no airport of its own (though one is, at the time of my visit, scheduled for imminent opening, only half a century after the debut of Branson's first live theatre show, *The Baldknobbers' Hillbilly Jamboree*; according to the literature I have been emailed, this show is still going, though without, I'm assuming/hoping, much of the original cast). The nearest place I can fly to is Springfield, which has no connections to any of the major coastal hubs (I travelled from Philadelphia via Dallas). Even once I've made it that far, I'm still an hour by road from my destination, and there are no buses (most people who go to Branson do so in their own vehicles, or on the coaches provided by whichever old folks' package tour they've booked). For a non-driving such as myself, the only option is to make some taxi driver very happy indeed.

Fortunately, however, I do really want to go to Branson, and the billboards lining Route 65 from Springfield do nothing to temper my anticipation. Most of these advertise live performances by people I'd have assumed, had I given them any thought in the last three or four decades, were long dead: Roy Clark, Bill Medley, Paul Revere and the Raiders. Others boast truly treasurably crass copywriting and/or inadvertent prompts to ponder such interesting questions as why some disasters become entertainment, and others do not: Branson's *Titanic* museum is touted as "a family experience," which is not a billing anybody would bestow upon a memorial to the Hindenburg or the Lusitania.

My lodgings in Branson are in the Hilton situated in the new Branson Landing shopping complex by Lake Taneycomo. Branson Landing is an attempt to combine the facilities of a modern shopping mall with the folksy charm of a small country town. Which is to say that Branson Landing is a reasonable approximation of hell. In a thoughtfully diabolical touch, muzak is broadcast through speakers mounted outside the shops—a looping selection of Yuletide standards punctuated, bafflingly, by Creedence Clearwater Revival's "Up Around The Bend," possibly a wry reference to where this soundtrack will swiftly drive a sane person. The racket is still audible in my hotel suite above the arcade, even after I've closed all the windows. It feels a bit like suffering the onset of a delusional psychosis in which one is convinced that one is receiving secret instructions from Mariah Carey, with specific reference to what she wants for Christmas.

In the middle of Branson Landing, an American flag flies above a fountain fitted with a battery of ten flamethrowers. At sunset, the festive hits are mercifully, if temporarily, silenced and the speakers bellow "The Star Spangled Banner" as jets of water and eruptions of flame roar towards the pinking sky. And all the shoppers shuffle to a stop, and hold their baseball caps over their hearts.

ALMOST EVERYTHING IN Branson is arranged along one road, a highway called Route 76, known locally as The Strip. A drive along The Strip offers sights including—but by no means limited to—a museum in the shape of the *Titanic*, a motel resembling a riverboat, a souvenir barn painted in the black and white patchwork of a Friesian cow, a replica of Mount Rushmore featuring the heads of John Wayne, Elvis Presley, Marilyn Monroe and Charlie Chaplin, a Veterans' Memorial Garden festooned with yellow ribbons, a statue of a horse draped in the Confederate flag, and one theatre (specifically, the Dolly Parton-owned Dixie Stampede) whose digital billboard promises a dinner show including ostrich-and-pig-racing (to my sorrow, if not surprise, tickets are sold out).

Two things are essential to the proper enjoyment of these and other attractions. One is resolve to appreciate Branson on its own merits— Branson is so disarmingly guileless that adopting any attitude of lofty aesthetic superiority, though the material to encourage same is abundant, would be as hollow a triumph as riffing wittily on the sandiness of the Sahara. The other is someone else: a course of three of Branson's Christmas shows in one day is not something that can or should be undertaken without moral support. I am joined in this enterprise by a friend of mine who lives in Missouri, knows Branson well and indeed goaded me into pitching it to the *Financial Times'* travel section in the first place, so it seems like the least she can do.

There's a third, though obviously optional, item of psychological equipment which feels necessary to us: that somewhat dazed, dulled, impenetrably bemused mindset that one can only bring to bear on a day's outing when one has prepared oneself carefully the night before by sleeping far too little and drinking far too much. Suitably fortified, which is to say burdened by hangovers which are a hazard to overflying birdlife, we report to the Branson Variety Theatre for the 10:00 AM performance of the *Spirit of Christmas* show (Branson theatres keep weird hours, to accommodate the schedules of tourist buses and the bedtimes of the city's mostly pensionable visitors—not much happens after 10:00 PM, and many venues stage three shows every day). From the carpark behind the Branson Variety Theatre, I can see another venue, a gleaming leviathan called the White House Theatre, upon which is painted, in immense blue letters, the definitive, reductive Branson enticement: "SHOWS & FOOD."

The reasons we have settled upon the *Spirit of Christmas* show to the exclusion of everything else on offer—Branson, population 7,435, has 53 theatres, 207 hotels and 458 restaurants—are the guest stars: Wayne, Jay and Jimmy Osmond. The latter still enjoys a certain infamy back in Britain, thanks to his vexingly unforgettable 1972 hit "Long-Haired Lover From Liverpool." Released when Little Jimmy Osmond, as he was then known, was just nine years old, it remains plausibly the worst UK Number One single ever: the sort of thing only grandmothers liked. It is a demographic that has remained loyal: an aerial shot of the pre-show throng in the lobby would resemble a crocheted quilt cover of blue and silver. It is doubtless in acknowledgement of the audience's age, and the bodily aches that time engenders, that the concession stand sells aspirin along with popcorn and ice cream, but all things—and by "all things," I mean temples throbbing like the bass guitar part in The Osmonds' "Crazy Horses"—considered, I am not ungrateful.

Most of the *Spirit of Christmas* show consists of a chorus line capering to numbingly predictable Christmas favourites in exactly the costumes you'd expect them to wear. The dancers are competent at best, but their rather overlong routines at least allow plenty of time for whispered-behind-programme speculations about the cast—which backing hoofer is conspiring to overthrow the female lead, which is the impressionable sidekick abetting her in this treachery, which male dancer has most often prompted his father to declare that "the boy ain't right," etcetera.

The Osmonds appear in intermittent cameos, and are great. They'd be even better if "Crazy" Wayne Osmond desisted with his jokes, several of which might even be older than most of the audience, but they seem to amuse him, if nobody else. When the three of them sing together they do so beautifully, especially on a medley of hits by other brothers (Mills Brothers, Everly Brothers, Doobie Brothers, Blues Brothers—though my prayers for something off The Louvin Brothers' 1950s gothic gospel classic *Satan Is Real* languish regrettably unanswered). Jimmy is an effortlessly charming host, his exhortation to "Keep this party going"—to a theatre largely populated by a pre-lunchtime crowd of grandparents—conspicuously lacking the laboured, mordant self-mockery of celebrities starring in British pantomimes. He is a man utterly at peace with his place in the world, even if that place is a remote Ozark town where he sells memories at inconvenient hours.

The same cannot quite be said of the next act we see—Roy Rogers Jr., at the Roy Rogers Museum theatre—but it is a nevertheless compelling spectacle. Roy Rogers Sr. was, during the 1940s and '50s, perhaps the most famous man in America, the occupants of the White House not excepted. He made movies, television shows and records (most of the latter are interesting only as period kitsch, but a couple, notably the early 70s albums *A Man from Duck Run* and *The Country Side of*, aren't bad at all, the latter featuring jarringly sincere versions of the semi-ironic Merle Haggard redneck anthems "Okie From Muskogee" and "The Fightin' Side Of Me," which manage to sound both amiable and belligerent: listening to them is like being threatened by your uncle). He lent his image to uncountable items of merchandise, many of which are exhibited in the museum: comic books, toys, breakfast cereals, board games. Also enshrined are Rogers' clothes, cars and guns. Roy Rogers died in 1998, aged eighty-six. He left his son these display cases of mementoes, his name and some awesomely big—and audaciously embroidered—boots to fill.

Rogers Jr. does this with a grace, humility and reverence that verges on the weird. The show Rogers Jr. performs is, substantially, a memorial service to his legendary father, to his mother (Grace Arlene Wilkins), and to Rogers Sr.'s second wife and co-star (Dale Evans). In a half-filled, semi-circular theatre adjoining the museum, Rogers Jr. croons cowboy ballads while his backing band make the quietest amplified music I've ever heard. In between tunes, he tells stories of his upbringing, which was both blessed by the fortune and fame of his father, and plagued by the death and misfortune that insistently stalked the family. Rogers Jr.'s mother died of an embolism days after he was born. Rogers Sr. and Evans' first daughter was born with Down's Syndrome and died in infancy. Two of the children Rogers and Evans subsequently adopted also died young. One, a Korean war orphan, was killed in a road crash at age twelve, when her church bus collided with a car. Another choked to death while serving with the US army in Germany.

Rogers Jr. discusses these tragedies from the stage in detail that feels all at once forensic and dispassionate, and which leaves us altogether unsure how we're supposed to react. It's all rather odd. Rogers owns a pleasant, Jim Reeves-ish baritone, and his a capella version of the ancient spiritual "Wayfaring Stranger" is terrific. But it's hard to separate from the knowledge that it was, as he has explained at some length, the last thing he sang to Dale Evans before she died in 2001—and that he's still singing it twice a day, five days a week, in what is essentially his family mausoleum. He wishes his audience a "happy Branson cowboy Christmas" as artificial snow descends from the ceiling, and we leave thinking Jimmy Osmond should take him for a drink.

Neither the Osmonds nor Rogers would deny that we saved the best for last: indefatigable crooner Andy Williams, at his own Moon River theatre. His timing in comic set-pieces is faultless, his supporting cast brilliant, especially the astonishing mimic Bob Anderson, whose singular genius is for channeling the voices and mannerisms of lounge singers, including Frank Sinatra, Dean Martin, Tom Jones, Ray Charles—and, for one memorably surreal duet, Andy Williams. Williams looks, sounds and seems five decades short of the eighty years he racked up the previous birthday. When he signs off with a sumptuous "Moon River," the few hairs remaining on the heads of his audience are thrilled upright, quite rightly.

WE SPEND SATURDAY at Silver Dollar City theme park, whose attractions include the opportunity to pose for sepia portraits in antique costume (the woman running this operation agrees when I observe that they have a wider range of Confederate costumes than Union uniforms, and confesses that when people ask to dress as Yankees "they tend to kinda whisper"). That night, we attend a show by Kirby VanBurch, a magician with a Dutch pop star's accent and haircut. VanBurch is a Branson veteran. This theatre is, he notes, with perhaps understandable weariness, the ninth Branson venue he has played in. "I'm the only performer in Branson," he announces, "who is actually touring Branson."

It's the rest of the world's loss. VanBurch is fantastic. He produces bottles from empty tubes, cavorts with tigers, teleports a motorcycle and causes a helicopter to appear from thin air. His performance is also noteworthy for two defining moments, one very Branson, one not. The extremely Branson act is VanBurch's solemn presentation of one young assistant from the crowd with a dogtag inscribed with Isaiah 54:17 ("No weapon that is formed against thee shall prosper; and every tongue that shall rise against thee in judgement thou shalt condemn. This is the heritage of the servants of the Lord, and their righteousness is of me, saith the Lord"—which is at least more rarefied than "My grandmother went to Branson and all I got was this lousy t-shirt").

The jarringly un-Branson thing, which sums Branson up by being everything Branson is not, is a reflexive mis-step into sarcasm. Introducing an escape trick, VanBurch mentions Houdini. The crowd applaud. "Clap all you want, he's not coming out," smiles Kirby. "Not at these prices."

It's a good joke, but it dies, crushed by the truth it is bearing: that maybe we'd all rather be in Vegas, but realise that Sin City is just too brash, too cynical, too much, for any of us.

27

LEMON ON A JET PLANE

Around the world with U2
APRIL 1997-FEBRUARY 1998

WHICH IS, IF you've been reading this book sequentially, where we came in, more or less. By accident and by design, my path crossed with U2's *PopMart* tour of 1997-98 fairly frequently. What follows is–if you will–kind of a director's cut of a sequence of articles written about the tour, largely for *The Independent* and *The Independent on Sunday*.

The *PopMart* tour was entirely preposterous–which was, of course, at least half the point. There was no doubt that U2 were in on the joke they were playing on themselves, their heritage and their reputation, even from the off. Their road crew certainly bought into the spirit of things early on. The afternoon before opening night, at Sam Boyd Stadium in Las Vegas, a few of us journalists covering the show had wandered down to the venue to watch the final pieces of the immense and ludicrous set being erected. As we arrived, some or other prop was being gently lowered on cables from the rigging overhanging the stage. The roadie on the mixing desk beat us all to the punchline. "HEWN!" boomed a voice through the bank of bright orange speakers. "FROM THE LIVING ROCK! OF . . . STONE'ENGE!"

A few months later, in an irony too perfect to contrive, U2 ended up wearing their most ironic guise as they played what was–at least, perhaps, until their three-night stand at Madison Square Garden in October 2001–their least ironic concert. Their show at Sarajevo's Kosevo Stadium, on September 23, 1997, remains an absolute highlight of your correspondent's gig-going experience. On its own merits, it wasn't a great show, for the fairly fundamental reason that Bono's voice deserted him more or less completely (at time of writing, a YouTube clip of U2's performance of "Pride" captures his struggle acutely). But it was a resonant example of what U2 do—and what rock'n'roll does—best: elevates naivete into an inspirational, if wretchedly temporary, reality.

★　★　★

"THE highest art will be that which in its conscious content presents the thousandfold problems of the day, the art which has been visibly shattered by the explosions of last week, which is forever trying to collect its limbs after yesterday's crash. The best and most extraordinary artists will be those who every hour snatch the tatters of their bodies out of the frenzied cataract of life, who, with bleeding hands and hearts, hold fast to the intelligence of their time."
—DADAIST MANIFESTO, BERLIN, 1918

"WHAT's Boner's problem?"
—*Beavis and Butt-Head*, USA, 1994

ABOUT A HUNDRED miles from here, about a decade ago, four young Irishmen stood amid the cacti of Death Valley and gazed grimly towards the dusty horizons while Anton Corbijn took their pictures for the cover of *The Joshua Tree*, an album that remains a benchmark for ascetic introspection. Tonight, the same four Irishmen will perform songs from an album called *Pop* on a stage decorated with a fifty-foot-high lemon-shaped mirror ball, an enormous glowing olive atop a towering swizzle stick, and a giant golden arch obviously intended to signal associations with populism and disposability. U2's reinvention, first flagged with 1991's *Achtung Baby* album and subsequent Zoo TV tour, has been an act of total auto-iconoclasm. It's been like watching a Pope touring the world's cathedrals with a tin of kerosene and a lighter and has, as such, been well rock'n'roll.

However, there's self-destruction and there's self-destruction, and when U2 open their *PopMart* world tour tonight in Las Vegas's 37,000-seater Sam Boyd Stadium, they deliver an excruciating example of the wrong kind. Beset by technical hitches, grappling with material that seems even less familiar to them than it does to the audience, U2 play a shocker. That they make little attempt to disguise their own disappointment is some mitigation, but not much—it's difficult to extend much sympathy for first-night nerves when tickets are $54.50 a shot. It's perhaps only this consideration that compels the band to grit their teeth and go the distance. If this had been a fight, it would have been stopped.

LAS VEGAS, WE press junketeers have been told, is a logistical rather than a conceptual choice for opening night. If this is true, it's the happiest of coincidences. Las Vegas is the city in which the characteristic American refusal to acknowledge that such a thing as vulgarity exists has reached a triumphantly crass apotheosis. In the arcade leading into Caesar's Palace, I stop, entranced, in a foyer where a faux-marble Aphrodite stands among the ten-cent slot machines. "Wow," says a camcorder-encumbered American next to me. "Isn't it beautiful?"

Vegas's casinos are fleetingly amusing but eventually terribly depressing places. At the endless rows of slot machines, people lose and win thousands with a total lack of emotion. I wonder how many of these dead-eyed people feeding in money, pulling a lever, feeding in money, pulling a lever, feeding in money, pulling a lever, are on holiday from repetitive, menial factory jobs. As I sit around the roulette tables, every so often someone will swagger along, throw a ludicrous amount—five hundred, a thousand dollars—on one number and then, when they lose it, shrug and walk away, bearing a strained no-really-it-didn't-hurt-at-all expression. It seems bizarre to spend so much money to impress total strangers; there again, I've come to Vegas to watch U2 do exactly that.

If U2 have decided to see what happens when you submit to, even revel in, the junk, kitsch and flash of popular culture, they've come to ground zero. The only problem is that bringing a fifty-foot lemon-shaped mirror ball to Las Vegas, of all places, and expecting anyone to impressed, is a bit like trying to attract attention in London by driving around in a red double-decker bus. In a short walk along the

Las Vegas Strip from my hotel, I see a pirate ship, King Kong, a blue glass pyramid, the New York City skyline, a volcano that erupts every fifteen minutes and marble dolphins frozen in mid-leap above the fountains next to an automatic walkway. To create a stir here on a purely visual level, U2 would have needed to invest in an entire fifty-foot mirror ball fruit salad.

Of course, for all the gaudy window-dressing of *PopMart*, it's the music that's supposed to carry it. Tonight, it mostly doesn't, though things start well. In fact, only rarely since the ancients of Babylon finished work on the Ishtar Gate have people made entrances this spectacular.

To a remixed fanfare of M's lone hit "Pop Muzik," U2 enter the arena from under one of the stands along the side. A spotlight tracks their progress through the crowd. Bono, his hair cropped and dyed blonde, is wearing a boxer's robe and sparring furiously. Edge is clad in a very Las Vegas rhinestone cowboy outfit and looks like an escapee from The Village People. Adam Clayton has drawn the short straw in the outfit department for roughly the thousandth time in U2's history—he wears an orange boiler suit and a facemask and looks like one of those poor Chernobyl technicians who were given a shovel and ten minutes to shift as much glowing rubble as they could off the roof of the reactor before they started growing extra heads. Larry Mullen Jr., consistent throughout U2's image rethinks, has come dressed as Larry Mullen Jr. (I've always imagined that, stuffed in some Dublin filing cabinet, there must be the dozens of extravagant costume ideas that the band have presented to Mullen over the years, only to be rebuffed every time with, "Well, I thought I'd wear the leather trousers and a t-shirt, again.")

At the back of the stage, on the largest LED television screen ever built, the word "Pop" appears in red letters taller than your house, or taller than your house if you're not a member of U2. They start with "Mofo," the most explicitly dance-oriented track from the new album. Immense images of the band fill the screen. It looks fantastic, and sounds twice as good.

The wires start coming loose almost immediately. Having established a giddy forward momentum, U2 stick a pole in the spokes by exhuming their 1980 rabble-rouser "I Will Follow" and follow that with two relatively undemanding newer songs, "Even Better Than The Real Thing" and "Do You Feel Loved." When they go from those into

"Pride" and "I Still Haven't Found What I'm Looking For," there's an almost audible grinding of gears. These two songs were among the most exciting parts of Zoo TV—the former was graced with a spectacular guest appearance by its subject, Martin Luther King Jr., testifying from the ether on video, and the latter sounded like a raging defiance of the temptation to rest on lucrative laurels. Tonight, they just sound tired, the evening is turning rapidly into a bewilderingly timid exercise in nostalgia, and I'm thinking of that episode of *Yes, Prime Minister* in which Sir Humphrey is advising Hacker about his address to the nation, counseling that if he's got nothing new to say, he should wear a bold modern suit and fill his office with abstract art.

It gets worse still when U2, hamstrung by sound which is killing the bottom end and making everything sound like it's being played down the phone, move down a catwalk to a smaller stage in the middle of the arena. "If God Will Send His Angels" is lovely, but "Staring at the Sun" is a disaster, lurching to an abrupt halt in the middle of the first chorus. "Talk amongst yourselves," says Bono. "We're just having a family row." They get all the way through at the second attempt. Edge leads the crowd in a karaoke sing-along of "Daydream Believer."

Some hope that *PopMart* is going to be something more than watered-down Warholia is provided by "Miami" and "Bullet The Blue Sky." Both are played with an intensity that verges on the deranged, and the latter is illustrated with a dazzling animation of Roy Lichtenstein fighter planes, chasing each other across the immense screen while, around the stadium, perpendicular lasers point towards the summit of an immense pyramid of light. It's an unabashed steal from Albert Speer's Nuremberg illuminations: that the only lasting cultural legacy of Nazism is stadium rock is an irony U2 underscored during the Zoo TV shows by getting the crowds to clap along with a Hitler Youth drummer boy excerpted from Leni Riefenstahl's *Triumph Of The Will*. Bono has at last found his voice, along with a bowler hat and a stars'n'stripes umbrella, and is goosestepping along the catwalk in the style of Chaplin's *Great Dictator*. This is more like it: if Zoo TV marked the first time a band of U2's stature had acknowledged their own absurdity, this may be the first time such a band has asked its audience to do the same.

The rest of the set is an inevitable comedown, and the encores are flat enough to putt on. The giant disco lemon putters slowly down the catwalk in a tornado of dry ice fog, and U2 emerge from inside it. On a better night, this might look like endearing self-mockery, but given what has preceded it, it's a little too close to the pods scene from *This Is Spinal Tap* for comfort. U2 proceed to make rather a madwoman's custard of "Discotheque," follow that with an inconsequental "If You Wear That Velvet Dress" and then engage in an ungainly race with each other to the end of "With or Without You." They come back on once more, do a shambolic "Hold Me, Thrill Me, Kiss Me, Kill Me" and a desultory "Mysterious Ways" before locating some form to close with a beautifully turned-out "One," illustrated with a touching Keith Haring sequence.

U2 are about the only famous people on earth who don't make an appearance at the after-show party at the venue, or the after-after-show party in Vegas's Hard Rock Café. At both of these gatherings, there is much excitement about the presence of R.E.M., Dennis Hopper, Bruce Willis, Kylie Minogue, Helena Christensen, Winona Ryder, etc., etc., but I'm more interested in the large inflatable *PopMart*-logo-branded lemons suspended from the Hard Rock's ceiling. The more daiquiris I drink, the more convinced I become that one of them would look great on top of my fridge. With the help of some passers-by, a table and two chairs, I get up high enough to get a grip on one and, despite the warnings of a bouncer shouting at me from the ground, remove it from its moorings and climb down.

"Sir, I must ask you . . ."

I was leaving anyway.

My hard-won souvenir nearly goes missing on the way back to the hotel, when I am diverted towards a roulette table somewhere en route. Using an infallible new system of my own instant and inebriated devising, I do okay, turning ten dollars into 500. Continuing with the same infallible system, I lose nearly all of it. I totter off to collect what remains of my winnings.

"Sir!" the croupier bellows across the casino floor. "Sir! You forgot your lemon!"

THERE IS ONE building in Sarajevo that would fit in nicely along the Las Vegas strip. The Holiday Inn, a distended cube of lurid purples, yellows and oranges, can only have been the work of an architect who was totally insensitive to the city's architectural heritage, or a chronic glue-sniffer, or both. The first time I came to Sarajevo, in March 1996, this absurd building, stranded in the open boulevard known as Sniper Alley, was a wreck, shot to pieces. It sat incongruously amid the ruins of the city's other, relatively demure, buildings looking like some bumbling spacecraft that had been brought down by crossfire.

The Holiday Inn has been repaired since Sarajevo's war ended in late 1995, though some twisted fragments of stubborn shrapnel still pock the walls. On a grey autumn morning, in a room decorated entirely in brown, a singer, who looks in need of some restoration work himself, is trying to explain what he's doing here.

"There is a history," croaks Bono, "of artists having a response—and they ought to have a response—to situations like this. Dada and surrealism were responses to fascism."

Last night, U2 brought *PopMart* to Sarajevo's Kosevo stadium, making good on a five-year-old promise to play in the Bosnian capital. Bono's voice didn't quite make the journey with him.

"They call it Las Vegas throat, did you know that?" says Bono, tentatively rubbing his neck. "It's the desert air. When seasoned old crooners hear of a new boy coming to Las Vegas they all giggle, because they know what's going to happen. We even rang Sinatra's people about this thing, and they just went naaaah, just keep drinking and smoking, it'll sort itself out."

When I first heard that U2 were definitely coming to Sarajevo, I assumed they'd be playing a scratch show with the bare minimum of equipment. When I heard that they were bringing the entire *PopMart* circus—500 tons of equipment carried by seventy-five trucks, operated by 250 personnel on sixteen buses and one Boeing 727, with a total daily operating cost of £160,000—I assumed they'd been out in the sun without hats on. It was less than a year since I'd come to Sarajevo with China Drum, all of whom fitted into one truck, and that had degenerated into the most ludicrous expedition undertaken by man or beast since Scott's to the Antarctic.

"The idea," explains Bono, "was that we'd flash bastard it into town—you know, the big private plane with the lemon on the side, the police escort from the airport, the lot, you know, you saw it, you were there—and play a rock'n'roll show like rock'n'roll bands do. Don't patronise these people, just do it. That was the plan. I was gonna give 'em the full whack, you know. I just wasn't able to, because my voice kind of . . . went. But, you know, what happened last night. . . it dwarfed *PopMart*. That's what I thought was interesting. Arches, lemons, fucking drive-in movie screens, all kind of disappeared, because . . . something else went on, something that I, as an outsider in this city, probably can't fully understand. I just have to say that those were the cards we were dealt, and the crowd made it very special."

I'd been in Sarajevo a month previously, doing a story for *The Sunday Times* about the rebirth of the city's tourist industry. Just about everything that wasn't moving was upholstered with U2 posters. The concert was all anyone was talking about. Even the staff of Sarajevo's newly reopened tourist office, whose average age was around seventy, said they were going. The excitement was about more than a big rock group coming to town: Sarajevo was going to be on CNN because something good was happening in it.

"Well," shrugs Bono, "I don't, as a general rule, suffer from any Catholic guilt, even though I'm half Catholic, but I think for any person who finds success, the instinctive reaction is to try and level the pitch a bit, with your friends, and your family, and I guess in the wider world, which is when you become a real pain in the hole. Or I guess the other extreme is to just put it all up your nose, and I thought I had a great nose, so I wasn't interested in that."

U2 had played a smart game: tickets were sold in Croatia, Slovenia and Yugoslavia, but there was no concert scheduled in Zagreb, Llubljana or Belgrade. Anyone between Austria and Greece who wanted to see U2 was going to have to come to Sarajevo, and they did, in their thousands. On the day of the show, trains had run into Sarajevo for the first time in four years. The city's roads were full of cars bearing Croatian and Yugoslav license plates. The bars were crowded with people with subtly different accents. There was no trouble—although, earlier this morning, I did see a local market trader knock on the window of a Belgrade-registered car, say something to the clearly affronted driver and walk off looking terribly pleased with himself; a friend translated the pedestrian's remarks as, "I've just fucked your Hungarian mother with her dead horse's dick."

"So no, it wasn't really what I'd planned," continues Bono, in what sounds a painful rasp. "I'd planned to be in fine voice. I have been in fine voice, of late, and I'd probably have been a terrible pain in the arse if I had pulled that off. It was very humbling, actually. But maybe that allowed room for Sarajevo to kind of take the gig away from us, which is what they did. They could see that things could go very horribly wrong, but they'd come here, and they'd gone to a lot of trouble, and they were going to make it happen. And they did, and they just kind of carried me along. And the band also played with some real spunk, I thought. When I lost it on 'Pride,' and Edge started singing it, I thought, fucking hell, now see what it feels like, you bastard, but he did it, you know, he got us there."

The first act on last night had been a local choir. They were followed by Protest, one of the better acts to have emerged from Sarajevo's wartime rock scene. Sikter followed them, starting their set by tearing up the Bosnian national anthem in the style of Hendrix's "Star Spangled Banner," and playing a blinder after that. When U2 made their entrance, and the *PopMart* stage lit up on cue, the roars had been as much of relief as excitement. In a city which has come to view delivery on promises as very much the exception to the rule, there had been a general view that something would go wrong at the last minute.

In the event, the only thing that went wrong was Bono's voice. On any other night, this might have been catastrophic, but as Bono says, last night it really didn't matter. By the time the giant disco lemon rolled out for the encores, it felt less like another stadium concert, and more like a very, very large party with a band playing in one corner of it. Standing in the middle of it on the mixing desk was an overwhelming experience, if one leavened with a guilt at the privilege of being there without having suffered the same suspension of everyday life that everyone else was celebrating the end of. "Concerts are one of those things that happen in normal cities," Sikter's drummer Faris had said backstage before the show, twitching with nerves. "Tonight is one of the most important things that's ever happened here—way bigger than the Olympics." Faris is not, in my experience, prone to overstatement. "My father made me some new shoes especially," he laughed.

Two parts of *PopMart* had been tailored to the location. The karaoke singalong was replaced by Edge delivering a lovely, mournful solo reading of "Sunday Bloody Sunday," and the encores included the first-ever live performance of "Miss Sarajevo"—the gorgeous song inspired by Bill Carter's film about a wartime beauty pageant, and recorded by U2, Brian Eno and Luciano Pavarotti under the name Passengers. Last night, Eno joined U2 onstage in person, Pavarotti on tape. It had been a tentative performance. "Well, we wrote that song for you," Bono said, as it stumbled to a close, "and we can't fucking play it."

When the lights came up at the end of the show, and the crowd started filing out, something strange and wonderful happened. The stand along the left of the stadium, which was filled with ranks of uniformed soldiers serving with the multinational NATO-led Stabilisation Force (SFOR) stood, as one, and applauded the crowd, the people of Sarajevo. The punters leaving the ground stopped, turned around, and clapped back. A self-conscious, embarrassed silence followed, eventually broken by the Spanish SFOR contingent, many wearing their national flag as bandannas, leading an impromptu massed military choir in "Y Viva España" and, then, an altogether surreal line dance to "The Macarena."

With me on the mixing desk was the only other British journalist who'd flown out for the show, Mat Smith of the *NME*.

"It's amazing," he said. "Every time some idiot musician starts with that hippy-dippy music-bringing-people-together-as-one stuff, we just laugh at them. But look at this . . . they've actually done it. What the hell are we going to write?"

At the Holiday Inn the next morning, Bono tries to give me a hand with that one.

"In the mid-80s," he says, "we were involved in America, and the concept of the two Americas, and that brought us on the one hand to Central America, Nicaragua and 'Bullet The Blue Sky' and on the other hand to Sun Studios. But it was all part of the same . . . it's sometimes helpful to make a parallel between bands and filmmakers. You go for whatever you're doing and just focus on it. And that's one of the reasons our records have real . . . they're caught in their time. When people look at the 80s, they will pick out one of our records, and they'll say that if you want to know what was going on in music, and you want to know what was going on . . . you know, America was what was going on, and this was a response to it. *Achtung Baby* and *Zooropa*, again, that paints a picture of what was going on. I guess we should start just writing tunes, and just shut the fuck up, but if you're curious, and that's certainly my strongest suit, the tunes get set into a context of some kind . . . and here we are."

Someone comes to tell Bono to get a move on, as U2's plane has to leave.

"I've had, I guess, a few holidays in hell, but I hate that—and you should be careful with that yourself—but the way it works with me, the way it works with the group, is whatever you're doing, you look under every stone of it. So Zoo TV brought us into that world of television, news, cartoons, Dada, and you end up following that through, and if you do that you end up in Sarajevo one minute and hanging out with some of the most beautiful women in the world the next, and you just get fully into it."

TWO MONTHS LATER, by the pool in the exquisite garden behind the impeccably renovated and uproariously expensive Delano Hotel in Miami's South Beach, we are hanging out with some of the most beautiful women in the world, getting fully into it. Photographer Rankin introduces me to Helena Christensen, and one of my chats with Bono is interrupted when he is distracted by Veronica Webb wandering over to say hello. I am inclined to forgive Bono for this, as Veronica Webb wandering over to say hello would be enough to distract a man performing an emergency tracheotomy on his brother.

U2 have pitched camp in the Delano for a couple of weeks while *PopMart* tours the south of the United States. The band's families are here as well—there are seven U2 children—and U2 are flying back to Miami every night on the lemon-spangled 727 after shows in other nearby cities. Various friends have flown in for the Miami show, Elvis Costello among them. George Clooney is also staying here ("Hey," says Bono, as we leave the hotel to find a bar showing the Ireland vs Belgium World Cup playoff, "there's Batman playing basketball. Cool.") and though he hasn't come as a friend of the band, he seems to leave as one.

Rock tours are not usually such relaxed things to visit, especially not after they've been six months on the road. Most seethe with tensions and paranoias comparable with the last weeks of the Nixon administration, and most regard an itinerant journalist as little more than a handy outlet for those pressures. U2's organisation has the feel of a large and almost suspiciously happy family. It may help that many of their closest staff have associations with the band going back most of the twenty-odd years of U2's existence. It may also help that many of those closest staff, whether by accident or design, are women.

The four members of U2 are themselves unfailingly courteous and pleasant, certainly more so than men regularly credited with a combined wealth of £300 million really have to be.

Edge, the permanently behatted guitarist, first sees me at some distance past my best when, not long off the flight from London, I descend on his table on the Delano's back porch, jetlagged and margarita-sodden, and interrupt someone else's praise of The Spice Girls with a lengthy rant outlining their defects. Edge cheerfully puts up a case for the defence while I mutter things like "cynical," "vapid," "worse than the plague" and "the Nolan Sisters," and drink someone else's drink, becoming dimly aware that I am talking no sense at all, know nobody here and that everyone has gone very quiet. A hope of salvation arrives in the shape of Elvis Costello; while I don't expect him to remember the nervous nineteen-year-old who interviewed him in Sydney nine years ago, I do expect that the curmudgeonly elder rock'n'roll statesman will take my side. "I'm in the Spice movie," he grins. "I play a barman." I decide that discretion is the better part of valour, and go up to bed, my attempt at a dignified exit hampered by the way the garden furniture keeps jumping in front of me.

Larry Mullen Jr., the strangely ageless drummer whose high-school noticeboard advertisement bought U2 together, introduces himself after a few days and apologises for not wanting to speak on the record on the grounds that "I only feel comfortable sitting at my kit hitting stuff," and besides which, his young son, Elvis, has pulled a table over on himself and hurt his foot. Adam Clayton, the bass player who comes nearer than any of them to mustering the traditional hauteur of the rock'n'roll aristocrat, seems generally thoughtful and oddly shy.

Bono flits between tables in the Delano's garden, dressed all in black with silver sunglasses and the leopard-print loafers Gucci made him to go with the interior of his Mercedes, chatting to those he knows, signing things for those he doesn't. He's a prolific and entertaining talker—I can imagine he gave the Blarney Stone the one kiss it still talks about. Unusually, for someone as famous as he is, little of what he says is about himself—he talks seven beats to the bar about things he's read, people he's met, places he's been. In two espressos flat, he can do Picasso, the Reverend Cecil Williams' Glide church in San Francisco, Daniel Ortega and liberation theology and whether or not Ireland really stand much of a chance against the Belgians. Even more unusually, for someone as famous as he is, he's also a generous and genuinely inquisitive listener.

"I like that generosity in Americans," he says, later. "We haven't the cultural baggage that other bands in the UK would have, because we're Irish. We don't see America as the devil like the English do, so we came here early on and we spent a lot of time here. Being on the road feels like an American idea—you grow up on Kerouac, and the poetry of the place names, and what it was like being nineteen or twenty and looking out the window of a tour bus and thinking it was more like the movies, not less."

U2's love affair with America has been one of two boundlessly ambitious entities falling hopelessly for the endless possibilities of each other. Of the seventy-seven million albums U2 have sold, thirty million have been bought in America.

IN MIAMI, U2 are playing at the ProPlayer Stadium, home of the Florida Marlins baseball team. *PopMart* has come a long way, in every respect, since its inauspicious beginnings in Las Vegas. A workable tension has been located between the gleeful satire of consumer culture that flickers on the giant screen, and the songs from *Pop* which are, beneath the beats and effects, some of the most intimate and troubled U2 have recorded. During the Miami show, just before U2 play "I Still Haven't Found What I'm Looking For," Bono makes a short speech thanking the crowd for their patience with his band's unpredictability. "If we keep it interesting for us," he says, "hopefully it won't be bullshit for you."

After a triumphant show, in a suite somewhere in the warren of dressing rooms inside ProPlayer Stadium, Edge can just about laugh at the memory of Las Vegas; the encore, when he was forced to his knees to fossick hopelessly for his dropped plectrum in the dry ice while the other three started "Discotheque" without him and his signature riff, was, he says now, "about as *Tap* as it's ever got." Edge is genial and amusing company, and only makes about a dozen slighting references to my inebriated performance at the Delano the previous evening, which is sweet of him.

U2 have kept Edge's solo "Sunday Bloody Sunday" in the set since Sarajevo. He's kind enough to let it go when I explain that I'd never liked the song much in its original, martial-drumming, foot-stomping, flag-waving incarnation, that it had seemed to sum up everything that I used to think U2 were: pompous, earnest and a whole bunch of no fun at all. Stripped down and delivered in a bare whisper, it had worked in Sarajevo, and even removed from that emotive context, it had worked in Miami.

"I thought the song would have a different resonance in Sarajevo," he says, "but not as a band version. I thought if I showcased the lyric and the melody, it might fly. What I discovered was that the song had a completely other side. That's what I find with a lot of our songs, that you can fiddle about with them, but you can't change the essence of them, and it was nice to find a song that we thought we might never play again could still do that. We dropped it on the 'Unforgettable Fire' tour, so it's been nearly ten years."

This must be the weirdest part of the musician's job. Most of us scream at pictures of ourselves a decade ago, cringe at the memory of things we thought, said or bought when we were younger. But a successful musician never escapes it. Everything ridiculous you did or wore as a youth is a matter of record, part of the fabric of other people's lives.

"Yeah . . . playing the old songs is a bit like what I imagine travelling back in time and meeting yourself would be like. We're quite lucky in that when it comes to the early embarrassing moments, we have so many that it's actually just pointless even trying to defend ourselves. There's so much there that we just have to laugh at, and be thankful that we're still growing, still getting better at what we do. The first few weeks of *PopMart* were . . . well, we'd jumped in at the deep end and hadn't prepared as much as we should have. But now . . . on previous tours, I remember Bono being under such a cloud for hours after coming on stage, but on this tour we're just laughing so much. It's the most fun we've ever had on the road."

Adam Clayton, when he's wheeled before the tape recorder after Edge, offers a similarly sanguine view. As the only member of U2 to have racked up the traditional rock'n'roll accoutrements of court appearances, tabloid scandals, supermodel girlfriends and excess-induced absenteeism (at the end of the Zoo TV tour in Sydney, U2 had to play one show with Clayton's guitar tech on bass), Clayton has perhaps had a better view of the bottom of the abyss than the others, but he doesn't have any complaints this evening.

"You can have bad days," he allows, "and every day is a challenge, because the preconceived ideas you had, as a sixteen-year-old joining a pop group, as a twenty-year-old releasing your first album, as a twenty-seven-year-old releasing *The Joshua Tree*, you have to battle against those, you have to get to the essence of what being a musician is, and you have to remember that, well, tonight I could have been playing in the Holiday Inn. By the time showtime comes around, you've got yourself centred. There is a discipline involved, and—I mean, this sounds very Californian—you have to reduce the number of stimuli in your day in order to become a sort of hollow vessel, so by the time you go on stage, you've actually got some energy to run off."

Clayton has a strange accent that isn't quite English and isn't quite Irish.

"What's fun about this now," he continues, "is that an awful lot of the uncertainties have been removed by the fact that we have a history, by now, that indicates that this is probably what we're going to be doing for the rest of our lives. We have a history that says we've done something very hard and very unnatural, for four men to grow together and live with each other for twenty years. I think everyone's a lot more rounded and settled, and I'm realising that this is the most interesting musical engagement I could be involved in."

That's the thing about great bands, though: they're always more than the sum of their parts. Lennon and McCartney's post-Beatles efforts ran the gamut from the adequate to the excruciating. The Smiths splintered into an occasionally inspired session guitarist and a risible self-parody. Even the ones where you'd think it wouldn't matter go this way, like Pixies—Black Francis wrote all those fantastic Pixies songs, but listening to his solo albums was like wading through knee-deep mud in loose wellies.

"That chemistry," nods Clayton, "is gold dust. If we went off and tried to make solo records, I'm sure they'd be as crap as everyone else's solo records. For some reason, each of us works best in this situation. And that's a nice thing to have figured out. We still all live within twenty minutes of each other. We spend a lot of time with each other, so we can chew a lot of ideas over. Other bands, when they get to our age, there's a couple of divorces, there's a couple of jealousies between members, there are management problems, and it's very hard. We've been lucky, or wise, and we can devote most of our energy to being in U2. We keep a full-time staff on, which a lot of people don't. We're in a unique position, and we do take those risks, and we look like fools sometimes, but other times people say 'Yes!' and that's the kind of band I always wanted to be in."

BONO IS A restless interviewee, physically and mentally, sitting up and lying down as ideas occur to him. It's the afternoon of the day after the Miami show, and we're sitting in the sunshine in the Delano's garden, roughly equidistant from the swimming pool, the cocktail bar and the giant-sized lawn chess set. Things could probably be worse.

"Are you enjoying Miami? It's a very interesting city. It's kind of the crossroads between North America and South America . . ."

In Bosnia, Bono had said something about his attraction to the idea of Sarajevo as a cultural crossing place, though in Sarajevo's case it had been between east and west . . . trying not to sound too much like a hack in search of an underlying theme, I wonder if he sees similarities.

"Exactly. Well, here you have the Catholicism of South America, which is the sexy end of the religion, you know, carnivals . . ."

I'm starting to get used to Bono's associative monologues.

". . . which is something I'm becoming more and more interested in, the carnival, the celebration of the flesh—you know, carne meaning meat—before the denial, which is Lent, going into Easter, that kind of thing . . ."

Keeping him to one theme is like trying to cage water—like a lot of people whose understanding of the world has come largely from going places and finding out for themselves, the connections he draws tend to be as individual and eccentric as his experiences, and as he's one of the most famous people on earth, it's safe to assume that his experiences are more individual and eccentric than most. When transcribed into cold hard print, Bono can occasionally read like a stereotypical cosmic rock'n'roll mooncalf, but in person, his intellectual promiscuity just feels like the vigour of a compulsive conversationalist. It's also something I've noticed in a lot of Irish and Scottish friends—a fondness for constructing elaborate, even absurd, theories out of bugger all just for the fun of seeing where the pieces land when the edifice topples over.

". . . and you just get this sense that South America is coming through, you can see it in the writers and filmmakers, and this is its interface. You know, South Beach looks like lots of blocks of ice cream, Neapolitan, or . . ."

I'd been thinking that earlier. The violently clashing pastel paint on the beachfront apartment buildings looks ghastly and ridiculous all day, until sunset, when the sky behind them becomes daubed in the exact same colours. Then it looks like heaven, or at least like Ernest Hemingway's idea of it. Except I'd been thinking that the ice cream was more like tutti-frutti. U2 recorded some of *Pop* in Miami.

"Tutti-frutti, okay. Well, we came here to see if there was something here for us, but in the end our record wasn't going to be about any one location. Because sometimes there's almost a physical sense of location, Berlin for *Achtung Baby*, the US for *The Joshua Tree*."

While we talk, passers-by stop to ask Bono for an autograph, or mumble terrified hellos. Bono's lack of annoyance or condescension is startling (I mean, the interruptions are annoying me, and I've only been putting up with it for an hour). U2 started young—it feels like they've been there forever, but Bono is only thirty-seven—and they've been U2 all their adult lives. It may be that because of this they really don't know any better, but they seem remarkably free of cynicism. They still get excited—they would scarcely have sunk a tidy fortune in taking *PopMart* to Sarajevo otherwise.

"Well," muses Bono, "when you get what you want, what do you do? But we haven't got cynical, you're right. We're still trying to make that record that we hear in our heads, and can't quite play. I guess when we were twenty-three or twenty-four we went through that

phase where groups move out of their flats, and into houses, and start
wanting to put paintings up on the walls, and they don't want to look
like rednecks, so they start reading up on what sort of paintings they
should have in their houses, and what Chinese rugs . . . I guess we must
have gone through Chinese rug phases, but we were over it coming out
of our twenties. The weird thing is that you're left, in a way, with only
the right motives. If the reason you joined a band was to get laid, get
famous, get rich, well, they all went by the way fairly quickly, so all
we're left with is . . . make that record."

U2 in general, and Bono in particular, have often been scoffed at—
indeed, back in the dusty-leather-and-white-flags pre-*Achtung Baby*
era, I had, occasionally, been party to that scoffing. Scorn is not unusual
for a successful rock group. What is unusual is the equanimity with
which U2 shrug it off—many are the millionaires who will, given
half the chance, bitterly recite every bad review they've ever had. I
once spent an afternoon in New York listening to Gavin Rossdale of
Bush relate chapter and verse of the critical batterings his band had
received, mostly in publications that sold a hundredth of what his
records did. I suggested that a) next time, he send the journalist a
statement of his net worth and a photo of his big house in the country,
or vintage car collection, or whatever, and b) perhaps he could lighten
up; "You don't understand," he replied, and rarely has a truer word
been spoken.

"Oh," says Bono, with a dismissive wave of his cigarette, "bands at
our level deserve to be humbled. But it was the very gauche nature of
where we were at that allowed us entry into a world where much more
careful and cooler acts couldn't allow themselves, or depending on your
point of view, were too smart to want to visit."

The trouble is that most artists—most people, come to that—
condemn themselves to mediocrity because their fear of looking like
a fool outweighs their potential for greatness. Hoping that Bono will
forgive the impudence, I think it'd be fair to say that this has never
looked like a problem for him.

"That's right," he says. "Obviously, it's better to do it in private, but
when you're growing up in public, that's hard. People who . . . people
who jump off, like . . . like Jimi Hendrix trying to put Vietnam through
his amplifier, or like the way Lester Bangs wrote about rock'n'roll, that

takes a certain courage. I think one of things I found difficult in the 80s was this din of voices telling me, 'But you can't fly, you arsehole.' But that's the kind of thinking that results in restrained, reasonable music—or, for that matter, restrained, reasonable writing. You must not find yourself tiptoeing."

Pop contains at least two songs, "Staring at the Sun" and "Please," that appear to address the Northern Irish peace process, and concludes with an open letter to Jesus, titled "Wake Up Dead Man."

"Well . . . look. As far as what I actually believe myself goes, I'm not up for discussing it in any detail, because some subjects are too precious for interviews. I let them come out in songs. Also, I haven't got it all figured out, so I don't want to make an arse of myself. But yes, I do feel that there is love and logic behind the universe, and that in recent years that instinct that we all have has been written off, we're reduced to being two-dimensional. There's a heartache that goes with that, or if not a heartache, then certainly a soul-ache, that music . . . I mean, I have great admiration and respect for atheists, though. I feel God would have a lot more time for them than for most people who are part of a religion, who seem so odd, to me, or doped, or just believe because they were told to. I think atheists have a certain rigour. In the absence of God, people have promoted a lot of lesser types to the same position, which is quite confusing. Film stars, pop stars, royalty . . . are not actually heroes. Nurses are. Mothers are. Firemen are. Some things are arse about tit."

It must also be difficult trying to maintain a conventional view of religion when you've spent so long being worshipped yourself.

"That's . . . good," he laughs. "I'll have to have a little lie down after that one. Wow, that's great. I'll get out of bed for that. No, basically, but most musicians I know say that the great stuff they kind of stumble on, and the average stuff is what they can claim authorship over. I do still feel that U2 write songs by accident, and maybe that's why we keep shifting ground, to stay out of our depth."

The hapless metaphor is left to try untangling itself. Bono's away again.

"It all started with the Psalms of David," he continues, with a smile that indicates that he knows he's being preposterous, but is determined to see where this goes. "They were the first blues. There you had man shouting at God: 'Why have you left me? Where have you gone? Who do you think you are anyway?' That's basically what music has been doing since. I'm still a student, so I'm still knocking on Bob Dylan's door . . ."

Ouch.

". . . no pun intended, and I'm still going to turn up to Al Green's church, I'm still going to invite Bob Marley's mother to our gigs, talk to Frank Sinatra, talk to Quincy Jones, just trying to figure it out."

It could be argued that this reverence for their forebears was what got U2 into trouble on *Rattle & Hum*, when they recorded with Dylan and B.B. King, effectively sneaking into the rock'n'roll hall of fame and hanging their own portraits on the walls. *Rattle & Hum* was derided, and not without reason, as work of epic humourlessness and egomania. Though it did, buried somewhere beneath the homage and piety, contain the line "I don't believe in riches but you should see where I live," which might have been the beginning of U2's rebirth, an acknowledgement that they badly needed to resolve a few contradictions.

"I think you're trying a bit hard, there, but . . . for us, revenge is getting better. I don't think John Lennon ever got over the fact that he was in a pop group, that The Beatles were the girls' group and The Rolling Stones were the boys' one. And that was the greatest gift, in a way, because he was constantly trying to recover from that. So I think that maybe when we were younger we didn't have the brains to say fuck off, what we're doing is more interesting than what you are. Today, to some degree, I can back that up. Back then, we just wondered did people hate our haircuts this much? The answer was yes, of course—and the haircuts were terrible, awful—but it was that very lack of style in this group that led us to soul."

Bono borrows another cigarette from another autograph-hunter. The sun is beginning to set now, and South Beach is enjoying its daily hour of visual harmony between ground and sky. Rankin is making wind-up gestures in the distance, worried that the light will vanish before he gets his photo session, so I ask Bono if he can imagine a life beyond being the singer in U2, the only job he's ever had.

"Yeah . . . I'd like to be alive. I'd like to chase little children across the street with a big stick. I am curious about. . . I love people like Willie Nelson, and Johnny Cash, there's something about their voices

as they get older. Bob Dylan's voice on his new album is just . . .
I love to write, and I think that's what I'd do if I couldn't sing, or
perform. The deadlines that you have to deal with as a journalist are
something I'd obviously have a problem with, but I like people who
write. Where I'd be writing from, or where I'd be living I don't know,
but it's something I'm getting more interested in, and you don't get
to do much of it when you're in a band, because the lyrics are your
attempt to put the feelings of the music into words."

As we wander down the beach to do the photos, I comment that it
can hardly have escaped his notice that, back home in Ireland, there
might be more exciting career opportunities awaiting someone with
his credentials. After all, if Dana can give the Presidency a shake on the
strength of one long-past Eurovision appearance . . .

"Naw," Bono says, and rubs one eye under his silver shades. "I
wouldn't move to a smaller house."

FOUR MONTHS OR so later, after another *PopMart* show, I'm in a big
room full of free drink and freeloading people somewhere underneath
Waverley Park, an Australian Rules football stadium in an inconvenient
suburb of Melbourne. I'm in Australia on holiday, reminding my
parents what I look like. I'm about to get a fine demonstration of the
famous law devised by another great Irish thinker, Murphy. By which
I mean that if I ever take someone to a U2 concert whom I'm actually
trying to impress, I just know I'll be lucky to sneak in to the one-beer-
and-a-hundred-straws C-list wing-ding for local radio drones, record
company deadwood and spotty competition winners. But the night I
take my mother . . .

"Andrew? Bono wants to say hello. Follow me."

Mum, fair play to her, is very cool about the whole thing. She bows
her head just slightly when Bono swoops low and kisses her hand,
and when he asks her whether she liked the show, she just says she
thought it was amazing how much of a racket four young men could
make. Someone else I know waves at me, so I go and say hello to them,
leaving Mum and Bono to it.

I've seen some weird stuff. But when I look over from the other side
of the room at the pair of them still yammering away to each other, I
wonder if it gets stranger than this.

28

I WANNA BE YOUR ZOG

The Blazing Zoos in Albania
JULY 2006

T IS AXIOMATIC that all music journalists are frustrated musicians. It is also untrue. By early 2006, I had been writing about music for some or all of my living for nearly twenty years, since a Sydney street paper saw fit to print, and pay me for, a 300-word assessment of the merits of a show by Ed Kuepper & The Yard Goes On Forever at the Mosman Hotel (don't look for it—it isn't there anymore). I had also, during all that time, generally had a guitar about the place. Despite being equipped, therefore, with everything one might need to write songs—an ability to place words next to each other, and a musical instrument—the idea of doing so had never occurred to me, much less the desire to then perform such things in public. Until, for reasons outlined below, it did.

It is important, however, that my decision—or, really, in the circumstances, somewhat demented instinct—to mount a stage relatively late in proceedings should not be interpreted as an expression of any sort of inferiority complex attached to being a rock journalist. The idea that rock journalism is by definition inferior to rock music is curiously commonplace, and often expressed by the deployment of that annoyingly quotable quip, usually—though I'd prefer to be believe erroneously—attributed to Elvis Costello, to the effect that writing about music is like dancing about architecture. This assessment is wholly correct, though not for the reasons believed by the lackwitted dullards who generally cite it. Rather, it acknowledges, explicitly, that rock writing and rock music are discrete and uncomparable means of expression—as different, indeed, as ballet and building. Just because rock writing is about rock music doesn't invalidate it as an arena in which great things can be created—any more than rock music counts for anything less than whatever it was the rock musician in question was making rock music about. And, you know, like dancing about architecture would be a bad thing to do.

Great writing is great writing, whatever the subject—even a subject as dominated by mediocrities, chancers, scoundrels and buffoons as rock music. The works of the finest rock writers—an echelon, incidentally, of which I do not claim membership, being a dilettante in this as in all other realms of my trade—are, by any sensible measure, of greater worth than the output of 99 percent of all rock artists. This is a less provocative assertion than it might sound, once it is considered that 99 percent of all the CDs I've ever been sent have been useful only as emergency shaving mirrors—and that recent technological advances have made it easier and cheaper than ever for utterly talentless acts to inflict their hapless racket upon the commonweal.

By the time this volume appears, my own band, The Blazing Zoos, whose unlikely gestation is detailed below, will have done exactly that—our debut waxing, "I'll Leave Quietly," should be generally available for virtual or physical purchase. To those who ostentatiously sneer at the scrawlings of even the best rock writers while reflexively genuflecting to the creations of even the worst musicians, I will concede this much: that attempting, after nearly two decades of writing about other people's albums, to make one of your own, is an instructive experience. Though it didn't cause me to regret any of the harsh—or, indeed, downright abusive—judgements I have passed upon various recordings over the years, it did inspire some previously un-thought thoughts, which is always a useful blessing. I observed—and, during some longeurs in the final mix stages, slept through—the lonely diligence of the producer, in our case Mark Wallis, who has worked with everybody ever, but most humblingly from my perspective, had made several albums with my favourite band of all time, The Go-Betweens. I marvelled at the process by which colossally gifted musicians—that is, everyone in the band except me—can take a half-baked, barely-composed, ill-considered notion and turn it into something with a tune you can whistle. Most importantly, I laughed quite a lot.

Whether or not what we did is any good is a decision for others to make (I remember, during my time at *Melody Maker*, how we used to groan, and subsequently mock, whenever some gormless indie wastrel mumbled, "We just do it for ourselves, and if anyone else likes it that's a bonus," but I kind of understand, now, what they meant). What I can say for certain is this. If, especially as a consequence of finding yourself unhorsed by some or other caprice of fate, you should find yourself entertaining ideas that you would normal consider unworkable, ridiculous or palpably insane, don't dismiss them instantly (as long as, of course, they don't involve taking automatic weapons to your school or workplace). Let your id run wild for a spell. You never know where you'll end up.

★ ★ ★

WE'RE BARRELLING DOWN the mountain in the dark when I start to worry that the wheels are coming off, certainly metaphorically and perhaps literally. For most of the day-long run south along the coast from Tirana, the driver piloting our minibus has, by Albanian standards, been reassuringly decorous—more or less slowing down for red lights, parking at less than thirty miles an hour, that kind of thing. Not now, though. Something has spooked him, sufficiently that planting his accelerator foot seems a reasonable course of action in circumstances which are more suited to proceeding gingerly in first gear, possibly with a chap bearing a red flag and a torch walking ahead of the vehicle. There are no streetlights up here, and the only mercy of this absence is that it's impossible to gauge how far we'll fall, and onto how many jagged rocks, if we part company with the poor and unfenced road. And we're going faster and faster and faster and faster.

The driver speaks no English. I don't speak much Albanian, beyond the phrase "Nuk flas shume Shqip," which means "I don't speak much Albanian." From my perch at the back of the van, I yell towards the only duoglot aboard, an emissary of Albanian youth activist organisation Mjaft!, who is clinging to the passenger seat up front. My enquiry, the essence of which is the expression of ardent desire for some sort of explanation of our sudden and potentially fatal haste, prompts a response as uncertain as it is unwelcome.

"There are bandits. . . he thinks."

A tersely worded request for further elucidation yields little.

"There was a car. . ."

The narrative is punctuated by sharp intakes of breath and whimpers, some from him, others from the members of my band, The Blazing Zoos, who are all probably wondering, like me, if the bizarre and glorious pageant of rock'n'roll history contains an example of a group wiped out in a calamitous accident on the way to their first gig. If not, we may accomplish something this weekend.

". . . he thinks it might be following us."

This strikes me as unlikely, which I don't believe is just wishful thinking on my part. We're coming off the back of a vertiginous range overhanging our intended destination, the small resort town of Himare, where The Blazing Zoos are due to play at a festival on the beach. This part of Albania is generally reckoned relatively civilised (or so I'd assured my bandmates prior to embarkation). If we were negotiating the proper hillbilly country in the north, I'd concede that that driver had a case, but as things stand, it seems that the person most likely to get us all killed in the near future is in this minibus, not any of the other cars on the road—which might, after all, just be heading to the same event we are.

"He thought he saw guns."

We're in Albania, I mutter to myself. This is probably the only unarmed vehicle in a three-country radius.

"I am going to make some calls," yells our translator, shakily prodding the buttons on his phone.

There's clearly nothing for it but to hang on, hope and direct the same sort of water-testing entreaties to the God one usually disdains that one usually pleas when on an aircraft stricken by turbulence. Against this hypocrisy I offer upward the mitigation that my prayers are all on behalf of my bandmates, decent and reasonable people who have, unlike myself, sensibly chosen lives that usually necessitate little of being chauffeured at knuckle-whitening velocity by paranoid kamikazes and/or pursued by Kalashnikov-slinging ne'er-do-wells. Take me if you must, Lord, but. . .

"They're sending some people up from Himare to meet us," informs the latest yelped bulletin.

An all but two-wheeled lurch right, another one left, another one right again and we come to a rest in an impressively thick cloud of tyre smoke in a happily brightly lit service station forecourt on the outskirts of some species of settlement. The white sedan that was either carting malevolent brigands or blameless motorists sallies blithely past. Our driver recuperates. My bandmates dismount, swig water, swat aside the mosquitoes, and engage in conversation that amounts to variations on the question "What the fuck was that about?" Heart rates are beginning to return to normal when a black car, with ominously tinted windows, roars up the hill from town, screeches to a halt in front of us and emits, with all the exuberance and none of the panache of a showgirl erupting from a cake, a sweaty, bald apparition brandishing a pistol. His black t-shirt declares "Security," so I assume that he's nominally on our side (even in the Balkans, it would be surprising to discover that the local highwaymen have their own bodyguard service). I thank him for his concern, and make what I hope are gestures placatory enough to encourage him to holster his weapon. He misunderstands me.

"I help you!" he announces. "I here for your protection!" With that, he strides towards me, ignores my warily outstretched hand, seizes the waistband of my jeans, tucks the pistol into my trousers, steps back and salutes. I return the courtesy, hoping as I have never hoped for anything that the safety catch on the automatic is engaged. It's at times like this, when you're standing next to a van containing two former members of a platinum-selling rock group and a cultishly regarded Shetlandic chanteuse in a remote part of southern Albania with a maniac's gun barrel tickling your knackers, that one can find oneself asking: how did I get here?

IT'S A FAIR question, which merits a frank and detailed answer.

Forming a country & western band in one's late thirties is obviously something one is only going to do in the deranged extremis of heartbreak, and indeed that's why I did it. The reader may therefore wonder as to the identity of who is to blame, may be curious to know the identity of the spectre responsible for my decision to seize a guitar and set my sorrows to three chords. This seems an appropriate place to reveal it: Colonel Muammar Abu Minyar al-Gaddafi, Guide of the First of September Great Revolution of the Socialist People's Libyan Arab Jamahiriya.

I should stress that I didn't break up with Colonel Gaddafi, as such:

in fact, I've never met the man (I did once interview his son, Saif, and quite liked him, but he isn't my type). Gaddafi's culpability for the existence of my country band is, at best, tangential. It is apportioned only because at the point in the tiresome drama of having one's heart torn from its moorings at which one would normally avail oneself of the recourse of drinking oneself to sleep, I was on assignment in Gaddafi's capital, Tripoli, where alcohol is prohibited. This meant that I couldn't drink, and this meant that I couldn't sleep.

Native Americans believe sleep deprivation useful. Extended sleeplessness often forms part of what they call a Vision Quest—a rite of passage during which the individual undertaking it wilfully subjects himself to decomposing hardships in order to connect with a greater power, and develop an understanding of his higher purpose on this corporeal plane. The quester traditionally meanders off into the wilderness for a few days, abjuring such comforts as food, company and sleep, that he might liberate his mind of its workaday clutter and focus his consciousness on what truly matters to him (my admittedly cursory research into the subject has, sadly, failed to discern what percentage of vision questers return from the woods determined that what truly matters to them are food, company and sleep).

I do not, as a rule, have much time for traditional beliefs, or indeed any sort of empirically untested wisdom—we Sagittarians are very sceptical of such things. But there is something to be said for the potence of sleeplessness as a promoter of innovative thinking, though I don't recommend it for air traffic controllers. Unhinged from the stabilising ballast of rest, the mind does not so much wander as stagger and flail unpredictably, with often surprising consequences, much like a drunk slaloming between barstools. Which is, of course, exactly what I would rather have been, but with that option unavailable, I spent several wretchedly awake nights gazing blankly into the Mediterranean night from my 21st-floor eyrie in the Corinthia Bab Africa hotel, or huddled in foetal communion with my iPod—which is, and has always been, a veritable Fort Knox of solid country gold. At some stage, I reasoned—though "reasoned" is an overestimation of the capacities of my mental mechanics of the time, which were in a similar state to those of an engine which has just been thrown from fifth gear into reverse—that, really, the only sensible (everything's relative) response to my circumstances was to become a country singer. It is possible that I felt this course an appropriate submission to destiny. Just as the gluttonous Augustus Gloop in Roald Dahl's *Charlie and The Chocolate Factory* was punished for his chocoholism by being turned into fudge, so I'd been listening to country songs for years, and now my life had become one.

Over the next few days, I scrawled furiously by night, or quivered by day over coffees in the cafes of Green Square and the Medina, humming to myself and frowning at my notepad: the locals steered well and sensibly clear. I returned to London with red eyes, encroaching caffeine psychosis and about half a set's worth of completed songs. I bought a beautiful new acoustic guitar, and kept writing. In between executing more prosaic techniques of processing heartbreak—sitting in dark rooms, removing hair by the fistful, boring supernaturally patient friends to the brink of self-immolation, wailing pleas, and eventually threats, at a patently indifferent God—I cultivated dreams of a country album to file alongside George Jones' lachrymose classic "The Grand Tour," or Gram Parsons' "Grievous Angel." I'd construct a rueful and reproachful, yet poised and dignified, meditation on love and the loss of it, possibly to be titled "Cram This In Your Pipe And Smoke It, You Demented, Ungrateful Harpy."

It's still difficult for me to account for, or quite believe, the sequence of events that subsequently unfolded. It is possibly just that the universe reacts to the endeavours of a person clearly at the edge of their wits much as a householder would upon answering the door to a burly chap clad in a hockey mask, a Homburg hat and a bloodstained ballgown revving a chainsaw, i.e. with a somewhat nervous invitation to take whatever they want. Planets lined up. Tectonic plates shifted. Inexorable cosmic forces brought themselves to bear. A magazine commission enabled me to make my live debut at the legendary open-mic night at Nashville's Bluebird Café.

As is proper prior to embarking upon any serious or entirely ridiculous undertaking, I sought expert counsel. Just before I left London for Nashville, I was asked by a magazine to interview Elvis Costello. The inexorable cosmic forces were clearly at play again: it had been Costello's 1981 album of reverent country covers, "Almost Blue," which had sparked my long-burning passion for the genre. I asked

Costello what he'd advise a Nashville naif: "Go to Katy K," he replied, referrring to the celebrated western outfitter, "and buy a new shirt" (This I subsequently did, along with a complementing guitar strap from Gruhn Guitars, another Nashville institution). I asked my friend Astrid Williamson, a songwriter of no mean genius, for tips on playing live. "Visualise the performance," said Astrid. "Imagine yourself doing everything you're going to do." I spent the flight to Nashville, via Chicago, trying, but could only imagine myself cowering beneath a hail of empties, before being compelled under armed duress to re-enact key scenes from "Deliverance."

"That's unlikely," said Amy Kurland, the Bluebird's owner, when I visited the night before my debut. "It's a polite crowd, because the crowd is mostly each other. It's 40 people showing up wanting to play, they bring a couple of friends, that's your audience."

I was, I told Amy, under few illusions about my abilities. As a guitarist, I'm a semi-competent hack, and I'm a better guitarist than singer.

"Don't worry," she laughed. "The open-mic is like Russian Roulette with a full chamber—it's spinning the barrel and hoping you'll hear one decent song all night."

I solicited further guidance from Nashville-based singer-songwriter Billy Cerveny. He struck me as a smart choice of mentor not just because I liked his current album, "AM Radio"—a gorgeous, melancholic record in the John Prine/Steve Earle mould—but because before he was a musician, he was a journalist. Billy's elegant yet pugnacious way with words was embodied in the t-shirt slogan of his band, The Nashville Resistance: "Because the ass ain't gonna kick itself" (a sticker bearing this excellent advice has adorned my laptop keyboard ever since). In my room at Nashville's uproariously opulent Hermitage Hotel, I played Billy the MP3 demos of my songs. To my astonishment, Billy didn't emphatically proclaim these the worst things he'd ever heard. "They're rough," he said. "But they sound real, and that's what matters." I suddenly felt calmly, possibly foolishly, confident. I remembered that when I'd asked Amy Kurland how many open-mic contenders were certifiably delusional, she'd replied, "Oh, everyone's delusional. But sometimes, delusions come true."

That Monday night at the Bluebird, I was the fourteenth of the night's wannabes summoned to the stage—and, all things considered, it seemed to go pretty well. Nobody was thrown at me, nobody was injured in any unseemly stampede for the exit, and a couple of the more venomous zingers in the lyric promoted appreciate banging of bottles on table-tops. I was certain, during the climactic chorus, that I perceived an honest-to-goodness "Yeehaw!", though this may have been Billy being polite. I just wasn't sure, upon return to London, what—if anything—to do next. As it turned out, I didn't need to give it much thought. The inexorable cosmic forces were not done with me yet.

Robert Johnson famously became a blues singer after having his guitar tuned by Satan at a Mississippi crossroads. My country band owes its existence, possibly more prosaically but really not much less surreally, to being offered a gig by an Albanian politician in a London cocktail lounge. Shortly after I returned from Nashville, I went for a drink with my friend Erion Veliaj, then leader of a youth-oriented civil activist movement called Mjaft!, who was visiting from Albania. I'd met Erion in Tirana a few years beforehand, and entirely failed to conceive a lasting and violent dislike to him despite the tiresomely apparent facts that he's exactly eleven years younger than me, a dozen times smarter, a hundred times better looking and will almost certainly be prime minister before he's 35 and Secretary-General of the United Nations by 50. I told him about my recent escapades in Nashville.

"Mjaft! are putting on a festival in July," he said. "You should come and play at it."

I demurred, voicing concerns that my guitar-picking and singing, such as they were, were not anything anyone was going to want to sit through for longer than five minutes, at most.

"No," Erion agreed. "But you could bring your band."

I explained that I didn't have one. Erion, of course, had not got where he was by listening to excuses.

"Then get one," he said.

I thought about this for a few days. On the one hand, it seemed easy. I had been writing about music and people who make it all my adult life, off and on. So I knew loads of musicians. On the other hand, it seemed an incredibly awkward proposition. I would be asking talented people, possibly with reputations to consider, to line up behind a part-timing parvenu of sorely limited abilities who had clearly taken leave of his senses. Again, I thought advice was required. I mentioned the opportunity of the Albanian trip to another friend of mine, Mike Edwards. I'd known Mike since the early 90s, when he was the singer in Jesus Jones, and I was a writer for *Melody Maker*: my first visit to the US, and my first *MM* cover story, had involved rendezvousing with Jesus Jones' tour in Salt Lake City in 1991, when they were hovering about the top of the Billboard charts with "Right Here, Right Now."

"I'll do it," said Mike, instantly.

I wasn't sure he'd understood. I was asking for tips about recruiting. I wasn't yet recruiting.

"I'll do it," reiterated Mike.

I was both grateful and astonished, but also struck by a number of potential difficulties, which I thought it best to mention up front. Most obviously, there was Mike's attitude to country music. This fluctuated, judging by our wine-addled debates going back some years, somewhere between hostility and indifference.

"I can learn," he replied.

Also, he hadn't heard a note of any of my songs. They might all suck.

"I'm sure they'll be fine."

Plus, and I wasn't sure how to put this, Jesus Jones' mostly electronic pop records, fine though they were, had hardly been all about the lead guitar. And a country lead player, I explained, really had to be able to cut it, especially if he was also carrying a rhythm player like me.

"I'll manage," said Mike.

Then, you know, there was the fact that Mike had, within living memory, headlined major venues, indoors and outside, in front of a group which sold records by the million, in places people had heard of. This would be a sideman's gig buried down the bill in a band which could scarcely be more obscure in a country which didn't even get around to joining the 20th century until about 2003.

"It'll be fun," declared Mike. "And anyway," he continued, sealing the deal, "Gen [Matthews, Jesus Jones' original drummer] can play drums, and I've got a mate called Alec who'll play bass."

That seemed almost suspiciously easy. I felt able to push my luck. I called Astrid, and asked if she'd like to come to Albania to play piano in my country band, and maybe sing a bit.

"Okay," she said.

As the band now apparently existed, I needed a name. At the twilight of a long, liberally lubricated evening with another friend, someone mentioned a throwaway gag in a magazine column we'd both recently read (and the author of which, sadly, I have forgotten). Seeking to summon an image evocative of the chaos, hysteria, confusion and general shrieking nonsense that had apparently recently beset his personal life, the writer had likened the vexatious female he was bemoaning to "a fire in a zoo." It was cruel and vindictive, certainly, and altogether inexcusable, probably, but it made me laugh at a point at which little else was, and so the last toast hoisted before the waitress started doubting out loud that we had homes to go to was to The Blazing Zoos.

The next few weeks were, probably fortunately, necessarily too busy to ponder the folly of the enterprise. I stayed at Mike's house in Cirencester for a few days while we recorded some more demos. I emailed these to the band along with some MP3s of suggestions of the sort of thing I hoped we might eventually resemble—mostly my alt. country favourites (Old 97's, Robbie Fulks, Corb Lund, Todd Snider, Drive-By Truckers, Ryan Adams, Steve Earle), along with a few old-school throwbacks (Merle Haggard, Johnny Cash, Lynyrd Skynyrd, David Allan Coe, The Flying Burrito Brothers). After several raucous rehearsals in a reeking basement in East London, we sounded exactly nothing like any of the above—but, I thought, every so often, to the extent that I could concentrate on anything beyond not screwing up what I was supposed to be doing, we sounded okay. This was entirely due to everybody else: Gen and Alec were an instantly solid rhythm section, requiring no more, respectively, than suggestion of approximate tempo and the identity of the key we were aiming for; Astrid was, as I knew anyway, an almost indecently talented piano player, and blessed further with what I maintain is one of the half-dozen loveliest female singing voices ever recorded; and Mike was a revelation, every lick and solo sounding as I'd hoped, if not quite dared believe, that it would.

Our party of six—the band, plus Astrid's guitarist Dan Burke, who would be joining her for her own set at the festival—flew via Ljubljana to Tirana. I had no idea what the rest of them were thinking, and even less of a clue what I thought I was doing. But I clearly felt I was keeping some sort of appointment with destiny. Clearing passport control at Mother Teresa Airport, I was genuinely disappointed when the customs officer behind the desk neglected to ask the purpose of my visit. I had been looking forward, with peculiar intensity, to replying "country singer."

Outside the airport, we were chivvied aboard a white minivan, whose panelling was extensively and inexplicably decorated with pictures of The Teletubbies: it would have been an undignified vehicle to die in. On the drive down the coast, we played those games that musicians confined to each other's company do: coining, according to a preordained theme, puns based on song titles. We did geography ("Hungary Like The Wolf," "Ice Iceland Baby"). We did London Underground stations ("Sexual Ealing Broadway," "Solid Gold East Acton," "Theydon Bois Of Summer," "Rotherhithe Ho Silver Lining," "Wouldn't It Be Goodge Street," "Paint It Blackfriars," "Been Earl's Court Stealing"). We did foodstuffs ("We Could Send Lettuce," "I Fall To Pizza"). We did fish ("Hake, Rattle & Roll," "I Don't Like Barramundis," "Baby You Can Drive My Carp"). We did, briefly, the pornographic variant, but only got as far as "Fisting By The Pool" before Astrid told us all, quite rightly, to shut and/or grow up.

And then was when I noticed we were going too fast. And that's how I got here.

HE DOESN'T LEAVE his gun in my trousers long, and our journey to our lodgings, in a hotel snuggled in the hills overlooking Himare, proceeds without further incident. A late meal of excellent seafood and interestingly atrocious local wine takes the edge off the day's excitements. Mike plunges the table into internecine rancour with an assertion that no great records feature a saxophone. With characteristic steadfastness, he refuses to retreat from this position even when the forces opposing him mention "Born To Run."

Everyone emerges late the following morning to learn that we have a view: the hotel commands the heights overlooking Himare from the south, offering a vista of untidy scrub-country and half-built holiday homes trundling down towards a sea as radiantly blue as the sky. There being nothing else to do in the immediate vicinity, we pass the time before our ride arrives with an unplugged rehearsal on the verandah. The decision is taken to shanghai Dan and his acoustic guitar into The Blazing Zoos, in exchange for which Astrid claims Gen for a couple of songs in her set: Gen practises his parts by tapping the edge of a table with his drumsticks. Bemused holidaymakers gaze down from overhanging balconies, and are kind enough to applaud at the end of every song.

The road down to the festival site is the most precarious track we have negotiated yet, its perils illustrated by the crucifix memorials planted at what were apparently the last corners ever attempted by unlucky or imprudent motorists. The stage, when we find it, is gratifyingly large. On the right-hand side, the festival sponsors have inflated a tethered hot air balloon. On the left fester examples of Albania's distinguishing national landmark: a few of the countless concrete igloos built all over the country to ward off non-existent foreign predators during the bizarre dictatorship of Enver Hoxha, the paranoid dingbat who walled Albania off from the world from the end of World War II until his death in 1985. The beach, I notice, is one of those ones made of rocks rather than sand. If the crowd take agin us, I worry, this could get messy.

As befits our lowly status, The Blazing Zoos are the first act to soundcheck (the headliners on this, the second day of the festival, are German electronica collective Chicks On Speed and gloomy Austrian pop outfit Mauracher). For the rest of the band, soundchecks are a chore they have discharged times beyond counting: as such, they don't screw about untowardly, though Mike reels off the opening riff of "Right Here Right Now," possibly by way of reminding himself that he wasn't always an accessory to a friend's brainmelt. I, by way of contrast, have never had the opportunity to plug my beloved candy apple red Fender Telecaster into a sound system of these dimensions, and make the most of it to a degree which may be excessive: though I feel my solo surf rock medley of "Pipeline," "Wipeout," the theme from "Hawaii 5-0" and The Pixies' "Cecilia Ann" is appropriate to the seaside setting, Mike does not bother, as he dismounts the stage, to make his disconnection of my amplifier lead appear accidental.

As showtime nears, I surprise myself by failing to feel even slightly nervous. This is, I suspect, at least partly a reflexive vote of confidence in the abilities of the five people sharing the experience. It is also, I'm certain, due to the fact that the situation just seems too peculiar and improbable to take seriously. Eight or nine months previously, before it became clear that Cupid had not so much struck me with an arrow as planted a landmine in my path, I'd had some fairly firm ideas about how I hoped the immediate future might pan out. The spectacle of this group of people tuning up, copying out a setlist of my songs and shrugging themselves into recently borrowed or bought western shirts in a dimly lit tent behind a stage on a beach in Albania would have ranked low on my list of likely scenarios, probably in between being awarded the Nobel Prize for Physics and growing a beak.

Our introduction is not, with all due respect to the festival organisers, seamless. Ideally, the compere would have plied the few hundred bemused-looking people standing in the general vicinity of the stage with some sensational lies about our prowess, at which we'd have bounded on and hit the first chord of our opening number. While he does offer a lengthy peroration, the precise content of which is a mystery to me, being in Albanian and everything, the PA system subsequently refuses to transmit my initial A-flat, forcing us to stand sheepishly about for some minutes while a repair is effected. It is a humblingly impotent feeling, standing in front of a decent-sized crowd of people holding an electric guitar rendered incapable of broadcast. A little, I imagine, like reporting for firing squad duty with a pop gun.

After an interval long enough that I begin feeling certain that I can discern hair growth among the crowd, a shriek of feedback alerts us—and any passing shipping—to the restoration of power. My first swipe at my strings produces a satisfactorily belligerent clang, and we're away, starting with "I Didn't Have The Material (Before Now)," a song written as battle cry, statement of intent and ardent embrace of Harlan Howard's dictum that country music is "three chords and the truth": it's a Johnny Cash-style chugger whose lyrics announce the the late-blooming liberation of a performer whose ambitions of country stardom have been hitherto thwarted by a succession of lovely and fundamentally sane girlfriends who gave him nothing to write about. We all finish at more or less the same time, and the crowd respond with what even the most hostile witness would have to concede is applause.

Hubris meets nemesis with disconcerting rapidity, however. Our second song is one I wrote after the Albania show was confirmed, conceived as a frankly oleaginous act of populist bone-throwing: called "Like Tirana," it is a whimsical (and, for what it may be worth, altogether heartfelt) declaration of fondness for Albania's strange and engaging capital. While I don't seriously expect anyone, in this setting, to keep up with the arcane local references and excruciating puns that riddle the lyric, it'd be nice if they had the chance: the vocal microphones cut abruptly out somewhere during the first chorus, thus depriving all present of my brilliantly wrought allusions to Tirana's fabulously eccentric mayor, Edi Rama, and 15th century vanquisher of the Ottomans and Albanian national hero Skenderbeg. I look around at Mike, much as Lord Cardigan might have consulted a reliable sergeant-major as the Light Brigade first realised that their plans had been overtaken by events. "Just keep going," he yells back, much as one of Cardigan's NCO's might have suggested, if only in the hope that the chap out front will stop most of the shrapnel. We do: the song is, at least, great fun to play, and while it may not be quite so amusing to listen to, the crowd is, if anything, growing. Whether motivated by appreciation or curiosity I cannot say, and don't much care. This is fun.

With vocals restored, we attempt "Anywhere But Here," an upbeat shuffle inspired by—yet sounding in no way like—Buck Owens. It provokes actual dancing on the pebbles, which doesn't even taper off during "Waiting," a half-baked Green On Red pastiche whose clodhopping dreariness does not become fully apparent to me until approximately 15 seconds into this very rendition of it. Though barely three minutes long, it feels like strumming interminably along to a 45rpm recording of "Freebird" played at 33: it is a song whose first public performance will coincide with its last. Stupidly, I've chosen to follow that with three medium-pace-to-slow ones in a row, but the crowd is still building, dancing and cheering. Four possible explanations strike me: i) the guy playing in the DJ tent further up the beach really sucks; ii) the Kanun of Lek, a sort of Albanian bible of clan law, mandates the assembly of truly overwhelming force before chasing foreign interlopers into the sea at pitchfork-point; iii) the local beer is unusually potent; iv) we're doing okay up here. I decide to focus on the latter.

I'm pretty confident about "Do You Have A Sister?": it's the one I played at the Bluebird, a trundling ballad in deep inspirational hock to Robbie Fulks, in which a defeated, dispirited lover, unable to swallow his frustration that the apparently perfect object of his affections wasn't quite what she appeared, asks his vexatious paramour the eponymous, desperate question. And it sounds great. Astrid's sweet backing vocals take the edge off its essential poison, and Mike's solo is fantastic—so much so that I make what I guess is the rookie's mistake of enjoying it, and by the time he's halfway through I have no idea what I'm playing, and have to hope that by now the guy mixing the sound understands us sufficiently to bury my guitar appropriately. Still, everyone hits the key change for the coda, and as the last chord dies away I understand why people—like the ones on stage with me, for example—want to do this sort of thing so much.

The last four are a delirious blur: "This Isn't Love," a sort of anti-gospel tune, the lyric of which is a narration of everything said by an embittered wedding guest from the moment he answers the priest's request for any objections to the point at which he's heaved down the church steps; "Kumbo Prison Blues," our only happy song, an obvious Johnny Cash homage recalling my mercifully brief and altogether farcical imprisonment in Cameroon the previous November; "Boys Of Summer," the Don Henley mid-life crisis lament recast, probably not entirely convincingly, as Tom Pettyish southern-fried country rock, and inserted in the set in hope of eliciting some cheap Pavlovian ardour; "My Heart Won't Be In It," a sarcastic rant whose calamitously overloaded verses are intentionally sublimated in overwhelming squalls of Skynyrd-eseque guitar.

And we're done. I treat myself to a vainglorious fling of my plectrum into the crowd. A ferocious, clawing, eye-gouging struggle for ownership fails to ensue. But there is a quantity of clapping and cheering I'd have signed for gratefully before we went on, and I climb down the stairs at the back of the stage suddenly slicked with an apparently suppressed surge of nervous sweat, harbouring a heart hammering like an octopus's drum solo and yet on the whole strangely calm, suffused with the relieved serenity of having got away with it.

We've been playing for, I suppose, 45 minutes, give or take. It seems to have skipped by in seconds.

A few celebratory beers later, I head out onto the beach to watch Astrid's set. En route, I pass by the merchandising stall. There are festival t-shirts for sale, and our name is among those listed on the back of them. I buy one in every colour.

UPTOWN TOP THANKING
Acknowledgements

PROPERLY THANKING EVERYBODY who has commissioned, permitted and encouraged a trove of journalism stretching over nearly two decades would require the printing of a separate companion volume. So, with due apologies to the shortly-to-be-disregarded legions who've helped along the way, I'm going to attempt to keep this brief.

The first incarnation of *Rock and Hard Places* was published several centuries ago by Virgin in the UK. Thanks to everybody there who worked on it, especially Ian Gittins, who commissioned it, and Kefi Beswick, who ran the publicity. This second coming has been made possible by Soft Skull, and so thanks to everybody there as well, especially Anne Horowitz, Sharon Donovan and Denise Oswald. And neither version would have been possible had an assortment of editors not seen fit to send me off on these misadventures in the first place. I'm grateful to all of them, but in this context indebted more than most to Andrew Tuck at *Monocle*, Allan Jones, John Mulvey and Michael Bonner at *Uncut*, Caspar Melville at *New Humanist*, John Doran at *The Quietus* and Rahul Jacob at *The Financial Times*. I'd also like to thank P.J. O'Rourke, Bono, Patterson Hood and Bill Carter for their generous endorsements on the cover.

Observant readers will detect a theme of atrocious puns serving as chapter headings. These are not exclusively my fault. If memory serves, Simon Price, Maria Egan and Brendon Fitzgerald contributed several to the first edition, back when such things were done over a few drinks. In this bold new modern era that allows us to maintain human relationships without ever having to actually spend time with people, the periodic headline-writing challenges issued on my Facebook page were answered with greatest distinction by Matthew Dupuy, Sean Kemp, Ariane Sherine, Terry Staunton, Ian Watson, Holly Barringer, Shane Danielsen and Stephen Dowling. Another brisk, manly handshake must also be offered in the direction of Neal Townsend, who coined the book's title some while before the idea of writing it had ever occurred to me.

I am grateful, of course, to my family, for no end of things, but mostly for abandoning quite early the idea that I was ever going to pull myself together and get a real job. Finally, everybody thinks their friends are the finest and funniest people in the world, but everybody else is just plain wrong: mine are, and I thank them all, for being themselves.